The Jotunbok:
Working With The Giants
Of The Northern Tradition

Raven Kaldera

The Jotunbok:
Working With The Giants Of The Northern Tradition

Northern-Tradition Shamanism
Book I

Raven Kaldera

Asphodel Press

Hubbardston, Massachusetts

Asphodel Press
12 Simond Hill Road
Hubbardston, MA 01452

The Jotunbok:
Working With the Giants of the Northern Tradition
Northern-Tradition Shamanism: Book I
© 2006 Raven Kaldera
ISBN 978-1-84728-729-8

Cover art © 2006 Abby Helasdottir, http://www.gydja.com
Back cover photo © 2006 Sensous Sadie

Printed in cooperation with
Lulu Enterprises, Inc.
860 Aviation Parkway, Suite 300
Morrisville, NC 27560

Dedicated to Fuensanta, who insisted that it happen,
Loki, who made it possible,
Hela, mistress of my head, who gave the order,
and all those who bravely contributed
their gifts of words and devotion.
Hail to the Gods and Wights; let them hear
Their names honored in voices uplifted to the sky.

Contents:

Giants of the Northern Tradition

hen one thinks of the word "giant", one usually comes up with the fairytale giants of the late medieval period— enormous to the point of silliness, usually stupid and destructive, hankering for human flesh or at least for whole sheep, and easily dispatched by the slingshot to the head, or the Jack's tricks. Giants have become, in the world of the Brothers Grimm, an allegory for all that is dull, slow, huge, and nearly mindless.

Yet in the ancient Norse and Germanic tales, the giant-race was not nearly so simple. There were many kinds of "giants"; some were honored as deities, others feared as monsters, and still other sought out for their great wisdom and knowledge. To this day, a reading of the Eddas and sagas will show the Jotunfolk—the Jotnar of the Northern Tradition—to be keepers of deep elemental knowledge, whom many of the Aesir gods sought out for their wisdom, or feared for their powers.

The giant-race comes under many names. They are referred to with the following words: Old Norse *jotun* (plural *jotnar*), *gýgr* (giantess), and *Thurs* (Middle High German *türse*); Anglo-Saxon *eoten*, *ettin*, or *ent*,; Swedish *jätte* and *troll*; and German *Riese* and *Hüne* (in Westphalia and part of Drenthe). While some scholars have attempted to sort these names out by moral division—the giants under this name are friendly to the Aesir; those with that name are enemies—it is clear from any compilation of giant-references that the ancient Norse and Germanic peoples were nowhere near that precise. Any of the terms could be applied to any sort of giant in any sort of relationship to the Aesir, or humans. Some, however, did seem to be applied more often to specific sorts of giants sorted not by their attitudes toward outsiders, but by their elemental nature. While even this is hardly universal, I have tended, in this book, to refer to "fire-etins" and "frost-thurses" and such.

As scholars have pointed out, although the giants are less of a focus of worship than the elves, they are also more individualized in personality; few of the Alfar are known to us by name, but dozens of uniquely characterized Jotnar take part in the Eddas and sagas. They are embodiments of and allied to natural forces—storm, fire, mountain, forest, stone, the raging sea. They are constant shapeshifters and come in a thousand different forms— some beautiful, some hideous, and every gradation in between.

Among today's modern practitioners of the various religions of the Northern Tradition, reverencing and working with wights other than the "standard" Aesir deities (Odin, Thor, Frigga, etc.) is beginning to come into its own. As one example, the cult of the Vanir (agricultural deities of Vanaheim) is blossoming slowly but surely. As another example, some folk are working openly with the Alfar (elves); a few are forging links with the Duergar (dwarves). These are seen as races of beings who dwell in the Nine Worlds that surround the World Tree, but who can reach across time and space (or be visited across that gap by knowledgeable tranceworkers) and forge alliances with the humans of this world. Here on this plane, it is becoming more common to honor and bond with the land-wights, the spirits of a given piece of Earth beneath our feet.

Yet of all the various pantheons—and I believe it is fir to call them pantheons—the Jotnar are the ones approached with the most trepidation, or perhaps even reviled. The Northern Traditions are still finding their feet with regard to all the creatures known by our ancestors, and people are often unsure of what they do not know—and, to be fair, there is insufficient information in the much-touted lore when it comes to the Giant race.

First, what do I consider to fall within the "Northern Tradition"? I consider any religious group who worships and works with the Gods and wights of the ancient Norse, Germanic, and Anglo-Saxon peoples to fall under that umbrella. In practice, this generally means two main types of religious groups: First, religious reconstructions of these practices, who tend to refer to themselves with the umbrella label of "Heathens", and who encompass such other labels as Asatru, Vanatru, Rökkatru, Heithnir, and others. Second, reconstructionist-derived groups who use the same Gods and wights, who tend to refer to themselves as Norse Pagans or Northern-Tradition Pagans (not to be confused with Norse Wicca, which is a Wiccan-derived tradition, not a reconstructionist-derived tradition).

Scholar and Mystic

In reconstructionist traditions such as Heathenry, a great deal of emphasis is placed on using the mythos described in the remaining scraps of lore, for obvious reasons. Leaving aside the complicating factors that the lore is garbled, patchy, sparse, and written by people who were Christians writing with Christian perspectives about an already fading tradition, there is the fact that if one treats this as a living religion with real deities, not just an academic exercise or the religious version of a historical-recreation society, there will be some people who will make personal, individual contact and communion with certain deities. Or, perhaps, one could say more accurately that certain deities will make personal individual contact and communion with the mortals in question.

When this happens, the inevitable clash of the mystic and the scholar fills the air. It is one thing to argue questions of lore, but when someone walks up in the middle of the argument and says, "Well, I talked to Freyja last night, and she said..." it pulls the very ground out from under the feet of the debate. Such proclamations are referred to in northern-tradition reconstructionist circles with the acronym of UPG, meaning (depending on the level of intended insult) either Unusual Personal Gnosis or Unverifiable

Personal Gnosis. In general, UPG is not trusted, as there is supposedly no way to verify it.

However, that personal contact with Gods and wights inevitably leads to UPG, whether anyone likes it or not. The more that people actually work with the Gods rather than merely talking about them, the more that personal observations and communications not covered in our patchy scraps of lore will come up. This is what makes the difference between resurrecting a dead religion and practicing a living faith.

There are, sadly, many holes in the extant lore, especially where the Jotnar are concerned. The scanty references that exist often tantalizingly point to the possibility of the giants being an older race of Gods, much like the Hellenic Titans, who were deposed by the Indo-European Olympian deities. This may mean that we are burrowing through a double layer of obscurity—first, the loss of the oral-tradition pre-medieval pagan religions to Christianity, and deeper than that, the muffling layer of a conquest several millennia old of a people whose only records survive in pottery and linguistic hints. This means that for those whom the Jotnar, and the Jotun Gods, are contacting, UPG is our only choice in filling out the enormous gaps in our votive practice. The Christians who wrote about the pagan religion that they were supplanting had enough of a tendency of demonize Odin and Thor and their ilk; the already-supplanted Jotnar Gods were even more easily made demonic in their black-and-white world view.

Yet there is always the gnawing question of how much is fantasy, or even the voice of the Gods coming through the complex puppet theaters in our heads? Those of us who struggle with the issue, especially those of us in reconstructionist-derived (rather than strict reconstructionist) traditions where UPG is less reviled, have come gradually upon the concept of PCPG, or Peer-Corroborated Personal Gnosis. This is the idea that if the same pieces of information, the same stories, are being imparted to separate people—especially ones who have little or no contact with each other— then something real is going on here. The corollary to this is, of course, that if we don't write down and share these pieces of UPG, then how are we ever to compare them?

I have been collecting UPG—my own and others—about the Jotnar for many years. I didn't have a choice about my own; I was claimed by Hela, the Death Goddess, as a child. As an adult, She sent me around to her relatives and friends to learn lessons. Some were similar lessons to those of spirit-workers who were taught by the Aesir and/or the Vanir (or deities of other pantheons); others were unique in their goals and methods. Many times I had experiences with deities and wights whose only mention was a word or two in a saga; sometimes I would get no name at all. Of the latter category, I would occasionally find a scrap of lore and realize who that dead Jotun woman in Helheim who'd been teaching me actually was. In every case, I learned far more about them than those written scraps describe. It was when I began to speak to others who had worked with those same entities, and found similar—or even dead-on identical—traits that I knew this body of knowledge needed to be written and disseminated. There should not be so many of us wandering around with the same knowledge, afraid to speak of it, and believing that we are the only ones who have it.

Therefore, this book is a work of UPG about the giantkind of the northern-tradition, not a book of compiled lore. It is the collected experiences of many people, gathered through interviews, through private conversations, through personal experiences. Many refused to allow their names put into this book, or even pen names; they asked me to merely incorporate their observations into the meat of the book. Other brave folk wrote long and detailed essays about the Gods that they are devoted to; where it is possible, I've used these in their entirety. Some wrote poetry, invocations, or simply stories of their experiences.

Not everything that was given to me was used in this book, or it might have turned into a veritable encyclopedia, and taken nine years to produce. I had to draw the line somewhere, so I reverted to PCPG. If a given piece of information about a deity A) severely contradicted the lore in a place where the lore held no contradictory information within itself (such as vastly differing information on who was whose parent or child) and B) severely contradicted the experiences of at least two spirit-workers I trusted with regard to that deity, I decided not to print it. Information that was simply not present in the lore, or that followed one rather than another conflicting tale in Edda or saga, was simply put to the test of passing B; if there was no one else who had dealt with that particular entity, I often put it in anyway, in a discrete essay by its source.

So this is my disclaimer: Assume that anything you read in the main text that is not directly footnoted is PCPG. Assume that anything you read in specific essays by labeled people is somewhere on the continuum from UPG to PCPG. With that in mind, take what you will from this book. It is not a scholarly work, nor is it meant to be, which may limit its usefulness to strict reconstructionists, but those who are being contacted by the Gods and wights cannot afford to stay within those too-narrow boundaries. This is a work of personal experience, of devotion, of revelation. It is a work designed to bring aid to those who are called to work with the Jotnar, and information to those who are interested in such things.

Here is the point, also, where I must give profound and profuse thanks to all the northern-tradition folk who gave their essays, stories, poetry, and personal experiences to be used in this work. To lay out in print one's personal spiritual beliefs and experiences, especially when you know that they may be ridiculed or reviled, is an incredibly brave act. I have been overwhelmed by the number and quality of the pieces offered to me for this book. Whether they came as attachments from experienced professional writers or were hesitantly thrown out as musings in private emails to me, I am amazed at the intensity and clarity that they contain. They prove that this body of worship is a complex and continually growing phenomenon. Although this book started out as simply my offering to the Gods and wights that grace my life, it quickly grew into an anthology of devotion that spanned continents and traditions. Thank you, all of you. This work would have been so much poorer without any one of your words.

Polytheistic Boundaries

One major difference that we have found between those whose interest in the Gods and wights is more academic and those whose interest is personal is the conundrum of which deities to consider as merely forms of the same deity, and which are clearly separate. All the Northern-Tradition religions have strongly polytheistic values, which means that the underlying theology prioritizes that every deity is real and separate and Their own individual selves, neither merely an archetype, nor merely an amalgam of Godhead turning different faces to the light, nor dependent for its existence on the belief or the attention of human beings. Yet even with this, questions of garbled lore arise when trying to figure out where one deity ends and another begins. Many deities have titles added to their names, or even extra pseudonyms, which refer to a particular aspect or power; these are referred to as *heiti* in Old Norse, and many obscure mythic figures are claimed as merely the *heiti* of more popular gods.

Where to draw this line is problematic and difficult, and there is no perfect answer. Some folks are iffy about even considering Odin and Woden the same deity; others are clear that Odin is Woden is Odin, but that Odin Grimnir is an entirely different "face" from Odin Jalkr. On the other end, there are those who claim that Frigga and Freyja are the same deity, or at least interchangeable. Many internecine wars are waged over these questions, but the truth of each of them will never be discovered by studying lore. There is only one true answer, and that requires dealing with the deities themselves, a skill which not everyone has, and which is not to be done on demand.

There seems to be a strong desire among those at the more academic end of the spectrum to prefer to have as few deities as possible. By lumping together any who are even remotely similar, and by demoting those who cannot be lumped together as "not really gods", they try to decrease the number of deities in a pantheon to a "decent" number, whatever that is. One senses that this is a holdover from monotheism, not unusual in religions of converts; although they may have come to terms with the fact that this is not a properly monotheistic religion, something in them still feels that fewer deities are more "proper" than many deities. I've seen echoes of this protest in the way that western anthropologists treat the religions of tribal peoples; once they discover that they may have literally hundreds of "spirits", all different, variably powerful but not a one to be entirely dismissed, that tribal faith is redistributed from the box labeled "religion" to the one labeled "superstition".

At best it may be referred to as "the religion of the peasants", or the lower classes in general, with the implication (or sometimes the bald statement) that the educated, less ignorant upper classes would of course limit themselves to a suitably compact number of supreme deities who would divide all of creation up neatly between them. There is even a sort of peevishness at the idea that anyone would be able to remember and keep straight a pantheon of fifty gods, much less a hundred. The average tribal member in a Third World country, however, can probably name off at least that many spirits large and small, and if he forgets any, there is likely a local spirit-worker around who can certainly name every one and everything that is known about them. As the Northern-Tradition religions grow and slowly come alive again, we are gaining more and more of these spirit-workers, those who work directly with the Gods and wights and are beginning to be able to answer these questions. We are also learning that true polytheism is just that: having relationship with many gods.

So this book is written from a polytheist perspective, by people who, rather than assume that a particular mythic figure is just a *heiti* of an already-known deity, assume that it is more likely a different entity, and go in search of them with that attitude. Occasionally we are surprised that calling a name pulls up a god that we already knew, but usually it means the start of a whole new relationship with someone that we don't know, and who may not have spoken with a human being of our world for a long time. We value knowing the divine reality of an actual deity, even a "minor" one, over limiting the numbers of Gods that we work with. This means that many of us work with dozens of "minor" deities and "major" wights— and we acknowledge that the line between one and the other is more like a wide grey area—and we have plenty of obscure names to call on at sumbel.

Opposite Numbers

As I researched this third pantheon of the North, I began to notice something interesting. Several of the wights on either side of the "line" mirrored each other in interesting ways. They held similar functions, but in a different "flavor". For example, the most obvious and easy pair of "opposite numbers" is Mordgud and Heimdall. Both are gatekeepers and Guardians, Heimdall of the Bifrost bridge upwards into Asgard, and Mordgud of Helheim's Gate downwards into the land of the Dead. Both are armored warriors known for their stalwart, loyal, indomitable nature; both are inflexibly impossible to wheedle or bribe; both are also, as Guardians of the liminal space and shepherds of the arriving Dead, possessed of unique wisdom and counsel. Yet they are also very different: one a golden-haired cloud-dwelling man, the other a dark woman in black armor.

It is not unusual for different peoples to have separate deities that oversaw the same natural and archetypal functions—a weather god, an earth mother, a trickster, a Guardian deity, and so forth for each—and for those deities to vary a good deal within the limits of the archetype involved, such as the cultural differences between Frey and Tammuz. Each tribe of humans, everywhere in the world, finds the Gods that are right for them to describe these important things. What is surprising is that northern-tradition religion contains more than one pantheon that mirror each other in many ways, and yet are strongly culturally different.

Looking at this pantheon-overlaid-onto-a-pantheon, it is not difficult to imagine the people who were conquered by the Indo-Europeans, who might already have had a multitudinous pantheon of spirits, which was overlaid by the waves of invaders—first agricultural peoples, then horseback warriors speaking the same or at least a similar language. Lest readers assume that "primitive" means having fewer gods, be assured that tribal societies frequently have large pantheons of spirits that they revere and fear. The ascendance of the Aesir and the Vanir over the World Tree may have been mirrored in our world by the ascendance of their worshippers over the Jotun-worshippers. It would account for the interesting redundancy of deities in different cultural versions on both sides of an opposing line.

Looking into the other possible pairs, we have of course Odin and Loki, the two major powerful male figures on both sides. They are blood brothers, but the bond is broken over inter-tribal policies and the sacrifice of both their sons, and Loki alienates Odin's people. In a way, their blood-brotherhood is similar politically to other European integrations of old and newer pantheons, where the matriarchal goddess of the conquered tribe is married to the patriarchal god of the conquering one. While Odin and Loki are both male, they are brought together as blood brothers (an acceptable substitute), and there is strong intimation of a further bond. Certainly Loki turns into a mare and seduces a stallion for Odin, and bears him Sleipnir, the mount he will ride; one would have to be blind to the sexual—and power-dynamic—implications of that myth to miss the comparison. Yet in the end, Loki rebels and refuses to be submissive, in a way that echoes instead the relationship of Zeus and Prometheus, also respective leaders of conquering (Indo-European) and conquered (indigenous) pantheons. Like Prometheus, Loki is chained and tortured for rebelling on reasons of principle; like Zeus, Odin cannot bring himself to kill him for personal reasons, and eventually he is set free (as many of the spirit-workers who deal with Loki claim has happened).

They are also alike in other ways. Both are canny, clever, well-spoken, and givers of the gift of words. Both are male and virile, with many lovers, but both spend time being in a female role for reasons of magical gain—Odin spends time dressed as a woman learning seidhr from Freyja and being called Jalkr (Eunuch); Loki often shifts gender to appear as a woman, and actually talks Thor into cross-dressing. Both take pride in their skill in tricking enemies into doing what they want, whether through illusion, fast-talking, rules-lawyering, or outright lying. Both have been known to do ruthless and even apparently cruel and unethical things for some sense of the future good of their tribe, or sometimes merely out of anger. Either can be benevolent and friendly, or fly into a terrible rage—Loki is a fire-god, and Odin is the Master of the Berserkers. Both are associated with wolves, and both are wanderers on the road—Loki is Fleet-Foot, Odin is Way-Tamer. Both work and teach shamanic magic; both suffer ordeals. In fact, except for their respective archetypal statuses as All-Father/King and Outcast/Rebel, they are frighteningly similar.

Another similar pair might be Freyja and Angrboda. Freyja, the Lady of the Vanir, has at least four different areas of divine office: she is goddess of love and sex, she is goddess of fertility, she is a warrior who takes the honored Dead into her hall Sessrumnir, and as Mistress of Seidhr she is a witchy, spooky goddess who aids spirit-workers in gaining oracles from the Dead. Similarly, Angrboda, the Hag of the Iron Wood, is said by those who work with her to be powerful in teaching women's sex magic. She is the Mother of Monsters who brings forth many; it may be aesthetically different from Freyja's forms of fertility, but it is still fecundity. (Indeed, the comparison between Freyja's emphasis on fertility of the fields, and Angrboda's on the fertility of wild animals, may echo an ancient conflict between agriculturalists versus hunter-gatherers.) She is a wolf-warrior, head of the Wolf Clan of the Iron Wood, and she is just as witchy and spooky as Freyja, if not more—her daughter is the Goddess of Death itself.

Frigga, the Queen of the Aesir, is a mother goddess to her people, but she is not the fecund earth so much as the Lady of the Hall, bringing *frith* to the people. On the Jotun side, we find Loki's mother Laufey who fulfills much the same peacemaker role to those who work with her. Both are gracious and maternal, and both are associated with trees—Frigga with the birch, and Laufey is "Lady of the Leafy Isle".

Another interesting similarity is between Tyr and Surt. Both are warrior deities, and the genealogy of both is in doubt—Tyr is sometimes a son of Odin and sometimes a son of two Jotnar, and Surt has no parents that anyone knows of. However, in terms of mythic rather than literal heritage, Tyr is an avatar of the ancient, primal Indo-European sky/war god Tiw/Ieu/Dyaus who was once the central figure of the Indo-European pantheon as they made their way across the wide steppes under the great sky. Surt is the oldest known being in the Nine Worlds; before there was anything else there was Muspellheim and Surt, wielding his sword. Both are primal gods from the Beginning Days in their own way. In personality, both are grim, daunting, laconic, impenetrable warriors known for their prowess in battle and the terrible doom of their word.

The Norse goddess Iduna is the gardener goddess, in charge of the orchard; rather than the great fields, her place is more in the small domestic fruits around the farm, and her apples give long life to the Gods. On the other side, Gerda is the goddess of the walled garden and the wild herbs, married to a Vanir fertility god. Eir is the healing goddess of the Aesir ("the Norse Hygeia" as one writer put it); Mengloth is the healing goddess of the Jotnar. Thor and Farbauti are both gods of thunder and lightning—and also both large, burly, red-bearded, hotheaded types prone to striking first and thinking later.

Probably the most interesting and controversial of these pairs of opposites is the dichotomy between Baldur and Fenris. In a very real way, both are sacrificial deities held hostage by opposite sides—the Aesir hold the god who is the "darkest of the dark", metaphorically speaking, and the Jotnar hold the god who is the "brightest of the bright". While they are as dissimilar as is possible, their very opposition in identical places confirms their pairing. Both are only to be released at the end of the world.

The school of thought which sees the Jotnar as the Gods and wights that were revered by pre-Indo-European folk is a small one, with only fledgling theories as of yet. And what of those people themselves? We know little about them; the tiny scraps we do know about come from the existence of their words in our language (they gave us the basis for such words as wife, child, house, and slave, so we know that there was a good deal of intermingling), and what archaeological evidence we are able to turn up. We know that they had a Mesolithic-to-Neolithic culture, but not much more than that. (Some of the folk that I interviewed had independently had sudden inspiration upon seeing the museum exhibit or the book or TV show about Otzi the Iceman, and strongly felt that he was an example of this pre-Indo-European shamanic culture, and that it was known to and taught by the Jotnar, under various names.) As can be seen by the Titans in ancient Greece, and the Fir Bolg of Ireland, the old gods of the conquered people become the demons of the conqueror's gods. This theory has been put forth by Liljenroth, although I am still anxiously awaiting a good English translation of his work.

There's no question in my mind that it was the Jotnar who first befriended the people of northern Europe, before the Aesir or even the Vanir got around to dealing with them. Back when agriculture was spotty, when we were hunters and gatherers and herders who were just settling into villages and doing some planting—or not yet, even—that was when we learned from Them. Their involvement with us goes back that far, and they remember it, all right, even if we as a culture have forgotten. Their cultures are much more shamanic, one might say, and so are their practices...and so were ours, in those days.

—Ari, spirit-worker and spamadhr

Political Considerations

But back to real and not theoretical life. In the past few years, rumors have come around about Norse/Germanic-religionist people (besides myself and my friends) who work with, or are called by, the Jotunfolk. This growing tendency has shown itself to the dismay of the general Heathen populace. Some protest under the excuse that there are few references to our ancestors actually worshipping these Gods, but most strongly feel that the Jotnar are the enemies of the Gods—meaning the Aesir—and thus of mankind. There is an intense need for an enemy in their cosmology, for a clean black versus white theology, and one can clearly see the hand of a Judeo-Christian upbringing in the imprint of these reflexive assumptions. However, as this phenomenon is growing, Norse/Germanic religionists as a whole need to come to terms with it. People are coming into the Northern Traditions saying things like, "Loki talks to me; he's a Norse god, right? Do I belong here?"

They are met with widely varying responses. At this time, the Norse Pagan reconstructionist-derived folk tend to be open and tolerant about which deities from which pantheons are acceptable to worship. Reconstructionist Heathen groups have a wider variance; some are tolerant, others will discourage contact with any Jotun or Jotun deity, and a few of the most conservative have policies to expel anyone who is found even to be contacting them in their private devotional life. The rationale of this is that any mention of them will bring their notice and their wrath, and thus they are bad luck to invoke in any way. (At least they do recognize the power of the Jotnar, if only as the proverbial rejected fairy at the christening.)

At the same time, a number of solitary practitioners have been working with these deities and wights intimately for a long time. Comparative practices have been shared, merged, and melded, and a unique theology with its own pantheon is beginning to emerge. In the mid-1990s, Abby Helasdottir of New Zealand coined the term "Rökkr" for the deities of the Jotnar, the most powerful among them who were revered even by their own race—Loki, Hela, Angrboda, Jormundgand, Fenris, etc. (Abby's explanation of the many layers of the word "Rökkr" is explored in the chapter of that name.) At the same time, some Northern-Tradition religionists were arguing against the label "Asatru" as an umbrella-term for their collection of faiths; some felt that its literal meaning—"those who are true to the Aesir"—left out worshippers whose focus was more on the Vanir agricultural gods. Soon after, the term "Vanatru" was coined, and "Heathen" became the umbrella-term of choice for Northern-Tradition reconstructionists. It is hardly surprising that the term "Rökkatru" followed, referring to those whose practice centered around the Jotun Gods and wights.

The most important thing for Heathens to keep in mind, and the one thing that we who work with the Jotnar would most like readers to come away with, is to understand that the Northern Tradition is not a dualistic faith like Zoroastrianism, or Christianity. The Aesir are no angels, and the Jotnar are not demons of Satan. It's not that simple, or that black and white. To fully understand and live this faith is to get beyond dualistic good and evil. Whatever else it may be, the faith of my ancestors was based on keen observation of the nature of this world and the Otherworlds, and nothing in nature—in any world—is good or evil. While there may be tension between opposing forces, to rank one side as "good" and the other side as "evil" is a holdover from an idea that sprang from Zoroastrianism to Manichaeanism and finally into Christianity, and that worldview is not reflective of the way our world (or any of the Nine Worlds) works.

We dare not forget the effect that Christianization had on the only surviving heathen lore, and that its first effect was the forcing of this dualistic worldview onto the people. From their perspective, the Jotunfolk were especially easy to demonize, even more so than the Aesir or Vanir. Regardless of what our ancestors came to believe, the denizens of the Otherworlds don't see things that way. Individuals are judged, not entire races of beings. Thor may kill one giantess and have an affair with another one. Skadi aligns herself with the Aesir; Sigyn with the Rökkr. In real life—and for those of us who are tranceworkers or spirit-workers, the Nine Worlds are very real and not just archetypes or myths—things aren't black and white.

The three major pantheons (and their assorted minor spirits) of the Norse/Germanic peoples are engaged in a complicated dance. They war with each other, yet they marry each other. They denounce each other and befriend each other. They battle over some territories and respect each other's claim on others. They act, in other words, like neighboring tribes. Sometimes they act like the Sharks and the Jets, or the Crips and the Bloods, or the Hatfields and McCoys, but those are actually rare compared to the general peaceful coexistence. Those of us who work with them, and are followers of the deities of the three different pantheons, must remember this...and must not attempt to project the tales of those oversimplified battles and alliances onto each other.

One spirit-worker that I spoke to whose primary alliance is with Odin, the chief Aesir god, told me that she wears the valknut, a symbol composed of three interlocking triangles, which followers of Odin have chosen as a mark for themselves. Her feelings on the matter are that the three triangles represent the three pantheons of the Northern Tradition—Aesir, Vanir, and Rökkr—and that their interwoven nature symbolizes the reality of the interdependence between these three tribes, three sets of divine powers, and three ways of being which have grown together into one great spiritual organism. While they may battle with each other—the Aesir had a terrible war with the Vanir, and habitually skirmish with the Jotnar—they are locked together, and this is how it should be.

As with all things to do with the Jotnar, there are no absolutes. Some Jotnar marry into Aesir and Vanir lines, and ally with them. Others oppose them implacably. Most are somewhere in the middle. The ones who consider most of the Aesir honorable enemies—and remember that the emphasis is on "honorable"—will sometimes extend that opposition to followers of the Aesir. While the lore calls them "enemies of mankind", from what I've seen, they only count as enemies those humans who are committed to the side of the Aesir. They have nothing against humans who do not have primary allegiance to the Aesir. (For that matter, there is very little lore about the Jotnar actually harming humans at all.) They have much less of a beef with the Vanir, and more frequently marry into their ranks.

It's a difficult situation. On the one hand, insults have erupted in religious groups from Asatruar who closely serve their deities, and who feel that an enemy of their Gods must be their enemy as well, sight unseen. I understand the pressure involved. The Aesir themselves do see the Jotunfolk, for the most part, not only as lesser creatures but as a dangerous force to be restrained. There is a strong undercurrent of... do I dare call it racism? Yes, I do dare... among them. Heimdall has said flatly to myself and to other tranceworkers, including Asatru spae-workers, that he sees humans with Jotun blood as being unworthy to ever enter Asgard. Odin has gone back and forth on the subject, canny old man that he is.

However, some of my best friends are wives of Odin, or followers of Aesir gods. And we are sensible human beings who have absolutely no need to have any kind of feud between us, just because our bosses have issues. In fact, I think that this is a way in which we can teach Them something. (I know, the very idea that we could, over time, change and teach the Gods will make some people's eyes spin around in their head. But I think there's something to that! And I intend to live as if this, at least, this example, is a gift that I can give.) I will serve my Lady while not carrying on the feud that some of her people are involved in, and I encourage Asatru folk to do the same. After all, if I, with all my Jotun-blooded handicaps, can do it, surely so can they?

In some ways, the Aesir are proponents of forcing order on chaotic Nature, which two thousand years ago was necessary for the survival of the species. They are the force of civilization. However, the pendulum in our world has now swung so far in the other direction that our imposed "order" has thrown things out of balance and is now causing harm, a theory gently put forth by Diana Paxson in her essay "Utgard", which follows this chapter. We have a greater problem from pollution than from most actions of nature these days. I agree that there is a balance to be had here. However, we humans need to remember that our place is in the middle of that balance, always—after all, the one of the Nine Worlds that we are closest to is Midgard—and not at one end or the other.

> I find that a lot of Seidhworkers (particularly Hrafnar/Harner-type Seidhworkers) are learning to get along with the Jotnar. They are frequently working with landwights, which of course leads them to Jotnar, which always seems to surprise them that they didn't find Freyja at the end of the string they pulled on! Not to mention that they didn't stop to think that the Norns are giantesses…. As I traveled about I met a lot of different Jotnar, and learned about their elemental natures. I learned with Rock, and Wind, and Forest, and so many others. The forest Jotunfolk teach how to see in all directions at once, the weather giants teach a lot about thinking patterns, the rock giants are great for protection and healing…That was when I began to understand that the Jotnar are very active in Seidhr. In Seidhr, whatever style you choose, you are dealing with dead things and ancient things. Well, let's face it, sooner or later you gotta deal with a Jotun to do that. The Jotnar, the Alfar, all of these are so connected, but so many Asatru people are afraid.
>
> —Lyn, spirit-worker

Darkness and Wilderness

One thing that is unavoidably true is that the Jotun-wights, and their Rökkr Gods, are "darker" and "wilder" than the other two pantheons. This is partly a problem with our modern assumptions about the nature of the Divine. It's not that we misread them as dark and wild; they are that, no question. It's that in ancient times, these qualities were not seen as something that ought not to be present in a Deity. These days, there is an assumption that Deity ought to be the culmination of all that is good, and nothing negative or frightening (or, perhaps, even challenging) ought to be part of the Force that you are deigning to honor. In the Neo-Pagan religious communities, this conception of deity is satirized by referring to "the Barbie Goddess Who Gives You Stuff".

Up until a decade ago in both Pagan and Heathen communities, the "darker gods" of any pantheon were demonized as scary figures whose rituals and energy would bring down the tone of any hearty festivities. However, as the various European-descended religions have matured, their acceptance of the "ending" parts of the cycle of life has grown. Deities such as Kali, Hecate, Hades, or Lilith are now routinely accepted in most Neo-Pagan circles, although in some places they are euphemized (a practice possibly just as insulting, if not more so, than banning them entirely). Some Pagans seek to make them less frightening and more friendly by downplaying their more destructive aspects and planting kindlier and more parental motives onto them. It is not that the Dark Gods of any pantheon lack a kindly side, but it is dishonest to ignore the balance of their nature.

For that matter, any deity has a dark side. Odin is both the wise, benevolent All-Father and the power of destructive wrath; the leader who speaks truth and the conqueror who is not above telling lies. Tyr is the power of Honor who strikes down those he deems dishonorable with grim, uncompromising persistence. Thor is both the loyal warrior who loves the common man, and the belligerent drunk. Regardless of what the dogma of Christian cosmology would have us think, there is no such thing as a deity that is all-light. When you find one who purports to be one of those, there is always another deity with whom they are inextricably bound up, who acts as the keeper of darkness, the alternate personality, the shadow to the light.

The ancient Norse/Germanic peoples understood the benevolence and danger of their deities, regardless of which ones they chose to worship for reasons of tribal loyalty. It was the Christian overlay—so much of the lore is seen through the eyes of an already Christianized world-view that accepts the God=good/Devil=bad division—that tried to press the idea of the Aesir as entirely benevolent and the Jotnar as entirely evil upon a much more complex and ambivalent situation. The Jotnar bore the shadow of the glittering Aesir, even more so in the post-Christian legends.

But it is a fact that the Jotnar are not always beautiful or nice or even benevolent, and the Rökkr Gods are, indeed, dark and scary-looking at first glance. Was the original pantheon worshiped by the pre-Indo-European folk always this dark, or was it like most other pantheons, with a variety of natural-function gods who were the usual ambiguous mix of benevolent and dangerous? Was Hela originally another mostly-undifferentiated Great Virgin Goddess, with Angrboda as yet another primitive mother-figure, Farbauti yet another weather god, and Loki yet another Sacrificial Trickster? Did they gain their specific character traits through struggle with the Gods of the conquering people, a struggle that, while it cast them in shadow roles, differentiated them from other similar "generic" deity-pantheons? Or was the culture and the aesthetics of those pre-Indo-European peoples, about whom we know so little, such that they naturally built a pantheon around a Virgin Death Goddess, a devouring wolf-mother and her totemic wolf-children who try to eat the world, and all the other Rökkr deities in their disturbing glory? We will probably never know for sure, as they lost the war of history long before the age of written records reached the North.

Whether we are looking at the Hellenic story of the Olympians and the Titans, or the Sumerian tale of Marduk and his followers slaying Tiamat and her people and carving up her body to make his world, or the Norse creation myth, it seems as though that many-thousand-year-old conflict of invaders versus indigenous people has left an enormous scar on the spiritual history of the Eurasian continent. It seems to have been such a hard turning point, especially in the North, that it has shaped the entire basis of the worldview. Much has been made of the fact that Western pagan traditions center around a balance of conflict, rather than the quest for harmony and the erasure of conflict that characterizes Eastern religions.

One could even posit that the artificial light-good/dark-evil duality lifted from Zoroastrianism into Judeo-Christian monotheism was a reaction to this balance of conflict, an attempt to resolve it by drastic unbalancing fiat, stopping the scales by permanently weighting down one arbitrary side.

It may have happened many thousands of years ago—the Indo-European migrations lasted from 6000-4000 B.C.E.—but its legacy remains like an indelible stain, even if the source of that mark is forgotten. We who study and practice the Old Religions can only forget the crucible of our ancestors' experience at our peril, if only because it has shaped even our modern Western culture so thoroughly that we seemed doomed to keep repeating it every time we forget.

Synchronicity

But now that I've spoken of the Gods in theoretical ways, and posited their mythology in terms of historical process, I am now brought up short, as I always am, by the reality of their existence. As a shaman, I do not have the luxury of suspending literal belief in the Gods in order to theorize about the origins of their human-recorded history. What does it mean, that I believe that they have a literal existence, independent of mine, or of the belief of any human; that the Otherworlds are just what they are, other planes of existence which touch and cross ours, yet are not dependent on our ever-so-physical plane; and yet even further, that our human history seems to reflect a series of events that a scholar would claim caused these myths to be created by humans to metaphorically describe their lives? How can the worlds of shaman and scholar be resolved?

While I don't have a full answer to that—and I think that there may not be one—from the shaman's perspective, these events do not have to be mutually exclusive. The very fact that our world spins close enough to the Nine Otherworlds that spiral about the World Tree is enough. Our world would not be in a position to experience so many crossings-over, so many gateways and "soft spots", places where (and times when) the boundary between worlds is thin and easily accidentally permeated, if there was not an essential quality of "likeness" between them in some way. Even if the peoples are different, the landscapes are different, the laws of physics are different, we have some kind of spiritual synchronicity that allows for periodic linking of our world with Theirs.

Part of this synchronicity is expressed in time and events. Although time in the Nine Worlds is very different from time here—it seems much slower, for the most part; centuries or millennia pass here and only a few generations pass there—their time moves along a pattern similar to ours. From the perspective of spiritual synchronicity, it is not unthinkable to imagine that the Indo-European invasions took place perfectly timed with the murder of Ymir and the overthrow of the thurses...because the cosmic pattern drew both worlds into the same major turn of conflict at the same time. One could see it as a place where the threads of Wyrd for both cosmoses ran through the same narrow space, and knotted together. Similarly, the war between the Aesir and the Vanir may have been cosmically timed with the conflict in our world between earlier waves of earth-worshipping agricultural Indo-Europeans with later sky-worshipping horse-warrior waves.

This worldview presupposes, of course, that the Nine Otherworlds are not a static place frozen in their own time, like some Disneyworld ride that repeats the same moment over and over. It assumes for progress and regress and change, according to their own timescale, but perhaps also linked to ours. It assumes that just as our history is not finished, neither is that of Aesir and Vanir and Jotnar and Alfar and Duergar...and that the changes of their future may also be interwoven with ours. One could speculate that the long centuries (for us) of Christianity-induced lack of connection with the Nine Otherworlds might indicate a period where the threads of Wyrd spun apart for a time. If so, what does it mean that they are seemingly drawing back together again?

Not only is connection with the Old Gods increasing, they are clearly beginning to have an active, transgressing impact on some humans of this world, without those humans seeking them out and inviting that impact. It is also telling that we are approaching a crisis point again in the Western cultural world. As Diana Paxson suggests in the section following this one, when we last left the Gods, the Aesir were acting as the forces of civilization and the Jotnar were taking the part of the implacable powers of nature aligned against it, and humans were desperately siding with the fragile structure of civilization that promised them sanctuary. In this day and age, civilization has, in many ways, won... to the detriment of Nature, and the parts of us that are inextricably a part of Her, which would include every particle of our physical flesh bodies.

We are finding ourselves in a place and time where civilization has run out of balance, creating pollution, diseases, and overpopulation. We are as menaced by the side-effects of progress as our ancestors were by the feral wolf pack, and we are finding that a new respect for and partnership with Nature is now necessary for our survival. At the same time, the Jotunfolk and the Rökkr are making unexpected connections with many of us at a rate that may be unprecedented, or at least unknown for something like eight millennia. To attempt to convince myself that these things are unrelated strikes me as an enormous mistake. If the threads of Wyrd are drawing us closer together again, it would be foolish of us not to consider the possible slant of this new turning point in our histories.

This is, above all other things, a book of faith. To study these Gods and wights, whether through the lore or through the experiences of others, is to expand our understanding not only of their humanlike traits, but of their divine characteristics as well. Through our Gods, we gain understanding of the workings of the Cosmos, and our place in it, however small.

> *Hail the North Wind, bitter with frost,*
> *Hail the fire that leaps and bites,*
> *Hail the oceans that birth and devour,*
> *Hail the mountains that rise to the sky,*
> *Hail our brother beasts that run,*
> *Hail the Wights who are the gateways to all of Nature.*

Utgard:
The Role of the Jotnar in the Religion of the North
by Diana L. Paxson

nyone who has ever picked up a book on Norse mythology knows about the conflict between the gods and the giants. It is pictured as an endless dualistic struggle between the forces of order and chaos, or good and evil, which will culminate in the epic struggle of Ragnarok. And yet, despite the gusto with which Thor bashes etins, the old literature leaves one with a curiously ambiguous picture. Ancient and terrible the Jotnar may be, but are they simply destructive, or does the conflict between them and the lords of Asgard have a deeper significance?

As I explore the spiritual ecology of the North I have come to believe that far from being the eternal enemy, the Jotnar may have a crucial role to play in the survival of the world and its inhabitants, including human beings. An analysis of their origins and functions not only illuminates their relationship to the gods (and therefore the meaning of the Æsir as well), but suggests a new way to interpret some of the ambiguities encountered in Norse attitudes towards the feminine and the natural world.

The mythologies of other early cultures reveal a pattern which may be paralleled in that of the North. Bearing in mind that traditional cultures do not have a single, canonical, "creation myth", still, almost everywhere we find a first generation of deities who are responsible for the creation of the world and who are later supplanted by their children, the pantheon whose worship becomes the religion of the land.

The Graeco-Roman creation myth tells how Gaia, Mother Earth, arose from the empty "yawning" of Chaos and conceived the Titanic powers by Ouranos, who suppressed them before they could be born into the world. The last of them, Kronos, attacked and emasculated his father, separating him from the earth. The Titans who were then released were powers of the sun and moon, darkness and the dawn. Monsters of various kinds were also created. Kronos (Time) married his sister Rhea (Space) and they became the parents of the Olympian gods. Eventually the gods, aided by monstrous allies and the counsel of Mother Earth, defeated and imprisoned the Titans in Tartaros. Nonetheless, the time when Kronos and the Titans ruled was considered by the Greeks to have been a golden age.

Despite the theological sophistication of Hinduism, traces remain of a pre-Vedic system in which "The gods and the antigods are the twofold offspring of the lord-of-progeny (Prajapati). Of these the gods are the younger, the antigods, the older. They have been struggling with each other for the dominion of the worlds." (Brhad-aranyaka Upanishad 1.3.1.[205]). These antigods are sometimes called *asuras* (later construed as *a-suras*, or "not-gods"), although this term, derived from the root *as*, "to be", or *Asu*, "breath", was originally used to identify the most important gods. Although the *asuras* are seen as opponents, many among them are described as wise and beneficent and aid the gods. Among the *asuras* of the Mahabharata include *daityas* (genii), *danavas* (giants), *kalakanjas* (stellar spirits), *kalejas* (demons of time), *nagas* (serpents), and *raksasas* (night wanderers, or demons) They live in palaces in mountain caves, the bowels of the earth, the sea, and the sky and are said to be powerful in battle and magic.

In Egyptian religion, the oldest company of gods seems to have represented properties of primeval matter. According to E.A. Wallace Budge, "in primeval times at least the Egyptians believed in the existence of a deep and boundless watery mass out of which had come into being the heavens, and the earth, and everything that is in them." (The Gods of the Egyptians, I: 283). These powers were represented by four pairs of gods and goddesses. The world as we know it was created by the action of the Khepera aspect of the sun-god, who says in the Book of the Overthrowing of Apepi, *"Heaven did not exist, and earth had not come into being, and the things of the earth and creeping things had not come into existence in that place, and I raised them from out of Nu from a state of inactivity."* (295)

This bears a remarkable resemblance to the opening of "Voluspá" —

In earliest times did Ymir live:
was nor sea nor land nor salty waves,
neither earth was there, nor upper heaven,
but a gaping nothing, and green things nowhere...
Was the land then lifted by the sons of Bor,
who made Midgard, the matchless earth...
    (verses 3-4, Hollander's translation)

Unless one is prepared to believe that the author of the Edda read hieroglyphics, one must accept this idea as a way of conceptualizing creation common to many early peoples. The "inactivity" of Nu is a reasonable southern parallel to the eternal ice that encased Ymir. In both cases, the earth we know is "lifted" into a state of manifestation by the action of a more clearly personified power. In the Younger Edda, we learn that the world was fashioned from Ymir's skull and bones, freed from the ice by the tongue of Audhumla, the primal female principle in the form of a cow.

In all of these mythologies, the elder gods are the world creators and elemental powers. Myths about them have to do with their origins and their battles against the race of gods who supplanted them. They may be portrayed as monstrous or fair, but always they dwell in wild places— "Utgard"—or in the element to which they belong. Although they are the opponents of the gods, they do not appear to be hostile to men. In fact they have very little to do with human concerns.

A number of theories have been offered to account for this cosmic struggle. A hypothesis adopted by many scholars has been that the elder deities, such as the *asuras*, were the gods of races conquered by the people who worship the gods. The *asuras* were the gods of pre-Vedic India, and presumably the Jotnar and Titans would be the deities of the pre-Indo-European peoples of their lands. However, this theory does not explain why gods and giants should differ in function.

Although some of the Jotnar are allies of the Æsir—Ægir, for instance, who brews ale in his cauldrons so that the gods can feast in his undersea hall, or Mimir who teaches Odin wisdom—their functions clearly have to do with natural forces. Ægir is a god of the ocean; his wife, Ran, rules the depths beneath the waves, who are their daughters. However it is the Van, Njord, who watches over ships and those who make their living on the sea. Fjorgyn is Earth, but Frey and Freyja, the *alfar* and *ármadhr* ("harvest man") are invoked to aid in farming. It is not the gods who are the personified natural forces beloved of 19th century folklorists, but the Jotnar.

The gods, be they Æsir or Olympians, can be seen as the product of evolving human consciousness. Odin, first of the Æsir to arise, gives us the runes, the symbols and words of power by which the human intellect is enabled to comprehend the world. The Jotun expresses the natural power, while the god embodies the qualities needed for humans to deal with it. In the myths, the Æsir are able to interbreed with Jotnar or humankind. The stories of interaction between the gods and the giants can almost serve as a chronicle of the changing relationship between evolving human consciousness and the natural world.

Of all the Æsir, Thor, the thunderer and great slayer of giants, is the most elemental. He is the Son of Earth, and his rune is that of the *thorn*. He joys in the chaos of the storm, but he can use its energy to protect humankind. But his is not a war of extermination. In "The Lay of Hárbarth," Thor tells us, "much might had the etins if all did live; little might had men then in Midgard's round." (verse 23, Hollander's translation). As Gro Steinsland points out (1986), this is not a war of extermination, but of balance.

For a long time it was assumed that one distinction between Jotnar and Æsir was that the giants were never worshiped. However, Steinsland has demonstrated that the giants, or more particularly the giantesses, did indeed receive cult worship in the Viking Age. She proposes that Snorri's account of how the gods gave part of the roasting ox to Thiazi while traveling to visit Utgard-Loki reflects an ancient ritual in which offerings were made to the wilderness powers. Skadi's reply to Loki's taunts in "Lokasenna" refers to her holy groves and hallowed shrines, a boast supported by many place names, and she is not only the daughter of a giant, but the home she inherited from him is located in Asgard. However for the most part, the hallows of the Jotnar are to be found in Utgard—"outside the garth"—in the wilderness beyond the fields we know.

The Jotnar are elemental in character and force, associated with the regions or environments in which they live (cliff-thurses, *berg risi*, or mountain giants or trolls, rime-thurses, sons of Surtr, Ægir, Ran and the waves). They rule the realm of Nature, and can thus be viewed as chieftains of the orders of nature spirits appropriate to various environments: the *skogsrar*, or "wood-roes", of the forest, who can bestow blessings in exchange for offerings; the *näckar*, or "nixies", *sjöra*, lake spirits, and *forskarlar*, the falls-men, in the water; the *duergar* (dwarves) who live under the earth, and the *landvættir,* or land-wights, for a region in general. These are what the people at Findhorn in Scotland call the devas, the spirits which inhabit and give health to the environment, ranging from entitities that express the spirit of a place or a group or species of living things (such as a forest), to the spirits of individual flowers and trees. Even during the Christian period they survived in Færie, in which noble races of elves are accompanied by all kinds of sprites and goblins. In medieval folklore, the Jotnar devolved into hags, giants and trolls, and their attendant nature spirits into dwarves, dryads and the like, but they continue to dwell outside the boundaries of the human world.

But not all of the Jotnar live in the wilderness. Giantesses are co-opted into the world of the gods as mothers and mates; in fact a majority of the Æsir are the children of Jotnar on one or both sides. Indeed, when an As or Van seeks a bride outside Asgard, his only source of mates is in Jotunheim. Scratch a goddess, and you are likely to uncover an etin-bride.

The courtships of Skadi and Gerda are particularly noteworthy, and it is significant that they are married to Vanir, the gods most closely connected with the natural world. Odin himself sires children by a number of giantesses, most notably Jord, or earth, the mother of Thor, and Rind, who bears him Vali. On the other hand, those female Jotun who are not co-opted by marriage appear to be more feared by the Æsir than are the males.

The male Jotnar slain by Thor are viewed as worthy antagonists who can sometimes be tricked into sharing their wisdom or powers. But the females, even Hyrokkin, whose strength is required to push Baldr's funeral ship out to sea, evoke a primal terror. They are not only wild, but female, with all of the suppressed power of both the feminine and the wilderness. In his analysis of prayers to Thor, John Lindow identifies eight killings of female Jotnar and four of male.

"Thor was the defender of Asgard, as Thorbjorn himself put it, against the forces of evil and chaos. These forces seem, in the reality of peoples' lives... to have had a very strong female component... If those who fight for order are male, then it is appropriate that those who fight for disorder should be female." (Lindow, 1988, p. 127)

At this point a good feminist should say, "how like a man", but I think that the causes of this hostility lie deeper than simple misogyny. Norse culture in general approaches the feminine with a mixture of emotions, seeing it as irrational and equating loss of status with loss of control while at the same time retaining the memory of a long tradition of reverence for women and belief in their superior spiritual powers. This attitude is paralleled by equally ambivalent feelings about the world of nature. Is it therefore surprising that the Jotnar—the primal powers of nature—who are most feared should be personified as female?

Female biology makes it harder for women to suppress awareness of their physical nature in the way that men often do, and though women are less likely to seek battle, a woman once enraged may fight with a fury that ignores the rules by which men like to conduct their wars (certainly some of the women in the sagas are first-class bitches, and the men might have been better off if their wives had been allowed to fight the bloodfeuds).

These generalizations reflect the social stereotypes of our culture; in reality there is a considerable overlap between the genders in this regard, and intellect, intuition, and the like are uniquely mixed in each individual. Given this caveat, such social and biological factors may explain why men have tended to link the feminine with Nature, which can be both terrible and nurturing, as well as with the irrational, the unconscious, and spiritual power.

Steinsland makes a good case for the survival of rituals addressed to the Jotnar into the Viking Age. Rather than identifying this as a lingering superstition, let us consider what function retaining a reverence for powers first conceptualized at the birth of human culture might serve in a supposedly more "civilized" age. The scholars who look upon myths of the passage of power from Jotnar or Titans to the shining gods as a reflection of a historical process may be seeing only part of the picture. A more accurate way to describe the change might be as evolutionary. Evolution does imply change over time, but this change can consist of alteration within a continuing group as well as the replacement of one culture or species by another.

The human brain is an excellent example of an organism which has developed by adding new structures and functions to older ones. Most people today have access only to the newer levels of consciousness, and are disturbed by the "irrational" emotions that shake them when the older parts of the brain are aroused. In the same way, our civilization thinks of itself as "modern", and has trouble understanding the social movements that arise when deeper needs revive older ways.

A major paradigm shift in our relationship to Nature is taking place in this century—a change that must occur if humanity is to survive. Ours is the first generation to be aware of the fragility of the environment. "Primitive" people retain an instinctive awareness that the only way to survive in an environment that is more powerful than they are is by learning to live in harmony with its forces. But as civilization and the development of technology have given humans more control over their surroundings, Nature has become an adversary. In the natural world, birth and death, creation and destruction, are parts of a continuing cycle in which both are equally crucial to long-term survival. Modern man can accept this in theory so long as he remains insulated from its realities by his technology, but especially in the ancient North, where the climate is unforgiving, it is understandable that in the Viking Age the world outside the walls of the garth should have often been seen as something to fear.

And yet, as Kirsten Hastrup shows in Culture and History in Medieval Iceland, access to the actual or psychic wilderness was necessary for magic. The outlaw, or "out-lier" is banished outside the boundaries of the community, and yet that position may enable him to serve it in ways impossible for those who stay safe within walls. In the cases of both *hamrammr* and *berserkr* there is a movement, in body on the one hand, in personality on the other. Such movement seems to have been easily imagined, in a world where every man had his *fylgja*, his double in wild space. (Hastrup, 1985, 153)

The tension is not only between order and chaos, but between control and power. This is why Thor never kills all of the giants, why the Æsir seek Jotun-brides, why Odin goes to Vafthruthnir to seek wisdom—and why worship at the shrines of Skadi and other Jotun continued into the Viking Age. From wilderness comes the energy that humans, like other species, need to survive.

What will happen if humans forget how to balance this energy? Ragnarok acquires a different meaning in each age. The "Voluspá" foretells a simultaneous breakdown in the natural balance and the social order. Odin marshals the Einherjar and the gods march out for the last time to meet their foes. When all is destroyed,

> 'Neath sea the land sinketh, the sun dimmeth,
> from the heavens fall the fair bright stars;
> gusheth forth steam and gutting fire,
> to very heaven soar the hurtling flames. (verse 56)

The order of creation described in the early myths is being reversed. The world will return to its primal elements once more.

For the ancient Norse, the fear was that natural forces would grow too powerful. But science shows us that it is equally dangerous to suppress a powerful force too far or too long. The film *Koyaanisqatski* presented a frightening picture of a world out of balance. Whether the Jotnar are allowed to rage unchecked or suppressed too completely, disaster will follow. Today's vision of Ragnarok is of an age when natural cycles have been pushed so far out of balance that only the most chaotic and destructive of the powers of nature will remain.

Can this disaster be avoided? Early cultures, living in a world in which the seasonal alternation of birth and death was more accepted than it is today, tend to think in terms of cycles rather than of a linear progression. But though the Völva foresees destruction for the gods, the victory of chaos is not final–

> *I see green again—with growing things,*
> *the earth arise from out of the sea...*
> *again the Æsir on Itha Plain meet...*
> *again go over the great world-doom,*
> *and Fimbultyr's unfathomed runes.* (verse 59)

The process of creation is repeated, and once more Odin's runes give meaning to the world.

In a world of vanishing rainforests and global warming, it may seem that the Time of Earth Changes foretold by more recent prophets such as Sun Bear is unavoidable. In the long run this is probably true, for why should either a physical body or the world be expected to last for ever? For the world, as for us, death should be viewed not as an extinction but as a transformation so that the cycle can begin anew. Still, just as abuse of one's body can shorten, or healthy living extend. a human lifespan, humans have the power to hasten Ragnarok or to lengthen this age of the world. With that power comes responsibility.

Environmentalists have provided us with more than enough information to start work on the physical plane, and there should be no need to repeat their instructions here. But those of us who follow the Way of the North have an additional opportunity. We are already vowed to stand with the gods—what we must do now is to understand their relationship to the Jotnar so that we do not end up sabotaging our own side.

We need the giants as we need the wilderness, as a source of the nourishment required for our physical and spiritual survival. They provide psychological stability by aligning the powers of nature and protection at the species level, for they are the spiritual ancestors of all living things. Even apparent chaos may hold a hidden harmony. This does not mean abandoning intellect and technology and returning to the primitive, but as we use the gifts of the gods, we should remember that even Thor does not attempt to completely exterminate his enemies. These days perhaps we ought to be supporting the Jotnar rather than fighting them.

Jotun myths have to do with creation and cosmic patterning. In recreating the myths we recreate the world. Along with the land-spirits, they should therefore receive offerings and honor. When we seek to work in trance, to draw on the deepest powers that lie hid in our own inner Utgards, the Jotnar may even be invoked first in the ritual.

Like other forms of paganism, the Northern branch of the Old Religion is an Earth-religion. As Steinsland puts it, "After all, it would be more remarkable if Norse tradition should miss any ritual dealing with powers on whom the whole of existence finally depended. The giants are as necessary to the world as the gods are." (ibid, p. 221). In recreating the practice of Norse religion, we must not forget to honor those powers.

References

E. A. Wallace Budge, The Gods of the Egyptians, I. N.Y.; Dover Press, 1969

Alain Danielou, The Gods of India N.Y.; Inner Traditions Internation, 1985

Kirsten Hastrup, Culture and History in Medieval Iceland. Oxford, 1985

C. Kerenyi, The Gods of the Greeks. N.Y.; Thames & Hudson, 1951

John Lindow, "Addressing Thor", Scandinavian Studies 60, 1988:119-136

The Poetic Edda, trans. Lee M. Hollander, Austin, University of Texas Press, 1986

Gro Steinsland, "Giants as Recipients of Cult in the Viking Age?" in Words and Objects; towards a dialogue between archaeology and history of religion. Norwegian University Press/Institute for Comparative Research in Human Culture, 1986.

On The History And Nature Of Giantkind

otunfolk, taken as an entire race, are more numerous in the Nine Worlds than any other type of being. Of the Nine Worlds, three of them—Jotunheim, Muspellheim, and Niflheim—are entirely ruled and populated by them. A fourth world, Helheim, admits the Dead of many races, but is ruled by Hela, a Jotun goddess. They are a power to be reckoned with.

In the lore, the giants are pictured with a dizzying variety of characteristics. Some are beautiful, some grotesque; some are simple to the point of dullness and some are blessed with wisdom of divine measure. Some of them are the sworn enemies of the Aesir; others marry into their ranks, or those of the Vanir, or have affairs with them. Many an Asa-god was mothered by an etin-woman, although few women of the Aesir marry etin men—Sigyn being a notable exception in that regard.

The Jotnar have some habits, as a species, that we humans find difficult to deal with, and we tend to demonize them for these things. It's hard to get beyond our own cultural imprinting and appreciate that these people are members of a different species from us. Some of their cultural practices—cannibalism, duels, sexual violence—may upset or horrify us if we see them through human eyes. What we need to remember is that they are not human, and cannot be held to human morality. They have their own moral code(s), which work for them; their nature is different and could not be

best served by human rules. It is the ultimate in ethnocentricity to assume
that we can judge them by our standards.

What I have seen is that the Jotnar are all different. They have
distinct personalities, motives, and preferences. They are
individuals, not some mindless screeching horde. They are not
stupid; many of them are cunning and intelligent. Some are hostile to
everyone but their own, some are benignly inclined toward others
but not inclined to care much, and a few are actively interested in
outsiders. Some will give their word and stick to it no matter what,
while others are simply not to be trusted under any circumstances.
Some are wise and fair, others cruel and vengeful, but most are
somewhere in between. I don't believe they can all be painted (or
tarred) with the same brush. In short, they remind me a lot of human
beings in many respects.

However, I think the etins should be accorded caution,
circumspection and respect, no matter whether you're well- or ill-
disposed toward them personally (if nothing else, they can be
viewed as worthy enemies by those so inclined). No one has to like
or admire them, but they shouldn't be dismissed as insignificant.
After all, I doubt Thor would've made it his business to fight them if
they were all just a bunch of sniveling weaklings.

—Elizabeth, spirit-worker

All of the Jotunfolk in the Nine Worlds were descended from two very
different ancestors—Ymir and Surt, the progenitors of frost-thurses and
fire-etins respectively. Surt is spoken of as being there before any other
beings, when there was only Muspellheim and Niflheim floating in
Ginnungagap. He fathered the race of fire-etins, and little is said about
them, as they did not have the tumultuous beginnings of the frost-thurses.

On the other hand, the story of Ymir, or Aurgelmir as the Jotnar refer
to him, is the classic Norse creation myth. Originally, Niflheim (Land of
Mists) was a frozen chunk of ice, its only moving water the primal river
Elivagar, whose waters were a poison that froze anything it touched. As
Muspellheim drew closer to Niflheim, the solid ice of the Land of Mists
began to melt, and to this day it is half water, blending into the frozen ice.

The ice began to recede, and the sleeping body of Ymir was brought into the air.

In his book *Our Marvelous Native Tongue*, linguist Robert Claiborne explores the origins of the word *Yule*, referring to the Winter Solstice, the darkest part of the year. This word seems to have been brought into the Indo-European lexicon by contact with the indigenous Scandinavian peoples that the Indo-Europeans conquered and intermarried. Most of what we know of these people—which is very little, to be sure—comes from these words which were passed into Old Germanic and into no other Indo-European-descended language. The descendants of some of these words we use every day, such as *husam* (house) and *skuldar* (shoulder). We know that they intermarried with the more populous Indo-Europeans, because they also bequeathed us the words *wif* (wife, originally meaning merely an adult woman) and *kiltha* (child)... and, ominously, *skalkhaz* (slave). They also left us *Yeowhla*, the word for the Winter Solstice, which must have been a crucial time for a people living in a subarctic area, where the nights are painfully dark during the winter months.

According to Claiborne, there is some evidence that parts of the Norse creation myth were also passed down to us from these distant ancestors; specifically the part of the story with the ice melting with the coming of warm winds from the south—Muspellheim, the warm place—and the "birth" of Ymir, the mountain-like giant ancestor, from his icy bonds. His theory is that this description is very like what people would have experienced during the end of the Ice Age, when the glaciers might recede many miles in a single man's lifetime, exposing the mountains which then began to bloom with green, and creating tumultuous rivers that flooded the lower areas and created lakes and inland bays. This would suggest that these proto-Scandinavians had been present in the area since well before the melting of the Ice Age...and that the Jotnar may well have been their Gods. The Scandinavian scholar Liljenroth has put forth similar theories, tracing the name of the goddess Hel to pre-Indo-European sources.

When Ymir appeared from the ice, according to what we can figure out he was an enormous proto-giant, unable to move much, and without much intelligence. He could not speak or shapeshift; it seems that his nature was more mountainlike than anything else. He got his nourishment from the udder of Audumhla, an immense divine cow who appears suddenly, unexplained, in the story and then vanishes again soon after. Ymir mostly slept, and while he slept two frost-thurses were born from the sweat of his armpits—one male and one female—and another male frost-thurse was born of the friction of his legs rubbing together. These were full-fledged first-generation frost-thurses, with all the powers that they would pass to their descendants; they grew, worked, spoke, and bred a new race.

Audumhla the cow, as her final act in this play, tries to lick away the ice of Niflheim. In doing so, she uncovers yet another body which comes to life—that of Buri, the first Aesir. He is of a different race than the thurses, but he takes one as a wife and sires children, including a son named Bor. His children are Odin, Vili, and Ve, and these three plot and carry out the murder of the great giant Ymir, causing his blood to flow out in a great rush that floods all of Niflheim. Many giants are swept away, and those who remain repopulate Niflheim and the newly created Jotunheim, while Bor's sons busily remake the rest of the cosmos to their liking, using the dismembered pieces of Ymir's body.

Looking at this myth from the perspective of that long-ago conquered people, it is easy to see it as reshaped, rebuilt, remodeled to reflect the new reality. The conquering Indo-Europeans swept in and took over, and the myth changed to show the eponymous ancestor of their Gods appearing jarringly like a Johnny-come-lately in the story; his grandchildren murder the eponymous ancestor of the Gods of the conquered people, and rebuild things to their liking. Those who rebel hide out in the wilder areas, the poorer and less accessible lands, and fight an ongoing guerilla war with the new regime. The murderers divide up their ancestor's legacy—the earth that is his physical body—among themselves and their allies.

Odin, the grandson of Buri and the chief of Ymir's murderers, ceremonially takes to wife a giantess—Jord—whose name means Earth and who is practically the embodiment of the land; there are strong echoes of this practice in the myths left behind by other Indo-European conquerors. To the south, once Zeus has firmly conquered the giant-race referred to as the Titans, his first wife is Metis (Wisdom), a woman of their race taken to wife as a symbol of his dominance and sovereignty over their land, as well as a ritual melding of their races. He then divorces her and marries Themis, another Titan who symbolizes social rule, and then divorces her, too, for a wife of his own people—Hera—who is a goddess of marriage and who becomes his consort and ruling Queen. Odin, too, does this; although he may breed with various giantesses, his Queen is Frigga, a lady of the Aesir.

The next section of Jotun history is spotty, and glossed over in a line or two in long paeans to the Aesir's creations. It is said that only Bergelmir and his family, alone of the first-thurses, survived the flood, but every piece of PCPG we have on that subject disagrees. According to the Jotunfolk who have spoken to us about it, a good portion of Bergelmir's tribe survived, and there are some Jotunfolk even today who were born before the Flood; they are listed in Bergelmir's entry. Surt and his folk in Muspellheim were apparently little bothered by the Flood. Except for those who crossed their bloodlines with frost-thurses and left their hot realm, the fire-etins in general seem to have had a much more clannish and well-guarded history. The frost-thurses, perhaps due to their elemental association with Wind and Air and Weather, spread out and populated the new world of Jotunheim, some with fire-etin spouses, cross-bred children, and children who adapted to the new worlds and their ecosystems. By the time of the war between the Aesir and the Vanir, the giants are the most populous creatures in the Nine Worlds.

Giant Characteristics

We will discuss the issues of Jotun genealogy and breeding in the next chapter; first it is important to examine those characteristics that form "giant nature"—those traits that they all have in common regardless of their elemental attributions. What the Jotunfolk are like varies widely—frost giants are not fire giants are not Jotunheim mountain-etins are not Iron Wood Clan etins. But they all have certain racial traits in common:

1) Powers that are strongly linked to nature and the elements—wind, water, fire, snow, rock, trees, animals. Some curious researchers have asked me what the difference is between a Jotun and an elemental spirit. Although it's a tricky concept to tease apart, I have tried to make sense of the clear difference between them.

It's difficult for us as ordinary human beings, caught up in the bias of our own existence, to understand what it is to be fire, or ice, or some other natural phenomenon... difficult, but not impossible! Shamanic-types the world over have studied "becoming one with the natural world" as a way to gain knowledge and power. One of the things that Hela is having me do, as part of my shamanic training, is to "master" the elements. This does not mean being able to wave my oh-so-wizardly hands and call up storms and lightning. On the contrary; this means being familiar with them, understanding them inside and out, having had the experience of being as close to them as it's possible for a human to get. You meld with them and understand the essence of them. Working with Jotun nature is very helpful for this.

To explain the difference between a wight/elemental and a Jotun, I could use an example from the Finnish Kalevala, where the sorcery is all about learning the "true name" of something—like cold, or heat, or the sun, or fire, or whatever. The "true name" isn't a magic word, it's a magic feeling, a way of being, an intimate knowledge of that element. When you've made that intimate connection, something of it is in you, and you can work with it far easier than someone who's standing back and working with it from a safe distance.

To be in the presence of the elemental Jotuns is to see this up-close and in action. Take a fire-etin, for example. It is not that he is just fire, otherwise he'd just be, well, a fire like any other fire. It is not that he knows the true name of fire. It is that he embodies the true name of fire. It is not that he embodies the *spirit* of fire, it's that he embodies the true name of fire, that experience of being one with fire yet being oneself as well, separate. The fire that knows itself, in essence. An elemental has a much more limited understanding of itself as a conscious being. An etin is fully as conscious and complicated as a human (and perhaps more so), while having the experience of being a part of nature as an integrated part of themselves.

As part of their affinity with the forces of Nature, there does seem to be something of an antipathy to civilized farming among many of the giants. In an old Alsatian myth, the daughter of a giant playfully captures a farmer in the act of ploughing and puts him in her apron, but her father tells her to put her new toy back, as even giants need bread. On the other hand, giants such as Baugi and Hreidmar are farmers themselves, perhaps their location on the eastern Vanaheim-ward coast has something to do with that.

2) A wild, primal temper, and the ability to berserk easily. Some have excellent self-control, some don't. Their various cultures have boundaries for this racial tendency, which include strong rules around what is and is not an acceptable reason for challenging or killing someone. Weregild is very important to a wounded Jotun, and part of that weregild may be the visible suffering of the trespasser, in order to satisfy their anger. Not all are quick to anger; old mountain giants can sometimes have a somewhat more phlegmatic attitude.

3) Strong passions in general—high emotions, harsh violent lusts, wild ecstatic joys, loud crude humor, overkill vengeance. Their one mark is their intensity. They live life at high volume and deadly seriousness. There is no such thing as a boring repressed Jotun, or a flighty noncommittal Jotun. (Loki can pass as that last one, but he's faking it when he does it.) Even with the ones who have the mask of polite courtesy and iron self-control (like Utgard-Loki and Mordgud and Gerda), you can sense that roiling volcano underneath. If they become invested in you, they will defend you against any enemy (unless they feel that you are being stupid, and sometimes even then), and perhaps even kill for you, but they expect the same intensity of commitment in return.

4) Strong clan and tribal loyalties. With a few exceptions, Jotunfolk all live in tribal societies and generally feel a stronger kinship to their blood family than to whomever they might marry. One example of this is Gerda's insistence that Frey give up his magic sword as a bridal-gift to her family;

besides the fact that an expensive bridal-gift shows the value of the bride, she also increased her family's power in this way. Their loyalty is another example of their intensity; this is where the Swedish term *trolltryggr* (faithful as a giant) came from.

5) Jotunkind have an almost casual familiarity with shapeshifting. All of them can do it to one extent or another, all that I've spoken to about it have been doing it since birth, and the really adept ones whip their physical forms around like we change clothes. They consider it a cultural art form. Most of the time, you'll see them in their "force of nature" form, which means that you might walk right by one and not notice them. They have perfectly usable humanoid forms as well. In general, though, Jotnar vary wildly in size and shape, not just between subraces but between individuals in the same family. As an extremely physically homogenous race, we are often made uncomfortable by the multitudinous differentiation among Jotunfolk.

This shapeshifting seems to be inextricably linked with their nature-affiliation. Those who change into animals have a totemic feel to them; the names of many giantesses, especially, are animal-names such as Hyndla (Hound-bitch), Ktt (Cat), Kraka (Crow), or Trana (Crane). Others are named after their natural powers, such Kari the North Wind and his bevy of children whose names are different terms for snow, or Aegir's daughters who names are mostly different sorts of waves.

6) Their cultures vary, but all seem to be more bloodthirsty, more intense, more primal than humans. They have codes of honor, but those codes are much harsher—they have to be, or they'd all kill each other. (One seidhr-worker commented, "To use a terrible pop culture reference, they are much more like Klingons than humans.") Certain things are acceptable in their culture that are not so in ours—one example is cannibalism, which they do for both funerary and vengeance reasons. Just as I wonder if many Pagans who have visions of some utopian dark-age agricultural past are actually unconsciously tapping into Vanaheim, I wonder if some folk who have visions of the fantasy "barbarian" tribes are actually tapping into Jotunheim.

7) Jotnar are fighters, all of them. The natural forces that they are most in tune with are the most powerful of Nature's forces—the hurricane, the brush fire, the earthquake, the storm at sea. (While we, from our perspective, tend to assume that these are entirely negative and even evil, that's coming at it from our perspective. Nature would disagree. She might even say that these moments are when She is at Her most awesome, even if they are inconvenient for us.) They fight for territory, for tribal justice, and for sport. Some will even humor us and fight for sport with us. One tranceworker commented, "I've dealt with several of them in varying capacities. Several times, being the martial individual that I am I've challenged them to 'test my mettle.' This seemed to greatly amuse them. I have won and I have lost. I can honestly say that I've walked away from all of them on my own two feet. I think this is why it was so easy to 'test my mettle' against them. They saw it as entertaining that the little human wanted to tussle."

They will also fight for dominance, to see where people are in the "pack order". This is especially true for the more animal-oriented Jotunfolk. On my first visit to the Iron Wood, I was surrounded by werefolk, and one of them jumped me. I shapeshifted to a fighting form and knocked him down, and he retreated. It was just a challenge, to see how I should be treated. Often, it seems, passing human tranceworkers will be challenged, either for this reason or because they are trespassing on someone else's territory and are being legitimately warned off. Instead of realizing what is happening, they may think that this is a life-or-death battle, and that this strange beast is challenging them out of nowhere for no reason except to eat them. They lash out instead of thinking, and things get worse from there.

8) Jotun sex is wild, rough, and violent, but not sexist; in general, male and female Jotunfolk tend to be equal in size and ferocity, with no sexual dimorphism. The idea of females submitting to or being overpowered by males is ridiculous to them. Jotun female nature is not any more frithful than Jotun male nature. They are much less prone to any sort of rigid gender role than any other race in the Nine Worlds, including humans.

Ordinary sexual activity among the Jotunkind is as passionate as anything
else that they do, and as violent, and is often accompanied by a great deal of
wild shapeshifting during the act. The one time where there are
active/passive partners is during Jotun sex magic, and strangely enough, it is
the passive partner who is considered the primary magician, with the active
partner as their assistant.

The marriage customs of Jotunfolk vary from place to place, but there
are strong differences between their generally accepted customs and those
of, for example, the Aesir. There is no taboo against nonheterosexual
relations in any Jotun tribe that I have found; although heterosexuals tend
to have a somewhat higher status in tribes where childbearing and siring is
important, there is no penalty for engaging in any sort of relationship that
does not cause trouble in the tribe. This is especially true in the Iron Wood
where there are a high percentage of hermaphroditic or gender-ambiguous
births. Many humans who work with Jotnar find it surprising that even the
largest and most "macho" male Jotun warrior, if he isn't interested in ever
doing it with another large macho male warrior, probably has a friend who
has done just that, and is likely just fine with the general concept even if it
isn't his own preference.

Monogamy as a standard is variable; among most of the Jotun, one may
take as many spouses as one can A) afford to house and feed, and B) keep
from fighting with each other. Multiple spouses don't generally live
together unless they are related, such as a pair of sisters or brothers, which
means that those with two or more spouses also have two or more
households and need to wander between them. The much-whispered-
about difficulties between Angrboda and Sigyn, Loki's two wives, have
nothing to do with objections to polygamy, but more from Angrboda's
resentment of his taking an Aesir wife instead of sticking to his own clan.

Jotun marriage ceremonies will vary from formal religious ritual to
simply stating one's intentions in front of the tribe, but what they all share
is some form of blood-sharing. If there is no blood publicly exchanged
between the two people in question, the wedding is not legitimate as far as
the Jotnar are concerned. Even a finger-prick is essential, although
generally both partners give their hands for a blade-cut that will make a

scar. These scars are shown off in the same way as wedding rings might be to a human; if there is a breakup, both partners might disfigure the scar with many lines across it. Sharing blood seems to be less about drama and gore, and more about kinship relations between tribes; it's how you make your partner ritually into part of your family by placing some of your family's blood into their body.

Whether or not a married couple will live together might also vary. The idea that all partners ought to live forever under the same roof and spend every night in the same bed is foreign to Jotunkind; they might prefer to live with their own tribes or families, and simply get together in one place or the other for part or most of the time. Some might live with one spouse and visit another. Some permanent wanderers might have no home at all save that of their spouse, but be on the road much of the time. When you do find a couple living together long-term, it may be because they have small children to raise and are isolated from their tribes, or have built a hall together, or are working a piece of land together, or simply prefer each others' company.

> In a way, I find that although the Jotnar are beneficial to work with, particularly in this day and age, it is much, much more delicate to work with them in some ways. By this, I do not mean that they are delicate as entities, but that they must be approached with total awareness of the entire relationship. I find that they are a bit touchy, and caution must be used. This is important, and perhaps this is something that can be seen as one way in which some folk don't work well with them. Jotnar don't like to be ignored, they don't like being overlooked once you've started to work with them and they take an invested interest in you, and they claim a lot more responsibility on my part than any other God or wight has. What do I mean by this? I have to do the work. I have to work with them, I have to do what they say, I have to keep active to keep them present. They also don't allow much laziness in my work, either. Another way they demand responsibility is they seem (at least for me) to require a lot more patience and awareness and politeness to the rest of the world—human, animal, plant, you name it.
>
> —Lyn, spirit-worker

For most folk in the various northern-tradition religions, the main question will be, "Why should I bother to deal with the Jotnar at all? What can they teach me that the Aesir or Vanir can't?" Leaving aside the fact that everyone has something to teach that no one else can, there's certainly no reason why any particular person ought to work specifically with trolls and giants, especially if they make you uncomfortable and they are not speaking to you personally. For the same reasons, there's no reason why I should work with the Aesir particularly closely. However, I have been known to talk to them on occasion, when I needed something—especially when I needed to learn something. Similarly, some of my friends and acquaintances who follow the Aesir or Vanir have been known to consult Jotunfolk when they required teaching in a particular area.

One of those areas is shapeshifting. Although the Gods and the Alfar can shapeshift, to an extent—Odin is reasonably good at it, as is Freya—no one is quite so accomplished at it as a Jotun. It's part of their nature. Shapeshifting—for us in our more material bodies, that means changing the shape of our *hame,* our astral body, at will—can be a powerful learning experience. In a very real way, you can't really understand what *you* are until you have gone by way of what you are *not.* That's why such a large part of the shaman's path is shapeshifting, and/or gender changing, and/or body modification, and/or playing with neurochemistry. It's deliberately putting yourself into the deep knowing of what you are not, and by this you learn more about what you are—although that's not the main point, it's only a side effect and a preliminary teaching (something that the core shamans often miss). Of course, becoming what you are not has this tendency to change what you are, starting the whole process over again.

Another area is the understanding of the elements on a deep level. By elements, I refer not only to the standard four elemental forces of earth, air, fire, and water, because the Jotun work with and embody other natural forces as well—death, decay, rebirth, balance. While there are many other lessons in the world to be learned about esoteric things, no one teaches about the natural order of things like the Jotnar. I could not really begin to master my first element, Air, until I had an intimate (although short-lived) relationship with the North Wind. I despaired of fully understanding Water, my most recalcitrant element, until the Nine Mermaids got through with me.

Nowhere in the traditional lore does it deny that the Jotnar are wise in many ways; they are frequently consulted on their "specialties" by the Aesir and Vanir, and some (like Vafthrudnir) are deliberately sought out and destroyed because their wisdom is a threat. It has been noted by Kvedulf Gundarsson in his work "Spae-Craft, Seidhr, and Shamanism" that the shamanic descent to the Underworld in search of wisdom is almost exclusively practiced by giants, and specifically giantesses when it is mentioned in lore sources.

This brings us to another fairly controversial issue, which is in many ways central to this book: the relationship of the Jotnar to northern-tradition shamanism. This practice, still in its early stages of rediscovery, seems to be strongly linked to the Jotnar. It is distinct from the practices of seidhr or spae, which are late-period Norse/Germanic psychic/spiritual practices still mentioned (however sparsely) in the extant lore. Seidhr may well have grown out of shamanism, but shamanism as an entire practice died out in Norse/Germanic areas well before the appearance of any written records (although the same practices, with different wights, are still going on in nearby Saamiland), and thus cannot be reconstructed from Scandinavian lore per se. Instead, it is an almost entirely spirit-taught tradition, because even if we have forgotten, the wights have not. The Gods and spirits who seem to be the most involved in choosing shamans and teaching this spiritual practice seem to be, with a few exceptions, among the Jotnar. This is not surprising when we consider that the last time that northern Europe was primarily religiously a shamanic culture was probably also the time when the Jotnar were most revered.

Whether any of the reconstructionist religious communities accept the validity of a spirit-taught tradition of shamanism (which is not unusual in other shamanic traditions; the Mongolian Buryat word for a spirit-taught shaman is *bagshagui*) is entirely irrelevant to those of us who are practicing it. Indeed, by the time of the Viking era (which seems to be the era that most northern-tradition reconstructionists are reconstructing) it was almost entirely gone except for the few practices which remained as part of seidhr-work, so a claim that such a long-dead tradition has no place in a "period" religion may well be accurate. However, whether or not it is ever accepted into a spiritual community, it is still slowly growing, and the Jotnar are the key to mastery of this tradition of shamanism. Although this book was written with many different folk in mind, it is my brothers and sisters in this tradition, those of us drafted by the Gods and wights to struggle through this rediscovery, who are the primary recipients of this gift, and the books that will follow it. Have courage, and don't give up, because for us, giving up means insanity and death. This book is my first gift to you, and to the Gods we serve.

I guess what I'm saying here is that one of the major things I've learned is that you learn a lot more by sitting still and opening the door and letting the things that want to talk to you come, and those that don't, let them be. The other big thing is to approach each entity with an open mind, regardless of your pantheon/party alignments. Aesir, Jotun, heck, anything and anybody are very different when you approach them and let them define themselves. Let a giant be who they see themselves as, and you'll get a lot more than if you look at them as some chaotic-evil-rock-thing. Trees can teach us to see in all directions. Rocks can teach us patience. Soil can teach us growth. Water can teach us so much as well.

That is one way to figure out how to give them good offerings. Work with them for a bit. The amount of plain-out work they demand—like scrubbing, sewing, general house work and gardening, most people don't have the patience to do these sorts of things, especially in a world other than ours. Most people, I think, would be outraged if their deity told them to clean something for them. They would take it as degrading rather than the lesson it really is. Nor would they understand the whole 'pay as you go' idea. You have to work for them to get them to work for you. I think it is so funny how so many people want to return to a tribal lifestyle but cannot figure out the barter system. Yeah, many entities like a touch of beer, wine, ale, mead, alcohol, etc... but let's face it. What do you want more? Someone to bring you a bottle of wine when you visit, or someone who brings you a bottle of wine, cooks your meal and cleans your kitchen before they leave? This may be that I grew up in a household where it was expected to clean up the relatives home we were visiting before we left. If you don't like doing the dishes, there is always firewood to be cut.

What I am saying is that you need to look at this as though you are a guest in their home—which you are. We aren't entitled visitation rights to the other worlds. In fact, tourists get killed where I usually go. But I will say that there are a lot of people out there doing a lot of crappy things in these worlds. They get what is coming to them. So treat the thurses like they are respected relatives that you are visiting. Kiss Aunty-Ice-Beard when she bends down to you and her breath smells like rancid rotting rat, give Uncle Avalanche a quiet afternoon for his nap, help around the home with what needs to be done—they don't have time for moochers and free-loaders—be respectful and bring them a gift you made for them.

—Lyn, spirit-worker

The Problem Of Jotun Blood

racing the genealogy of the giants strictly from the lore is difficult, because the Nordic lore often has stories where people of the same name (and sometimes with children who might randomly have some of the same names) are presented here as giants or elves, and there as actual kings or famous human beings, and sometimes the two intermingle. While we are not averse to the idea that once, long ago, the two mingled much more than they do now, it does make tracing a genealogy difficult. In the end, perhaps only Hyndla knows the many threads of Jotun bloodlines, and it was to her knowledge that I turned to understand the phenomenon of Jotun breeding.

What she taught me about Jotun breeding was this: Just as Jotun bodies are not as solid to a single form as ours are—they are, after all, shapeshifters—they also take far less time to adapt and evolve than ours do. Where the various races of mankind gained their particular racial differences over hundreds of generations of living in strange climates, the Jotnar respond to a change of climate much quicker, especially while they are still in the womb. The development of an etin-fetus is a battle—or a combination—between the race of each of the parents, and the environment where the mother's body dwells.

This means that if a frost-giantess gets with child by a fire-giant, the child might be all or mostly frost-thurse or fire-giant, or it might be a combination of both. If she moves to a forested island in the ocean for the duration of her pregnancy, the fetus will sense and adapt to the new environment, and possibly end up an earth-etin. If she swims frequently in the ocean, the baby may develop into a sea-etin. Several children by the same two parents may have entirely different racial characteristics. Throwbacks are common, and wide variations can occur even among siblings. An example might be Kari, Logi, and Hler/Aegir, three brothers with the same frost-thurse father who are a frost-thurse, a fire-giant, and a sea-giant respectively.

The ability of the etin-fetus to understand and adapt to its mother's new environment is partly due to the fact that the mother must shapeshift to function well in a new environment herself; a form that is useful on a lava-beach or in a frozen waste will need some alterations in order to be comfortable on a leafy isle or a rainforest. It is also due to the fact that Jotnar are always aware of and in communication with the landvaettir; even a half-grown etin-fetus has the ability to touch and understand the nature of the land-wight that dances under its mother's feet, and to absorb information from that spirit. Actually, it may well be that when any Jotun adapts themselves to a new climatic environment, they first get the proper information from the land-wight.

The malleable, shapeshifting nature of the etins has created a wide array of characteristics, and representatives of each of them live in various places. Intermarriage is rife; there are no taboos against one sort of etin marrying another sort of etin, and in fact bringing new bloodlines to a tribe is considered a good thing, so etins often "go wandering" when the urge to settle down with a mate seizes them. As monogamy is not mandated culturally among them, they may have more than one wife or husband, and may or may not live with their spouses. Even incest taboos are less firm among them as they are among other races, as it isn't necessarily the breeding issue that it might be elsewhere. This makes tracing Jotun genealogy something of a tangle. As a race, though, the giants are vigorous, hardy, and wonderfully diverse.

Jotun bloodlines, however, concern us in many more ways than just genealogy. It is becoming increasingly apparent that their blood is circulating in the humans of our world as well, and in fact the number of Jotun-descended humans is rising. One of the questions that many northern-tradition spirit-workers have been asking me is why the Jotnar (and especially the Rökkr) are contacting people in escalating numbers. The truth of the matter seems partially to be about the fact that increased workings with the Northern Gods in general has stirred up their interest, but the heart of it seems to be centered around those of us with Jotun bloodlines mixed into our human blood.

I certainly can't speak for all of the people who have been approached by giant-wights and giant-Gods, but of the ones where I'm absolutely sure that the individuals are really talking to a Jotun, I find certain things that we all have in common. We all have Jotun-like personality traits, more so than in the rest of the population, and those traits were present in our family history as well. In many cases, we struggled with them for much of our lives. According to the etins, some of us share blood with them, however thinly.

How nonhuman blood gets into a human bloodline is a long and complicated situation. To make it short, suffice it to say that when a deity or wight or other powerful creature borrows (as in god-possession or spirit-possession) the body of a human being, whether the human is conscious of it or not, and that human being conceives or sires a child during that time, the embryo's genetics shift to mimic some of the nature of the possessing spirit. Some people may find this unbelievable, but I believe it, and find merit to the idea, and it has consistency in my experience of the situation. Until I come across evidence to disprove it, I will go with it. (Besides, the one time I met Odin, I asked him about it, and he was silent for a moment and then acknowledged that it was true. So did Heimdall, the one time I met him; in fact, he said that he would prefer never to let any humans with Jotun bloodlines into Asgard, but it wasn't his decision. Hyndla, the Goddess of Bloodlines, makes no bones about it being truth.)

According to my own boss, bringing Jotun bloodlines into humanity has been a long, slow process that is finally starting to peak. Apparently some of the Rökkr deities, particularly Hela and Loki, felt that the Jotunfolk ought to be more invested in humans. This may be because of Hela, who deals with human souls on an everyday basis, as well as Jotun souls (and a very few Alfar/faery ones). There is some evidence that Hela may also be recycling Jotun souls into human bodies, but I can't comment on that for certain. However it goes, some time back they started a full-scale breeding program to get more Jotun blood into humankind, and thus have Jotunkind recognize humankind as valuable "brotherkind", so to speak.

So as far as I can tell, they are approaching those of who smell like family. It does seem as if they treat us honorably, at least according to their codes. They are not always as nice to those who don't have those bloodlines. A few of them may also be approaching other humans for less savory reasons—likely feeding off their energy, because many of them can do that; it's a common Jotun gift. (And a not uncommon gift among humans with Jotun bloodlines.) I'm not pretending that they are nice. Nice is the last thing that they are. They are dangerous, but then so is any deity if you anger them. Real religion, and especially real spirit-work, comes with danger.

The question of "why should anyone deal with the Jotnar if they approach you?" then gets reframed as "what do you do when they, not the Aesir or Vanir, are the ones who approach you?" And the answer is, you deal with them. If it's their door you're sent to, that's for a reason. Ask the Nornir; they know, although whether they'll give you a straight answer is debatable. Godhis, gythjas, and seidhworkers need to remember this when someone with Jotun blood shows up at their door. Give them the list of cautions and etiquette, and let them go their way.

It does seem that if you have enough Jotun blood, or certain types—it has not yet been established whether it's quantity or quality—the Aesir will simply not deal with you. It's like you have "reserved for something else" written all over you astrally. Before I had even heard of the heathen community, I was talking to all sorts of pagan gods. The ones who responded were useful or noncommittal or supportive, but clear that I was reserved. However, I could never get any of the Aesir on the phone, so to speak... except for Hela, who owned me. Then, when she revealed herself and her name (all that time from the age of four on she's just been the Death Goddess, and I played a Rumpelstiltskin-like game to figure her out—"Are you Kali? Are you Hecate?") I started getting visits from Loki, Fenris, etc. I never touched the Aesir until I was sent there directly on an errand (although some of the Vanir would talk to me). It was like I didn't exist for them. Now they acknowledge me, but only as Hela's servant.

So I can well understand the chagrin of someone where Frigga won't return her calls, but here's Mordgud appearing in her dreams. And would such folks have a place in a religion called Asatru, if this was chosen for them before they were even born? It's a hard question. Some heathens and Asatru, determined (and perhaps conditioned by a Christian upbringing) to turn their religious beliefs into an "Us vs. Them" war, would say that no, there was no place for them in places where the main votive activity was worshipping the Aesir. And, to be fair, there is a small minority of folks called by the Rökkr who are restricted in that way as well. For some, they simply may not enter any northern-tradition religious place where it is forbidden to invoke their deity at blots or sumbels. Others—again, a small number—may have a strong aversion to the Aesir in general; some reported that this aversion started before they knew anything about them except for the names (read in some mythology book) and well before they discovered any Jotun bloodlines. (Those folks generally don't ever make it into the Heathen or Asatru communities, although one does find them in northern-tradition Pagan groups where there are no restrictions on which deities one can honor.)

I've noticed, also, that folks with Jotun blood tend to have certain personality traits. One, not surprisingly, is anger management difficulties. Those of us with Jotun blood so often have an internal Fenris-part, so to speak, that has nowhere to be and go in this world, this time, this space. It's hard for us to deal with that part, and dealing with Him, the ultimate expression of that, is useful and healing. So is learning to be around folk who have that in themselves, but have had to bind themselves to social codes that clearly state when and where their rages, their passions, their hungers are acceptable.

Most people don't understand what it's like to go around boiling all the time, or to be very cold and yet strongly passionate, and have that be an integral part of your nature from birth rather than having it stem from some damage. They tend to give bad advice about how to handle it, ranging from "Just don't be that way," to "Heal yourself and it will go away," or "I refuse to believe that this is really just the way you are," or "If that's really what you're like inside, you are dangerous and ought to be locked up." This is unhelpful at best and can be downright damaging at worst. Talking to the Jotnar can help you understand how to live with this kind of nature, even if you do not live in a society where there is any place for it.

Others may find that tracing specific personality traits—not only in themselves, but in their parents, grandparents, and other close family members, especially if it's "known" that "the people in our family are just like this" can show them not only Jotun blood but which tribe. While anyone with any kind of Jotun blood may find themselves naturally evidencing some of the characteristics listed in the prior chapter (and let's make it clear that Jotun bloodlines are by no means the only reason for those behaviors!), the different tribes of etins have their own particular additional attributes.

Frost-thurse characteristics that have been passed on through human bloodlines include (anecdotally), antisocial behavior, extreme introversion, ingrained misanthropic distrust, coldness of personality, and a lack of compassion in general. Fire-etin blood may give a much more extroverted personality, including hyperactivity, athleticism, and the urge to be generally rowdy, but may also escalate the fiery temper. Either may (or may not, depending on how the genes manifest) have a strong, large-boned, undelicate frame; frost-thurse types may be prone to being heavy in general, and endure cold temperatures well, while fire-etin types may prefer warmth.

Island giant blood may give a strong wanderlust and an urge to travel, and perhaps a longing for the seashore. Of the lot, they tend to be the least likely to manifest physical body-clues. Ocean-giant blood, which is very rare, would exaggerate these qualities further (except that ocean-giant blood does bring with it the tendency to odd facial and internal-organ deformities). We have no anecdotal evidence regarding sky-etin bloodlines in humans (assuming that there are any), but since they are all descended from fire-etins, one might assume for fire-etin qualities plus a good deal of wanderlust.

Mountain-giant blood also gives one the frost-thurse qualities of introversion and antisocial behavior, but it can also generate a strong sense of wanting to hole up in a "cave" and not leave (which becomes agoraphobia when exaggerated), whereas frost-thurse types, while not necessarily liking people all that much, are fine with wandering about. One of the few places mountain-giant folk feel comfortable being outside is in thick woods or mountaintops. Mountain-giant blood is even more likely to give a large, square (or squat) frame and a heavy build. Many of the giant bloodlines may give a strong love of music and the urge to sing, but the mountain and ocean giants are the most likely to actually be talented at it.

Iron Wood blood seems to be both the most powerful and the most problematic of the Jotun bloodlines when added to human genetics. Humans with Iron Wood blood have all the problems of Jotun blood, plus the likelihood of physical deformities and birth defects. One of the most common birth defects is some form of intersex condition, mild or severe, as well as other hormonal defects such as polycystic ovarian syndrome and early menopause. We have also seen extreme hirsutism, polydactyly (extra fingers and toes), facial deformities, and general skeletal deformities. Chronic genetic health problems are much more common with Iron Wood bloodlines, not surprisingly.

Our observations of interviewing a whole lot of people over a period of several years is that introduction of nonhuman blood into human bloodlines inevitably gives a certain chance of health disorders, including both physical and mental disorders. This does not mean that everyone who evidences the psychological and spiritual qualities of these bloodlines will end up with physical or mental illnesses, but it does mean that there is a higher chance of it. While we have by no means managed to chronicle and compare a definitive list of problems (except for the astoundingly high level of birth defects among Iron Wood-descended humans, which includes those with Loki's blood, and the astoundingly high number of intersex conditions within that micropopulation), we have noticed some interesting anecdotal groupings, including autoimmune diseases, blood sugar problems, and hormone disorders such as pituitary gigantism.

The various mental illnesses associated with nonhuman blood seem mostly to be exaggerated versions of the personality characteristics involved. For example, when people with Alfar bloodlines suffer from mental illnesses, they seem to suffer from the disorders that detach them from the "real" world and send them into an imaginative world of their own— perhaps through visual and auditory hallucinations, perhaps through alcohol or drugs—and make them increasingly unable to care for themselves, until they quite literally waste away. In contrast, when Jotun bloodlines manifest as a mental health problem, the first weak spot is that of anger management issues, difficulty with impulse control, and a tendency toward violent urges. They are less likely to die emaciated in some alley of exposure, anorexia, or heroin overdose, and much more likely to go down in a hail of police bullets. However, we stress again that these incidents are rare. It may even be that with more knowledge by spiritual clergy about the existence and side-effects of nonhuman bloodlines, some of these potential endings might be headed off.

Of course, not all the side-effects of Jotun bloodlines are negative. It can bestow a wide array of psychic abilities, most reflective of the type of etin-blood involved—astral shapeshifting, spellsinging, affinities with weather and earth and stone. It can also bestow rock-solid faithfulness, zest for living, and great persistence and intensity, of the sort that can keep going when others fall and work wonders through sheer will. It is unwise to underestimate the willpower of giant-blood.

One note of hope: If you are close to someone who is strongly connected to Jotunfolk, and perhaps has the personality characteristics that suggest Jotun blood, an excellent deity to call on for aid in understanding is Frey, the fertility-god of the Vanir. Frey fell madly in love with Gerda, who is a cold, reserved etin-woman from a bloodthirsty family, and was willing to give up his sword to her family and thus be evermore defenseless in order to win her. Frey is a god of Light who loves and appreciates Darkness; he loves it and is drawn to it, in Gerda's nature as well as that of others. According to some partners of Rökkatru folk, Frey can be extremely helpful in coming to not only an understanding, but a (perhaps even erotic) appreciation of their nature.

> "You and I are more alike than you think," Frey said to me. "I know about sacrifice. Ha! Yes, I know about sacrifice." And I saw him as the pure golden god who is cut down at his height, approaching death not with a grim acceptance or dutiful obligation but a big smile and that ever-present erection, celebrating even this aspect of life. And more... "I also know what it is like to love one of that blood. There could be no Asa bride for me. No, I needed someone dark, someone wild. And I too know what it is to willingly be completely defenseless for that love." I recalled the irony of this gorgeous god desperately courting a fierce giantess who scorned his beautiful home and people, accepting only when he gave his sole weapon as a bride-price, and my defenselessness against my own lover with his murky twisted Jotun bloodlines.
>
> —Joshua, spirit-worker's partner

As the marriage between Frey and Gerda was condemned by the Aesir and the Alfar, it has become traditional among many northern-tradition folk to call upon them at weddings that are not quite socially acceptable (as opposed to Frigga, the Aesir goddess of marriage, who is in charge of more acceptable unions). These might include weddings between two very different people (the sort where everyone says, "That'll never work!"), people of different traditions, or the wedding of an Asatru/Vanatru with a

Rökkatru. Because Frey has since ancient times been fond of nonheterosexual folk, and since the Jotnar have no taboo against nonheterosexual relations or polyamory, Frey and Gerda have also been honored for the weddings of people of various alternative lifestyles.

The issue of bloodlines is an important one throughout all the Nine Worlds. Ancestor reverence is important to all five races, and genealogy is almost a sacred task. This is reflected in the eddas and sagas, where ancestor lineages are often recounted; the lay of Hyndla is a clear example of the value Nine Worlds folk set of ancestry and genealogy leaking out into our world. Having had the equivalent of many millennia to watch the results of the interbreeding of different species, the folk of the Nine Worlds are well versed in what happens when this sort of genetic code mixes with that sort.

Indeed, one of the subtle and generally unspoken reasons that the Aesir give for the inevitability of their place as rulers and conquerors of as much of the Nine Worlds as they can manage is the uniqueness of their bloodlines. When an Aesir breeds with a Jotun, or a Duergar, or even one of the Alfar, the offspring carries far more qualities of its Aesir parent than of its other parent. In other words, their genes are more likely be dominant over nearly every aspect of the other parent. That is why although most of the Aesir are descended as clearly from giants as any giant, they still consider themselves to be a separate race... and that delineation is based on clear genetic fact and obvious physical characteristics. Buri's blood is amazingly dominant; there is no question about that, and this is used covertly as a reason for the Aesir's opinion of themselves as the "true" gods, with everyone else further down the scale. Part of the almost-instant animosity of the Aesir to the newly discovered Vanir may have been due to the fact that Vanir bloodlines are every bit a match in dominance characteristics to the Aesir; the first "challenge" to their superiority to come into the cosmology of Yggdrasil.

One reason for the emphasis on bloodlines is because certain things are known to be passed down ancestral lines: magical gifts, curses and knots in the threads of Wyrd, and even reincarnated souls. When I first began to work with the wights of the Northern Tradition, this emphasis on ancestry and genealogy troubled me. It seemed to smell of the sort of racist teachings that I had been worried about encountering when I first began to read up on modern northern-tradition religion. I was made profoundly uncomfortable not just by the far-right end of Asatru practitioners—the openly racist neo-Nazis—but also by the practices of those who claimed that these deities should only be worshiped by those of Norse, Germanic or Anglo-Saxon blood, and that everyone else should stay away. (The one time that I inadvertently got into an argument with one of them, I actually won it by pointing out that the Gods I was serving—the Rökkr pantheon—were ones that they weren't using anyway, and were in fact reviling, so did it matter if someone without northern-European bloodlines worshiped *them*? This entirely seized up the other person's train of thought, and he wandered away, speechless.)

Part of my discomfort was that the northern Gods and wights were clearly bothering people who had little or no northern blood in them, and just as clearly ignoring others who did. I figured that it was one of those divine mysteries that I just don't understand and probably never will. I also figured that I shouldn't be deciding for the Gods who they ought to talk or listen to, as that seemed not only laden with hubris but utterly futile. Yet the more that I read about the northern-tradition Gods and wights, and the more that I studied with them, I realized that working with bloodlines is extremely important to them, at least. Ancestor reverence is strong in them, and most are very aware of their entire genealogy. Although there is no widespread agreement on whose race was better (though the Aesir have occasionally intimated that they believe that the genetic dominance of their race is a sign of superiority), there is a good deal of acceptance that certain bloodlines give certain gifts, and that some magics and wisdom are passed down along ancestral trees.

There is also an emphasis in northern-tradition spirit-work on what we refer to as "untangling people's threads of Wyrd". This is the acceptance that some actions can tangle people's destiny, and also be passed down to future generations of their family, and that certain (often drastic) acts need to be done in order to untangle them. This is not a punishment of one's innocent descendants; it is just a spiritual mess that someone has left for their descendants to clean up. While there may be other religiocultural spirit-work traditions that emphasize such things as bloodwalking and the untangling of ancestral as well as your own threads, it seems that this tradition is particularly strong in these things. In fact, we even have a patron wight of such things; Hyndla is the undisputed mistress of bloodwalking and genealogy. (Which techniques, I should point out, work just as well for you no matter who your ancestors were.) I suppose that just as a faith with strong warrior gods is going to attract a lot of military types, and a tradition with strongly ecstatic deities is going to attract folks who do a lot of drugs, a tradition with a revered place for the sacredness of ancestral bloodlines is going to attract a lot of people with racial issues they have not yet worked out.

In the meantime, the only way to know for sure whether or not you have Jotun blood is to ask them, and get an answer. Even then, that doesn't necessarily mean that you are special or have superhuman powers; in fact, it may mean that you have extra challenges in addition to rest of the ordinary human challenges in your life. That's why it's important to work with the source, as They know best how to handle these things. And, of course, no matter who your ancestors are, the Jotnar have useful lessons to teach about a great many things.

Primal Fire:
The Fire-Etins

uspellheim, the World of Fire, is one of the two oldest worlds in the Northern-Tradition cosmology. Its inhabitants are the fire-etins, tall and strong, elementally aligned to flame. Compared to frost-thurses, the fire-etins of Muspellheim are slightly more civilized and friendly, but just as bloodthirsty. They build buildings out of black volcanic stone rather than simply hewing rough caves in mountainsides, they do some relatively complex handcrafting, and they might actually ask your business and wait for an unsatisfactory reply before eating you.

Fire giants are also much more social than frost-giants, if they like you. They dance wildly, laugh loudly—even while fighting—and fight as wildly as a raging fire. Their fire-forms can be pillars of flame, or shooting balls of sparks, or coal-glowing human shapes. Ari, a spirit-worker, writes: "Fire giants love to be sung to, and they can get some pretty complex background harmonies going. Actually, all Jotnar love to be sung to. Singing is one of the best gifts you can give them, which means that musicians like me are generally expected to trot our stuff out and perform for them whenever we show up."

The leader of the fire giants is Surt the Black, the oldest Jotnar still living. All the fire giants, and thus a good deal of the giants of Jotunheim, are descended from him. For some, like Farbauti and Loki, the descent is pretty clear; for others it is many generations back. Descendants of the fire-giants tended to end up in the warmer southern rain forests, or among the islands of the western coast, rather than the cold northeastern mountains. There is a good chunk of fire-giant bloodline in the Iron Wood, as evidenced by the Lightning Tribe and its offspring.

Fire-etins are useful for learning to work with fire—well, obviously. They can help you with learning to make fire from an older method, such as tinder and flint, and with deciphering the subtleties of the rune Kano/Kaunaz/Ken, and with learning to heat your body with your own energy. They are very good for people who tend to throttle their aggression to the point where they get stepped on; they can help folk get in touch with their inner fire. They are also good for people suffering from burnout, who have lost enthusiasm for life. Their courage and confidence is contagious, almost to the point of blind enthusiasm, but it's a nice change for the tired and cynical.

Fire-etins are territorial, and curt and abrupt with outsiders. They take offense fairly easily, and react in an appropriately fiery manner. It is best not to travel there without first getting permission. In their human form, they stand six to eight feet tall, and their skins are usually blackened with soot. When they flip to their fiery forms, the soot is shaken off, and so you can see them with unblackened skin for a little while after they change back. They wear very little clothing—usually just a tunic or loincloth of some sort of tanned reptile skin—and there seems to be no clothing difference between males and females. They will put on Jotunheim-style clothing when leaving home. In their fiery form, they are like great pillars of fire, sometimes vaguely humanoid-shaped, and sometimes not. They can fling fireballs a good way, so running away from them is not recommended, nor is attempting to fly in. Like all etins, they are cannibals, and are not averse to eating visitors. Unlike other etins, they eat all their food cooked...because they can cook it in a matter of seconds.

Fire-etins are generally cheerful and wild, except when they are being suspicious and cautious. In fact, if they are subdued, you're probably in trouble. They have infectious laughter and love to shoot sparks, competing with each other to create fireworks that illustrate their moods. They are the most confident and courageous of etins, and they always laugh during battle. They do some of their own metalworking, but for the more intricate and delicate things they trade with the Duergar, who are the undisputed masters of forging.

When working with fire-giants, remember that just their presence can cause burns and overheating; take care not to have a lot of flammable things around, and to wear appropriate clothing. Mark the rune Isa for coldness on you for protection. Fire-giant bloodlines, as noted, can give extra weight to impulsivity, hyperactivity, and anger management issues. Children of humans with fire-giant blood should be closely supervised around flame and explosives, as they will be fascinated with them.

Offerings: Food that they wouldn't normally get—raw fruits and vegetables, especially if they are full of juice, like citrus. Don't comment if they cook or char food offerings that we tend to eat raw. Whole grains and ale poured into a fire is another good offering. They like booze poured onto the flames more for the fireworks than the booze itself, so it should be high-proof, although it doesn't have to be high-quality.

Surt and Sinmora

The Lord of all fire-etins is Surt, and the Lady is Sinmora. Surt is a lover of music and dancing, as is Sinmora. One of the odd things about them is that you will almost never see them together, and when you (rarely) do, only one of them will speak to you. It is rumored that they are actually the same person, in different forms, and that Surt happens to like flipping from male to female form, and having a separate female persona, but the fire-etins consider it rude to ask personal questions about their ancient ruler, and you won't get an answer anyway. Many folk have reported something androgynous about Surt's energy, though. In the Eddas, it is said that Surt was there guarding Muspellheim long before Ymir and Audumhla broke from the ice. As such, Surt is the oldest living being in the Nine Worlds, and may well be some kind of primal androgyne, although he does not make this a public issue. It is true that I've never seen them both at the same time, but it's another issue that I don't think it's polite to bring up and discuss.

In spite of this, most people see Surt as being quite masculine, gruff and laconic. He is the single oldest surviving being in the Nine Worlds. According to the lore, in the beginning, before there were any other living beings, there was Surt lighting the place up with his great sword—or, rather, wand—of fire and light, Laevateinn. Surt himself will rarely discuss where he came from, or what brought him forth; in fact it's another of the questions that you shouldn't be foolish enough to ask. He does have a temper, and if it rages, you may be in for fire hazards in your life over the next several weeks.

Surt is rather short for a fire-etin, which shows his great age—not that they get shorter with age, but more that the younger generations are taller. His manners are more courtly than the average fire-etin, and his wrath is a little more controlled. He is extremely intelligent, although he has on occasion acted less so in order to gull visitors into making rude comments, and thus having a reason to fry and eat them. He is not to be underestimated. Surt has a close relationship with (and a great respect for) Hela, with whom he is building Naglfari as a joint project; in spite of the fact that he is much older than her, he refers to her as "Her Ladyship", as many etins do. He has said that he is Loki's godfather, and that Laufey came to Muspellheim to give birth to him, because nowhere else in the Nine Worlds was hot enough, and that she lay in Surt's biggest fireplace to bring him forth.

Surt is knowledgeable in the ways of all kinds of fires, and especially—although few speak to him of this—the kind of primal fire that stars are made of. In fact, his knowledge of suns and stars outside the Nine Worlds is enough to take one aback, and seriously wonder about his origins. It goes without saying that he knows a great deal about moving heat and energy.

Sinmora, according to lore, has a close relationship with the healing Jotun-goddess Mengloth, the mountain-dwelling lady has a special room in her high fortress just for the safekeeping of Laevateinn. Considering the role of heat in the healing traditions of the North—steam-baths, hot stones, etc.—this makes a certain amount of sense. Sinmora is known to love dancing and music; she does certain ritual dances for her folk at different times throughout the year. It seems that while Surt appears as the temporal leader of the fire-giants, Sinmora appears as the ritual leader.

Surt the Black
by Abby Helasdottir

Surtr shall ride first,
and both before and after him burning fire;
his sword is exceeding good;
from it radiance shines brighter than the sun.

The origins of Surt seem to date back to the very beginning of the cosmos, amongst the first primeval fires of Muspellheim. This primacy has been interpreted as signifying that, in the pre-Æsir and pre-Vanir pantheons, Surt was originally a god of some great importance, perhaps in partnership with Hela. He was the very embodiment of the fires of Muspellheim, just as Hela embodied the ice of Niflheim. In later mythology, we find Surt as the ruler of Muspellheim and its deep dales. He also acts as the sentinel of this home of dry earth, standing outside its gate and brandishing his fiery sword, the light of which outshines even the sun goddess.

Muspellheim is the realm of creation and destruction, out of which emerged the sparks that were set in the sky as the stars, and two fire-disks that were harnessed to a twin set of chariots and traveled across the sky as sun and moon. As such, Surt also possesses this creative potency; his is the fire of invention, but more importantly, he is the spirit of such creation. It is from his realm that the primeval fire arose to meld with the primeval ice of Niflheim in the void of Ginnungagap, but it is he who also finally destroys all that Nature has created. At the end of the battle of Ragnarok on the field of Vigrid, Surt throws his fiery brands throughout the heavens, earth, and the nine worlds, setting the entire cosmos alight.

> *Fire's breath assails The all-nourishing tree,*
> *Towering fire plays Against heaven itself.*

All life is destroyed, except for those few who are hidden within the hollows of the World Tree, and those other beings that are the purest expressions of Wyrd. Surt also survives, for as fire he cannot be destroyed by fire, and the Rökkr spirit of creation and destruction must continue into the new world as a manifestation of cosmic law.

The fiery brands of Surt, and Surt himself, have been seen by some as signifying a comet. In the Gylfaginning, there is a description of Ragnarok which says: "In this din shall the heaven be cloven, and the sons of Muspell ride thence: Surtr shall ride first, and both before and after him burning fire; his sword is exceeding good; from it radiance shines brighter than the sun" This vivid image does seem to suggest a blazing comet. Like Surt, a comet is both a destructive, and creative force. Surt is also linked to volcanoes, so much so that one of the world's most recently-formed volcanic islands off the coast of Iceland is called Surtsey.

Astrologically, Surt is represented by the constellation of Bootes, and notably also by its brightest star, Arcturus. Appositely, Pliny referred to it as "horridum sidus," while Hippocrates claimed that its rising had a detrimental effect on anyone unfortunate enough to have a disease at the time. This inauspicious character carries over into Lappish mythology, where Arcturus performs a similar role to that of Surt at Ragnarok. It was believed that "when Arcturus shoots down the North Nail with his arrow on the last day, the heaven will fall crushing the earth and setting fire to everything." This prophecy recalls a common motif in astral mythology, in which bows and arrows perform an important role as the tools of cosmic change. But what is truly remarkable about this prophecy and the role of

Arcturus is how closely it resembles the Norse account of Ragnarok, and the role of Surt.

Because he instigates and oversees the destruction of the Æsir's order, Surt is also important in establishing the reborn and regenerated world. This role has been willfully ignored by Æsir-centric authors from Odinic times up to the present, but a trace of it can be found in Snorri Sturlusson's Elder Edda, although only in the version known as the Uppsala Codex. In this, it tells how "there are many good abodes and many bad; best is to be in Gimle with Surt." Gimle is a hall, thatched with gold and fairer than the sun, as the Voluspa describes it, which lies at the southern end of heaven. It is from here that the new cosmic order arises, where human life is reborn through the new primal parents Lif and Lifthrasir. The ruler of Gimle is Surt, who is described as the king of eternal bliss, at the southern end of the sky. There has even been a suggestion that it is Surt who is implied in references about a mysterious great one who comes following Ragnarok. This is usually assumed though to be a late Christian interpolation of the messiah myth.

Surt carries the epithet of The Black, and similarly, the name of the Egyptian god Set means the black, or burnt, one. Like Surt, Set was also associated with volcanoes, having amongst his many titles one of God of Volcanoes. This provides a meaning to both gods' epithet of black, because when the bright red magma and lava of a volcano cools and hardens, it turns a striking jet black. It is interesting to note in connection to the identifications of the fires of Muspellheim as a creative, life-giving force that, according to Marija Gimbutas, the colour black symbolised life in Old Europe. Black was the colour of the fertile soul, whereas white was the colour of death. The black of Surt and dried lava can be seen as a symbol of life.

Surt and Healing

by Tamara Crawford

My initial interactions with Surt came as something of a surprise. I'd never considered calling upon Him before and certainly hadn't sought Him out, though I bore Him no ill will. I simply hadn't made His acquaintance. So a few months ago, I was doing a healing on a friend of mine and she asked for a Reiki session. I don't generally like to do Reiki but I can, and have the third degree attunement. So I've got my hands on her hip, she's in serious pain and suddenly Surt shows up and asks me "Do you want some help?"

He was friendly, outgoing and asked for nothing in return for his aid. I was surprised but agreed. My patient told me later, after the session, that she'd never had a Reiki session in which the healer's hands got so incredibly (yet not painfully) HOT and that it eased her pain almost immediately. I told her precisely Who she had to thank for that. Since that time, Surt has offered His aid in several healings and I've developed a pretty good friendship with Him. With me, He's forthright and down to earth and has been teaching me how to control my own internal energies better.

He seems to appreciate the Jotun part of me, the rage-beast that I keep strongly locked away. He is teaching me different ways to communicate with fire etins and He appreciates my dance background (I was a dancer for 13 years). He's been showing me things about the interrelation of energy and rhythm, heat and movement that in the end, have been helping me recover from a nasty, two year bout with elfshot (even though it's removed now, my energy patterns were shot and needed much healing). He's even offered me hospitality in Muspellheim. I half think that His initial overtures toward me had much to do with my friendship with His foster-son Loki.

Visit to Muspellheim
by Elizabeth Vongvisith

This morning, shortly after sunrise, I went to see Surt. It was different this time; I didn't use my stang. Loki said I should make the offering beforehand and initially offered me the use of his altar, but eventually he told me to set the plate of fruit in the fireplace. I lit some candles around it, having no means to get a fire going. As I did so, I could feel something paying attention to me. I offered the fruit to Surt, the Lord of Muspellheim, and saw, just for a second, two glowing eyes in the back of my hearth.

I was going to go to sleep thereafter because I had been up all night, and then go pay my respects after I awoke, but then Loki told me that we were going right then. *I fear you'll be too tired and groggy to do it later,* he said. I protested that I was tired and unready, red-eyed from being upset the night before, and still wearing my tatty old black T-shirt dress. *It doesn't matter what you look like, just come on. But put your charm on before we go, so that you don't get lost.* He meant the bone and silver pendant with the stang symbol engraved on it, which I have worn on every journey I've taken since last summer. I put it on, then dragged my bean bag before the fireplace, wondering if this was such a good idea. But Loki was insistent.

Get comfortable, and don't be frightened, my sweet. I shut the blinds, then lay down. *I'll tell you a secret. Fire – any fire – can be used to get to Muspellheim. But it's tricky, and if you're not careful you'll wind up in a place you didn't intend to go, and probably get burned to death. If you have the hang of it, though, you don't need a stang or anything else to get there. Come.* He took my hand and pulled me to my feet, leaving my body lying there. I saw that he had changed form—he looked far less human than usual, and everything about him suggested flames and embers. I've only seen him like that once before. But he was wearing the ring I gave him last year, when we made our marriage-oath. *It's still me,* Loki said, grinning. *Now...look into the flame.* I gazed at the largest of the candles, a red one within a glass jar, and I saw the flame swell in my gaze, pulling me into it.

It was like that Johnny Cash song. The ring of fire opened, and I saw smoke and ash in the air, and a black-sanded beach, barren next to a gently steaming shoreline. Loki and I sort of folded ourselves out of thin air. I winced; the sand was very warm and stung my bare feet. *Oh, sorry. Here, love,* he said, and from nowhere he produced a pair of flip-flops, which looked exactly like a pair I used to own as a child, with red straps and rainbow-colored layered soles. I put them on, looking around. My back was to the water. There was not much to see except steam and smoke. And then Surt appeared.

His demeanor was completely unlike what I expected. I heard a gruff voice saying Loki's name, and then my husband, to my immense surprise, ran up and threw his arms around Surt, like a child scampering to his father. Surt was considerably taller and broader than Loki. Surt returned the embrace, with a laugh that was more like a growl than anything else. He put Loki down after a moment and turned to me. *So. You're her, my godson's new consort.* I nodded, too awed to speak. He surveyed me up and down, but I got no sense of disapproval, as I'd expected. Apparently the offering had softened him up considerably.

Surt was very tall, as I said, and there were sparks floating in the air around him, but for all that I couldn't really see what he looked like. I had the impression of the same fiery eyes I'd seen in the back of my fireplace, and equally fiery beard and hair, but other than that he was indistinct-looking, hazed in smoke, with skin that looked blackened by soot and ash, but I never got a clear sense of his face or expressions, as I generally do with other beings I encounter in the Nine Worlds. What was distinct was his voice. Surt's was rough and gravelly-sounding, and his diction was both strangely enunciated and oddly inelegant. I could sense keen intelligence behind it.

The visit was brief. I don't actually remember much of what anyone said at first because the heat was immensely uncomfortable in a way that surprised me, since I hadn't been so affected by the cold in Niflheim, for instance. My shoes kept melting and sticking to the sand, so Loki had to give me new ones. The air smelled of brimstone, and somewhere in the back of my awareness, I knew that inexplicably, my eyes were burning and my throat was itchy as my body lay lifelessly before the fireplace.

Then Surt picked Loki and me up and set us on his wide shoulders, and with a few long strides, we were in his dwelling. He showed me the place where Loki was born, Surt's fireplace—it looked as wide as a room with fire burning continually all inside it, glowing red-hot so that I had to stand far away. And I had—a vision? I don't know what—of Laufey giving birth to him, Loki, in blood and fire, sparks all around, and Loki as an infant, with a thatch of red hair and eyes far too intelligent and knowing for such a young child. The vision was brief, and when it was over, I saw my shoes had once again melted and had left tracks across the floor. I exclaimed in dismay, but Surt said not to worry about it, the marks would soon burn themselves away.

"Can't you make me asbestos shoes or something?" I said as Loki picked me up so my feet wouldn't touch the red-hot floor. He only smiled.

I need to take her away from here, Father, Loki said deferentially. *It's too hot for her.*

Surt bent down close to me, squinting through his own smoke and haze. I gazed up at him, but then I felt myself shaking and the next thing I knew, I was on my back, my head in Loki's lap, on the beach. Surt was nowhere to be seen.

I told him so, Loki said, shaking his head. *Go into the water. It's not very hot and it will make you feel better.* So I got up and wobbled into the ocean, which was blood-warm and thus felt cool by comparison. There was a shadow over me I took to be from cloud. It wasn't. I looked up and saw Naglfari looming very nearby, half-built, a sort of whitish-gray, and terrible-looking. I gasped, almost drowning myself in my shock. I didn't think I had gone that far out into the water...and looking back, I wasn't. The thing was just that big.

Yes, that's it, love, the famous ship of doom. Loki was beside me in the water. He put his arm around my waist, holding me steady, and gazed up at it coolly, as if the sight of it — and everything it represented — didn't bother him in the least. *Impressive, isn't it?*

Impressive wasn't the word I would have used. Its sheer size was terrifying; no matter how I looked at it, it was as if I couldn't take it in all at once. Overcome, I turned around and splashed back to the sand, Loki following me. Then Surt appeared again out of the smoky air.

He told me that yes, he had appeared to me this way because he was pleased with my humble yet thoughtful gift, and because something had happened recently which pleased him, which he said was none of my affair before I could ask what it was. What he didn't say, of course, and what I understood, is that usually he's much more awful-seeming, so I was glad he was in a good mood today, because I'd been feeling weak and vulnerable and not at all bucked up enough to face a scary fire giant and be brave.

Surt then bade us farewell. He seized Loki in another bearlike hug, which was both touching and strange, since Loki had not displayed half as much affection toward Farbauti, or Laufey, for that matter. *I spent a lot of time there with Surt when I was very young,* was all he would say later when I asked. Surt eyed me again, then bent down and pulled me close enough for sweat to break out over my entire body at once. He kissed my forehead. I braced myself to feel as if a hot iron had been put there, but Surt's kiss was only pleasantly warm. *There. That'll keep you safe.*

"From what?" I asked, fanning myself involuntarily with my hand.

From fire. Oh, if you go and stick your hand in a lit candle, it'll still burn you, but you need not fear the flame so much after this. After delivering this curious statement, Surt winked at me. I started to stammer out my thanks, wondering what exactly this meant and feeling like somebody from a fairy tale who gets strange gifts from everyone she meets and doesn't know what to do with them, but he made a dismissive gesture before I could say any more. *Family,* he said, as if that explained everything, and I guess it did.

Far, far away, my body was suffering. I was half-afraid something really was burning, other than the candles, in my apartment. *You need to go back now,* Loki said, and poked me again, hard in the ribs, as he had once before. It had the same effect. I jolted violently awake, coughing heavily. The whole episode hadn't taken more than ten or fifteen minutes of "real time" at the most.

Loki was half-sitting, half-lounging next to me on the bean bag, which is quite big enough for two people even if one of them is unseen. *Told you it wouldn't be so bad, sweetheart,* he said, but this time there was the faintest trace of relief in his voice. I was extremely disoriented for a few minutes after, though it faded relatively quickly, leaving me very tired. The whole experience was so short and so very odd that for a while I doubted I had actually experienced it, until Loki told me I was being stupid. Then I noticed there was a faint acrid smell in the air, like brimstone.

Invocation to Surt

Hail, Master of Muspellheim,
Guardian of the Wand of Light,
Eldest of the elders, first upon the World Tree,
Primal Flame that shines in the dark,
Your soul is of the power that births universes,
Your heart is the power of the fire beneath the earth,
Your flesh is the molten stone pouring forth,
Your hands are the flame that leaps forth,
The smoke of your hair is as dark
As your sight is bright and blinding.
Hail, Master of Muspellheim,
Keeper of the Eternal Flame,
Bringer of the first red light
Into the darkness of Ginnungagap,
Bringer of the first red warmth
Into the frozen cold of Niflheim,
Melter of ice, destroyer of worlds,
Spark of hope that begins life again.
Bless us, Surt the Black, Obsidian Lord,
From birthing coals to funeral pyre.

Poem to Surt

by Corbie Petulengro

The clink of chipping stone,
Black stone-glass turned to razor edge,
I hear it in my dreams
And know that you send the message.
Ancestral clink of flint against steel—
Or, further back, the whir of bow on stone
Praying for smoke, or further still—
Twig spun in the desperate dance
Between chilled hands that whisper your name,
As my lips whispered your name,
Your runes, your words of power.
Ken, ken, ken, kano, kaunaz, ken,
Like the hammer on the grey-white stone,
Like the chipping of the black-glass stone.
Cweorth, cweorth, cweorth, like the whisk
Of spinning twig on log, the wisp
Of smoke that escapes, chokes the breath
That prays in gratitude, nurtures each tiny flame,
Feeds it the delicate grasses, watches it suckle them
Giving it breath with my own breath,
Coaxing, coddling, and then as it grows
From infancy to childhood in seconds
As your red babies do, then solid food—
The twigs, then sticks, then logs to gnaw.
It is the dance that saved my ancestors,
That I dare not forget. My word on it,
I will care well for your children, O Surt,
So that my own may survive.

Primal Fire (Surt Speaks)
by Ari

you think you know me
but you know nothing
or, rather, you know not nothingness
but I do, I know it well.
I was the first spark in the dark
born from the womb of my eternal mother
you name her Ginnungagap.
I am named to be Her child.
I held the wand of fire
and the lava beaches flowed
and there was warmth in the cold
light in the darkness
as it was before, so shall it be again.

the great cloud births stars
the stars explode with light
and burn until they burn away
to the perfect intensity of a white cinder.

I watched the giants born of wind and water
but wind and water are ephemeral things
so I sent my blood to them
I sent my sons and daughters to them
to warm their blood, to prepare them
for the Flood I saw would come
that they might be ready for the exodus
that they might become the heirs
of mountains, the masters of forests,
that other races might take this spark
and let my children teach them survival.

understand,
this tree of nine worlds
is not the first world I saw born
the first torch I lit
the first ice I melted
nor will it be the last.
old? old? You know nothing
of age. You know nothing
of the intensity of a perfect white cinder
lying in wait to birth new stars.
I do not speak of these things
for even the Gods do not understand.

do you understand?
do you understand?
do you understand?

all that is born in fire
ends in fire...
and nothing ever ends.
you think you know me
but you know
nothing.

Sinmora Dances

by Ari

Black like a charred stick
coming up from the ash
only no stick could move so graceful
undulate like a flame
which always seems pulled upward
by its tip, by the air.
Arms pointed up, she dances
undulates hips, ripples body,
the center of the singing fire
surrounded by her stamping, clapping sons.
I see through eyes so watered by smoke
that in this vague vision
she seems an artist's stroke
on the palette of the flame.

Logi

Logi is the second son of the old frost-thurse Mistblindi, also known as Fornjotr, born of a fire-etin mother just after the Flood. He is a fire-giant, and later entered into the sworn service of Utgard-Loki. He appears in the story of Thor and Loki meeting the sorcerer-ruler Utgard-Loki; they were challenged to beat the lord of Utgard's various friends and family members in random contests. Loki was challenged to beat one of his courtiers in a contest of eating; the giant soundly trounced him, as he not only devoured the meal but the bones and the plate as well. He was then revealed as Logi—the old fire-giant against the young one.

Logi was sometimes called Halogi (High-Logi) by his friends and family, because he was very tall, even for a giant. His wife was named Glut and she bore him two daughters, Einmyria and Eisa. They have long since passed away, and Logi lives alone in his black-rock cave. The lore also recounts a mortal name Logi/Halogi, who gave his name to the Scandinavian kingdom of Halogaland. Whether there was a mortal Logi/Halogi who lived a life similar to the giant's—perhaps living Logi's archetypal pattern—or not is something that we may never know.

Logi is a very old etin, one of the original magical triplicity of Kari-Logi-Hler, and those who have worked with him claim that he is associated with not only flame but specifically volcanic fire, the fire of the earth. He lives on the volcanic lava-beaches of Muspellheim, where he is a crusty and cantankerous presence. He will teach those who come to him with respect, although he reserves the right to turn them away for no apparent reason. He has a great love for the volcanic cliffs of Iceland, and pieces of black Icelandic lava rock are best for contacting him.

On Logi

by Jessica Wulff

There are only a couple of references to Logi in the lore. We know from Gylfaginning that he can be found in the company of Útgarda-Loki, on whose behalf he defeated Loki in an eating contest. In the time it took Loki to eat all the meat on his wooden plate, Logi devoured the meat, the bones, and the trencher too. This speaks to his substantial appetites, which I understand to be as much for knowledge and novelty as for sensational experiences.

The Prose Edda, Ynglingatal, Orkneyinga saga, and Hversu Noregr byggdist all attest to Logi's kin relationships. He is the son of Fornjót and brother of Kári (wind) and Ægir (sea). Logi's name is the same as the noun for "fire" or "flame", and Útgarda-Loki refers to him as "wildfire".

According to Þorsteins saga Víkingssonar, Logi (here euhemerised, but still said to descend from giants) is referred to as Hálogi and is the eponymous ruler of the Hálogaland, the northern-most district of Norway, historically inhabited by the "Háleygja ætt", or the family (more likely "people") of Hálogi. This source also tells us that Hálogi is the husband of Glóð (red-hot embers), father of Eisa (glowing embers) and Eimyrja (embers), said to be the fairest maidens in the land.

The Hálogi epithet is usually given as High Logi, but it may also be related linguistically (at least, via folk etymology) to the root for "holy" (*hailagaz). Linguistics aside, a connection between the god of fire and holiness is consistent with the Norse view of fire as possessing hallowing (holy-making) and protective properties, as evidenced by the use of fire in land-taking rituals.

My friendship with Logi is still very new; I do not pretend to be an expert but rather present the remaining material from the standpoint of that first flush of discovery and delight that heralds the beginning of any significant relationship. Everything hereafter is based solely on my personal experience, although it does not contradict the little we know about Logi from the extant lore.

I met him while doing journeywork as part of a local class, during which the leader spoke of Loge as being first bound and later banished. I was already in trance and suddenly confronted with an profoundly pissed-off fire jotun. He appeared as a wall of flame that coalesced into a roughly man-shaped pillar of fire. I apologised immediately for the offense on behalf of the class leader and, by extension, the group affiliated with her and offered weregild. He agreed to accept "blood, bogwater, and a bitchslap". "Bogwater" I understood to be Laphroaig, a single malt scotch with very strong elements of peat and smoke, blood I have a ready supply of, and "bitchslap" was negotiated to "a clear explanation of her error and the offense caused thereby", which he deemed acceptable after I explained that this was more likely to effectively communicate and hopefully correct the problem.

I bought him a bottle of 15-year-old Laphroaig, a special glass dedicated to his use, and a package of diabetic lancets. I did not buy a lancet device because I'm terribly squeamish about needles and part of the power in the sacrifice was forcing myself to penetrate my own flesh deeply enough to draw blood. After speaking to the woman who'd inadvertantly offended him, I gave him a burnt offering of blood and whiskey and sang to him.

Since then, he's been a constant presence, slowly revealing himself to me. While I still see him in his fire form, he's more often shown himself to me as a tall and slender man, with sharp, fine features that are androgynous without being overly delicate. His hair is shifting reds and golds, with darker ash and shadow at the nape of his neck. His skin is pale, but his cheeks are almost always flushed. His eyes are long and narrow, burning the bright blue of a welder's torch beneath red-gold lashes. Sometimes, he is covered in soot, and his eyes smolder like embers. Other times, he seems to be made of lava, streams and currents visible between the cracks of his skin. He is always in motion; even when he seems to be still, there are sparks rising from his hair or skin. His voice can be soft as smoke, crackling with laughter, or the angry roar of an inferno.

He likes fire colors, reds and golds as well as the hotter blues and whites, but he also likes ash grey, charcoal and soot black. He likes Laphroaig specifically but any single malt scotch is fine. He likes strong black coffee or plain espresso, hot mulled wine, glögg, anything smoked or flambéd (smoked salt is a favorite), spicy foods, incense or simple smoldered herbs (cedar and sweetgrass have both been popular). He's made a specific request for dried red chili peppers dipped in bittersweet chocolate, probably inspired by previous offerings of Dagoba "xocolatl" candy bars.

He prefers burnt offerings, and fire itself can be an offering as well as a focus for meditation or communion. Divination by fire, smoke, coals, or melted wax can be useful tools for communicating with him. Other burnt offerings that may help to connect with him are letters, drawings, or poems created with a charcoal medium (pencils or vine charcoal). He loves obsidian, jet (fossilized coal), and fire-colored stones or other sparklies. Sparkly things in general are a big favorite, especially glass, metal, and other things that require fire in their creation. Learning to use fire in crafts (glass, smithing, ceramics, etc.) can be a powerful devotional act. He also loves music and dance, preferring live music or dancing (however amateurish) to recorded performances.

It is too simplistic, almost insultingly limiting to think of him as an elemental or even a personification of fire although he certainly has an elementally fiery nature. Like fire, he can be as dangerous and destructive as he is useful and nurturing. He can be as warming as a blazing hearth and as bleak as a cold charred cinder. He must always be approached with respect. He is passionate, primal, mercurial, contrary, warmly affectionate, searing in his scorn, wicked smart, indecently funny, hypnotically sensuous, unfailingly voracious. He demands heartbreaking honesty and unwavering loyalty from his friends, and returns these gifts, and more, in kind.

Invocation to Logi

Hail Logi, Fire-Master,
Hottest of the Three Ancient Brothers,
Tall as a tree on fire
With flames leaping to the sky,
Tall as the black mountain
That gouts red rock toward the sky.
Hungry as a pack of hounds,
Always devouring, ever-thin,
Hungry as the molten earth
That devours the land around.
Hail Halogi, tricking the Trickster,
Warming our blood with your eternal spark.

Glut, Einmyria, Eisa

The confusion surrounding these three giantesses occurs largely because they are sometimes listed as being the wife and daughters of Logi, and sometimes as Loki's. What seems to have been the case—and this was received as a UPG from a chuckling Logi—is that there were two of each of them. Glut (Glow) was the original (now deceased) fire-etin wife of Logi, the daughter of a giant named Grim, and she named her two daughters Einmyria (Ashes) and Eisa (Embers). They were said to be the fairest giantesses in Muspellheim, and were both abducted by young giant-louts trying to make their fortune. Later, this story was reset in Norway, with mortal protagonists by the same name.

Those names were common among fire-giantesses, and many generations later another Glut came out of Muspellheim as a young giantess. She settled in the Iron Wood and was adopted as a younger sister by Angrboda. The wolf-chieftess and Loki were in love with each other at the time, but the two of them were playing a game of each pretending to not care for the other. Knowing that Loki had spent his childhood in Muspellheim among the fire-etins, Angrboda offered Glut to him as a bride, and convinced him to marry her, against his better judgment. She bore him twin daughters, and sentimentally named them Einmyria and Eisa after the children of her long-dead ancestress. When Loki lost interest in her after about a year, she left him and returned to live with Angrboda with her baby girls.

Spirits Of Storm
And Wind:
Frost-Thurses

he frost-thurses (or "rime-thurses", Old Norse hrimthursar) of Niflheim are the oldest and most feared of all etinkind; by that I mean that they are feared by nearly everything that isn't a deity, and by some of them as well. They are certainly feared by other Jotunfolk, some tribes of whom ban them from parts of the other two worlds (not that they could survive long in Muspellheim, anyway). They are the largest etins; their humanoid form is something like twelve to fifteen feet tall, and their other forms—generally pillars of whirling snow—are even huger. They can easily be seen in the distance of Niflheim, which gives travellers time to avoid them, but they move exceptionally fast in their snow-forms, so if you are in Niflheim and see one, go in the other direction as fast as possible. Hiding in caves and crevices too small for them to enter has been useful for some people.

The frost-thurses can be very problematic. Perhaps I should just change that to automatic-problem. They are the least friendly of giants, but they also will ignore you first, until you present a problem. They can smell intent pretty damned fast. They also don't take kindly to humans in their physical form, so be aware of that when you enter. If you find that you are more of a fire-blood type, then they may find you difficult in other ways. For me, I am frost-etin-blooded, so I don't find their basic disposition all that bad, but perhaps that is because I am a lot like them. I don't like people when I meet them for the first time, I hate going out to where people are unless I need something, and noise can set me off like nothing else. Actually, if you can think about an avalanche as an entity, you'll see what I mean here. An avalanche zone can be seen or not, but if you so much as make too loud a noise, step in the wrong spot, or don't take heed, it will come crashing down on you. As for offerings, they seem to like milk, tea (green tea and white tea especially), and work. Hard work. People often forget that the Norns are frost-thurse.

—Lyn, spirit-worker

There is no reasoning with a frost-thurse if they decide that you don't belong in their territory, and often at that point, you become food as far as they are concerned. Their environment is harsh and cold, varying from frozen snowfields to tundra, so this attitude may have been honed by the general lack of food in the vicinity.

Frost-thurse blood gives a certain amount of coldness to the disposition. As Lyn notes, the Norns are supposedly of frost-thurse lineage, and they need to be cold-blooded to do what they do. Compassion for its own sake isn't something that Jotunfolk in general are strong on, but this goes even less for frost-thurses. On the other hand, no one can teach you about weather as well as they can, and they are excellent teachers for learning outdoor survival as well.

The frost-thurses of Niflheim are like a thirty-foot screaming, whirling blizzard in their weather-form. In humanoid form, they have pale skin, almost blue for some of them, and hair that ranges from snow-white (and has nothing to do with age) to black. If they wear clothing, it is usually skins and leather, although some have woven fabric of some sort that they have traded for. In some cases, they may wear the entire skin of a huge animal, like a white bear. This may make it difficult for travelers to figure out whether the bear-thing coming for you out of the snow is an actual bear or a bear-clad frost-thurse.

Although Niflheim frost-thurses are the most territorial and least friendly to strangers of any of the Jotunfolk, fortunately, if you are just passing through, they will usually not bother you. Things that attract their attention: Hunting without permission on their doorsteps. Starting fires close to their homes. Carrying fire, in general. Littering. Invading their caves, thinking that just because it's an empty cave means that it doesn't belong to anyone. If you must use a cave, leave an offering for whoever might own it, perhaps with a note thanking them, or the Gyfu-rune.

There is no one ruler of all the frost-thurses in Niflheim. They are organized into a bunch of loose tribes, and come together for moots and decision-making. Any of the wise elders of any tribe is respected as much as any other. Frost-thurses are keenly aware of the fact that they were some of the first intelligent beings to be created in the Nine Worlds, and they are proud of that fact. One of their strongest oaths is swearing by Elivagar, the primal frost-river of Niflheim, some of whose nature runs in their veins. In personality, the frost-thurses are private, retiring, suspicious, and somewhat cold. They hunt silently rather than noisily, and they are superb hunters. It is said that they have a certain amount of power over the weather in Niflheim, and can bring down storms, which is another reason not to anger them.

If you are spirit-traveling in Niflheim and you run into hostile frost-thurses, one way to get out of being attacked is to tell them that you are looking for the Helvegr, the Road to Helheim, and are lost. They have a great deal of respect for the Land of the Dead that borders their world, and for the Lady who rules it, and they will not molest any pilgrim who is going to that dread land. On the other hand, they are not unaware that some folk lie about such things in order to escape retribution, so they may well call your bluff and insist on escorting the traveler who invokes the Helvegr right to the road, at least within sight of Mordgud's tower. At that point, you have no choice but to walk the Hel-road, so this excuse should only be invoked as a desperate last resort, or if it was actually one of your intended destinations. As harsh as Niflheim is, it is less difficult to extract yourself from than Helheim.

The non-Niflheim-dwelling descendants of frost-giants are the storm-giants, who may live anywhere in the Nine Worlds. Thjazi is one example, as are Thrym and Kari. There is a good deal of blurring as to what is a frost-thurse and what is a storm-giant or wind-giant; it seems that even the Jotnar themselves don't draw those lines tightly, except that the permanent denizens of Niflheim are always referred to as frost-giants; those who migrated out or were born elsewhere may have any combination of names and powers.

The storm-giants of Jotunheim are descended from the Niflheim tribes; a few, such as Thrym the Old, titular king of Jotunheim, are elders who emigrated directly from the Land of Mists. The more frost-thurse blood a mountain Jotun has, the more likely they are to prefer the northeastern mountain chains, where the weather is warmer than Niflheim but not by much. The Jotunheim storm-giants also tend towards being masters of winds rather than ground-storms; some have learned to command the winds and fly.

Offerings: Any food, or small item made of wood (preferably something that is both useful and beautifully made) that will not rot and degrade in the cold. They aren't so much for metal, preferring stone and wood (when they can get the latter). Fruits and vegetables are especially valued, as there isn't much in Niflheim. An elderly frost-thurse once wept with joy when I gave her edible flowers, which was pretty impressive, as I've never seen any of them make such an emotional display before or since. They are very fond of cake and bread (and other food items that they don't normally get), but they don't like caraway seed. It may be that they are allergic to it.

Aurgelmir/Ymir, Thrudgelmir, Bergelmir

As is told in the chapter on the history of the giants, the first frost-thurse was Ymir, whose blood runs in all giants today except for Surt and the purest of his children. Aurgelmir he is called by his descendants; he is known as Ymir by all others. He was created out of the living rock of the land of Niflheim as the ice slowly receded, warmed by the approach of Muspellheim. Apparently he was a primitive, helpless creature; he did not know how to shapeshift, and retained a huge and unwieldy body made mostly of earth that he never truly learned to use. He survived because the great cosmic cow Audumhla wandered over periodically to feed him from her udder.

Three frost-etins grew parthenogenically from his body; a man and a woman from the friction of each of his armpits as he thrashed, and another man from the friction of his legs rubbing together. While lore cannot give us the names of the first two—although the giants know them, and they are sacred names to them—the third was named Thrudgelmir, and he had six heads. Both he and his parthenogenic brother bred with their sister, and thus the race of frost-thurses was born.

The second generation of frost-thurses were much smaller than their enormous, nearly world-sized comatose creator. As far as we can tell, Ymir never really woke up, at least not to speak and walk, but his children had speech and movement and intelligence. They revered the immense body of their progenitor, and cared for it as best they could. The first child born of the three was named Bergelmir, and became the chieftain of his third generation.

As the world of Niflheim came periodically closer to the world of Muspellheim in a sort of dance, a bridge would be made of water which thawed and then froze again. Frost-thurses began to cross the bridge and meet with the sons of Surt and Sinmora, and some of them wedded each other and had children. And in this way, the race of giants increased.

Meanwhile, the great cosmic cow Audumhla had licked at the salt-ice until it finally uncovered yet another being. He was male, yet differently formed than the giants. He named himself Buri, and the giants at first welcomed him among them. He took a wife from their tribes, and bore a son, Bor. It was noted by all that Bor very much resembled the race of his father, yet showed little of the race of his mother. Bor in turn chose for a mate the giantess Bestla, daughter of Bolthorn, a son of Bergelmir and grandson of Thrudgelmir. Bestla bore Bor three sons: Odin, Vili, and Ve. They, too, took more after their father's race and looked almost nothing like that of their mother.

It is unknown exactly why bad feelings broke out between the growing Jotnar tribes and the tribe of Buri. Both sides tell a different story, and both are suspect, tangled with old emotions, and garbled with retellings. The sons of Buri have said that they feared the Jotnar would increase too quickly and use all the food and resources in meager Niflheim, and it is true that the Jotunfolk have always found it easier to breed than the descendants of Buri, who often can only have few children, or none, unless they mate with the Jotun race. The Jotnar have always been hardier than the Aesir, and outnumbered them by a thousandfold, and perhaps this grated on the smaller, slower-breeding tribe of Buri.

On the other hand, the Jotnar claim that the sons of Bor, seeing that their bloodlines nearly always triumphed over those of their Jotun neighbors, claimed indeed that those bloodlines were superior and gave them superior magic, and that they ought to be the rulers over all. They say that Bergelmir, the chieftain of the frost-thurses, challenged this claim, and called on Surt to back his challenge, and that the sons of Buri were to meet him on the plain of ice to fight for the rulership of Niflheim. They say also that instead of coming to the appointed place, where all waited to witness, the sons of Bor, accompanied by their wives and daughters, stole instead to the unguarded body of Aurgelmir and hacked it into pieces. So much blood flowed from his severed neck that all of Niflheim was flooded, and indeed parts of Muspellheim were waterlogged for the first time, and the light was dimmed. Only the Underworld, Jormundgrund, was dry and safe, but most of the folk there were Dead.

On their part, the sons of Buri have long claimed that it was necessary to murder and dismember Aurgelmir, as his body was the largest single source of magical regenerating earth-stuff, and they needed a large supply of that stuff to rebuild their world to their dreams. The frost-thurses claim that they deliberately attempted to drown everyone else in the flood; that the killing of Aurgelmir was not only ancestral murder but an attempt at genocide. If so, it was entirely unsuccessful, as many of the giants survived with teeth-gritted persistence in spite of the danger of the flood.

Surprisingly, the elder giants have no animosity toward Buri and Bor, the eldest Asa and his son. According to their account, Buri and Bor honorably arrived to witness the duel, and were drowned with most of the giants. We will likely never know if they knew about their sons' plan and rejected it as dishonorable, or if Buri's sons were perfectly willing to sacrifice their father, mother, and grandparents in order to carry through their scheme.

What we do know is that the sons of Bor, standing on their one high place, put together the greatest magic ever done around the World Tree. Three worlds already existed, but they used Aurgelmir's dying flesh to build four more. His legs and lower spine were built into the mountainous Svartalfheim for the duergar, and his upper spine floated off and became the even more mountainous Jotunheim, which was claimed immediately by the surviving giants. His belly became the plain of Midgard, with protruding bones as mountains. His eyelashes and eyebrows were made into a stony hill-fence around the continent of Midgard, and around this gushed the ocean that had come from his blood. His teeth were scattered far and wide as sacred boulders. His skull was brought up into the heights of the Tree and made into a world for the Aesir, Asgard, with his brains strewn about as clouds. Thus were four worlds crafted from the one huge ancestral body of Aurgelmir.

Aurgelmir's grandson Bergelmir, and many of his folk, survived the flood by making a boat out of an enormous hollow tree trunk, and floating until they found land. In one legend, Bergelmir sees the shrieking, drowning experimental humans Ask and Embla, and plucks them out of the water, setting them into the branches of a tall tree to wait out the flood. Another legend says that the humans weren't created until after the flood, by the Aesir, so there is a discrepancy of myth here. At any rate, Bergelmir and his tribe repopulated not only Niflheim (when the flood-waters partially receded; Niflheim is still about one-third open water) but Jotunheim as well. Every giant not purely of the blood of Surt can trace their bloodlines to this small, ragged band of survivors, perhaps fifty or sixty giants in all. Of these, a few still remain alive who can remember those days—Thrym, Kari, Logi, Rym, Bolthorn, Bestla, Mimir, Hymir and Hrod and Hymir's nine-headed mother, Hyndla, and although he does not speak of it, Tyr.

Bergelmir himself is long gone, after having lived and ruled for a very long time as the Lord of Niflheim and Eldest of the Jotnar. Regardless of how much of his blood was inherited, his lineage encompasses all of the Aesir, through his granddaughter Bestla. He is revered among all his Jotun descendants as being wise, practical, and resourceful, a leader who rebuilt two worlds from an overwhelming disaster and renewed the race of his people with even more vigor than before.

Mistblindi/Fornjotr

Mistblindi is a chieftain of the old original frost-giants, who with Bergelmir escaped the Flood. His name refers to a kind of fog so thick that you can't see your hand in front of your face. His other name, Fornjotr, is translated by scholars as meaning "old giant", or possibly "old Destroyer", "Old Howler", or "the receiver of sacrifices". He later wandered the world with his three wives and sired three sons—Kari, Logi, and Hler (later renamed Aegir). The three brothers were all different, as they came from different mothers and were born in different places.

Some scholars, including H.A. Guerber in his Myths And Legends Of The Norsemen, conjecture that these three giant-Gods were part of an older creation myth that predates the myths of the Aesir and Vanir. Together, they make up a triplicity of the primal elements working on the Earth; the interaction of Sea, Flame, and North Wind creating and shaping the world of the North. The Scandinavian scholar Preben Muellengracht has suggested that these three elements of Sea, Flame and North Wind were an alternative model to the magical quadriplicity of Earth, Water, Fire and Air. The sea-kings of Orkney historically traced their descent from these three brothers. Logi's information is listed with the fire-giants, and Hler/Aegir's with the sea-etins; Kari's is below.

Kari, and his descendants

Kari is the oldest son of Mistblindi, born of Mistblindi's first wife, another frost-thurse. He was born before the Flood and was a storm-giant of wind and snow. After the Flood, when things settled out, he stayed with his father Mistblindi through many wanderings and returned with him to Niflheim, where he inherited his father's title and tribe after Mistblindi died. Kari is the Giant of the North Wind, and is a powerful Lord of Niflheim and the wind elements.

One of the interesting things about Kari, if one works with him, is that he regresses in age and then ages again. In the spring he returns to the form of a slender, androgynous youth, and he ages throughout the year until he is a hoary, bearded old man in winter. On a natural cycle, this mirrors the change of the North Wind from cooling breeze to bringer of bitter blizzards. In his young phase, he is often amorous, taking on wind form to stroke a lover; it is said that he loves to blow up women's skirts. In his older form, he is more reclusive—when not doing his job as North Wind—and stays home in his cave is Niflheim with his great-granddaughters.

Kari has two sons, one named Frosti (Frost) and one named Jokul (Icicle), who is in turn the father of a frost-thurse named Snaer (Snow) the Old, who is another of the chieftains of Niflheim. Snaer in turn has a son named Thorri (Frozen-Snow), and three daughters named Fon (Snowfall), Drifa (Snowdrift), and Mjol (Powder). This last daughter is a powerful sorceress and seer of Niflheim who can fly through the air. Frosti, in turn, seems to have married into an Alfar family; his son was the half-Alfar Raum the Old, whose son was Finnalf (or just Alf), one of the kings of Alfheim. Finnalf's niece married a mortal descendant of Kari's brother Logi, who was named after the fire-giant.

Invocation to Kari

Hail, North Wind, coldest of breezes,
Bringer of Winter, Blizzard-Bearer,
Youth who cools the blazing summer,
Bearded storm of the autumn rains,
Old Man of the icy knives
That slice the uncovered flesh to blue ribbons.
Hail, Chieftain of Niflheim, son of Mistblindi,
Brother to Fire and Sea, father of many,
Singer of songs of power,
Give us your gifts of the wind's music
And spare us from your cold embrace
That we may willingly sing your praises
Back to you again through the whirling snow.

Bolthorn

Little is known about Bolthorn save his name, which means "Evil Thorn" (and is pronounced "Bol-thorn", not "Bolt-horn"). He was a frost giant from before the flood, one of Bergelmir's sons who escaped, one of the very first generations born, in fact. One of his sons was Mimir, and his daughter was the giantess Bestla, the mother of Odin.

Hymir and Hrod

Hymir is a warrior frost-thurse, living in the northern mountains of Jotunheim. Hrod, his wife, is of fire-giant extraction. The two of them go back before the Flood; they met on the bridge of ice that formed between Muspellheim and Niflheim, and fell in love. Theirs was the first union of fire and ice, and between them they bore a son, Tyr. They escaped the Flood, Hrod with her little son in her arms, and Hymir carrying his aged mother, a frost-giantess whose shapeshifted form had nine heads. Their son grew to be the famous warrior-priest Tyr, who would become an avatar of the Great War God and eventually join forces with the Aesir and be adopted by Odin.

According to the Hymiskvida, Hymir owned a great cauldron, huge enough to boil several oxen. The Aesir were used to hitting up Aegir for food and beer, but when the sea god failed to produce enough at one sitting to satisfy them, he remonstrated that it was because of the lack of a big enough kettle. Tyr remembered his father's kettle, and suggested that he and Thor find a way to win it from him. Thor would have happily stolen it, but Tyr, the more honorable of the two, insisted that it be fairly won. The two visited Hymir, who was not happy to see his long-defected son, accompanied by a noted giant-slayer, and smashed a pillar to rubble in typical frost-thurse rage. Hrod stepped in and made a temporary peace.

Hymir grumblingly killed three steers to feed his guests for dinner, but to his dismay Thor ate most of the feast, and left so little food that they would have to go fishing the next day. Thor offered to help, but while Hymir was pulling up whales to eat, Thor bumblingly tried a fishing-charm to hook something really big. He managed to hook Jormundgand, the Midgard Serpent, but before he could kill the sacred Snake, Hymir cut the line and the Serpent sank back into the sea. Hymir, in frustration, asked Thor to at least carry the boat back to the hall. Thor did so easily, boasting of his strength; Hymir snapped that if he were as strong as he claimed, he ought to be able to break Hymir's goblet. Thor gleefully bet the frost-giant the great cauldron if he could break the goblet.

Unfortunately for Thor, the goblet was enchanted, and couldn't be broken, even when he hurled it several times through Hymir's walls and pillars. Finally, to stop the trashing of the hall, Hrod told him that the charm would be broken if he threw it at Hymir's head. Thor promptly beaned the old giant with it, and it broke, although Hymir's exceptionally hard head was undamaged. Fuming, the old giant let Thor heft the cauldron and leave his hall, but when he and Tyr were a good way down the road, he felt quite taken advantage of, and sent a warband of giants after them anyway. Thor leaped into battle and killed off the etin-band, and then brought the cauldron to Aegir, who was then obliged to keep brewing beer for the ever-greedy gullets of the Aesir and their warriors.

This particular episode was the last straw between Tyr and Hymir; the frost-giant cursed his son and refused him hospitality from them on. Some say that Tyr's loss of Fenris and his hand came from that curse, from denying his bloodline and incurring the wrath of his father. Either way, they ended up implacably on opposite sides. If Ragnarok comes, Hymir has promised to captain the great ship Naglfari, created by Hela and Surt out of the nail clippings of the Dead, with its great boatload of dead souls. He will dismount at the plain of Vigrond with several thousand dead Jotun warriors behind him to fight in the battle.

Prayer to Hymir and Hrod

Hail to Hymir
Ancient rime-thurse
With ice in the fringe of your beard.
Hail to Hrod
Ancient fire-woman
With sparks in the glint of your eye.
Hail to you who held out your hands
Across the gap of worlds,
Hail to you who touched and held,
Who built the first bridge of flesh,
Whose love was the meeting of fire and ice,
Whose passion made Honor,
Made the Lord of Swords, walking tall,
Made the Hand by which so many swear.
Help us to remember
That reaching across a great gap
And building a bridge of Love
Always bears a reward beyond imagining.

Thrym

Thrym The Old, as he is known among then Jotnar of Jotunheim, is a frost-thurse, born in Niflheim, who was elected High King and Chieftain of all Giantkind. He is one of the handful of surviving thurses who go back to the time before the Flood. His home is Thrymheim, high in the snowy northeastern mountains of Jotunheim; he is still more frost-thurse than anything else and prefers the cold northern areas.

Thrym's greatest role in the lore is the story of how his agents stole Thor's hammer, Mjollnir, and attempted to ransom it back in exchange for marriage to the Vanir goddess Freyja. This created the rather slapstick adventure in which Thor cross-dresses as Freyja in order to get into Thrymheim, and as soon as he lays his hand on the hammer in order to take the wedding vows, he begins to lay about him and smash the place. While Thrym survived the episode with only a bruised ego and a mess to clean up, he is still resentful about it and it is best not to bring it up with him, should you attempt to contact him.

As King of Jotunheim, his duties are largely ceremonial, although he is called upon to mediate disputes between tribal leaders, and make decisions on problems that they might find too large or impactful to handle themselves. (What decisions Utgard-Loki or Surt wouldn't choose to handle themselves, I can't imagine, although I suppose there might be some.) Thrym is a jovial, white-bearded giant with a generous table who throws fine parties. The best offering to give at his table is that of entertainment—songs, stories, juggling, etc. In fact, if you announce at the door that you have entertainment to share, you will likely be let in immediately. Remember that the best songs and stories are ones that they likely wouldn't have heard, but that would be understandable to them and their culture, and choose your repertoire carefully. Laugh at Thrym's jokes, smile and nod when he tells war stories, don't talk politics, and don't get drunk and say things you'll regret. If Thrym or any other Jotun there challenges you to a drinking contest, turn them down with good humor, perhaps saying modestly that you are a lightweight and could never win against their obvious prowess. Which, frankly, is likely to be completely true.

Keep in mind, however, that under his jovial manner Thrym is much colder and more hard-hearted than you might think. He hates the Aesir with a passion, and if you are sworn to them, you'd better not talk about it. Avoid the subject, and don't challenge him on it. Even if he knows that you wear a Thor's hammer about your neck, he'll let you in if you are entertaining, but leave your politics at the door and talk about neutral subjects. This is another reason not to get drunk while visiting.

The beer brewed at Thrymheim, by the way, is some of the best around, and is extremely strong for beer. Its recipe was started by Olvalde (see his entry), two of whose sons are still alive and brewing it. Be careful when you drink it; it tends to give mortals a terrible hangover.

Hymn to Thrym

Hail Thrym, frost-father,
Lord and Chieftain of Etin-Home,
Keeper of the snowy passes,
Generous host and passionate storm,
You who are not afraid to dare, to risk,
To be audacious above your station,
Lead our footsteps skillfully
Through the blinding storm of white,
Give us safe passage over the mountains
And the haven of light and warmth
Where we least expect it.
Hail, Thrym, frost-father to your people,
White-bearded warrior, hale of hand,
Grant us good wishes and spare us your wrath.

Thorgerdr

Another giant-figure who often lives at Thrym's court (although she has a modest hall slightly to the north of it) is Thorgerdr. While she passes as a frost-giantess in Jotunheim—she can throw wind and rain and hail with the best of them, and often does—she is actually Finnish in origin and spends part of the year in Lapland with the Saami. Somewhere along the line she started spending time in Scandinavia, and got inducted into this pantheon as a patron deity of Halogaland in north Norway. Like Kari the North Wind, her age waxes and wanes from sturdy maiden to iron-grey-haired matron throughout the year.

Mimir

Mimir is the son of Bolthorn and grandson of Bergelmir, first chieftain of the frost-giants. Before the death of Aurgelmir, he went to the Underworld of the time, Jormundgrund, and became the consort of the original death goddess, Hel. (This is not to be confused with the modern Hela, Loki's daughter; see her entry for more information.) When the flood came, Hel released him and told him that he must guard a particular spring, a sacred well that had formed in Jotunheim next to a protruding root of the World Tree. Mimir stood in the spring for so long, up to his neck in water, that the Kjolen mountains grew on his shoulders.

Finally he decided to leave the spring, perhaps because he wanted to see the world. He had been gone long enough that he recognized few of the new post-Flood generation of giants. His father Bolthorn had been killed in the Flood; he heard that Bolthorn's daughter Bestla dwelt in Asgard, the honored mother of its All-Father. Mimir traveled to Asgard and sought her out, and was welcomed by Odin as his uncle. After having been immersed for so long in the spring of knowledge, Mimir had learned much, and Odin made much use of his wisdom.

When the Aesir discovered that the space around the Tree had been invaded by yet another race—the Vanir—who had made their own world and were prepared to defend it, war broke out. For several years the struggle went on with no clear winner; finally, the Aesir wisely called for a truce, and agreed to exchange hostages as part of the agreement. Odin asked that Njord, the god of sailors, and his two children Freyja and Frey, be the Vanir hostages; he was especially eager to get his hands on Freyja, who was a love goddess with knowledge of seidhr-magic. In return, the Vanir asked that Odin send them hostages of equal knowledge and wisdom.

For reasons of his own, Odin chose his giant uncle to be the sacrifice, and also sent along his youngest brother Hoenir, a shy young Aesir who was good-looking but neither bright nor loquacious. Mimir resented being traded off by Odin, and refused to play the part of the wise counselor to the strange Vanir, to whom he had no kinship links. When they would ask him questions, he would give them long-winded and deliberately cryptic answers. For his part, Hoenir was mostly silent, except when parroting Mimir.

After some time of this, the Vanir became angry and chopped off Mimir's head. They sent Hoenir back to the Aesir, carrying the severed head with him as a message of their ire. It was also a message of power; although the Aesir could have taken the murdering and rejection of their hostages as an excuse to declare war again, or at least to kill their own Vanir hostages, they did neither. Odin valued Njord and his children too highly to murder them, and he dared not start the war again, and the Vanir knew both these things. The Vanir went on with their lives, independent of the Aesir, and meanwhile the Aesir councils had strong Vanir voices in them that could not be ignored.

Odin took the severed head of Mimir and treated it with magical herbs, bringing it back to life so as to have access to Mimir's wisdom. When Mimir cursed his nephew, Odin flung the head back into the Well of Memory in Jotunheim, and there Mimir floats today—old, tired, cantankerous, and resentful. When Odin went on his epic journey to find knowledge, eventually his footsteps led him to Mimir's Well. Mimir offered him control over Thought and Memory—and gave him the two ravens of those names into the bargain—but in exchange, he demanded that Odin rip out one of his own eyes and throw it into the well. As we know, Odin acquiesced. To this day, one of his eyes glows like an underwater star in the well, providing what light there is to see in the depths of the waters there.

For journeyers, Mimir's well is probably one of the most-visited tourist attractions in Jotunheim. The Tree's root extrudes from the ground like a vast earthwork, curling around to the southeast, and in the small valley made by its knotted bulk is the mouth of a cave. The well is just inside, and floating in it are a number of skulls and severed heads. Some are offerings that folk give to Mimir; some are trophies that he takes when folk fail to answer a bargain-question properly. The heads are a ward-off; many folk become frightened at the sight and leave, which is fine with Mimir.

Sometimes one of the heads will turn and speak, which means that Mimir has decided to make the first move. His head is old and wrinkled, with long white hair floating in the water like a cloak all around. More often, though, he will be underwater and you will have to call him up. Pouring good booze in the water is one way to start. Good offerings for him, before and afterwards, are alcohol and food with strong, sweet flavors that dissolves easily in water. While he gets no nourishment from it, he enjoys tasting it.

Mimir is the god of underground waters, and like them his wisdom runs deep and hidden. He has a fairly direct line into the Library of the Akashic Records as well as a good relationship with the Norns, which is why people bother him with questions. He is also old, tired, capricious, embittered, and spiteful. Cranky doesn't even begin to cover it. Being a floating oracular head down a well is a lousy job, and several journeyers have noted with compassion that the kindest thing that could happen to Mimir is to be released into death. He might like you, in which case he might actually be cooperative, although possibly sarcastic and insulting. If he doesn't like you—and whether he takes to you or not seems to be less about you and your offerings and more about whether he's just in a bad mood that day—you might think about coming back another time.

If Mimir says that the only exchange for your question is for you to answer one of his, do not take him up on the challenge. First of all, there is no way that you can beat him at this game. He will always come up with something you don't know. He's especially good at finding things that you ought to know but don't, so that you are groaning and slapping your forehead and feeling stupid in the moments before you die. That's right...the price for losing is beheading. Don't think that because he is a severed head down a well that he can't kill you. Floating blades will fall from the ceiling or fly from the walls before you can even turn around. Take those rotting, bloated skulls seriously. If he is in a bloodthirsty mood, apologize for disturbing him, leave your offering to perhaps sweeten his disposition towards you at a later time, and come back another time. (Remember that even Odin had to extract one of his own eyes to get some of Mimir's wisdom. This is not a god to be taken lightly.)

Even if he does answer your question, keep in mind that he may make it deliberately cryptic, or leave out important information that may trip you up if you act on it. He will not, however, lie. Mimir never lies. The truth is his weapon, to manipulate and strike with. If he offers to tell you the most likely date of your own death, I strongly suggest that you decline. While it may be tempting to know, the next temptation will be to attempt to stave it off, and that gets into messing with the strands of Wyrd and into the work of the Norns, and can often just dig you deeper into the hole. Besides, it wastes your question, and he may not be inclined to answer any others.

Invocation to Mimir

Hail, Grandfather of the Well of Wisdom!
Eyes that see through the darkness
Of the stone and water,
We honor your sacrifice,
We honor your pain,
We honor that which was hard-won
Only by losing.
Hail, Grandfather of the Sacred Spring,
You who have given much in service,
When the time comes,
May you bless us with your wisdom
And may we not be afraid to pay the price.

For Mimir

by Elizabeth Vongvisith

The waters of the Well are always rippling
And on their surface, you can see the sun,
A candle to light the dimness down
Where he dwells, living on after death, in
Simmering rage cloaked as resignation.

I wonder if Mimir dreams, floating
In his fluid jailhouse, his abbatoir where
The heads of the unlucky keep him company?
I am at least wise enough not to ask.
For then I might see a slow train of bubbles
Rising to the surface, conveyor-belt regular
As the heads shifted around to face me,
As Mimir opened his sleep-drained eyes,
Piercing the water and the air between us
Until I either run screaming from that place,

Or wait, frozen on my feet, for the old one
To speak the things I would rather not hear.

If I sang across the gently moving waters,
Would my song carry down to his ears
As well as the inevitable questions do?
And if I dared bend toward the surface,
Touching my mouth briefly to the chill water,
Would he feel the warmth of my lips on his face
Just before madness broke my brain in two
And drew me too early to Helheim's border?

If his sleep does permit it, perhaps
Mimir dreams of stark nothingness
In the silence and the depth of the Well,
An occasional blackout of sense
Cradling him painlessly there in between
Interruptions by the curious and the ruthless;
For now, until the end of the world,
He may draw only so close to release
And no further.

Vafthrudnir

In the Vafthrudnismal, Odin decides that he will riddle-spar with a particularly knowledgeable old front-giant named Vafthrudnir (whose name means "Mighty In Riddles"). Frigga would rather he not go, as the giant has made a rule about people coming to word-spar with him: if they lose, he takes their head. So far, apparently no one has won, because he still has his own head.

It is unclear why Odin feels the need to do this. Some folk see Vafthrudnismal as an entirely human-created saga, in encyclopedic form, as a teaching-tool: the question-and-answer structure allows the listener to learn many standard facts about Norse cosmology, including Ragnarok. If we assume that it is based on a real otherworldly event, however, the latter information (the final five questions are about Ragnarok) might be Odin's way of getting a second opinion, perhaps cross-checking the information of the dead giantess Volva in the hopes of getting a better outcome. Unfortunately, Vafthrudnir's information is exactly the same.

This means that Vafthrudnir is a seer, as Ragnarok is something that has not yet happened at the time of the saga, and might not happen; he is describing the possible future of what would happen should the Aesir take up full battle against the more numerous Jotnar, with their respective drafted armies of Dead. In the story, Vafthrudnir asks Odin a few questions about the standard workings of the Sun and Moon, and Odin then proceeds to ask a huge number of questions. The first few are clearly "testing questions" about Nine Worlds geography and cosmology, but the last bunch are Odin digging for information about the future, and particularly Ragnarok.

At the last, when Odin realizes that Vafthrudnir has answered correctly every one of his questions, and he is about to lose the bet, he asks an unanswerable one: "What did Odin whisper into his son's (clearly Baldur's) ear on his funeral pyre?" This is something that clearly only Odin could know, and it is rather reminiscent of Bilbo Baggins' final question to Gollum: "What have I got in my pocket?" One would think that this would be cheating, but apparently not, for after being unable to answer it—and subsequently realizing that he is facing Odin—the giant agrees that Odin is the wiser. His reference to himself as "fated" implies that he knows that Odin has the right to kill him now. Whether Odin does so or not is unknown, but according to other giants, Vafthrudnir is not alive today. (One has to wonder if the question about Odin's last message to his dead son was less of a cheat and more of a worry that some classified information about Baldur's death had gotten out, though.)

Vafthrudnir speaks of himself and his great age in the poem; he says that he was there when Bergelmir, the grandson of Ymir, was born floating in a boat on the River Elivagar, and that they had been friends before the flood. As Ymir produced only two frost-thurse men and one woman, it is likely that Vafthrudnir is one of the second generation, and thus Bergelmir's older half-brother; this would make sense of him seeing his younger half-brother born in a boat. He names his own son as one Im, about whom nothing is known.

Olvalde, Thjatsi, Ide, and Gang

Olvalde was a frost-giant whose name meant "Ale-Emperor", and he lived in Thrymheim as Thrym's personal brewer of fine ale. We know little about him except that his three sons were Thjatsi, Ide, and Gang, and that when he died they threw an immense wake that consumed the major part of his ale.

Ide and Gang, the younger two brothers, do not come much into the stories past their father's funeral; presumably they continue his loyalty to Thrym. Olvalde's eldest son Thjatsi (or Thiassi, Thjassi, Thiatsi, Thjazi; his name supposedly means "Water"), on the other hand, died famously by kidnapping the goddess Iduna.

Supposedly Odin, Hoenir, and Loki were out traveling in the forest, and they had trouble getting their cooking fire started. Odin noticed a wand in the grass next to the fire and smelled foul play; he looked up into the trees and noticed Thjassi there, shapeshifted into eagle form. Thjassi agreed to remove the spell on the fire in exchange for some of the meat, and Odin agreed. When the meat was cooked, however, he swooped down and grabbed the largest portion. Loki indignantly jumped up and whacked him with the magic wand, which he had taken from the grass. The wand stuck to both Loki's fingers and the flying Thjassi, who spent the next hour dragging the hapless trickster through tree branches and thornbushes. When Loki begged to be released, Thjassi offered him his freedom in exchange for luring Iduna out of Asgard, so that he might capture her and her golden apples.

Loki hesitated, for as blood brother to Odin, he had become used to the immortality offered by the golden apples, but after another hour of being banged off of mountainsides he capitulated was dropped to the ground. Having given his word, he now had to return to Asgard and lure Iduna out. He did so by telling her that he had seen golden apples like hers growing wild in the woods just beyond the Thund Thvitr, and that she ought to bring her box of apples to compare them. Iduna hurried out to the stand of woods that Loki indicated, and Thjassi swooped down and picked her up, carrying her off to his mountain fortress in northeastern Jotunheim.

However, Thjassi discovered that the apples themselves were useless without the cooperation of Iduna and her magic, and she refused to cooperate, even when he locked her up in a tiny cave on top of the mountain. Meanwhile, the Aesir were terrified at the loss of Iduna, and watched each other begin to age for the first time. Loki was suspected and seized, and he confessed, then offered to put the matter to rights if Freya would lend him her falcon cloak. The Aesir were suspicious, but had no choice.

In falcon form, Loki sped to Thjassi's mountain and found Iduna still holding out. He changed her into a nut, and seized the nut in one claw and her golden box of apples in the other. As he sped away with a falcon's speed, Thjassi passed them by returning home and saw the flash of gold against the setting sun. Knowing that his prize had been stolen, he sped after the falcon in eagle form. Being larger and stronger than Loki, he almost caught the trickster, but Loki made it just in time to the walls of Asgard, which had been enchanted to spout great flames if an intruder flew over. Thjassi was caught in the shooting flames and burned to death, falling from the sky. The Aesir thought that the matter was over, but soon afterwards Thjassi's daughter Skadi came to Asgard to demand weregild for her father; she married one of the Vanir hostages for a time, and managed to get a Jotun voice onto the Aesir councils. So in a way, Skadi inherited the gift of immortality that her father had tried to take by force.

Rym

Rym (whose name means "Old and Helpless") is an old frost-giant from before the flood who lives in the watery, flooded area of Niflheim. He is blind, but has a perfect sense of direction, and sees with his extra senses. Hela has made a deal with him that if Ragnarok comes, he will be the navigator of Naglfari, the great ship of the Dead made of corpse's fingernails. This is because a person with normal vision might not be able to guide the ship through the mist and fog that Ragnarok will bring down.

Hrimthurs

This giant, whose name simply mean "Rime-giant", more of a title than a name, and who introduced himself to the Aesir simply as "Blast", was a stonemason of some note. We may never know his true name, but he wandered up to Asgard soon after the war between the Aesir and the Vanir. The Vanir had thoroughly shattered the great wall around Asgard, leaving it in rubble. This meant that if anyone else—meaning any Jotun tribe—decided to attack, the Aesir would be at an extreme disadvantage. To rebuild the wall themselves would take years. Hrimthurs, on the other hand, told them that he could do it in six months. As a price, he asked for Freyja as his wife, and ownership of the Sun and Moon. He agreed that if he could not finish the wall in the time allotted, they would pay nothing.

As the Aesir were sure that his claims were entirely exaggerated, they agreed out of desperation. However, Hrimthurs began his work at the winter solstice, and as the summer solstice drew near, it became clear that he was indeed about to succeed. Much of his strategy depended on a great magical stallion, likely bred and bought in Alfheim, named Svadilfari, who hauled the stones as fast as he could cut them.

When the Aesir saw that they would have to pay up, they became furious. Odin detailed Loki, who was at that time his "fixer", to do something about it. Loki turned himself into a beautiful mare in heat and lured Svadilfari away, mere days before the deadline. Without the horse, the angry Hrimthurs could not finish in time, and lost. Smelling foul play, he stormed into Asgard and raged at them for unfairness. Odin called in his other "fixer", his son Thor, and ordered him to slay Hrimthurs, which he did.

Some months later, Loki appeared again, leading an eight-legged foal. Apparently his Iron Wood blood had asserted itself; although he was able to take on a female (animal) form and bear a child, it was just as oddly deformed as many of his tribesfolk. He gave it to Odin as a gift, and Odin named it Sleipnir, or "Spider", and it became his favorite steed.

Byleist

Byleist is the second son of Laufey, the mother of Loki; he is a frost-thurse, but with a gentler temperament than most of them. His father is unknown; possibly a frost-giant whom she dallied with before meeting Farbauti and agreeing to come with him to the Iron Wood. Byleist is a member of Thrym's court and a trusted servant of his, when he is not wandering about the Nine Worlds. As such, he is often used as Thrym's messenger, courier, or just plain spy.

Skadi

Skadi is one of the most famous frost-giantesses in Jotun history, if only because she gained a place with the Aesir. Aside from that, it seems that she had her own cult in ancient times—in one saga, she refers to her shrines and worshippers. She is very much a goddess of the cold, snowy regions, a huntress with bow and arrows and sled pulled by white wolves. Some speak of her as the inspiration for the Russian Frost Maiden, and the Snow Queen of Hans Christian Andersen. She was apparently revered in ancient times by hunters who would ask her aid.

Skadi was the daughter of Thjassi, the frost-thurse who captured Iduna and was killed by the Aesir during Loki's rescue of her. Thjassi, the son of Olvalde, also somehow owned land in Asgard, due to complicated circumstances. As far as some of us can inquire, apparently Thjassi married an Aesir woman for a brief time, although he never came to Asgard; she apparently came to live with him in his cliff-fortress in northeastern Jotunheim, and died there after a short time of the cold. Although Thjassi technically inherited her Asgard estate, he never visited it because of the Aesir-Jotnar animosity; perhaps he knew that the Aesir would look badly upon his allowing his Aesir wife to die. When he was killed, his grown daughter Skadi (apparently no relation to the lost Aesir wife, but the child of a former marriage) claimed the estate, and also claimed weregild for her father's death.

She marched to the gates of Asgard in full panoply and fully armed, and demanded that she be given not only weregild and her father's inheritance, but also a husband. She hoped to win the beautiful Baldur, but Odin blindfolded her and made her choose from all the unmarried men in Asgard by feeling their feet. She chose the one with the finest feet, but it was Njord, the Vanir sea-king. He was good-looking and kind enough, so they married, but found after a while that they could not live together. Both Skadi's homeland—Thrymheim in Jotunheim—and her inherited package in Asgard were in the mountains, where she preferred to be, but Njord, could not bring himself to dwell long away form the sea. His home in Asgard, Noatun, and his Vanaheim home on the other side of the ocean, on the other hand, made Skadi uncomfortable; she complained about the noise of the sea-birds and the constant sound of the tide. The two separated amicably after a time, but by then Skadi had a place in the council of Asgard—the first Jotun to gain one.

It seems that shortly after this, she had an ill-fated affair with Loki. Some sources claim that Odin sent Loki to her in order to cement her bonds with Asgard; others merely suggest that the opportunistic Loki saw a chance to take advantage of the depressed Skadi. Apparently she had fallen into sadness, and Loki decided to cheer her up by making a spectacle of himself. He tied his testicles to a goat, and let the goat pull him around screaming and staggering, much to the amusement of the onlookers. At some point the rope snapped, and he fell headlong into Skadi's lap, and she laughed, finally. This rite is echoed in legends of sacrificial rites to the cold, implacable death goddess, where a man is castrated and flung bleeding into her lap, with the idea that only blood, not semen, can fertilize a death goddess. It may be that Loki was deliberately mimicking this rite as a way of offering himself to Skadi.

At any rate, she seems to have taken him more seriously than he took her, for they had an affair that did not last, and it filled her with a rage against him so bitter that when he was caught and bound after Baldur's death, Skadi placed a poisonous serpent over his head, to drip venom onto him until he was released. One senses not only the wrath of a woman scorned, but that of a priestess/goddess who was cheated. If Loki's courtship actions were an allusion to a traditional consort's sacrifice to a Goddess, and Skadi took that offering seriously, then Loki's casual discarding of her when he had had enough was more than callousness; it was outright sacrilege and the dishonoring of a ritual marriage. This may be why she felt that she had every right to make him suffer for centuries. Indeed, one could say that Loki's mistake with Skadi was the worst that he ever made.

Working With Skadi
by Lyn Skadidottir

Skadi was the first goddess that I began working with. I was living in Rhode Island at the time, and desperately seeking a mountain goddess. I found Skadi, or rather, she found me. I would meditate on her, and as a reward I was given snow. Not blizzards, just slight snow dustings as if to say 'hullo'. She taught me a lot about sacrifice, about offerings, about loyalty, and even, to some extent, about betrayal. Her land, Thrymheim, is a very, very sacred and beautiful place.

Skadi, much like Hela and the Nornir, is one of the best known and best loved of the Jotnar. It is not surprising to me in any way that she has garnered this type of affection from a multitude of groups. Her name finds her way into almost all aspects of the northern traditions, including Anglo-Saxon heathenry (which, though justified by etymology, is probably the farthest reach in my mind for her to have traveled). For me, my association with Skadi is extremely important, as she is the first Jotun I connected with—and, for that matter, the first being from the northern tradition that I encountered at all!

So, who is Skadi, what is her history, and what can be gained from knowing her? I mean, really, that is why you are reading this, is it not?

First, I must start with my usual "why are you here" question. This isn't a light question. In fact, it is one that is encountered on the Jotun path every day. I ask that of you now, only because I know that if and when you contact any Jotun being, you will be asked this. Why are you here? Is it because you want to prove that you can meet them? Is it because you have some Jotun-killing obsession? Do you think you are better than them? Do you have some Odin complex? By this, I am asking you a two-part question: Are you seeking their knowledge, or, are you seeking their things? Are you doing any of these things honestly, or do you have a hidden motive and agenda? Of all the questions, this is perhaps the most critical and important. Especially when you meet Skadi.

I'm going to assume that you know the lore and basic background of Skadi, of the story of her and Loki, and, of course, her father Thiazi. There are some important clues to Skadi in this story, and they are things that cannot be taken lightly. Her love of her family, for instance, and in turn, the love that Thiazi has shown for her, giving his life (and I fully believe that he knew what he was getting into) so that she could bridge the gap between Jotun and Aesir and insure her own immortality and godhood. These are not small portions of the mystery of Skadi.

She is a compassionate, and passionate, being. She can be one of the most loving and amazing wights you will ever know, but this does not come without its price, and it is not an easy one for most people. This price is not a sacrifice of the external. You cannot kill an animal, cut yourself for a self-blood animal, or give any material thing to Skadi to garner her affections and interests—or, for that matter, to learn from her. To work with her, to learn from her, to allow yourself to grow within her, requires a lot of work. I realize that at this point, you've heard "don't go into anything blindly", "watch your back", "be genuine", "know that they can hurt you, and will hurt you given the chance", and any other innumerable thing that is common to all of the Jotnar. You've probably glanced and read other sections that say, "Work is imperative." This is so very true, but with Skadi, it runs so deep that it cannot be denied. Accounts of the types of work she demands can be found almost everywhere, and most notably in Diana Paxson's article on Skadi, available on the Hrafnar website.

Her mythos is surrounded by dishonesty and half-truths. She has been lied to and deceived so many times that she has no patience for it. So what does this have to do with work? You can't lie to her about what you do or have done. She'll know, and then she'll test you. So what is this work?

She is a very physical being, strongly interested in physical health and stamina. The first thing to know about Skadi is that you will have to learn how to exercise, take care of your body, survive in the wild to some extent, and deal with winter in a constructive way. This is actually the hardest part of working with Skadi for me, and actually, for most people I know. She does not deal well with sloth and gluttony. She abhors any type of laziness involving the body—regardless of your health concerns. If you want to work with her, you need to know how to exercise, and you need to do it outside on a semi-regular basis. It is one of the hardest things, particularly in our current consumer society, to understand this. I think that this aspect of her is why so many unsavory groups have attached themselves to her. She lives by the axiom of might and survival of the fittest. This, unfortunately, attracts some of the crappiest people on earth. In fact, if you search for Skadi online, you will find a major fascist/racist group uses her name as the URL. Her cold, methodic and detached nature is magnetic to them.

She also shares certain connection aspects of Tyr, in that she is somewhat concerned with ethics and morality. This is not to say that she has the ethics or morality of Christianity. She is concerned with honesty, truth, fidelity, and, again, the truth of ones physicality is a portion of her morality/ethical concerns.

Fidelity is one of the more troubling aspect with working with Skadi. She is not opposed to polyamory, as long as it is honest and all persons involved are aware of the parameters of the relationship(s) that they are in. She seems to be uncomfortable with it, but this seems to only be connected with the notion of honesty and truth, and how poor humans are at these things, and that she little trusts them to do it rightly. Loyalty to your oaths, whatever they are, is important to her, as it is to Tyr.

She is associated with hunting and skiing, particularly cross-country skiing. This is important, too. Her huntress side is not that of the human hunter, particularly of today. It is a primal hunt, one of survival. There is no sport to her hunting. It is about eating, survival, and sacred death. I don't mean sacred death in the way that Hela is about death; Skadi is intrinsically linked to the act of dying, the death of the physical body. She is not concerned in the least about what happens to your soul complex; she is only interested in the carcass.

This is perhaps the most important part of this aspect of her. It isn't the soul she is concerned with. This is a difficult lesson, particularly if you are raised in an Abrahamic society, to understand. Why do I stress this? Because we spend so much of our lives being taught to focus on what comes after death, on what the next life will be, on what past lives were. This is not a concern of Skadi, at least not in my experiences with her. She is the huntress who takes down her prey with a bow, silent, in the woods, on her skis. It is the act of killing, the act of letting the life go, that is so important to her. There is some amount of compassion for the soul complex that is asked to travel away from the body, but that is not what her role is. It is her role to put the poison arrow into the body, to take the life. If you take the time to watch how predatory animals take their prey, you will learn a lot about Her. For those who are concerned with what happens after, she will allow you to open the doors to that mystery, but her place is not within that concern.

So how do you meet Skadi? I would suggest starting in winter, only because it is easier to connect with her energies then. Leaving out milk or red wine by your doorway is also a good invitation offering. Though I can find no literary references for this, she seems to have a strong connection with various wights, and it is always beneficial to treat the wights with good fortune and kindness. I can only assume that in this regard she is not too different from Artemis. Make it clear that your offerings are for Skadi and her folk/wights/beings. In addition, it is extremely important to leave a second offering out simultaneously for the "unknown" wights and beings in the area, on the opposite side of the door. This is because you want to keep your local landwights happy, even those of questionable nature. Do not invite the locals inside (unless you know them well), but you can go ahead and invite Skadi and her associates inside, with the allotment of being able to leave when they choose and when you choose. Repeat these offerings often.

In addition to offerings, it is important to do meditation workings that allow your mind to be clear. If you need guidance on this, American Zen Buddhism is a good place to start, and look into Zazen sitting meditation. The beginning meditative form is extremely useful for any type of work you do, particularly with Jotun work. Once you have the capacity to 'clear the mind' for the most part, invite Skadi to be present. If she wishes to come, she will. She does not manifest upon demand (and I highly recommend you do not demand any Jotun presence!); I usually meditate in my sacred space, designated in my small apartment by a very simple altar.

I generally do not use many serious altar tools and trappings of magic in my work. I have a small and simple setup—a few candles, occasionally a cloth or metal snowflake-shaped object. I don't work with visual representations or idols of the beings I work with, as I wish them to come in whatever form they prefer. I do not want to try and force them to be something they do not want to be. I recommend that others try this as well, as any being will be more giving and friendly if you let them show you who they are without forcing them to be who you want them to be. This is especially important with Skadi.

So, what about dealing with Skadi if you are a Lokian? A lot of Lokians I've talked to do seem to get the brush-off by Skadi. After talking to both sides about it, here is what I can seem to glean from both parties: First, Skadi doesn't hate Lokians because of their association with Loki. I doubt that Skadi and Loki have tea and biscuits every day together, but they are not mortal enemies. This being said, there are some things that Lokians who want to work with Skadi must know: She does not see being a Lokian as an excuse for being dishonest and shirking responsibility (and although the Lokians I am friends with do not act this way, I have met others who use an affinity with Loki as a license for irresponsible behavior). Leave your slippery trickster tendencies at home when talking to her.

Her relationship to Loki is not all dark and angry, these days. Yes, there is much anger, but she gained from the loss of her father. Thiazi's eyes will always watch her, and those that belong to her. She knows that he had to die, no matter what, that nothing could have stopped that. She understands the politics of the matter, and is will always be a little angry over that, but she also is very much aware of what Loki gave her—a chance for a Jotun presence in Asgard. Her footing there secured a lot for her people, both in Skandinavia and in Jotunheim. Yes, she is an etin-bride, but she won her own after that. She divorced and kept her honor and her place. Not all etin-brides fared the same. At least she, unlike some, kept her familial home and her Jotun identity.

Skadi is a Jotun that will make you work; she is concerned with safety, protection and physical well-being. She is a good deity to work with when traveling and doing any outdoor sports, particularly winter-based mountain sports. She is very much an *other*, and her notion of animal and body are crucial to understanding the natural life cycle of the human or any other being for that matter.

She is very linked with the stars, and parts of them belong to her. She can teach a lot about star lore, about astrology, about how to use the stars to the world's benefit. She knows a lot about maps, and is an amazing travel companion. She cares for her own, and she protects them fiercely. Under her watch, little harm can be done to me. She has a kind of peace about her, but it is cold. It is the same peace that is found in the dead of winter under gray sky with the sun in late day. She is brutal, and has her purpose, and cares for little else. She knows much about winter and ice.

Her tasks are demanding, they are slow, and they are not always clear. The road she offers is long, roundabout, and often not what you expect. Those things, however, are given to those who she chooses. She hasn't time for people traipsing about in her lands wanting her help. She will deal with those she accepts, and will not take on seekers who aren't going to be good for her. A good way to put it is this: People who go to her to take her knowledge of the stars and not offer anything in return are likely to get their stars, but get burned by them in the process. Her way of teaching can be difficult if you don't pay your way through, so a lot of people who think the gods are there to give to them without anything in return should just avoid her. She isn't a "loving" god in that respect. She has things to do, and if you can't help her in them, she hasn't the time for you. If you steal from her, you had better hope you can never be found by her.

And, like many other Jotnar, if you work with her as a primary, you had better be ready to talk to many other beings and gods. Be prepared to give multiple work-oaths, and be ready for a ride that will get you off your chair and into the wilderness.

Invocation to Skadi

Hail, Huntress of the snow and ice!
We who struggle between the tracks
Left by Your winter sleigh,
We whose bloody marks You track,
Skillful in your cold eye,
We hail you, Mistress of Survival!
Etin-bride of winter, Your cloak
Spreads white over the fields,
The icy wind Your breath,
White wolf in the snow.
Teach us of the narrow edge between
Living and dying, and of that struggle,
And the cold, naked truth that it reveals.
Catch us naked in the snow, Lady,
We shall bare our throats to your wisdom
And count ourselves lucky.

Snow Queen (A Song For Skadi)

The stars shine cold on the icy meadow,
The moon glints cold on the icy road
The track of the white wolf warns of her passing,
Bright blood warms the frozen snow.

Frost-crackled winds wipe bare the helpless trees
Then pile them high with crystal-crusted snow
She strokes your throat with loving icy hands
And whips your back in wrath as you turn to go.
The Green Man's children cower on their knees
As a velvet weight bends blackened branches low;
Earth's caterpillar life is at a close,
Chrysalis-cloaked, it seeks a time to grow.

The stars shine cold on the icy meadow,
The moon glints cold on the icy road
The track of the white wolf warns of her passing,
Bright blood warms the frozen snow.

We stand upon the bridge of icy metal,
We stare into the water dark below.
She calls us down into the perfect silence,
She shows us what we did not want to know.
We hear the cry of wind and screaming metal,
The glassy road, the helpless driver spins,
The quiet of the snowy bank that welcomes,
Her velvet arms that reach and take you in.

Can you touch that place within you,
The chill that came that frozen night?
This is her work, to preserve that spark

Until you are ready for spring's warm light.
Praise Her name, you who walk in the winter,
Praise Her cloak spread across the fields,
The teeth of the white wolf seize our souls,
Blood on the snow is the price we yield.

Rind

Rind, the daughter of the much-traveled giant Billing, Master of the Vanir Trade, is very much a throwback to her frost-giant bloodlines. While her father has become accustomed to the shore and the ocean, she prefers to live in his winter hall in the snowy northeastern mountain range of Jotunheim. Rind is a potent sorceress, cold and reserved; she works with weather and snow and frost, but her particular talent is the ability (like that of Unn the Undine) to move through time in limited ways.

Rind bore a son, Vali, to Odin, largely against her will; he was conceived just after Baldur's death, and grew old enough to avenge his brother by nightfall of that day. Rind's story, or the tattered scraps of it, raises many questions. Why did Odin need to sire a new son to be his brother's avenger? Why did he force himself on Rind, rather than simply choosing his wife or one of his willing mistresses? Why did Vali slay his blind, helpless brother Hoder when everyone knew Baldur's death was Loki's doing? The story is confusing... so I asked Rind herself, and she kept me up all night with her anguished, angered tale, which is chronicled in "Vengeance's Son" later in this book.

Saxo Grammaticus, who casts the Aesir not as gods but as historical mortals who made themselves rulers through superior magic, tells a story about a mortal Odin and Rind that may be a vague, garbled echo of the immortal version. In this version, Rind is a young girl who is the daughter of King Billing, Lord of the Ruthenians (translated loosely to Russians, who were at that time a Nordic colony). Odin is cast as a mortal sorcerer and king who sees the young girl and desires her. He comes to her in disguise as a great warrior, but she refuses him. He comes to her in a second disguise as a craftsman with fine wares, but she scorns him again.

Angered, he casts a spell on the girl to make her desperately ill, then presents himself to her father as an old wisewoman, saying that he can cure the princess's sickness. Her father consents to the treatment, which Odin tells him will be painful, and so the young girl must be physically bound to her bed. Once this is done and they are alone, Odin reveals himself, strikes the helpless Rind with a magic wand that paralyzes her, and rapes her. According to Saxo, the Aesir were so horrified by his act that they ousted him from the throne and put Ullr in his place.

Certainly the rape of Rind stands as one of the most blatant times that Odin discards honor and even ethics for his view of the long-term greater good. Scholars have tried to rationalize the story of Odin striking Rind with a paralyzing magic wand and forcing himself on her as a seasonal myth of the spring's fertilizing rains melting the winter frost, but it is an odd seasonal myth that casts the coming of spring as the rape of an innocent maiden. Some Asatru-folk have tried to justify Vali's act as necessary for Baldur's ghost to be laid to rest, but if Loki was truly the one responsible, then the murder of Hoder does little to solve the problem, and Rind is yet again left in the shadows with her pain and her own vengeance, which she takes into her own hands in a sort of victory.

Invocation to Rind

Winter to winter to winter.

Frost glitters cold on the leaves,
Preserving them for a sparkling moment,
More lovely than they have ever been before.
Yet this loveliness slays them
And they wither on the darkened branch.
Lady of the glittering frost,
Turner of time, winter to winter,
The mystery of cold's preservation
Flows from your fingers, as does
The mystery of withering in the cold.

All turns to glistening crackles
At the touch of your pale cold fingertips.
Lady of the chill wind, frost-giantess
Who holds your father's hall amidst
The snowy mountains, cool us with your touch
And freeze those memories we cling to
Into one perfect picture, so icy-clear
That we may savor them with indrawn breath
Like that which shocks the lungs on a
Winter morning. Teach us, also, the letting go
Of rage, of betrayal, for these things too
Are a part of imperfect life. May the memories
We do not wish to keep slowly wither,
Blacken and fall, lost to the misty centuries,
That we may be healed, as you were,
By the cooling winds of the Rime of Time.

Bestla

As the daughter of Bolthorn and the sister of Mimir, Bestla is best known for being the wife of Bor and the mother of Odin, Vili, and Ve. Here, Laure Gunnlod Lynch tells us about her dealings with the etin-bride Queen Mother of Asgard.

Bestla in the Lore and in My UPG
by Laure Gunnlod Lynch

(Partly adapted from the introduction to my book, *Odhroerir: Nine Devotional Tales of Odin's Journeys*.)

The short story Mother of Gods is the result of a vision I had late one night, of a beautiful white-haired woman dressed all in white tucking her three newborn babies into their cradle. When I realized who the woman was and who the babies were, the rest of the story came in a flash. This experience also marked my introduction to Bestla and the forging of a relationship with Her. Odin's mother is a formidable lady— gracious and queenly, yet iron-willed and with a piss-and-vinegar personality that tolerates no nonsense whatsoever. When She looks at you, you can sense the deep, calm, solid sense of knowing that is Hers, a trait shared by many of the great Jotun seeresses. I feel greatly privileged to know Her, as I have had the impression that She does not involve Herself much with humans—not even humans who belong to Her son. (Although I may have to revise that assessment, in light of new evidence. Last week I received a wonderful letter from a reader praising my new book, and in it he told me of a vivid dream experience he'd once had with a woman all in white with long snow-white hair who made it clear to him that he was to follow Odin. He assumed the woman was Frigga, but his description of both Her appearance and Her manner said "Bestla" loud and clear to me. It makes me wonder now how many people encounter a queenly matriarchal figure during visions or dreams and assume they have met Frigga when it is really Her.)

Bestla has considerable magical skill, especially in scrying and working with plant spirits, and taught these skills to Her son in His childhood, long before His other explorations in search of wisdom began. This early exposure to His mother's witchcraft later contributed to accusations that He was tainted by "womanly ways," (as Loki teases Him in Lokasenna), but Odin is the ultimate pragmatist, and uses whatever power or wisdom He can get His hands on, without regard for what anyone else may think. Odin has a closer relationship with His mother than most people realize, and relies a great deal on Her wisdom and experience, especially during crises. Although She spends a good deal of time at Her own residence in Jotunheim, She is quite secure and honored in Her position as Queen Mother of Asgard.

Although there isn't much to be found in the lore on Bestla, I've done quite a bit of scholarly detective work to back up some of my UPG concerning Her. Most people are familiar with the passage in the Havamal which mentions that in Odin's youth He was taught nine magical songs by "the son of Bolthorn, Bestla's father." Since most mythologists agree that the son of Bolthorn mentioned here can be none other than Mimir, in a roundabout way this passage confirms Bestla's identity as Mimir's sister. But things get more speculative from there on in. According to Viktor Rydberg, the origin of Her name may stem from *beizl* or *beisl*, which means bridle. This is interesting when compared to one of Mimir's epithets, Narvi, meaning "the one who binds." Mimir and Bestla are also closely related to the Norns, the three Jotnar who weave and bind the threads of Wyrd. As Mimir definitely has his own ties to the Well and to Wyrd, it seems fairly safe to assume that Bestla may also. On a smaller scale, In Germanic tradition a family's norns bind the wyrd of a child to it at birth, during a naming rite that involves sprinkling the child with water using a sprig of birch. If Bestla has a similar role, it would be appropriate to call on Her not only for the blessing of children, but also for all matters concerned with binding— such as naming rites, the formation of a kindred, blood brotherhood or sisterhood oaths, and even marriages.

But Rydberg's etymology of Bestla's name suggests even more than that. A bridle both constrains and guides a horse, directing it according to the will of the rider. This association calls to mind the runes Raidho and Ehwaz, as well as the partnership between Odin and His steed Sleipnir. So much attention is focused on Odin's ravens and wolves that we sometimes forget that the horse is also sacred to Him, and that His own horse is crucial to many of His activities. Sleipnir carries Odin in the Wild Hunt, is His companion on many of His journeys throughout the nine worlds, and bore Hermod to Hel to seek the return of Baldur at His behest. Far more than a mere vehicle, a horse is power, companionship, and support, an extension of the might of its rider. A bridle leashes and directs that power, much as Bestla—as Odin's mother—must have helped Him direct and control His own power in His youth, setting Him on the path that led to His continual journeys and explorations.

Rudolf Simek's Dictionary of Northern Mythology offers a different, yet not incompatible, translation for Bestla's name; according to him, it means "bark," as in the bark of a tree. The lore tells us that

Bestla was married to Borr, the son of the first of the Aesir. By him, she gave birth to three sons, known in the Prose Edda as Odin, Vili and Ve, and in the Poetic Edda as Odin, Hoenir, and Lodurr (who some Heathens identify with Loki). In both sources, the three sons of Bestla murder the proto-etin Ymir and use the pieces of his corpse to construct the nine worlds, after which they create the first man and woman by breathing life, spirit and form into two tree trunks. The connection between this story of the origins of life and the meaning of Bestla's name is intriguing, and adds weight to my previous speculations about her involvement with birth and the blessing of children.

The translation of Bestla's name as "bark" also calls to mind the World Tree. The nine worlds are often envisioned as being connected by or enclosed in the branches of Yggdrasil, and many practitioners of seidhr use the Tree as a vehicle or conduit for journeying between the worlds. In the prophecy of Ragnarok, the Tree will survive the end of all the worlds, and will ensure the continuity of life by sheltering a man and woman within its branches—and the Well of Wyrd, over which the Norns preside, is said to sit at the foot of the Tree and to provide water for it, so that the worlds that rest within its branches are continually being fed and formed by the layers of past, present and probability contained within the Well.

And yet, Yggdrasil is perhaps best known for being the Tree on which Odin sacrificed himself for nine nights in order to gain the runes, a set of symbols that encapsulate all the mysteries of creation, destruction and rebirth. Turning my attention to the runes provided me with still more insights into Bestla. The runes with the closest associations to the Norns are Perthro, which some see as representing the Well of Wyrd, and thus fate or destiny, and Nauthiz, which means constraint or need, and is often used as a rune of binding. My little bit of research has shown me that these (possibly in addition to Raidho, as mentioned previously) would both be appropriate runes to use when working with Bestla. In my own UPG, I have also come to associate Bestla with the rune Berkano, which means birch and is thus connected with the birch twig used in naming rites. Berkano is a rune of birth and renewal, as well as the transformative period of concealment that precedes rebirth; as such, it can also be interpreted as a rune of the symbolic death and rebirth that accompanies shamanic initiation. While it is more traditionally linked to Frigga, it seems especially appropriate—especially considering that one meaning of her name is "bark"—to associate it also with the mother of Odin, the God who endured death and rebirth on the World Tree. As Odin's mother, Bestla herself could be seen as embodying the roots from whence his wisdom sprouted, the wellspring of His might, and the protective bark that sheltered him until he was able to grow to the pinnacle of his strength and power. As Odin is considered All-Father of the Northern Gods, Bestla can in a very real sense be viewed as the All-Mother, the Mother of the Norse pantheon.

References

Caroline Larrington, The Poetic Edda, Oxford World's Classics, Oxford University Press, New York, NY 1996.

Viktor Rydberg, Teutonic Mythology, available online at: http://www.northvegr.org/lore/rydberg/086.php

Rudolph Simek, A Dictionary of Northern Mythology, D.S. Brewer, 2000.

Snorri Sturluson, Anthony Faulkes, Edda (The Prose Edda), Everyman's Library, Tuttle Publishing Group, North Clarendon VT, 1987.

Diana Paxson, Taking Up the Runes: A Complete Guide to Using Runes in Spells, Divination, and Magic, Weiser Books, 2005.

The Nornir

When one finds references to the Nornir (plural for "Norn", or "Fate") in old writings, the word seems to refer to different entities. On the one hand, there are references to a variety of Norns, sort of a lesser level of Fate employees, who are drawn from the ranks of many folk—the Aesir the Alfar, the Duergar, and human disir. The idea seems to be that the female protective ancestral spirits (disir) of any race/tribe/family watch over a woman of their descent who is in labor, and scry the fate of the child being born. This would suggest that each family has Nornir of their own, depending on their descent. Those humans with nonhuman bloodlines might have nonhuman Nornir, but most will be pulled from their majority racial makeup.

On the other hand, there are the Three Norns, the women who seem to be in charge of the whole Fate apparatus in the Northern pantheons. They live at the Well of Wyrd, next to the first exposed tree-root of the World Tree, in Asgard. They are named Urd (That-Which-Is), Verdandi (That-Which-Is-Becoming), and Skuld (That-Which-Should-Be), and they are mentioned as "the mighty maids from Thursenheim", or Niflheim, home of the frost-thurses. Urd spins threads, Verdandi weaves them, and Skuld cuts them short. Sometimes they appear to look identical; sometimes they appear with different ages. Unlike the Moerae, the Greek fates, Urd is the eldest and Skuld sometimes appears as a black-armored maiden who sometimes rides along with the Valkyries. Generally they do not appear as beautiful, however; most spirit-workers report them as plain, almost dowdy women, focused on their work.

The fact that the Norns are frost-giantesses reifies the fact that Jotnar did not merely represent hostile forces to our ancestors, but also the ancient and immutable forces. To the ancients, the same force that burned down your hut or froze you in a blizzard or drowned you in the sea also implacably named your destiny and held you to it. Fate was in the same category as natural disaster, as far as they were concerned. All were the wild and untamed mysteries, and all were equally easy to fear and to respect, and to hold wisdom that even the more "human" Gods needed to learn.

The Norns are very old; it is said that they are among the eldest of the Gods, and certainly they date from well before the flood that killed Ymir. There is some compelling but untested UPG on the subject suggesting that Urd, the eldest Norn whose name is cognate to Earth, may well be the oldest female frost-thurse of all—the thurse-woman who grew out of Ymir's armpit. If this is the case, then she is literally the mother of half the giant-race. It is also suggested that Verdandi is her eldest daughter, and Skuld her eldest granddaughter.

The word Norn has an ambiguous etymology. Some claims have linked it to the Swedish dialect word *nyrna*, meaning "to inform secretly"; others trace it to the Indo-European root word *ner* meaning "twist" or "twine", referring to the Norns twisting the threads of fate. In Anglo-Saxon, Urd became Wyrd, and the Norns were referred to as the Wyrd Sisters, wyrd taking on the meaning of one's ultimate destiny.

It has been speculated that the three Fate-goddesses of the Saami people—Sarahkka, Juoksaahkka and Uksaahkka—could have been the origins of the three Nornir. In the Norse sagas, it is told that the Nornir were there before the Aesir came, deciding the fate of all men, weaving the web of Wyrd. (If this was the case, it would suggest that they were of the frost-giants born in Niflheim, perhaps of the second generation from Ymir, before the appearance of Buri.) Like the Saami *ahkka*, the Norns were intimately connected to pregnancy, birth and rebirth. A tradition among the Saami is that a woman gets "Sarahkka porridge" as her first meal after having given birth; among the ancient Nordic people, "Nornagretur"— Norn-groat porridge—served the same function. It is likely that all the intermarriage between the Norse and the Saami people must have brought in these Saami customs. The intermarriage may have begun even before the melding of the Indo-Europeans and the aboriginal Scandinavians; there are several words in the Saami tongues that stem from early Indo-European, and it is not known at what point the two first crossed; certainly the Saami people would have been contacted first, before the aboriginals, by a people moving west across northern Europe.

Whatever their origin, the Nornir are often invoked by seidhr-workers, and anyone else who wishes to read the Threads of Wyrd, or work to change them in any way. This is called Threadwork. One's Thread of Wyrd contains everything one has done in one's life, and is knotted and tangled up with the Threads of others. When you make an oath or commitment to someone, when you give and receive deep emotions, when you give gifts and create obligations, when you wrong them and do not make amends (and when they wrong you and leave); all these things create knots and tangles that involve other Threads. In addition, your Thread can become knotted or tangled due to the leftover luck (good or bad) that you gain form past deeds, including, for some people, deeds done in past lives.

What a skilled spirit-worker can do, under some circumstances, is to trace a person's Thread through the tapestry, diagnose the origins of the knots and tangles that are creating obstacles, and figure out (usually by asking the Nornir or other deities) what would have to happen in order to smooth them out. It is especially useful for people who have lost or damaged their luck. Threadwork is advanced shamanic work—something only done after many years of being a spirit-worker—and it is only done with the leave of the Nornir. If you don't have a good working relationship with them, you won't be able to get very far with Threadwork. They'll simply start quashing your applications, as it were.

Spirit-workers who work with the Nornir are few; as far as we can tell, although they will teach and work with humans, they (perhaps alone among all the Gods) choose very few human spirit-workers as their own, have few human servants, and need no worshippers. It's likely that this is partly because they see every one of us as threads to eventually be cut—as their frost-thurse background suggests, they are quite cold-hearted—and partly because they have no need for them. They are every bit as implacable as any Death deity, and even more impersonal. Despite this, they have valuable skills to teach, and all the knowledge that Fate can offer—if they choose to do so. Offerings to them are traditionally pieces of fiber-art handwork, made by you, or commissioned at great price if you cannot make your own. Learning to handspin with a Viking-style soapstone drop spindle is very helpful in dealing with them, especially if you aspire to eventually learning Threadwork.

Working with the Nornir,
or Living in the House of Grandmothers
by Lyn Skadidottir

I knew at the time my spiritual training needed a change. I'd spent the past few years focusing on Dianic Wicca and Taoism, but knew that something was off. I'd been looking for a crone-aspect connection and a mountain goddess. One Samhain I'd decided to call on my paternal grandmother for guidance, so I lit a single white candle and placed out a glass of water (some Santeria website I found suggested this as a method to find your ancestors), and cast my wish into the wind. Within a month I was directed to work with Skadi, the Nornir, Hela and her kin. I was ecstatic and young, and dove right into working with Skadi and the Norns. Almost immediately, I found myself working on many projects for the Norns; Urda in particular.

My altar was small and nondescript. It still is. Through working with yoga and clear-mind-type meditations, I found myself often guided to the home of the Norns. Not "the home" at the base of Yggdrasil, but a small cottage out in the middle of a field, within walking distance of a forest. I journeyed there in my meditations, and sat by the fire each night, stitching away. Eventually, I was asked to put down my needlepoint and clean. For the next four years, I would go to the Norns' home and clean it. I knew intuitively that this was a special gift; I did not run into another human there for a long time, and, when I did finally meet another human there, I was sad and disappointed, finding that I had been replaced. It took two years for me to realize I had not been replaced; on the contrary; I had been given a promotion.

During the time leading up to my promotion, I felt lost, like I didn't belong to any god or goddess or giant or really anything but myself. I would do the work they asked in journeywork, and I would be rewarded in this world by the ability to give precision divination, advice, and lead others to the spiritual path they were on. Now, this was not a new thing for me—somehow, I'd always had the knack of guiding people to the options open to them. For some reason, however, I never had that opportunity myself. I never quite knew who my primary deity was. They would come, they would go, but never did I have that feeling that I belonged, and when I did feel like I could devote myself to a being, some voice would chime in "Go ahead, but your first oaths are to us. We gave you our fire, we let you touch our loom, you know where your path currently leads."

Time went by, and eventually I was lent out to fosterage with Hela. That, really, is one of the most important things I can tell you—it isn't like being given or sent to another god or wight. I was sent out for fosterage. And, as all things have been with the Norns, it takes a while to understand the what and why of the matter.

So what does it mean to work with and for the Norns? It can mean a lot of things. There are groups who do a lot of work with them, people who claim to channel them, and different ways to access their knowledge and to work with them. They are not like other gods and giants, and they are often seen as untouchable, aloof, and out of bounds. For most, they are. They stand as oracles to the cosmos. We view them as the three who keep track of what has been, what is, and what must be based on the other two. They have their own logic, and it can be infuriating to work with beings that do not have any agenda but to keep things recorded and moving. Motion of the cosmos is the first aspect of their mysteries—they are that which keeps things in motion. To stop that motion is to interfere with the entire cosmos—the worlds of men, gods, giants and even stars rely on motion. Without motion, we cannot continue. Even our cellular nature relies on motion, movement, progression, rebirth and death, and this is the first mystery of the Norns.

They also demand fierce independence in those who work with them. The knowledge that you are ultimately responsible to yourself, it is yourself that you must answer to, that you are making decisions that affect you, and that you must be able to work alone, of your own volition, without external aid is essential. You cannot truly call on the Nornir in time of need. You can call on them, beg them for assistance, but they will give none, only advice regarding the paths that exist and may or may not come to pass. This can be reassuring to some, but it is not the same as praying to a god and hoping to have your prayers answered. They are not like Valkyries, and do not involve themselves directly in the life and fate of humans. This can be difficult, and if you have a history with a god you can pray to, it is very discomfiting to know that no matter how hard you pray, it is not going to help you. You will have to find another outlet to effect change, or take it upon yourself to create change (which is what I would recommend in the first place).

In talking with Raven for this article, I learned that people are not forthcoming with information on the Nornir. I am not surprised; I can tell you that it can be extremely disheartening to talk of them, to write about them. You feel like you are giving up a piece of yourself, and that you are threatening the entire universe, and to a great extent, you are interfering with your own selfish desire to keep them for yourself. To work with them and be allowed to continue working with them is by far the most precious and sacred duty given to a spirit-worker. For me, it is the selfish desire to keep them for myself that makes writing this so difficult. But it needs to be known that all who work with them and for them are blessed.

The way that people work with them who are not devoted to them exclusively is very different from those of us chosen to run their temples and maintain their lands. They are often worked with to either attempt to learn the lay of ones personal wyrd, to understand Wyrd and its function, or wyrd manipulation. We will start with the most common, the lay of one's personal wyrd.

Accessing the information of one's personal wyrd can be done in many ways. Most often, we think of divination, such as rune readings, tarot readings, or astrology. These are probably the easiest to learn, least physically and emotionally damaging, and potentially viable. Lore tells us that it was at the base of Yggdrasil that Odin obtained the runes, and that he took them up screaming and near death. It was at the moment that Odin accessed the runes that he took upon himself what I call Urdaic consciousness—the ability to read the records that are stored in the well, on the tree, and in the threads and wood upon which the Nornir record all of existence. Odin's actions allowed a channel for humans and other beings to access the runes, by altering the insular nature of the recording technology. Of course, he is not the only one who can teach them, and there are many, many paths to learning the runes, but it is important to understand this myth in order to know what it means to work so closely to the mysteries of Urda and her handmaidens. You can choose to work through an intermediary (one of the gods, giants, deep mind, guiding spirit), and in all honesty, I recommend this method, as it is much less difficult than trying to learn the runes by either the method Odin chose, or by one's own Will (which is an eventual goal, but it isn't the place to start). Once you have accessed these keys, you will be able to utilize them in a myriad of ways, including divination. Other tools are available, and are much easier to grasp, such as tarot, scrying, astrology, etc.

Another method, employed by various seidhr groups (Hrafnar in particular), is oracular seidhr. Where most of the classic seidhkona's work involves going to Helheim, they also utilize the Norns in group oracular seidhr settings. This method is expanded on a great deal in Jenny Blain's "Nine Worlds of Seid-Magic: Ecstasy and Neo-Shamanism in North European Paganism"; however, there is a similar method that can be applied yourself. You can go to the edge of the Well of Wyrd and peer into it and see what you can. As with all forms of scrying, it is difficult but possible if you have the knack.

I have also found that working with the Norns is extremely helpful when making difficult decisions, and trying to cope with painful transitions and death. They are not comforting in any way, but it is possible to access their information to understand why certain events are taking place. This falls under the mysteries of Skulda. I once heard her called Obligation, and this is a very good term for her, as even death is an obligation at some point—we must do it, and every thread must end somewhere.

Wyrd manipulation is all too often the path of the power-hungry—not in its entirety, but most often I find those who seek to manipulate Wyrd are pulling a power play. Look to Odin's lore to understand this: When you seek out the Nornir to manipulate Wyrd, you will find that you are only creating wrinkles and knots. You are linking yourself into the Wyrd of others, and that is not always a good thing to do. It is hard on you, it is hard on them, and is extremely problematic for the Nornir in the long run. They will let you have your go at it, to be sure, but remember that Skulda is only preparing to shorten your thread. If you are interested in Wyrd manipulation, you must accept a certain amount of responsibility on yourself, whether you are doing it for the greater good or not, as there are problems inherent in this option.

Urda is by far the most revered of the three Nornir. It is within her that we find strength, foundation, and understanding of what has transpired. As a species, we have found a need to understand our past. We devote hours to lifetimes to the understanding of history of our world, our religions, and ourselves. We spend hundreds of dollars on therapy, peering into our personal pasts in order to create peace within this moment of our lifetimes. We spend hundreds upon thousands of dollars on historical research for our spiritual and recreational needs. Her power lies in knowing all that has been, and in this respect, she is associated with death goddesses. All things that have been go to her.

But she is more than this, much, much more. Originally, she was a singular entity, who controlled all the aspects of the Nornir, but as time progressed and the worlds grew larger and expanded outward, she needed to have help, and thus we find our current state with her handmaidens, Verdandi and Skulda. They, too are very powerful giantess figures, to whom we look daily for help though we may not comprehend that as our request. But, in the end, we always return to Urda.

For me, Urda is extremely complex. She extends beyond the basic lore concept of the woman who controls that which has been. Earlier in this writing, I used the term Urdaic. I utilize this term because I view the mysteries of the Nornir as Urdaic in nature; they are based on Her and Her responsibilities. As she has the ability to control all facets of Wyrd, and is the keeper of all things, I feel that her path (which, in my opinion, is the most pure form of the path Odin initiated) deserves its own name. Much as those who work exclusively with Hela call the path Helish, so I call this path Urdaic.

Verdandi is probably the least talked about and understood of the Nornir. She does not have Urda's power, and most certainly does not have the mystique that Skulda has. As the keeper of what is, meaning that which is occurring in this moment, she can be very difficult to comprehend. This may seem antithetical, as the moment in which we live is something we view every second of every day, but it is within its ordinariness that we find the truth of Verdandi. If you have a basic understanding of Buddhism, this is the "portion of the moment", the "living in the moment" that is often talked about. The moment as it is cannot be quantified, bottled or understood. This, in fact, is what Verdandi consciousness is. To comprehend the moment without looking ahead and without looking behind us is a powerful thing. It is within that instant that we are able to harness the ability to create change, to write our own Wyrd, and forge our own pathway in life. To root ourselves too deeply into the past or too far into our future forces us to take a predesigned path, not entirely of our own choosing. To accept the present, and to live in the moment, we are able to design and live a path free from the constraints of both what has been and what will be.

This is not to say that we should ignore the past or the future, nor what consequences our current actions will create. On the contrary, if you are fully bound by the immediate, the consequences will be felt immediately. What do I mean by this? If we choose, in the immediate, to eat, we can feel the effects of that food on our body. If we choose to cross the street, the action will be understood as crossing the street. I realize that this is difficult, and as an insular process seems silly or irresponsible and nihilistic. It can become that, but with the understanding of the other Nornir and what they embody, we can create a responsible living design.

To work with Verdandi is to work within the paradox of the ever-present. To live within this paradox allows us the ability to access the now, which, in my experience, is of the utmost importance in both daily mundane living and magical workings. I say this because we must understand the present clearly in order to act upon it, and create the next step in our path. It is the present that brings us to our next step in Wyrd, that of obligation. If we understand the present, we can choose to take action, be it physical, psychic or magical. For example, if you felt that you needed to create a magical change at work to help you towards a promotion or rise in salary, you should have a clear understanding of all of the present situations that change will impose upon. When you look deep into the situation and view all of the present circumstances of yourself and those around you who will also be impacted by the change, you may find that you are already going to get that promotion or raise without causing a change in Wyrdic patterns, or that a less fortunate colleague or more qualified colleague may be disadvantaged by your doing. This is where it gets tricky; by combining all three consciousnesses and personae of the Nornir, we can allow ourselves within the moment to make clear decisions about our actions and the actions we advise others to do.

Skulda is the most feared of the Norns. Colored by Greek mythology, we see her as the one who cuts the thread of our lives, but her job is much more complex then simply "cutting the final thread". She governs obligations, and is the one who not only cuts, but also marks the thread or wood for changes and conclusions. As she watches not only for time of death, she also is involved in marking other significant points, such as giving birth, changing careers, meeting and losing lovers. Though we often associate Verdandi with many of these, Skulda is present in these moments. Verdandi shows us the path we are on, but it is Skulda who truly marks those points of transition, killing one way of being in the world and starting another. Obligation and transition are the responsibility of Skulda, as she takes the records created by Urda, keeper of all things past, and looks at the work of Verdandi, that of the eminent present, and then places markers and cuts and color transitions for the patterns in the weaving. We fear her because she is the one who reads the patterns and dictates the changes that must occur, and as a rule, we don't like dramatic change. She is the path of inevitability, the one who governs when roads shall end.

Working with her has wonderful rewards. She is much like Skadi in that she is concerned less with what occurs after death than the event itself. In her marking of death she becomes also the marker of transition, for as the laws of energy have taught us, energy cannot be created nor destroyed. It is a continuum, and she is a part of that continuum. Translating the energy of conclusion into new birth, she imparts herself into the world of continuous creation. This is her paradox.

In my years of working for the Norns, I have found myself slowly learning and working towards creating a temple for them here, and maintaining an astral temple for them. Their temples are not like others; they are not set up to be a central location for worship. They are much more like a Buddhist monastery, a place for internal transformation and understanding. They require the ability to keep a clear mind, be as non-judgmental as possible, and to teach acceptance and the inevitability of suffering and death. Their clergy is made up of many types, but they are more or less mirrors or prisms into the mysteries they are assigned to study. Much like the Norns themselves, they are the magnification process into the world(s) and mysteries. This is where 'fosterage' comes into play. The Norns will send their own off to other places and gods to learn. In turn, the clergy will then act as a concentrated focus on that mystery for the Nornir as well as those who follow that path. For me, that is the Rökkr path. As I grow closer to the Rökkr, I find myself growing towards the Nornir and working more and more for them.

If you are interested in working with them, after you have established the ability to keep a somewhat clear and open mind, I suggest taking up needlework of some kind. If you have the means, spinning and weaving is best, but needlepoint will also suffice. Open your mind in meditation and let the answer to what the pattern you work on come to you; that will be the most important thing, as the pattern you are given will teach you much.

As for research, I would consider looking into the research of the cult of the Matronae. H.R. Ellis Davidson makes many references to them in her work, and the information of them can be found quite easily. Looking into their practices, combined with a clear understanding of Huldrefolk, can lead you to the door of the Nornir. This is not the only path, but the one that I have undertaken. As mentioned before, you can easily find the Norns via the path to Valhalla, but be aware that they will appear very different to you if you take that road. Much like a prism, the light they cast out depends on the light going into them. I chose to let the Nornir represent themselves as they wanted me to see them, and they did so quite eagerly. (I suggest allowing all of the Jotnar and other beings you encounter this courtesy, as it will help you learn faster, gain respect, and clear away any historical baggage that has been attached by other dominant cultures over the past few thousand years.)

I find that offerings of green tea, milk and fresh bread are very effective. In my experience, I have found that rye bread and any bread with caraway seeds are less desirable. Goat's milk seems to be preferred, but organic whole cow's milk seems to be okay. They do not seem as receptive to alcoholic beverages and ale, though that may work for you. Meditate daily, at the same time (I prefer evenings) and keep your mind clear, allowing the objective of the energy of the Norns to enter your home and mind. It may take a few days, but it should allow an opening to get information on how best to access them for you. I am not leaving you a recipe, as I find that your pathway is dependent on you, not on a precedent set by another.

Good luck, wipe your feet, and keep your house/temple area clean!

Invocation to the Fates

Spin truth into words,
Spin words into doom,
Spin doom into fortune,
Spin fortune into life,
Spin my life fine and strong,
O Lady with the spindle
Whose thread is my beginning.

Weave truth into vision,
Weave vision into mind,
Weave mind into spirit,
Weave spirit into life,
Weave my life with depth and color,
O Lady with the shuttle
Whose tapestry is my existence.

Cut truth away from falsehood,
Cut falsehood away from illusion,
Cut illusion away from matter,
Cut matter away from body,
Cut my body away from my life
When the time comes,
O Lady with the shears
Whose knowing hand is my doom
And also my truth.

Tyr

Another etin who has allied himself entirely with the Aesir is Tyr. In fact, he is so thoroughly enmeshed with them that we forget that according to the *Hymskvida*, he is the son of a fire-giant and a frost-thurse. Lyn writes again: "Tyr! What a difficult Jotun from a Rökkatru perspective. I've learned a lot about doing what had to be done from Tyr. I think that he is more of a priest than others know. I think that he was/is a priest for the Aesir, teaching them about the time before they wrote themselves into legend. I think it was aligning himself with the new, denying the old, that cost him his hand. I look at Fenris being bound as a changing of the guard, the last loose strings that need to be taken care of. As guardian of those strings, it was Tyr's job to put them in the closet. He still can be seen in the setting sun, and is the dying light over the land. He is the sunbeam that is the single ray on the way out."

In many ways, Tyr is a way for those who are unfamiliar with the Jotun to understand the Norse word "trolltryggr", which means "faithful as a giant". We think of trolls as nasty ugly creatures, due to centuries of human folklore and decades of fantasy novels, but when a Jotun says that they are going to do something or be a certain way, they are dedicated loyally to that in its entirety, sometimes beyond all reason. We humans, especially in this sound-bite age of convenience, could learn something from this.

There are two other origins of Tyr. In other lore, he is spoken of as a son of Odin. While this may seem irreconcilable with the *Hymskvida*, it is not entirely difficult to extrapolate. Tyr's visit to his parents' domain in *Hymskvida* is not exactly a happy reunion. If we assume that it is told from the point of view of Thor and (a rather young) Tyr, the latter seems somewhat ashamed of his giant parents, and especially his nine-headed grandmother. In fact, his entire reason for going there is to aid and abet Thor in robbing his parents of their huge cauldron. It is intimated that Tyr has not been home in a long time, and that this is the last time he ever goes there.

For a Jotun to ally himself so completely with the Aesir, to the point of rejecting (and robbing) his own kin, the cut must be complete. In joining the new tribe of the Aesir, Tyr lost his father figure, and it is not unimaginable that Odin stepped in, adopting the young Jotun and trusting him as a son. In many ways, even if he was born of Hymir and Hrod, he is still more Odin's son than theirs.

The other origin of Tyr is not one in the history of the Nine Worlds. The god Tyr is mythically descended from the Indo-European Teiwaz/Deus, the Sky Father who gave his name to the very word "god". Unlike the Rökkr, who may or may not be derived from deities worshiped by pre-Indo-Europeans, Tyr clearly bears the name of an Indo-European god. This makes placing him in Nine-Worlds history difficult. (One wonders if he bore a different name before defecting to the Aesir.) An added difficulty is that those who work with and speak to Tyr have long reported that he does not speak of his origins, preferring them to be none of anyone's business. However, nothing is neat and tidy when it comes to the nature of Deities, and we include Tyr here, in all his ambivalent glory, controversial as he is in this context.

Thoughts of Tyr
by Lyn Skadidottir

I sat on edge of the rock grouping, watching the sunset. As the sun descended on the top of the mountain peak facing me, I noticed the pristine light priming outward and breeching the sky forming the Anglo-Saxon Kenaz. At first, I thought of Odin, then of course because of the Kenaz rune, of Loki, and then, at last as I noticed the Blue of the Colorado sky against the black of the pine forest and the white-faced rocks, of Tyr. For some, he is the earliest form of sky god for the Indo-European peoples of Europe. To me, his mysteries lie within the world of his past, within his life as a Jotun entity.

It is easy to forget that Tyr is a Giant himself. We don't know much of his origins, but what little is written can be summed up within the lay of

Hymir. In this Edda, Tyr and Thor go to the home of Tyr's family, Jotun stock to be sure. Of his grandmother, who is mentioned to loathe Tyr, we hear that she has nine hundred heads. His mother is a bit different, as she is shining, all in gold and with white hair. Tyr's father, Hymir, is called the terrible one, with icicles hanging from his beard. He is seen as fierce, strong, and definitely of cold-stock, or frost-thurse blood. The histories of Tyr's bloodline past are not to be taken lightly. In fact, it is within this past of Tyr that we see the root of his betrayal, and in the trust that Fenris (and for that matter, Fenris' extended family) had in him.

This in and of itself is extremely important, and easy to forget. Why and what was the relationship between him and Loki's offspring? Why was it so easy for them, and in particular, Fenris, to trust him? Painted by contemporary lore, we are compelled to see him as a god of truth, of the Thing, of laws, order and war. We are told he once held the same position as Odin, as an Alfather and sky god. We will return to this notion of sky god later, but for the moment, let us focus on how he is viewed by contemporary heathens and Asatru. He is seen as a god of truth and order, and yet he is responsible in a large part for one of the largest betrayals in the history of the northern tradition. In an effort to keep what Odin had obtained in title, status and life, he chose to have Fenris restrained. The fact that Fenris knew better than to let them tie him up, and was coaxed by Tyr to do so by placing his own hand in Fenris' mouth, tells you the type of deceit that was and is possible within Tyr.

Given the fact that Tyr is also of Giant's blood, it is possible that he sacrificed his hand in order to prove to the Aesir that he was loyal to them. In that moment, he also took a side in Ragnarok that could not be denied. This, however, may not be as horrid as you may think. His deceit leads to the fulfillment of Wyrd that is predicted in the Voluspa, with the changing of the world through violent transition. In this regard, Tyr acts as a catalyst and seed early in the process of creating change within the worlds, and as such is acting in a truly Jotun fashion, particularly that of the Iron Wood thurses, who seem to entangle themselves most thoroughly in the manipulation of Wyrd.

Before this well-documented point, however, I believe that Tyr served a very different function. His role as sky god/giant is one that I believe he obtained from the earliest of times. In my own opinion, I believe it is very likely that Hymir is a direct descendant of Ymir, and that Tyr's (or Tiw/Zisa's) placement as a sky god has much to do with him being part of the crown aspect of Ymir as a member of family or son of Ymir. As the world developed and people wanted to have gods that resembled themselves, Tyr continued on in the role of a priest or godhi to the new gods, the Aesir, to guide them in the worlds they were now to inhabit. Within this priest-role, he served and serves to keep a natural order, continue to facilitate the path of natural Wyrd and transformation, and (through his newer aspect as a god of war) facilitate violent change through the manipulation of things around him. By taking on this role he acted not only as intermediary early on between the Jotun and Aesir (in particular Fenris), he eventually found himself in the role of betrayer. And how could one so high up betray his people by becoming a member of the new regime and not acknowledge his roots?

As a sky god, the fact that he is given the job of feeding the young pup Fenris is extremely interesting. In working with Fenris, I have found myself looking into his gaping jaws, and seeing the depths and eternity of the cosmos within him. If he (or his offspring) is to swallow the sun and moon, it makes perfect sense that within his body is the cosmos of eternity and never-ending universe. As I look into that terrifying space of infinity, it seems right that he is fed by the sky, for the sky is still present at night, but with a different face. Tyr is feeding the change that he is to become. In many respects, it could be seen that Fenris is the cosmological opposite of Tyr, as opposite as day and night can actually be. To understand the nature of either Tyr or Fenris, you must enter into an understanding of its "opposite." This dualistic nature, however, is heavily blurred by the actions of the two. Much like the mythical Greek king Laius and his son Oedipus, it is possible that Fenris would not have sought out Odin if the gods did not desire to tie him up, and the chaos that he levels during Ragnarok could have been avoided. All of Tyr's involvement within this really seems to support the idea that he acts in some respects as Irmunsil, and seeks to assist the change of the world as it spins on the axis of the North Star.

Within this concept, if we view the role of Tyr as a physicality of Irmunsil, the world pillar or axis, and take it one step further and attribute the north star to Hela (in her aspect as the Bear Goddess, found within Ursula Minor) we can see an interesting thing occur. They both seek to continue the spinning of the world (in the case of Tyr) and the rotation of the cosmos (Hela). We find that we have acknowledged an interesting and ancient dichotomy. Between the two we find the necessary means of change and stasis, and a balance between two dualistic natures, most basic of which is light vs. dark, or Day vs. Night. Though by many counts the Rökkr and Jotun entities are not wholly dualistic, we may view the basic relationship between the two in this way.

While I do not personally find their energies incompatible, upon talking about the two entities with Asatru seidhr workers, I have noticed that they feel most emphatically that Tyr does not like Hel, and does not like to be called upon when they are working Seidhr within the realm of Hel. The idea that he is uncomfortable with darkness suggests a few things to me, but primarily it shows that it is possible that he either feels he has committed a grave offense to Hela by betraying her brother Fenris (which He did) or that his position in their world view as a god of light denies him access to that realm. In my own experience, I do not see that conflict, though I have never asked the two to be in the same location at once. If I did, I would most likely call on much older aspects of the two, when they worked to keep the universe in balance following the destruction of Ymir and before the artificial construct of Irmunsil was necessary.

In my own work with Tyr, I find that he brings an insight into two separate things I would not access easily without his aid. First, He allows me to see into the changes of the world, as they changed from the hands of the Jotun and Thurse into the world of the Aesir. If you are able to view him as something other than the background figure of Odin, and see him as the son of Hymir (although he betrayed his family and father as well) and the figure of the priest who handled the "changing of the guard", you can obtain a lot of perspective into the transition from Jotun and Hel-centric society into an Aesir-centered society, one where man desired to have absolute control over the forces of nature and chaos. To take on that role, He had to have an understanding of the chaotic nature-oriented worlds that existed previously. His relationship with Hela can be seen as the inner mystery in that process, with the feeding of Fenris as an extension of that work. It is in these two mysteries that we can see Tyr's role as a valued Jotun entity, one that is intrinsically woven into the process of Wyrd. Where the Aesir seek to find a way to move away from and manipulate Wyrd, the Jotnar seek to carry out the path of Wyrd, regardless of the consequence to their own selves.

I realize that this theory is quite abstract and wholly undocumented in lore and "provable" texts. So what is it that makes it so I can feel comfortable making these bold assumptions? Over the past few years my relationship with Tyr has grown. Silent as he is, he holds many mysteries, both old and new, for us to understand. Much like Skadi, he has a purpose that lies politically between two peoples—you cannot ask a people to discard their favorite gods when you ask them to change. In this respect, Tyr has acted to smooth the transition between Jotun-centric belief and Aesir/Asatru-specific beliefs. In addition, as a Rökkr/Jotun centric person, I find that it is important to foster a relationship with this "accessible" Jotun as well, as it allows for better dialogue with other members of the heathen and Asatru community. I find no reason to argue and fight over trivial matters when our own personal transformative ideals are not entirely dissimilar.

Far-Flung Forest And Fertile Field: Earth Giants

s the frost-giants and fire-giants intermarried, and as they found their way into the woods and mountains and jungles growing up in Jotunheim, many of them shaped their bodies, souls, and children to the new land and its overwhelming new growth. Where Niflheim had been frozen and barren, with sparse resources, Jotunheim was wildly overgrowing with greenery. Giant-sized trees pierced and then blocked the sky; hills humped up to mountains covered in greenery, southern jungles put forth lush, steamy vines and fronds, delicate fruit grew forth in groves on jewel-like islands in the surf of Aurgelmir's blood.

It was more richness and survival-wealth than the half-drowned giants had ever seen, and many of them spread out across the unfamiliar territory. Their children, as we have seen, shaped themselves in response to the land-vaettirs of the new place, and many of them were born with shape and soul connected not to Fire or Wind, but to Earth. These children would become farmers, or foresters, or gatherers of herbs. Unlike their fire-and-frost parents, fertility would come forth from their hands... but it would be a wild fertility, unlike that of the Vanir. For the people of Vanaheim, fertility is something that is used for the benefit of the people, selectively; it was the farmer's friend, not that of the wild places. Vanaheim became the perfect ideal of the agricultural world, divided into fields and pastures, the stretches of woodland never overrunning their neat borders.

In contrast, Jotunheim still looks largely like wilderness to the untrained eye. Some areas sprout up with villages, and of course there is the great capital city of Utgard, but for the most part a bird's eye view over Jotunheim shows apparently-unbroken swaths of trees, with the empty mountain peaks jutting up from them. What the unknowing onlooker doesn't see is that those areas may just as well be populated with Jotunfolk, sheltering themselves in ways that do not disturb the environment, nourishing themselves with methods that take advantage of their natural resources.

Where someone else would cut down century-old trees thirty feet in diameter and turn them into boards for housing, the giants simply hollow out selected parts of them, making sure not to kill the tree, and live in the green, growing space. Where someone else would cut down trees and make fields for agriculture, the giants farm traditionally only those areas which are already mostly clear—the valley fields—and keep the upland forests for arboriculture. To a giant, the answer to wanting bread when you live in a forest is to interplant nut trees and grind them for flour. Their close relationships with the land-vaettir mean that they naturally do what is least disruptive to the area, working to fit into the ecosystem rather than remodeling it to their own needs.

This is not to say that they do not build out of stone; they do, and that will be touched on more in the chapter on mountain-etins. (Actually, there is a great deal of grey area between earth-giants and mountain-etins; some would say that there is no real difference, others would point to the essence of stone and clay being different from that of green, lush fertility, even though both partake of Earth.) When etins build out of stone, they do it in waste places without much life; the city of Utgard was built in such a place. The tops of mountains viewed from that theoretical bird's eye would show, if one were to fly closer, vast underground fortresses built into the sides of mountains. It is the giant's way: use what is there. One's works ought not to disturb the land-wight; they should blend seamlessly into the surroundings, and the land should hardly notice the subtle changes that you have wrought.

This is something that we, as a culture, have a need to learn. In America, three-quarters of what was in colonial times the most fertile farmland in the country is now under concrete; people settled on these lands in greater and greater droves, and finally citified and ruined the very fertility that had drawn them. The only way that we seem capable of not ruining any piece of land is to rigorously keep all humans and their dwelling places off of it. Anywhere we live, we seem to destroy. Working with earth-etins can help us to integrally understand what it is to live on a piece of land in harmony with that land's purpose. They can teach us that fertility is not just about one's cornfield, but about the many layers of humus that build up under the trees every few centuries, fertility that grows things not just for human consumption but for the nourishment of an entire ecosystem. It is a lesson that we desperately need.

Jord

Jord, as a goddess, is little mentioned in any of the myths. Her name means simply "Earth", and she is the daughter of Nott, the goddess of Night, and her second husband Annar, an island-giant whose name means "Water". One could metaphorize from here and see the daughter of Night and Water, dark and flowing, whose strongest connection is the fertile earth. In a way, Jord is the ultimate example of the earth-giantess, the being that is entirely in touch with the fertile soil. She is also not a "wifely" goddess. Jord seems to be very centered in herself and her fertility, and though she might willingly mate with a man, she would not build her life around being his partner.

Ari, a *spamadhr*, writes: "Ah, Jord! What can I say about her except to sing her praises? She lives in the area of Jotunheim that is the most fertile, and her very touch causes trees to fruit and seeds to sprout. In her own way she is just as much a mistress of fertility as any of the Vanir gods. Long hair and eyes the chocolate of rich, turned earth, skin darker than that of most Jotnar. Nothing small about her—belly of billowing female flesh, breasts that could drown a man, hips broad enough to spill forth triplets with ease. She is very often pregnant by her various lovers. It is probably impossible to calculate how many children she has borne. She is like the Earth itself, drawing you into her strong, soft, motherly embrace. Probably one of the most generous and giving etin-women in existence. I can see why Odin fell in love with her. I can also see why he left her—a man could get lost in her bed and never come out again to do any brave, heroic deeds. I have to wonder if Thor's ambivalent relationships with giantesses suggest how hard it was to cut the apron strings with such a powerful mother."

It is said that Jord was Odin's first consort, before taking an "official" Aesir wife. Perhaps he found her lushness irresistible; perhaps he was acting out an archetypal role of Sky-Father mating with the Earth-Mother. Their son, Thor, is certainly one of the Aesir, but he is in many ways the most giantlike of the lot of them, both in appearance and in behavior.

It is also said that another one of Jord's consorts is Fjorgynn. She herself is sometimes referred to as Fjorgyn, and as Thor's mother under that name, as well as by the name of Hlodyn. There is a good deal of confusion as to whether Fjorgynn is a male consort, or herself. Assuming for the moment that he is a male lover of hers, their daughter would have been Frigga. Since Frigga is an Asa goddess, the Fjorgynn-consort must have been an Aesir, or else Frigga might be the daughter of Jord/Fjorgyn and another unnamed Aesir man. Whichever it might be, if this is the case, Odin did the tribal equivalent of marrying his stepdaughter, trading in the motherly but independent Jord for her beautiful Asa daughter. Frigga, in her turn, was much more willing to assume the role of Royal Wife and Consort, making herself the mistress of Odin's halls and realms.

Invocation to Jord

Hail, Lady of the Dark Earth,
Fertile mother of the thunder,
Fertile mother of queens,
Fertile mother of many,
We reach out to you each spring
As the green begins its onslaught,
Wishing, asking for your blessing
On these our flocks and fields and lands.
May your touch bring new growth to our lives
As your touch makes the seeds to sprout.
May your touch bring fertility to our souls
As it brings fertility to our bodies.
May your touch nurture us into the future
As it has nurtured so many children.
Daughter of the night sky,
Dark as the turned earth;
Daughter of the deep well,
Reflecting stars in its depths,
Your thighs spill forth bounty
From between their dark cleft
Across the yearning land.

Gerda

Gerda is the daughter of Gymir and Aurboda, two mountain-giants. From her youth, she was very much an earth-giantess, and her great love was the enclosed, walled garden of herbs, flowers, and vegetables. Her name refers to a wall, a boundary, an enclosed space, and she is the Goddess of the enclosed herb garden, the domesticated fertile space in the middle of the wilderness, and the walls that enclose that space. However, she is also linked to the wilderness outside it. As an etin-woman, she is not about the clash between walled, "civilized" domesticity and open "uncivilized" wilderness; she is about the tended space existing comfortably within the wilder space, its walls well-kept but still trading back and forth seeds and spores over the wall. One of Gerda's lessons is that while some things require intensive tending and separate space to grow well, keeping them rigidly apart from the outside world is counterproductive. To the Jotun mind, anything that cannot survive on its own after careful tending should be culled out.

Gerda shares with many of the other farming and gardener deities of the Northern Tradition the magic of plant fertility, but her focus is different. Frey is Lord of the Grain and Freyja's specialties include ground-fruits and flowers; Iduna is Lady of the Orchard and loves fruiting and leafy vegetables as well. Gerda, on the other hand, specializes in herbs. Hers is the hand who carefully gathers the seeds from the wild plants and grows them in the garden, savoring their culinary and fragrance and medicinal uses, and breeding finer and more useful forms of them. She is also the force that lets them seed themselves back into the wild, perhaps strengthening their wild kin. Some herbs will not grow in her walled garden, requiring the humus of the woods or a wet stream-bank; these she respects for their wildness and gathers from the dark forests. The vegetable-plants that she is most in touch with are the roots, the goodness that grows underground and is pulled from the dark earth. Gerda's power goes deep, and is never far away from the wilderness.

As a goddess, she is quiet, dark-haired and pale-skinned, and has that introverted quality named by one writer as being "one-in-herself". Her soul has boundaries, and yet it touches wildness. One senses, under her quiet, self-enclosed demeanor, the watching tigress that could spring out suddenly when her private space is threatened. She is invaluable as a protector and teacher of those who have poor boundaries, whether it is failing to defend one's space against the encroachment of others, or allowing one's inner beast to escape too often. Gerda teaches the lesson of control of one's space and one's self, and of valuing that self enough to be effortlessly willing to defend that self's private, protective enclosure, with just enough effort to do the job and no wasteful overkill.

In the stories, it is told that Frey, the Golden One of the Vanir, stole one day into Odin's great tower to look through his magic window which sees far away. He was hoping for a glance of his sister Freyja, who was wandering in search of her missing husband, but the gaze of the window shifted and landed on a hall in Jotunheim, surrounded by flames. An etin-woman came out of the door for a moment, and with one glance at her, Frey fell madly in love. He sent letters, but her father Gymir returned them. Finally he sent his friend Skirnir as a go-between, and with some awkwardness, Gerda agreed to marry him. Their love story is told in "Gerda's Three Weddings" in this book.

Also discussed in that story are the reasons why Frey and Gerda have no children together. One of Gerda's powers is the ability to grant abortions, and to aid those who need to take that step. She is also the Lady in charge of comforting those who have miscarriages and stillbirths; she deeply understands the pain of the potential life that could have been yet did not come to fruition, and she does not judge the reasons. As a couple, she and Frey are very much complementary opposites: male and female; sunny extrovert and quiet introvert; sun-lover and nightwalker; light in the darkness and shadow in the light; pastoral and feral; civilized and barbaric; cultivated grain in the safe, open fields and weedy herbs in the enclosed forest garden; plants that reach for the sun and plants that dig into the earth; life that blossoms forth and life stillborn, culled out before its time.

Their marriage was archetypal in its complementarity, and yet unusual in that most of the folk on all sides—Jotun, Aesir, Alfar, and perhaps even Vanir—spoke out against it. As such, Frey and Gerda are gods of marriage, just as much as Frigga, the Aesir goddess of marriage with her faithfulness to Odin. Where Frigga symbolizes and blesses marriages that are favored by the community, Frey and Gerda bless those whose unions are condemned, and whose love makes them outcasts. As Frey was known to be favorable to followers who did not conform to heterosexuality or standard gender roles, and the Jotnar, being shapeshifters, are much easier with such things than the Aesir, they have in recent years been called upon to bless the unions of nonheterosexual weddings, as well as those between members of vastly different races, cultures, or faiths. Their love across all odds brings hope to star-crossed lovers.

Gerda is a goddess who is implacable in her own way. She holds to her boundaries and her standards, and does not waver, even for love; by respecting herself and her honor, she can better respect the love to which she is dedicated. It is a difficult lesson for many people, who usually overcompensate either in the direction of building walls or of being wild and lacking commitment. Gerda balances wildness and enclosed cultivation skillfully, with the giantkind talent of doing what fits best with the world around one. She is linked to the spirit of the earth in springtime, when the seed breaks forth from the dark earth and uncurls not only up, but downward as well, deeper into the darkness from whence it came.

Invocation to Gerda

Hail, Lady of the Walled Garden,
Hallowed in hedgerive and hammerwort,
Sacred in stonecrop and sowthistle,
Gifted and gifting in gladden and dragonwort,
You help us build the still, safe place
In which we can grow tender hopes to blossoming.
Hail, Lady of the forest paths,
Hallowed in hillwort and hindberry,
Sacred in cock's spur grass and sicklewort,
Gifted and gifting in gale and libcorn,
You help us bring those hopes into the world
To test and turn them into manifestation.
Hail, Lady of the quiet endings,
Hallowed in hulwort and whortleberry,
Sacred in ramsons and raven's leek,
Gifted and giving in viper's bugloss and boarfern,
You teach us to cull out what cannot be
While still keeping hope alive in the dark.
Hail, Lady of the hidden treasures,
Hallowed in mallow and meadowwort,
Sacred in sundcorn and stitchwort,
Gifted and giving in groundsel and sedge,
Cleansed in river-mint and lamb's cress,
You bring us deeper than we thought possible
Into the earth on which we depend.
Hail, Gerda, etin-bride of Frey,
Shadow to light, night to day,
All things balanced in your keen dark glance.

Gymir

The giant Gymir lives in a sheltered valley in the western mountain range of Jotunheim. His hall is surrounded by a wall of flames to keep out intruders, as he is extremely wealthy. He is one of the giants who trades regularly with Vanaheim, and the fact that his daughter Gerda is married to Frey, one of the lords of the Vanir, helps him a great deal in his trading. He is a doting and permissive father, and a canny businessman.

Aurboda

Aurboda is the wife of Gymir and the mother of Gerda and Beli; in some of the sagas she is confused with Angrboda, whose name resembles hers. As they are each Hags (Wisewomen), it is not surprising; Aurboda is the Hag of the Western Mountains while Angrboda is the Hag of the Iron Wood. Sorting out the tale which confuses the two of them is a difficult thing; one story claims that Aurboda A) was Gymir's wife and Gerda's mother; B) was Loki's wife and the mother of monsters; C) was Freyja's messenger; D) brought sorcery to Asgard; E) was burned to death three times, a fate which is also assigned to the Vanir goddess Gullveig; and F) started the war between the Aesir and the Vanir, which in all other lays was over long before the courtship of Frey and Gerda.

When faced with rampant confusions and mistranslations like this, sometimes the only thing to do is to ask the individuals involved. As far as I can tell from consulting and praying to both Aurboda and Angrboda, who seem to be very different individuals, Aurboda lays claim to A and C, but no others, and Angrboda lays claim to B, D, and E. F seems to be a spurious claim laughed off as chronologically incorrect by both of them.

So that leaves Aurboda as Gymir's wife and Gerda and Beli's mother, who occasionally worked for Freyja as a messenger. As her daughter was married to Freyja's brother, and her husband was known to have business dealings with the Vanir, this would make sense, although she claims that she has never been to Asgard but did her work for Freyja while the latter was in Vanaheim. This consisted of turning into a crow and bringing magical herbs to women who were praying for children. Aurboda is also listed as one of Mengloth's handmaidens; she sometimes works there in Gastropnir under the eye of the Jotun goddess of healing.

Beli

Beli is the son of Gymir and Aurboda, and the younger brother of Gerda. He resented his sister's Vanir marriage terribly, and swore vengeance. If Ragnarok occurs, he will kill Frey, who will strike him down in turn.

Fenja and Menja

Fenja and Menja are two giantess sisters whose story takes place not in the Nine Worlds, but in this one. They come into the tale in the land of Gotland, which is now part of Denmark. Gotland at that time was ruled by King Frode, whose father was Fridleif, whose grandfather was Skjold, and whose great-grandfather was Odin himself via some mortal Danish woman. The tale takes place, supposedly, at the time when the Roman Emperer Augustus ruled and Christ was living on the earth. In Gotland, of course, they knew nothing of such things, but King Frode's realm was reasonably peaceful—it was said that Frode's rule was so powerful that no man dared to kill another, even if he met his father's bane on the road. The penalty for thieving was so high that a gold ring could be dropped on Jalanger's Heath and no one would dare to take it, so serious was Frode about keeping the peace.

Frode had been given a magic mill named Grotte by a magician named Hengekjapt, or perhaps he had killed him and taken the mill. Unfortunately, the mill was such that it needed to be turned by two people of immense strength; horses and oxen would freeze it still, and no human beings were strong enough. Frode knew that Hengekjapt had probably used magical servants, and he set out to find some. He sent to King Fjolner, who ruled the neighboring kingdom of Svithjod (Sweden), and discovered that Fjolner had two magically-bound etin-thralls who were forced to serve him. They were a pair of sisters, Fenja and Menja, and they were large and strong. They were descended from the mountain-giant family of Hrungnir, Thjassi, Ide, and Orner, according to their song. Frode demanded them in tribute, and chained them to the mill-bench of Grotte, and bade them grind. This was how Frode discovered that the mill could grind out anything that was asked.

The name of the mill, Grotte, means "growth", and it is one of many magic mills in folktales that grind out grain, or salt, or riches, or nonphysical substances. The Sampo of the Finnish Kalevala is another example; both the Greeks and the Mayans speculated on a world-mill that churned out the stars. Either way, it is interesting that the three things Frode orders the giantesses to churn out are gold, peace, and happiness for himself. Gold, from then on, was referred to by the kenning of "Frode's Meal".

Fenja and Menja turn the mill, grinding out gold and peace and happiness, but Frode treats them cruelly in his greed for more of these gifts. They cry out to him in agony, screaming for him to lower the bin and lighten the stones, but he refuses to grant them any leeway. They try to stop grinding, but he refuses to allow them any more sleep than while the cuckoo was silent or the cock did not crow, and as they are magically bound, they must obey, hating the greedy, cruel Frode all the while. Their mournful song tells how grit tears their feet and frost covers their forms, but still they must keep grinding. It tells also of their lives as warrior-maidens, and the many services they had performed for men before being enslaved, from fighting in mercenary-armies to pulling boulders from fields.

Fenja and Menja are referred to as "the foreknowing pair", which suggests that even though they had been enslaved by mortals, they knew that sooner or later they would find a way to have their revenge. One thing they know that Frode does not is that a king "from over the sea", named Mysing, is coming to attack Frode, and they decide to use that to their advantage. As the sisters work the mill, they discover its powers and learn how to control it, creating a power-song referred to only as the "Song of

Grotte". This makes the mill grind out warriors, wave upon wave of them. When Mysing arrives the next morning, he finds a host ready to fight Frode for him. He leads the army against Frode and slays him, and ransacks the kingdom, and thus was the Peace of Frode, which had been so dearly bought, ended at last.

However, when Mysing discovers Frode's most precious possession—Grotte and its giantess slaves, which he inherits—he does no better than Frode. Fenja and Menja beg for their freedom, but Mysing sees the various uses to which the mill could be put, and orders Grotte and the sisters hauled on board his ship to be taken with him. Ignoring their pleas, he orders them to grind out salt, which was a valuable commodity. They are forced to grind, as their bondage has been transferred to Mysing, but they are more knowledgeable about Grotte than when Frode chained them to its handles. At midnight—the magical turning point of many stories—the two sisters ask him ominously if he is done with having them grind salt. He tells them to keep grinding and goes to sleep; while he sleeps, they grind out so much salt that his ship sinks. As they keep grinding, sinking to the bottom of the ocean, a great whirlpool is created by the sea spiralling through the hole in the millstone of Grotte, known as the Maelstrom (Mill-Stream). All Mysing's ships are pulled down and sunk, and thus the sea became salt.

The two sisters, no longer bound by any man, returned to Jotunheim with Grotte, which they use to grind out gold dust on a regular basis. They export it to the various worlds; the roof of Gladsheim is covered with it. One myth claims that these days, in order to grind out gold, Grotte needs living, screaming bodies to be fed into it while the sisters grind. Whatever the truth of that, many people have come to the house of Fenja and Menja, which is covered in gold dust, and tried to steal Grotte or their wealth. None have yet survived to tell the tale.

Song of the Sisters
by Ari

Grind, we grind, blood to gold we grind.

Humans are by nature
Greedy. We can attest to this.
The callouses on our hands will never fade
From the forced making of Frode's Breakfast
Served with the milk of our tears,
Until he too went between the stones.
We were the wiser, his bones
Were ours to grind away. Do not try us.
We owe no human anything, not wisdom,
Not teachings, not advice, and especially not
Gold. What we have, we earned, we keep.

Grind, we grind, blood to gold we grind.

He who followed Frode, he did not know
He was only our tool, though we were
In chains. He thought himself the master
Of us, our song, our power, the geas
Tight upon us, trapped by some venal
Human who thought he owned us.
Passed from one fool to another, all went down
In curses. Mysing drank seawater in his dreams,
And we made of his fleet a toy for Weed-hair
And her fanged daughters. We are the Mill-Keepers,
Sisters of the Maelstrom. Do not try us,
For we owe no human anything.

Grind, we grind, blood to gold we grind.

Asvid

Long ago, when Odin brought the runes into the world, at the same time the rift that the Norns opened to admit them, other runes spilled into the world. They were caught by various members of other races—Dain, a chieftain of the Alfar; Dvalin, one of the first fathers of the Duergar, and Asvid, a Jotun hermit who lived deep in the heavily wooded forests of Jotunheim.

All three, in their various worlds, were immediately moved to find the nearest branch or root or trunk of the World Tree and carve the Runes into it, thus making their presence fixed in the Nine Worlds. (The Futhark themselves, and Odin's special rune Gar, were graven into Yggdrasil by Odin's own blood.) Asvid thus brought magical runes to the Jotnar, just as Odin did to the Aesir and eventually to those who worshiped them. We know very little about most of those Jotun runes. There are some references to "Iottun villum", or "Jötna villur", which literally mean "the bewilderments of the etins" and refers to some unknown formula of "murk-staves" used by the etins to delude and confuse those who would attack them.

There are also the very Rökkr-like extra aett runes of the Anglo-Frisian Futhorc; modern users refer to these as Hel's Aett, to distinguish them from the Aetts belonging to Frey, Tyr, and Heimdall in the Futhork. These runes include Ear (Hel's Rune), Ac (Angrboda's Rune), Ior (Jormundgand's Rune), Yr (Aurvandil's Rune), Os (a rune much liked by Loki, Odin, and Bragi), Cweorth (Surt's Rune), Chalc (Gerda's Rune), and Stan (possibly Utgard-Loki's Rune). The final rune, Gar, not part of any aett, is clearly also Odin's just as the Futhark are. These might be some of the runes that Asvid carved onto the tree; all we know for sure is that the giant race has its own magical runes, and that there are probably many more than these.

Hreidmar, Fafnir, Ottar, Regin

Hreidmar is a farmer-magician; he seems to have been half Jotun and half Duergar. His sons are Ottar, Regin, and Fafnir. Of the three, Ottar and Fafnir were giants, and Regin was a dwarf. Ottar, the shapechanger, was a great fisherman in the rivers, taking the form of an otter in order to fish. Fafnir was a warrior, and inherited his father's love of money even stronger than that of his sire. Regin was small and not good with arms, but was crafty with metal and smithing, and wise and cunning in counsel.

There seems to be something troublesome about mixing Duergar and Jotun bloodlines; the Jotun intensity mixed with the Duergar love of wealth can create a great deal of avariciousness, and this shows up in two of the three brothers. The eldest, Ottar, was accidentally killed while in otter form by Odin, Loki, and Hoenir; all three of whom were out traveling and fishing. Hreidmar was furious at the death of his son, and demanded weregild. He spread the otter-skin of his dead son out on the shore and demanded that it be completely covered in gold. While Loki and the two Aesir could have fled, they felt that it would be more honorable to agree to the payment. Leaving Odin and Hoenir as hostages to his good faith, Loki sped off in search of money.

Loki went to a spring where a Duergar named Andvari dwelt, guarding a great treasure of gold, in the form of a pike. Loki borrowed a magic net from Ran, and caught Andvari in it; he then forced the hapless dwarf to ransom himself with the golden treasure. Andvari gave up the treasure willingly, but refused to part with one final gold ring which was his favorite, saying that whosoever robbed him of that ring would be cursed forever. Loki took it anyway, and covered Ottar's skin with gold, holding back only the cursed ring. When there was still a tiny portion of the skin showing, he added the ring, not telling Hreidmar about the curse.

After his prisoners were set free, Hreidmar became enamored of his cursed treasure, spending his days locked up touching and playing with it. And greed grew also in the hearts of his two sons, perhaps because of the curse, perhaps because of their bloodlines; but it was Fafnir the elder who slew his father and took the gold. Shapeshifting into a terrible dragon, he guarded his hoard and slew all who came near, until he had mostly forgotten anything except being a dragon and loving his cursed treasure.

Meanwhile, Regin, still craving the gold but knowing that he had no chance against Fafnir, went to work as blacksmith for a king in Midgard, Hjalprek, perhaps with the hope of eventually goading the king into fighting the dragon. He became the tutor to the King's foster-son, Sigurd, and raised him on tales of the evil Fafnir. When Sigurd grew old enough, he did indeed slay Fafnir and claim the treasure, with Regin behind him egging him on. Regin asked Sigurd to excise and roast the heart of the dragon for him, but while he was off fetching firewood, Sigurd ate most of the dragon's heart himself. He then discovered that he could understand the language of the birds, who were making jokes about the scene before them. The birds realized that Sigurd could hear them, and they taunted him, telling him that Regin would betray him in order to goad him into foolish behavior for their entertainment. When Regin returned, Sigurd struck off his mentor's head in a fit of paranoia, to the vast amusement of the watching birds.

Thus ends the stories of Hreidmar and his sons, although Sigurd goes on to get both much fame and much disaster from the Duergar-cursed treasure.

Aspilian

In the Thidrekssaga, a giant named Aspilian comes to a monastery in Lungbardi (Lombardy) and demands some of their lands as tribute. When they send Heimer, a retired robber-hero, out to deal with him, Aspilian kills the man. Then the robber's former boss shows up and kills Aspilian.

Stone And Clay: Mountain Giants

he mountain giants are the ones that most of us think of when we picture the fairytale giants of our childhood stories: huge, slow, craggy, and somehow rocklike. The mountainous nature of Jotunheim means that most of the land-wights are mountain-wights, and therefore most of the giants who shifted to be in harmony with them have the greatest affinity with stone and clay, cliff and peak, cascading waves of fir and pine down the mountainside. For some, like Hrungnir, their shapeshifting forms become so close to the land that parts of them look as if they are permanently made out of stone.

For some reason, certain sorts of places in our world are more likely than others to connect with "thin spots" in the barriers between other worlds, and make connections with harmonious places. This creates spots where one can quite literally walk in two worlds at once, and this may be the source of the confusion between whether certain spirits live in our world or another. One of these sorts of places is high mountain peaks; many of the peaks in northern Europe supposedly had giants living in them. One can imagine that these peaks lined up with similar mountains in Jotunheim, and unwary travelers who inadvertently and temporarily shifted worlds while traveling may have begun such stories.

The mountain-giants of Jotunheim vary tribe to tribe, depending on the ecology of their area. The giants who live on the peaks and rugged cliffs have been referred to as "berg risi". Some of the cliffs and mountains of Jotunheim "line up" with northern European mountains, enough that there is some moving between worlds. The majority of Jotunheim giants fall into the mountain-giant category, although since the mountain-giants are descended from both fire and frost giants, many will clearly show fire-giant or frost-giant bloodlines. In general, those with strong frost-giant blood tend to gravitate toward the northern mountain ranges, where it is still snowy most of the year. Thrym the Old, titular king of Jotunheim, is an example; he holds his court high in the snowiest mountains. Skadi also came originally from this area of Jotunheim.

In the more southerly forests, the giants live in the deep woods in treehouses or hollowed-out trees; wherever there are mountains (which is something like three-quarters of Jotunheim) they will aim for the highest parts, or live in caves dug into cliffs. Despite the idea of a cave being primitive and rough, these mountain (or tree, for that matter) homes are often quite comfortable and even luxurious. If you ask a mountain-giant why he builds his home on the highest peaks, he will tell you that it is to be close to the sky. Since many of them have frost-thurse blood, the sky and the wind are important to them. The perennial lightning storms that rage over Jotunheim do not bother them in their high stone lairs; on the contrary, many know how to use the storm-power to fuel their magic.

However, mountain giants can and do build great fortresses out of stone. They build these only on barren, rocky areas that have little wildlife to be disturbed, and pride themselves on building the structure in such a way that it blends in entirely with the mountain, with the various towers and turrets simply mimic peaks and outcroppings, providing camouflage and bewildering the tourist. Thrym's fortress is one of these; on the other hand, the city of Utgard is an unusual example of giant-building made to stand out and intimidate as a huge and obvious fortress that does not even attempt to blend into the landscape. (It is built on what was a wide waste place, and Utgard-Loki is a rather cosmopolitan sort, so he can be forgiven.) The *berg-risi* of Jotunheim were famed as builders, which is why they were hired to build the main city of Asgard.

In terms of appearance, mountain giants vary widely in size, but tend to be taller, bulkier, and stronger than any except for the huge old frost-thurses. Some—especially those who draw strongly from their home-mountains for power—can shapeshift into huge, slow-moving, incredibly strong forms. As there is no sexual dimorphism in their race, most etin-women of Jotunheim are tall, muscular, and large-boned, even if they are only of "normal" human size. (As the human race itself has grown significantly in height in the past centuries—just look at the size of our ancestors' clothing in museums—it is possible that the average Jotun in their humanoid form is no longer all that impressive to us in this way.)

In personality, the stony nature of mountain-giants comes out as well. While they are all subject to individual variances, they tend toward being stonily stubborn when they believe that they are right. It is almost a cliche that getting them to change their minds, or swerve from their goals, or leave aside a grudge, is a monumental task. Family infighting can create enemies who hold onto their resentments for centuries. However, mountain-giant blood also creates a strong homebody streak. These are etins who would rather stay home, holed up in their comfortable dens, than wander about looking for trouble, so there tend to be long periods of sullen peace between enemies rather than constant warfare. Some mountain-giants become so solitary and homebound that they will go for decades without speaking to another person, hiding on their familiar mountains. It is not surprising that humans with mountain-giant bloodlines tend to be homebodies as well, and in the worst cases can be agoraphobic.

Offerings to them will vary depending on the individual. In general, try food from agricultural sources that they might not have—grains from plains areas that would be rare for them, or tropical fruits, or foreign herbs that are not found in Jotunheim (but might be found in China, for example). Attractive handcrafted items are good too. And, of course, labor (skilled or unskilled) is always a good thing.

Utgard-Loki

According to the stories, Thor and Loki and their entourage once went to Utgard, where they were entertained by Utgard-Loki, the ruler of Jotunheim's capital city. Utgard-Loki was known to be a powerful sorcerer as well as an illusionist. However, he made them all sorts of bets that they couldn't do various things as well as his courtiers, and when they took him up on it, they lost. As he wasn't a malicious sort, or at least wasn't feeling malicious that day, they got off with merely a bruised ego or two.

Thor was invited to lift his cat, and to drain his horn, and to wrestle his granny; and failed. Loki was invited to out-eat his friend, and failed. Thor's page Thjalfi tried to outrun another courtier and failed as well. Utgard-Loki then told them that the cat and the horn were illusions; one was actually the Midgard Serpent in its waters, and the other was the ocean itself. His granny had the power of Old Age, his hungry friend was Logi the fire-etin who could devour anything, and his other friend was merely an illusion, being Thought itself. Besides being a clever story, it was an interesting lesson for those who would show off too readily for their hosts.

Utgard-Loki is probably the most influential man in Jotunheim. The one time that I spoke to him, I found him intelligent, canny, ruthless, sharp as a razor, a leader worthy of respect, but one who is much more concerned with the welfare of his people than the welfare or life of any given human whatsoever...as a good ruler of his people ought to be. When he spoke to me, he was also concerned with the growing numbers of strangers—"utlanders"—straying foolishly into his country, a telling comment for those of us who journey. The Nine Worlds must not be considered our personal Disneyland; it belongs to someone else, and we ought only to intrude with the greatest politeness.

Utgard-Loki took his name distinguish himself from Laufey's son. He is both warlord and sorcerer, a brilliant, canny leader who invokes deep respect from his people. He is known to be generous to visitors if he wants to impress them, or if they have something he wants from them; he is a faultless and courteous host, although he has been known to bait guests who seem too full of themselves. It is said that among all the great ones of Jotunkind, Utgard-Loki has never been seen to lose his temper. The kind of iron control behind that mask of flawless, regal politeness is awe-inspiring. He has mastered the ability to quell the most violent of drunken giants with his piercing gaze, and on the off chance that it doesn't work, he has a supremely competent, loyal, and well-organized cadre of city guards who can handle it for him.

While Utgard-Loki is nominally liegesworn to Thrym, the King of Jotunheim, he technically commands more power and respect than the King himself. Their relationship is reminiscent of that between the medieval Japanese emperor and the Shogun; one was the ceremonial wearer of the crown, and the other was the actual war leader who made most of the decisions.

Invocation to Utgard-Loki

Hail to the Lord of Utgard,
Hail to the Warlord of Jotunheim!
Hail to the Master of Illusion
Whose sorcery teaches Truth!
Eyes that see through hypocrisy,
Perceptions that see all secret motivations,
Judging us and our reasons
Clearly and with all due strategy.
Your gaze sees our usefulness
As well as our flaws, and assigns us
The best position to use our talents.
You who keep your unruly people together
In spite of all that would tear them apart,
Teach us to lead with honesty and clarity
And the wisdom of the even, iron hand.

Hyndla

Deep in the northern mountains of Jotunheim lies the cave of the giantess Hyndla, the Hag (wisewoman) of the northern mountains. She spends most of her time sleeping, or what looks like sleeping to some folk; actually, she is "faring forth", sending her mind out where her body cannot go. Her cave is guarded by a band of loyal etins, who will not allow her to be disturbed when she is unconscious, so seeing her is only possible during the short periods when she wakes up to eat and walk about a little.

Hyndla is small for a giantess—not more than human size—and wizened and old, with long silver-grey hair that drapes on the ground around her. She is pale from almost never leaving her cave, and walks with a stick. Her apparent frailty makes her guards all the more protective of her. She is a mistress of bloodlines; ancestry is her specialty, and it is rumored that she spends her astral-travel time walking up and down the bloodlines of many races. The Gods consult her when they want to know something about how someone is related to someone else, or for advice on their various human breeding experiments. Non-gods consult her about discovering unknown ancestors, tracing genetic disorders, dealing with blood-curses, asking about future children, or anything else that requires an ability to see into bloodlines far away. She is especially good for consultations about humans with problems from nonhuman blood, but you will have to go to her; she doesn't come to anyone who calls.

Hyndla is generally friendly, but can be cantankerous if she has just awoken. Flirting with her will usually soften her, but be prepared to go through with it if she decides to take you up on it; for all that she is old and wrinkled, she is also lusty. Her name means "hound" and she does indeed have a small pack of silver-colored greyhounds as pets, usually lolling about her and keeping her warm. She can shapeshift into a hound herself, or a dog-headed woman; it is in this form that she appears on a famous carved Icelandic stone. She has a stable of pet dogs and wolves; some of the latter are large enough to ride as steeds. In the lay *Hyndlujod*, Freyja comes in riding on a boar and suggests that Hyndla accompany her for a ride on one of her wolves while they discuss genealogy. This is another example of how powerful this little giantess is in her own specialty; for the Vanadis to consult her, she must be skilled indeed.

Jarnsaxa

Before his marriage to Sif, Odin and Jord's son Thor the thunder god had an affair with a merry mountain-giantess named Jarnsaxa. Her name means "iron sword" and she is said to be his co-wife with Sif, although she does not live with them in Asgard. It is unclear as to whether she is actually a wife, or simply the mother of his two extremely strong sons, Magni and Modi. It may well be that she is married to him by the rites of her people, which may not count as legitimate marriage with the Aesir, but which easily allow for multiple simultaneous marriages and living apart from spouses.

Writer Alice Karlsdottir has put together the story of Thor's courtship with Jarnsaxa in the last section of this book. Below are her reasons for doing so, which constitute an excellent discussion of the nature of the uses of personal gnosis.

How I Got To Know Jarnsaxa
by Alice Karlsdottir

Many Norse Pagan groups have a pantheon chock full of robust, manly Gods, but only a smattering of ill-defined Goddesses. This is not, as many Craft people have intimated to me, because Norse folk are inherently more chauvinistic or macho-mad than other Pagans. Rather, there is simply a decided dearth of material on the Norse Goddesses. Of many, only the names remain.

If one is an archaeologist or medieval historian, the matter would have to die there. But Paganism is more than history—it is a religion. No religion practices rituals in exactly the same form that they were done in 300 years ago. Religion, to be viable, must grow and expand. Besides, much of the old Norse lore was passed on orally, and many of the Norse Pagans passed on prematurely when the Christians moved in, so just because we can't find much material on the Goddesses does not mean they weren't worshiped. To the contrary, assuming that a religion reflects the culture it grew from and judging from what we know of Norse society, women played a strong role; therefore, it makes sense that the female deities would be equally strong in their world. Great mortal heroes like Sigmund and Sigurd took good strong women for their mates; would the great Thor, then, have some nebulous wimp (or wimpess) for wife?

So, accepting that Norse Goddesses should play an important role in ritual, how do you go about reconstructing a tangible personality from a mere name? What I have done for Oakrune Circle is this: first, I try to find anything and everything in the Eddas and Sagas and runestone inscriptions that even vaguely refers to the Goddess in question—who her husband, father, children were; any personal traits mentioned; any actions she is said to have performed. Next, I try to find out any etymological meanings that can be gathered from her name. And lastly, I make stuff up! Well, not really; but there is a degree of personal contact which can help you fill out the details that have been lost these many centuries, basing your work on the facts you have found.

If nothing is known about her but her husband's name, use what you know about her husband to give clues: what kind of wife would Thor have? Also, you can use comparative mythology (gasp!) to help you out (plundering other cultures in good Viking tradition): if the lady is married to a sky-deity or weather God, might she not be a Mother Earth figure? You can meditate, often in a very casual and playful manner, creating little stories about the Goddess, trying to see her interacting with Gods and Goddesses you know a lot about: what would this Goddess and Odin talk about? How would she get along with Loki? (Does anyone get along with Loki??) In this way you can usually get enough information to do some kind of ritual; and after several rituals, even more information tends to pop up (no surprise).

As an example of some results of this process, which may strike hard-core fact-finders as too cavalier a treatment but which I believe is valid, I am presenting here the material I did on Jarnsaxa, the Goddess Oakrune Circle invoked along with Thor on Midsummer (we usually like to invoke both a Goddess and God at any given ritual, which is why I embarked on this mission of Goddess-analysis in the first place). This is what I could find out about her from books: her name means "Iron-Sword"; she's a Jotun, or Giantess; she's referred to as "the co-wife of Sif" (Thor's wife) in the Prose Edda; she is the mother of Thor's two sons, Magni ("Might") and Modi ("Courage"), who eventually inherit the famous hammer. Period. From this, after much mulling and playing around, I wrote a little (actually it's kind of long) legend about Jarnsaxa and Thor, just to get a feeling for what kind of lady she is.

This tale makes no pretense at being sacred scripture, although it does have a little symbolism here and there; it borrows shamelessly from Germanic fairy tales; and it is as legitimate as many other myths which were created by Norse court poets for the amusement of their patrons. The second thing I wrote was an invocation to Jarnsaxa (one to Thor, too, but that's for another day).

Methods like this can be used to fill out any mythology for which few details are available. (Celtic mythology, for example, has been cited to me as being hard to track down.) It also never hurts to find out something new about well-known deities as well. I don't present these things as divine truth or absolute doctrine; I do present them as examples of a valid procedure for creating rituals out of very skimpy material. So, in good old folk-song tradition, "If you don't like it, you can sing some yourself."

Invocation to Jarnsaxa

by Alice Karlsdottir

Daughter of the Rock,
Daughter of the Storm,
Daughter of Darkness, mighty Jarnsaxa.
In Jotunheim
In the home of Giants,
In Chaos, there were you born.
Mistress of Thor
Co-Wife of Sif
Mother of the heirs of Heaven,
Magni and Modi, the Storm-God's children.
Straight and sharp as a sword;
Hard as iron;
Bright as the jewel on the hilt;
Strong as the runes on the blade.
Within the mountain, you stoke the storm of lust,
The fiery heart of the passive Earth.
Your heart burns,
Your arms reach,
Your loins hunger.
Stern as the cliff,
Wild as the heath,
Firm as the rock
You wait, and call.
Ancient Giantess,
We call to you,
We of Midgard.
Come, and fling your dark hair loose into the storm!
Come, and meet your lover, spark for spark!
Come, and strike the primal flame ablaze!
Come to the Circle, mighty Jarnsaxa!
Come!

Mengloth

Mengloth, who has been written about in the saga Svipdagsmal, is the healing goddess of the Jotnar, as Eir is the healing goddess of the Aesir. (In fact, although Eir is actually listed as one of the "maidens" who surround Mengloth, I suspect that this is either a different Eir, or that they simply get together and learn from each other periodically.) She lives on Mount Lyfjaberg in Jotunheim, and is married to Svipdag, a wandering hero who seems to be the son of Aurvandil and Groa. While we do not know her ancestry per se, the lay of Svipdagsmol names one of her father's parents as Svafrthorin, and her cloistered cliff-peak life marks her as a mountain-giantess.

Ari writes to us, "I've worked with Mengloth on her mountain, in the castle of Gastropnir. I was told that I needed to be a healer, but when I prayed to Eir—the obvious choice—she sent me off on this quest up a mountain in Jotunheim to visit 'a friend of hers' instead. I ended up on Mengloth's mountain, learning healing the Jotun way. She is famed everywhere for her healing abilities—she has very much the same standing among her people that Eir does with hers, and they consider each other equal colleagues, and trade clients that they are having difficulty with. The Jotun healing system is very complex and shamanic; it isn't crude, barbaric hacking about like I thought it would be. They are very wise and learned, in their own way."

Ari also points out that: "It was in reading the lore about Mengloth, and watching various intellectuals who had never met her argue over whether she was a Goddess or 'merely' a Jotun, that I came to the realization that none of us mortals are qualified to draw that line when it comes to powerful wights. Deity or simply powerful wight? How can we have the temerity and arrogance to decide that? I think that the people who are making those arbitrary judgments are people who haven't met very many wights, or perhaps any at all. For myself, I treat anything that is significantly bigger, older, and wiser than I'll ever be as a deity, and give them the appropriate respect. It's only correct to do so."

Mengloth can be prayed to for healing, and she is supposedly especially good with women's problems. She is very particular who she takes on as a student; usually she prefers that someone be referred by another deity that she trusts, such as Eir, Hela, Surt/Sinmora, etc. Her name means "Necklace-Glad" and she loves gifts of jewelry, especially unusual pieces that she wouldn't be able to get from the mines of Jotunheim or Svartalfheim. Those mines give her a good deal of crystals and polished stone, but items like shell beads, unusual stones, or cut gems would be much more difficult for her to come by. Linen for bandages is also prized by her; all linen in the Nine Worlds is farmed in Vanaheim and must be imported.

Mengloth is also the person to study with if you want to learn the Jotun system of healing. However, she does not give out her wisdom to everyone. She will likely want to know how you will use this learning, if you get it, and on whom. If no one that she considers important will be benefited—and don't assume that you know who she would consider important—then she may well refuse. If you seek her out for healing or for study, be prepared to pay for it, and you had better be serious on either count. Her fortress lies at the top of a mountain peak with high walls and many guards (and is named "Guest-Crusher") for a reason. She is not one to let her healing skills be exploited.

Gastropnir lies in the westernmost part of Jotunheim, near the shore of the Vanaheim Ocean, and is perched on the peak of Lyfjaberg Mountain. Lyfjaberg is easily visible from both the shore and from the mountain chain surrounding Utgard; it is the tallest mountain in the western chain. There is a twisting road that circles the mountain, but it is filled with hazards. The castle itself is said to have been carved from the bones of the giant Leirbrimir; the local story, however, is that Leirbrimir was a mountain Jotun who turned himself into part of the mountainside and stayed that way, and the jutting cliff that had been his body formed the foundation for the castle.

The front gate is enormous, of wrought iron shaped like twining vines, nicknamed Clanging Thrymgjol. It was supposedly forged by the three sons of the dwarf Solblindi. Two hounds, Gif and Geri, are constantly on watch outside and will not let anyone through. Attempting to bribe them with food will not work, as they are trained to deal with that: one will eat the food while the other watches. (It is quite likely that they are not ordinary hounds at all, but shapeshifted Jotnar.)

The gatekeeper, and general majordomo, of the place is Fjolsvid. He is a fairly large and intimidating-looking giant, but in actuality he is rather loquacious and enjoys chatting with passersby. His willingness to gossip, however, does not mean that he will be willing to let just anyone through. It is best to send a message to Mengloth first, asking to visit.

Mengloth's courtship with Svipdag (whose name means "Swift-Day") is retold in the story section of this book. Her six handmaidens are named Hlifthrasa (Help-breather); Thjodvara (Folk-Guardian); Bjort (Shining); Bleik (White); the twin sisters Blid (Mild) and Frid (Pretty) who are actually Vanir and younger sisters or cousins of Freya; Aurboda (Gold-Giver) who is the mother of Gerda, Frey's wife. A handmaiden named Eir is also listed; there is some argument as to whether this is the same Eir, goddess of healing, who serves Frigga. While I have not met Mengloth's Eir, being as the name is loosely translated as "healing", it could simply be another Eir. It could also be that Frigga's Eir herself comes to visit and trade learning; from my dealings with both of them, it is clear to me that they are colleagues at the least, and likely friends.

If you should get inside Gastropnir, you will see many halls around a courtyard that is open to the sky. One of them seems to be made of flame, or moving lava; the walls flicker as you look at it. This is Lyr, the Hall of Heat, a hall built specially for Sinmora the Lady of Muspellheim, who enjoys visiting Mengloth, by her godson Loki and a team of hired Duergar-craftsmen. Avoid going inside, as it is extremely hot in there; the floor is of burnished gold that is almost molten in places. Lyr is sometimes used for heating patients with chills, or water is poured on the floor and it becomes a purifying sauna. It is also the keeping-place for Surt and Sinmora's flaming sword/wand Laevatein, which is the source of all the heat. Laevatein was forged by Loki as a gift for his godparents, and it is kept in a bowl-shaped iron box sealed with nine locks. Don't get any ideas about stealing it, as no one without serious amounts of fire-giant blood could even touch it, and anyway the warders of Gastropnir keep an eagle's eye on it while outsiders are about.

Many folk who don't journey, and whose only view into the Nine Worlds is through the clouded lens of lore, have claimed that Mengloth isn't really a person unto herself but is actually a *heiti* or ritual name of either Frigga or Freya. Since I have had some dealings with all three of those ladies, I can assure you that Mengloth is indeed her own person, a tall Jotun-woman who loves jewelry and is usually draped in strings of beads, many of which seem to be healing amulets. (And, frankly, I think that it would be ridiculous to imagine that an Aesir goddess, or a Vanir goddess hostage to the Aesir, would be the keeper of the magic wand that Surt will wield against the Aesir at Ragnarok. Come on now.)

The friction seems to be caused by people who would like there to be fewer gods and goddesses, not more... and are disturbed by a line in Svipdagsmal that refers to women leaving offerings to Mengloth in return for her healing, as "everyone knows" that our ancestors never worshiped any of the Jotnar in any way. This argument is used, almost hysterically, every time that anyone brings up any of the several references to Jotnar deities being propitiated. So in her own way, Mengloth is a controversial goddess.

Invocation to Mengloth

Hail, Lady of Lyfjaberg,
Mistress of Gastropnir,
High on the highest peak
In the pure air of the north country
Atop snowy cliffs you dwell.
Lady whose roads are long and winding,
Lady whose roads are treacherous and fell,
Lady whose hidden fortress is sought
By the weak, the ill, the desperate,
Those whom all medicine has failed.
Lady of the Last Resort,
Healer of the wounds that cannot be healed,
This offering we make to you
And all the maidens that cluster around you;
Hlif and Hlifthrasa, Thjofvara, Aurboda,
Bjort and Bleik, Blith and Frith,
Colleague of Eir the Healer of Asgard.
We pray your healing hands, Jeweled One,
We pray your healing mind, Mountain-High,
We pray your healing magic shall shape us whole.
Svipdag's beloved, Keeper of the Wand of Light,
May your favor shine upon us
As we ascend to the trials of your high road.

Gilling, Suttung, Baugi, and Gunnlod

This family is one of the good examples of how the category of "earth giant" and "mountain giant" are difficult to separate, and indeed may blend and intertwine a good deal. While Suttung is clearly a mountain-giant, shutting himself and his daughter up in a stone mountain-fortress, his brother Baugi is an earth-giant farmer on the surface of the land. Their father Gilling is the brother of Billing, an island giant, but unlike his brother he dislikes the sea and cannot swim, implying an earthier nature. Thus even within families, and over lifetimes, the nature of each giant may change radically.

Gilling was an old giant who made an enemy of Fjalar and Galar, the two renegade Duergar who had recently stolen the Mead of Poetry. Gilling and his wife visited them at the shore, and quarreled over some small issue. The Duergar brothers, who were easily moved to anger, decided to do Gilling in. They suggested that Gilling might row out with them to enjoy the sea breeze and to keep tempers cool. As soon as they were out at sea, the Duergar brothers deliberately rammed the boat against a partially submerged rock, knocking Gilling out. He could not swim, not being used to the ocean, and drowned. When the Duergar brothers returned and told Gilling's wife the sad news, she went into a torrent of grieving and blamed them for it, so they struck her on the head with a large rock as she wept on the shore.

Suttung, their eldest son, found out and determined that he would avenge his dead parents. Unlike his trusting father and mother, Suttung was cold, canny, calculating, and also grieving the recent death of his wife. Life had been harsh to him, and it had made him hard. He drugged the Duergar brothers with a tempting bottle of herbed wine, and they awoke tied firmly to a rock at the seashore, the same stone that Galar had stood on to murder Suttung's mother. It was low tide, and the water was rising. The terrified dwarves begged for their lives, finally offering him the Mead of Poetry in order to escape. Suttung agreed to spare them, but took the Mead of Poetry to his mountain home, Hnitbjorg, and hid the mead in the center of the mountain.

Suttung's only daughter, Gunnlod, was much beloved by him. He preferred to keep her single, and set her to guarding the Mead of Poetry in its underground cave where no suitors would bother her. Unfortunately, Odin decided that he wanted the magical mead, and set out to get it.

His first stop was Baugi, the younger brother of Suttung, who worked the great farm next to his brother's mountain. Odin disguised himself as an ill-favored Jotun named Bolverk ("Evil Worker") and stopped by Baugi's farm. He noticed Baugi's nine thralls scything grass in the field, and stopped to talk to them. Seeing that their scythes were dull and the work was hard, he pulled a whetstone from his pocket and showed it to them. They offered to buy it from him, but he would not sell it. Instead, he enchanted it with a spell of chaos and death, and threw it up in the air. All nine of them ran to get it, and in the commotion they managed to cut each other's throats with their scythes—with Odin's magical help.

Having eliminated all of Baugi's farm help, Odin invited himself into Baugi's home and sympathized with him about the demise of his entire staff. He then offered to do the year's mowing himself, in exchange for a sip of his brother's magical mead. Baugi knew that he had no influence over his brother, but agreed to introduce them and make the offer. Odin, as Bolverk, did work hard all summer and get the fields mowed, but when they visited Suttung, he refused the stranger any part of the mead.

At this point, Baugi was ready to give up, but Odin convinced him to reluctantly help him gain the mead by guile and trickery. They spent a day crawling around Suttung's mountain until they found a point where they could hear Gunnlod's singing. Odin brought out a magical auger name Rati, and convinced Baugi to bore a small hole into the mountain. Odin then turned himself into a serpent and crawled through the hole, leaving Baugi to realize that this Jotun was really someone quite different.

How Odin seduced Gunnlod and got the Mead of Poetry from her, as well as fathering her son Bragi, is told in the story "Gunnlod's Tale".

Geirrod, Gjalp, Greip

Geirrod, whose name means "Spear-Reddener", was a mountain giant with a serious grudge against Thor the thunder god, slayer of many of his kin. One day Loki was flying about in falcon form, dipping in and out of the various halls of Jotunheim, and spying on things. Geirrod saw the falcon and sensed that it wasn't an ordinary bird; he set his men to capture it, but it was too quick. However, at the last moment he seized it out of the air and thrust it into a cage.

He tried to get the falcon to identify himself, but Loki said nothing. After three months without food or water, however, he finally gave up and revealed himself as Laufey's son, the great trickster. At this point in history, Loki was allied with the Aesir and living mostly in Asgard, and many of the Jotnar were less than pleased with him both for his defection and for his friendship with kinslayers. Geirrod called him a traitor to his race, but saw this as an opportunity to even the score with his old enemy. He told Loki that he would starve in that cage unless he gave his oath to convince Thor to come to Geirrod's hall without his hammer, sword, or belt of power. Loki, half-starved and hoping to figure a way out, agreed and gave his word.

Here the story goes different ways; some say that Loki returned home and convinced Thor to visit Geirrod's for a party, and assured him that there would be no repercussions or battle joined, and thus he should travel unarmed. Another version suggests that he confessed his oath to Thor and that the giant-killer agreed to go, sanguine in his ability to handle Geirrod and his men. Either way, they set out for Jotunheim. When night fell, Thor suggested that they take refuge at the home of Grid, a giantess with whom he had been having an ongoing occasional affair (and who had borne at least one child to his father Odin). Grid was pleased to see her Aesir lover, and took him to bed. Once there, she warned him that she had heard about his journey from Geirrod, and that Geirrod was planning to kill him.

Thor was determined to go on and fight Geirrod unarmed, but Grid persuaded him that this was not a good idea. Since it was too late to go back for his own weapons, Grid lent him her own—a magical iron staff, a belt of power, and iron gloves. As they didn't actually belong to Thor, it wouldn't technically be breaking Loki's oath, or so they all decided. Thor and Loki set out for Geirrod's place, but were stopped by the river Vimur which flowed in front of its door.

The river was strangely high and roaring, and no matter how much they tried, they couldn't get across it. Loki looked across the river and noticed a giantess—Geirrod's daughter—standing on the opposite shore with her skirts lifted. She was letting her menstrual blood—a powerful feminine-magic substance—drip into the river, and this was causing it to be unnaturally high. Thor picked up a rock and threw it across the river, hitting her in the head and knocking her over backwards.

Entering Geirrod's hall, they saw the giantess and her sister, and discovered that they were Gjalp and Greip, the daughters of Geirrod. Thor was shown to a chair, but the moment he sat he felt himself lifted into the air and saw the ceiling rushing towards him. The two giantesses were shoving his chair upwards, hoping to crush him against the beams. He barely managed to get Grid's staff between himself and the ceiling, and pushed down hard. His strength, and the unbreakable staff, forced him down onto the floor so hard that he broke their backs, killing them.

At this point Geirrod appeared with a roar of rage, seeing his dead daughters on the floor. He pulled a red-hot lump of half-molten iron out of the fire with tongs, and flung it at Thor with all his might; it would have slain the Thunderer if he had not grabbed it out of the air with Grid's iron glove and flung it back at Geirrod. The giant ducked behind a stone pillar, but Thor's strength aided by Grid's belt was so great that the iron lump smashed the pillar and shot into Geirrod's stomach, killing him. Geirrod's men tried to attack Thor, but he held them off with the iron staff long enough to grab Loki and flee; the roof gave way under the lack of the support pillar, and fell in just as they made it to the river.

Another mention of Gjalp and Greip is in a myth about nine maidens who turn a world mill, something like that of Fenja and Menja. In that story, Gjalp, Greip, and Sindur grind out fire through their turning of the mill. The other giant-maidens are Angeyja and Eyrgjafa, who mill mould; Jarnsaxa, who grinds the iron that comes from the water and clay of the world sea; and Atla, Egia, and Ulfrunand, who grind out fine sand for all the beaches. Little more is known of them except that.

Grid

Grid, a giantess, whose name means "Peace", once had a brief affair with Odin. Her son by Odin was Vidar, the strong and silent Asa, who went to live in Asgard with his father. There is some evidence that she might have been related to Jord, Odin's first etin-bride; at the very least, she had a soft spot for Jord's son. While traveling in Jotunheim, Thor helped Grid's young etin-son across a rushing river, saving his life. The young giant-lad brought him home for dinner to Grid's cave carved into the mountainside, and Thor told Grid that he was planning to visit the giant Geirrod without his hammer or magical gloves. (This was done on Loki's suggestion, as Loki had been recently captured by Geirrod and made to promise to lure Thor there weaponless as terms for his release.) Grid took pity on Thor and offered him the use of her old mittens, her moth-eaten staff, and a length of handspun string worn as a belt. He humored the old etin-woman by accepting them, and then realized upon donning them that they were magical implements and that she was a sorceress. Thanking her, he went out to have a successful adventure.

Hrungnir

Hrungnir was a stone-giant, one of the classic mountain-giants who have become so like their environment that they are living archetypes of it. He was said to have a stone head, a stone heart, and a mind of clay, and he carried a shield of stone. None too bright, but very determined, he spent his time on his mountain digging tunnels and caves. When he needed to travel, he used his one prized possession—a stallion named Gullfaxi, probably elf-bred, as are all the best horses in the Nine Worlds. One day while riding, he ran across a wandering Odin, who carelessly bet him his head that his horse couldn't outrun Sleipnir, who Odin was riding at the time.

Hrungnir, unfortunately, took him seriously. They raced so far and fast that they crossed the Thund Thvitr into Asgard; normally there was no way that a giant would have been able to do so, but Heimdall saw that Odin was neck-and-neck with the giant, and let them both pass, figuring that his father knew his business. The race ended at the walls of Valhalla, and Odin, not realizing that Hrungnir's horse would be so fast, laughingly claimed the bet to be a joke, and offered the hospitality of Valhalla to the surly giant.

The stone-giant came in, but he was still angry about the whole incident, and proceeded to get obnoxiously drunk. He boasted that if he wanted to, he could kill all the Aesir, bury Asgard, and carry all of Valhalla along with its residents (and Freyja and Sif as a side dish) back to Jotunheim. He also threatened to drink up all the mead in Asgard. As he got louder and more obstreperous, Odin called for Thor to act as the bouncer and get rid of him.

Thor stormed up to Valhalla, ready and willing to trounce Hrungnir, and the drunken giant—perhaps figuring that his end was near anyway, and wanting to at least get a shot at someone—challenged Thor to a duel on the border of Asgard and Jotunheim. As he was drunk and unarmed, and no giant had ever openly challenged Thor before, the audience drew in its breath. Thor accepted, of course, and even allowed Hrungnir the chance to go home and say his goodbyes.

Back in Jotunheim, the giants were appalled at Hrungnir's suicidal actions. While he was not well like by his neighbors and had no friends, many of them decided to pitch in and aid the drunken and cantankerous giant, more out of principle than anything else. Hrungnir was no warrior; he was an elderly stone-giant who knew nothing of battle, and many said that it was no honor for Thor to battle him. Some offered to take his place as his champion, but he would hear nothing of it in his drunken rage. Finally, the giants got together and created an enormous figure of clay, sort of a huge golem, bringing it to life by embedding a mare's heart in the clay. They tried to press weapons onto Hrungnir, but being no trained warrior, he refused them all and simply grabbed up a whetstone and several quarts of beer, which he drank en route to the Thund Thvitr, where the duel would be held. Escaping his would-be helpers, he hurried ahead of them to the appointed place.

Thor's servant Thjalfi, the elder son of Aurvandil and Groa, came running out and shouted to Hrungnir that Thor was attacking him from below, by tunneling through the ground. The drunken Hrungnir immediately put his shield on the ground and stood on it, and Thor hurled Mjollnir at him, striking him in the head and killing him. Hrungnir threw his whetstone at the hammer as it came, but Mjollnir shattered it. Fragments of the whetstone went everywhere, some embedding themselves into Thor's head. Hrungnir fell like a piece of stone, and his body fell across Thor's neck, pinning him to the ground.

The giants who had been hurrying to catch up with Hrungnir arrived at that moment, and saw that it was too late. They sent their golem-giant in anyhow, but it was not very well made and when Thjalfi ran at it screaming and waving a sword, it quailed and Thjalfi was able to chop its legs off, and then its head as it fell.

Meanwhile, Thor was being slowly choked by the corpse of his dead opponent, who lay on him like a rock. Thjalfi tried to move him, to no avail; just before Thor suffocated completely, his son Magni ran up and heaved the giant off of him. Grateful to his son, who had obviously inherited his strength, he gave the dead giant's horse Gullfaxi to him. Odin stepped in and tried to talk Thor into giving him the horse—giving rise to the notion that perhaps he had engineered the whole thing just as a way to get Gullfaxi—but for once Thor stood firm against his father and maintained that his son deserved the prize for saving his life.

To this day, the body of Hrungnir stands at the shore of the Thund Thvitr, an immense boulder, for this is what the stone-giant's corpse became. And to this day, there are pieces of whetstone in Thor's head, and it is bad to throw a whetstone, because it will cause Thor to get a headache, and possibly bring on a storm. One other interesting tidbit: The valknut (the emblem of the slain worn by Odin's folk) was historically referred to as "Hrungnir's Heart". We aren't sure why, except perhaps that Odin broke it.

Wanderers
On The Shores:
Island Giants

n order to be absolutely accurate, we are here classifying as an "island giant" not merely giants who live on the scattered islands off the coast of Jotunheim, but also those who live on the shores of that world, or who migrate back and forth between Jotunheim and Vanaheim. One might also include giants who were known to live by the ocean in Britain or the coasts of Scandinavia, since when a part of the Nine Worlds intrudes onto ours, the natural geographic features are usually extremely similar.

Island giants may have started as frost-giants or fire-giants or a mixture of the two, but they migrated to the shores and began to sail about in boats. At this point, their biology changed to meet their environment, as happens for Jotunfolk. Some changed more than others, depending on how solidly they connected with the land. Island giants became acclimated to a temperate zone, probably the most temperate of all the giant-lands, and became skilled seamen. In temperament, they became somewhat more "gentled" than etin-folk elsewhere, as well as physically smaller—if there are delicate-looking giantesses anywhere, it is in these areas. Some bonded with the ocean so well that they became sea-giants; it is clear that island giants are the intermediate step between the ancestral Jotnar and the mer-etins.

Island giants have the closest relationship to the Vanir, as the world-boundary between Jotunheim and Vanaheim lies on the ocean between them, and if a giant sails far enough, he ends up on Vanir shores. There is a thriving trade between the two worlds, orchestrated almost entirely by island giants and a few canny mountain-giants such as Gymir. Furs, feathers, tree fruits, nuts, wild herbs, and fine hardwoods are shipped across the ocean and the world-barrier, and grain, vegetables, and fine linen comes back the other way, to name just a few items. Billing, the Master of Vanir Trade, has married a Van woman and lives almost entirely in Vanaheim; he is not the only islander to have Vanir blood in his line, and some say that this is part of what has given the island giants their less fierce temperament.

However, not all island-giants are less than fierce, and some can rival any frost-thurse in ferociousness and bloodthirsty behavior. Grendel and his mother, in Beowulf, are often thought of as water-giants due to their seaside dwelling; as is the fabled giant Wade from Kudrun (Aurvandil's father), and the eight-handed giant of the waterfall in Norwegian legend. Certainly Grendel and his mother are good examples of seaside giants who are on the nastier end of the giant-spectrum.

Laufey

In the mountains above the Iron Wood, you will find a turreted stone cottage that belongs to Laufey, the mother of Loki and the sometime wife of Farbauti, Chief of the Lightning Clan. She lives by herself due to various disagreements with her husband, although he visits her often. Her three sons are all wanderers—Helblindi the island-giant who prefers the ocean islands, including the one from whence his mother came; Byleistr the storm-giant who attends intermittently on Thrym, and of course the infamous Loki. Any of them might be dropping in at any time, as they are all fond of their mother, and her cottage is really the only place that they might call home.

Laufey is slight, lovely, and very motherly. She is a tree-goddess, with a great affinity for the smaller understory trees. Visiting her home, if she is welcoming, will likely get you fed some soup and gently told some edifying tales. She is generally all right with visitors if they bring a gift and check first before coming. Planting trees in our world is always an appropriate offering for her.

But why is she listed in this chapter, under Island Giants, rather than Earth Giants, as she is so clearly an earthy figure? Her name refers to "The Lady Of the Leafy Isle", and this is where she came from originally, before Farbauti convinced her to come inland to his mountain. There is an island-giant delicacy to her; unlike the large and lavish Jord, she is frequently associated with slender, graceful trees.

Of Laufey

by Sophie Oberlander

I first encountered Laufey when I was in grave need of healing. I had been elfshot; my ability to ground and connect to any outer source of sustaining energy had been blocked and, by the time I met Laufey, completely cut off. For years, I have counted Loki amongst my closest friends. He has been good to me, often protecting and defending me with swift agility; so when He suggested that I seek out His mother, I didn't argue. I settled myself down and called upon Her—for while I was elfshot, I had been largely unable to journey. She was there immediately...it felt as though the room had been bathed in a golden light. She seems that way to me—Her presence feels goldish-green, the color of light filtering through a bower of autumn leaves, catching and refracting off the crisp, radiant colors.

She restored me, and began a process of healing that culminated with my being completely rid of the shot. Her wisdom was given with a firm clarity, a gentle detachment and deeply organic understanding of what constituted physical harmony for me. While not a Healer per se in the way that Eir is, Laufey has much to share about proper maintenance of what in Eastern esoteric traditions might be called 'chi.' She is all about proper flow, organic harmony, working with nature...

were I eclectic, I would say one might make strong comparisons about Her nature and that of the Native American Grandmother Spider. I've no lore to back this up at all, just the briefest wisp of a feeling that comes with Her presence.

Raven, in his introduction, mentions the surprising balance between the tribes in terms of function. We have Loki/Odin, Heimdall/Mordgud, Thor/Farbauti, etc. I would say that in Laufey, we have the Jotun equivalent to not only Frigga but Jordh. I could be mistaken, but there is that deep, intrinsic connection to the land, the flow of ley lines, the ability to center, ground and sustain oneself well. Symbolically at least, within Herself, She sustains fire and gave birth to change. Elementally, I would say Laufey is earth, fire and wood.

Her presence shines forth in places of solitude and silence, Her touch in the delicacy of spider webs, in dry, crackling leaves, and dew-drenched grasses. She is quietly contained flame, sunlight flickering through branches, the wood that sustains the flame and the deep reaching roots of trees. These are the images that come to mind with this Goddess. When I encountered Her, She never spoke much. She was very purposeful and moved with a clean, almost lyrical grace. The physical images that She brought to mind bore vague resemblance to Loki in coloring—one could definitely see the family resemblance: reddish/blond hair, pointed nose, pale alabaster skin—but there was a solidity that I have never sensed in Her son's nature; the opposite (not the absence) of mutability. She is not heavy in the way that many earth-oriented Deities feel heavy to me, rather She is expansive...holding forth not just in the soil, but the entire forest plain.

I would also say, given what I was permitted to observe of Her, that She has much to teach about mindfulness. There's something almost zen about her careful attention to detail and the smallest chore. I would also note that for all the gentle care She bestowed on me, I have no doubt of Her ferocity or power should She be challenged. There is might there. It is only that She does not wear it upon Her countenance for all to see.

I have a friend who keeps miniature willows in her garden in honor of Laufey, for we both see willows (miniature and weeping) with Her. It seems particularly appropriate for Her to honor Her in such a way that contributes to the good of the land. I myself frequently fain to Her and honor Her along with my household Deities. Suffice it to say, I do not know Her well, but I am forever grateful to Her for Her aid.

Invocation to Laufey
by Sophie Oberlander

Laufey, Wise Goddess, I hail You.
Mother of Loki, Nurturer of the flame,
I honor You.
You are rooted and ancient wisdom,
The strength of the trees that wind their roots
Deeply into the earth,
Of rich dark soil,
Of solitude, and seasons,
Dissolution and quiet change.
You are patient endurance,
Wise weaver of the threads of fate,
Luck-warder, mother of warriors,
Fierce defender, skilled healer.
All of these things You have been.
You restore and rebalance.
You sustain
And grant to Your children
The enduring strength of the forest,
The quickness of flame,
The swiftness of light, liquid and untouchable.
Lady of the Leafy Isle, no ornament
To Farbauti's hall but to Your own alone
Wherein You shine, ever shall I speak Your praises.
Hail, Laufey.

Fjolvar

Mentioned in only one lay, Fjolvar is an island giant whose domain is the island Algron (All-Green). He has seven daughters and a very large brothel, of which his daughters are the stars. The brothel is famous throughout the Nine Worlds, with workers of almost every race—Jotun, Duergar, Vanir, Midgard human, and the occasional hapless Alfar. He has no Aesir employees yet, but he is always on the lookout for talent. Odin discreetly visits his island from time to time, and once taunted his naive son Thor about his dealings there.

Billing

The giant Billing is the "Master of the Vanir Trade". He is Gilling's brother, Rind's father and Vali's grandfather. Although he is a giant, he has strong ties with the Vanir—one of his wives is a Vana—and he is in charge of handling the trade between Vanaheim and Jotunheim. He is mediator and bargainer, working towards the best deal for both sides, and both sides respect him for his fairness and neutrality. His hall is located at a large port on the Jotunheim-facing coast of Vanaheim; it is as much warehouse as living space, and he lives there with his Vanir wife, whose name we do not know. He also has another winter hall in the northeastern mountains of Jotunheim, but he rarely goes there, preferring to let his daughter Rind (the child of an older marriage with a frost-giantess) take care of it. Billing is technically a frost-giant, but he is that rarest of things: a rime-thurse who has grown accustomed to warm weather and the ocean. Although he is well-disposed towards human travelers, he is very busy and has little time for their questions.

Billing was sometimes also referred to as the King of the Ruthenians; this is an old term for the Scandinavian Rus tribe who settled in Russia and took up the speech of the East Slavic peoples.

Aurvandil/Egil

Aurvandil (also known as Orvandil, Orwandil, and Earendel) is a difficult figure to trace and discover, although his legacy lies in many different mentions from the Norse to the Anglo-Saxons to modern-day Tolkien. In some accounts he is a giant; in others it is not mentioned and he has non-giant relatives. Certainly his wife, Groa, is listed as a giantess; their son, Svipdag, the suitor of Mengloth, is conversely seen as a human hero.

In the Prose Edda, he is Aurvandil the Bold, friend of Thor, who carried him across the freezing and poisonous Elivagar river in a basket on his back. When Aurvandil's big toes protruded and froze, Thor obligingly snapped them off and threw them into the sky, where they became two stars—Alcor in the Big Dipper and Rigel in Orion. Thor recounts this story proudly to Aurvandil's wife Groa.

The figure of Aurvandil is generally seen as an archer, aiming for the stars; he is associated with the Futhorc rune Yr, which is a bow and arrow. He is also identified with Egil (pronounced Ay-ell), the brother of Volund/Wayland the Smith. The third brother is Slagfinn. On the Frank's Casket, a carved ivory box circa 700 A.D., the figure of Volund is shown with an archer-figure labeled "Aegili". In the Hymskvida, Thor leaves his goats with Egil and Groa while going off on his latest adventure, bringing the names of Aurvandil and Egil together again. While we generally prefer not to syncretize clearly separate deities and wights, Aurvandil and Egil do seem to be two names for the same star-archer hero.

If Aurvandil is the brother of Volund, who is a human hero, he may well be simply the husband of a giantess rather than a giant himself. Volund, who learned his magical smithcraft from the Duergar, is the son of Wade, who is the brother of Nordian, an alternate spelling of Njord. That would make the brothers Vanic-descended, and younger cousins of Frey and Freyja. Being the nephew of Njord would make sense given that

Aurvandil and Groa are coastal-dwellers, and Aurvandil is also associated with ships and sailing.

On the other hand, Wade is also spoken of as a giant—actually a sea-giant, which adds to Aurvandil's shore-dwelling position. As the Vanir gods are more likely to wed giantesses than the Aesir, for a variety of reasons, it might make sense to see Wade—and possibly Aurvandil—as half Vanir and half Jotun. Also, there is a reference in Anglo-Saxon folklore to a giant named Wendil or Wandil who steals a magic spring. The UPG that some folk have gotten from working with Aurvandil is that his background is complex and multiracial, and that this is part of what gives him his heroism. Like his son Svipdag who is racially uncertain but who is magically destined to win the heart of the famed giantess Mengloth, Aurvandil is a hero who can connect his kinship with more than one race of people.

Another, possibly more famous reference to him, is in an Old English Christian poem where "Earendel" is seen as not only a star but "the brightest of angels over Midgard". Scholars believe that this references a pagan mythological figure, inserted into a Christian poem for camouflage and syncretism. J.R.R. Tolkien was fascinated with this poem, and used it as the basis for the Earendil character in *The Silmarillion*. Svipdag (known as Swaefdag to the Saxons, who counted him as an ancestor of one of their royal dynasties) himself first names his father by the nickname "Spring-Chill", showing echoes of the Wendil story, then names him "Sun-bright", which reflects the star-solar Earendel poem. He also names as his father's father Fjolkald, or "Much-Cold", which would imply a frost-giant heritage behind his island-giant father.

Aurvandil makes another appearance in Saxo's *History of the Danes* as Horwendil, a hero who son, Amleth, inspired the myth for Shakespeare's original Hamlet. Son of Gerwendil and brother of Feng, he is supposedly a king of Jutland who goes a-viking, kills the King of Norway, and marries his daughter Gerutha (remarkably similar to Groa). His brother Feng kills him and takes his wife, and his son Amleth avenges him. In medieval Germany, Orentil was the hero of a poem by the same name, the hero of which is first shipwrecked at sea and then returns home as a mysterious hero.

It has been suggested that the second half of his name is a reference to the tribe of the Vandals, and that he was their divine ancestor just as Ing/Frey spawned the Ynglings and Saxnot the Saxons. However this might be, the star that was known as "Aurvandil's Toe", and sometimes just "Aurvandil's Beacon", was said to have been loved by sailors as a navigation point. Theories as to which star this was vary widely. Some claim the constellation Orion, some have even named Venus. Either way, Aurvandil survives as a figure of hope: the archer forever aiming at the star on the horizon, doing heroic deeds in order to achieve it, and eventually becoming the symbol of that very star. As a giant with Vanir and human connections, whose good friend is Thor of the Aesir, he is a figure that crosses boundaries as well, and can be called on to build bridges between warring spiritual groups through the bridge of heroic deeds.

Groa

Aurvandil/Egil's wife Groa was an island giantess, but she was also a sorceress and healer. Thor consulted her in the hopes that she could remove the battle-shrapnel of Hrungnir's whetstone from his head, but he wouldn't stop talking, and while he regaled her with tales of how he had gone on an adventure with Aurvandil, had crossed the icy poisonous river Elivagar, and had snapped off Aurvandil's big toe and thrown it up into the sky to make a star, Groa became distracted and couldn't finish her spell. The result was that Thor had to live with shrapnel in his head.

Groa is mentioned as the mother of Svipdag, and in the poem Grougaldr he raises her from the dead in order to ask her how to win the giantess Mengloth. (The other one of her sons by Aurvandil, Thjalfi, spent a good deal of time as a page for Thor.) It does indeed seem that Groa is dead and dwells in Helheim—although the cause of her death is unknown—but in order to speak to her, one must have the permission of Hela. She is not unwilling to teach people magic, but one must visit Helheim and receive one's teachings there, which can prove difficult. When raised from the Dead, Groa teaches her son Svipdag nine charms to use in his quest to find and woo Mengloth.

The first charm is the rather awful paralysis-enchantment charm that Odin used to rape Rind; although not very ethical, one can see why she included it for her son's wooing of a proud giantess. The second charm is for being lost on the road, and calling on the Norn Urda to show one's destined way. The third parts the water of dangerous streams; the fourth makes foes suddenly wish to be friends; the fifth will burst chains, fetters, and bindings; the sixth is for calming the sea under your boat; and the seventh is a charm against freezing. The eighth charm is interesting, and its purpose is open to speculation—it is to guard against the curse of a dead Christian woman, whatever that might be. The ninth is to provide a headful of ready wit in case one has to go at a game of riddles with any Jotun. All in all, it is a fine toolkit of magic to protect the wanderer in Jotunheim.

Helblindi

Helblindi is the eldest son of Laufey by an island giant who died before she met Farbauti and agreed to journey with him to the Iron Wood. He is a wanderer, moving from island to island in a small boat, trading and traveling and telling stories. He prefers his family connections to not be known, as he is rather overshadowed by the reputation of his younger brother Loki.

Ocean's Depths:
The Sea-Giants

he presence of the ocean giants in the Nine Worlds is a tribute to the amazing shapeshifting evolutionary qualities of the Jotun race. Of all the types of etins, the sea-giants are arguably the most altered from their initial form. It is speculated that they may have started out as island giants and quickly went further into the ocean, changing irrevocably. Although this theory is only due to observation, it does seem true that although other sorts of giants can adapt to various climates, at least enough to survive and be temporarily comfortable, the sea-giants are permanently formed to live in the ocean. They can breathe both air and water; they can shapeshift enough to form legs with which to walk or tails with which to swim, but they do not come out of the ocean for long. It seems that in so thoroughly transforming themselves as to be able to survive in the alien element of the sea, they have reached a point of no return.

In the historical myths of the northern tradition, the sea was both revered and feared. The ability to sail with reasonable accuracy and safety was what built the short-lived Viking empire (and before that, brought in a important survival food in the form of large-scale fishing in the North Atlantic), yet the sea itself was a constant source of threat. This is where we find the differences between the Vanir god Njord, who is in charge of ships and coastlines, and the Jotnar gods Aegir and Ran who move with the energy of the ocean itself. Both were propitiated, but Njord was generally friendly, while the ocean-giants could swing from friend to foe with a moment's notice.

All the countries of northern Europe border on the sea, and fishing and seafaring are an important aspect to the economy of every one, especially fjord-surrounded Scandinavia. (The Vikings called the River Eider, a main water-channel leading to the sea, "Aegir's Door".) However, the Age of Migrations, as it is now referred to, brought a huge upswing in shipbuilding (as can be seen in the ship museums in Oslo and Roskilde) and changed the face of Europe. Seafaring became even more crucial, and even more propitiated. Sailors threw gold (and sometimes sacrificed animals or humans) over the side of their ships in order to ask for the aid of Aegir and his family.

With our modern forms of travel, we tend to forget the importance that the sea and its gods had for our ancestors. We put the sea-gods aside in our worship, ignoring the fact that three-quarters of our planet is still their home, not ours. I have been to many a blot where Aegir is referred to merely as "the beer-god" and thanked briefly for his gift of booze, while nothing is said about his awesome oceanic power, nor his wife and daughters. It may be that many modern northern-tradition groups place a higher priority on becoming intoxicated than in revering the forces of Nature that surround us.

Sea giants seem to be more capricious and playful than the other varieties of etin, which is not unusual considering the general notion of the sea as a capricious entity. However, their ideas of playfulness tend to be a little more bloodthirsty than most—remember that mermaids seduced sailors into drowning themselves, and mermen liked to pull down small boats or incite shark attacks. They laugh more than other etins, and sing more even than fire-giants. They have developed their own underwater language, which sounds rather like dolphins or whale-song, although they can all still speak the old etin-tongue.

Besides Aegir's family, there are other Jotnar who could be considered water-giants. Jormundgand, the Midgard Serpent, clearly has some sort of water-giant throwback blood. The mermaids of the northern tradition are all considered etins of one form or another; unlike popular conceptions of them, they are not always considered beautiful—some are pretty ugly—although the mer-women are able to put on an illusion of beauty in order to lure in the unsuspecting.

We tend to think of water as being the most gentle of the elements. The adjectives used to describe it symbolically all tend to center around things like "nurturing" and "healing" and "comforting". The truth is, though, that the largest single body of water on the planet comes not in the form of warm hotsprings or gentle babbling brooks. It's ocean, and ocean is wild and ferocious and drowns people. It is also the source of life, something that is no conundrum to anyone who understands Jotun nature—and thus, through them, nature itself.

This can be seen in the nature of the sea-giants, particularly Aegir, Ran, and their daughters the Nine Undines. They are not (or not merely) the nurturing, welcoming waters; they are the sea that eats people. As in all things, when you confront the elements through Jotun nature, you start with the natural disasters. The sea-etins can bear you up and teach you all about the powers of water, or they can drown you.

Our European ancestors understood this as well. The sea gods—from Aegir to Poseidon to Tiamat—may have been propitiated, perhaps even desperately, but their powers were rarely invoked. The sea was seen as too dangerous an entity to attempt to harness or control. Today, when global warming is raising sea level and creating more tumultuous weather, we may again find ourselves in the situation of regarding the sea with its original ancient mix of fear and respect, which it has never really ceased to merit.

> Sea runes you should know to save from wreck
> Sail-steads on the sea:
> Carve them on the bow and the blade of the rudder,
> Etch them with fires on the oars:
> Though high the breakers and blue the waves
> You shall sail safe into harbor.
> —*The Lay of Sigdrifa*

Aegir

How shall the sea be referred to? By calling it Ymir's blood, visitor to the gods, husband of Ran, father of Aegir's daughters, whose names are Himinglava, Duva, Blodughadda, Hevring, Unn, Hronn, Bylgja, Bara, Kolga; Land of Ran and of Aegir's daughters and of ships and of terms for sea-ship, of keel stem, planks, strake, of fish, ice: Sea King's way and roads, no less ring of the islands, house of the sands and seaweed and skerries, Land of fishing tackle and of sea birds of sailing wind. As Orm Barteyiarskald said: 'Out on the sea-bank of good vessels Ymir's blood roars.'

—Skalskaparmal

The oldest—and likely the first—sea giant is Aegir, the Lord of the Ocean. He has most certainly gained enough power to be considered a deity, and not just because he has alliances with the Aesir. Aegir commands the entirety of every ocean in the Nine Worlds, with the possible exception of the stretch of dead, empty ocean between Helheim and Muspellheim. If you want to cross the big waters, you have to propitiate him, or his wife or daughters.

The oceans of the Nine Worlds are largely connected; the largest lies between Jotunheim and Vanaheim and brushes against the shores of Asgard; the Vanaheim ocean is where he keeps his underwater palace, Aegirheim. The second-largest ocean is the one that surrounds Midgard, in which the Great Snake lies. The third (and oldest) lies between Jotunheim and Niflheim, and freezes into ice at the far end. The fourth, as we have mentioned, is the stretch of dead, quiet water between Helheim and Muspellheim that borders Dead Man's Shore on one side, and the lava beaches where stand the half-built Naglfari on the other.

Aegir's original name seems to have been Hler, which scholars translate as either "shelterer" or "concealer", and he was the third and youngest son of Fornjotr by an island-giantess. Later, after becoming the chief of the growing number of sea-giants, he took on the name Aegir, which simply means "ocean". Even today in parts of the world, Aegir's name is called before faring out to sea, and a certain type of storm-wave is referred to as an "aeg".

Aegir is generally shown as a middle-aged Jotun crowned with seaweed, with blue-green skin and green hair and beard. He carries a spear—one of the poetic names for the sea in Old English is *garsecg*, or spearman. (In this way he much resembles Poseidon, who looks and acts similarly, although his "spear" is the trident.) The sea god himself comes across as very jovial— he is the brewer of the best beer in the Nine Worlds, which is imported all over and highly prized, as is the fine table that he sets for visitors. His beer is brewed in a mile-deep kettle that Thor and Tyr took from Tyr's father Hymir, in order that they might extort him for even more food and drink.

Of all his connections, Aegir is most closely allied with the Vanir. Indeed, his alliance with the Aesir seems to be largely one of business, and rather shady business at that. In the saga of Hymir, Aegir is seen as being blatantly shaken down for food and ale by the Aesir, who routinely move in on him in the winter, demanding his hospitality and stripping his supplies. Aegir is himself a generous and magnanimous host, and his famous food and beer, more than anything else, has gained him alliances. His hall is accessible off the coast of Hlesey Island, where merfolk escort visitors down to eat, drink, and be merry. Nixies and mermaids serve and hang around the hall, seducing visitors. The cups in his hall are always full, magically refilling themselves with his copious beer. As no fire can burn there, light and warmth is provided by a pile of enchanted gold in the middle of his floor, which led to "Aegir's Fire" being yet another kenning for gold.

The other side of Aegir, however, makes us remember that he is still a Jotun god. A ship that was wrecked at sea was referred to as having gone "into Aegir's jaws". He caused storms at sea, either to do in the ungrateful or just because he felt like it. Sailors both loved and feared him, often making elaborate sacrifices to him; fifth-century Saxons routinely sacrificed a tenth of their captured victims to Aegir when they were ready to leave a conquered land over the sea. "The sea has snapped the ties of my kindred," says Egill in the great poem of mourning, the Sonatorrek, composed after his young son was lost at sea. "Could I have avenged my cause with the sword, the Ale-Brewer would be no more." Behind the jovial front lies a relentless deity who demands sacrificial victims of one sort or another. Aegir's fingers are clawed, reminding us of that part of his nature.

While his hall is beautiful, bedecked with coral and gems, it is also laid about with the wealth that he has taken from every sunken ship, which is quite a lot of stolen plunder. If he is pleased with you, he may give you some of his collected valuables to take back, although this is rare—he likes the physical plunder as much as his wife enjoys the plundered souls.

Offerings to Aegir might include bread, or polished stones, or anything that he would not be likely to get otherwise. If you don't live near an ocean, make a large bowl of salt water and drop food into it for him. Don't try to give Aegir beer; you couldn't make anything that would rival his, and he seems vaguely offended by modern chemical-soaked beers.

Ran

Ran, the wife of Aegir, is a delicate-looking sea-etin with blue-green skin. Her long black hair drags on the ground behind her when she walks through Aegir's hall; its ends trail off into nothingness, and this is because her hair is magically linked to all the seaweed that grows in all the northern oceans. Like her daughters, she can appear in mermaid form or with legs, although she is more likely than they are to take the latter shape, perhaps because her job as hostess of Aegirheim requires her to spend more time walking on mother-of-pearl floors than swimming. Her weapon is the net, with which she drags people down to their deaths; her name is translated by scholars as meaning "robber" or "ravager" or "plunderer" (though Alby Stone has proposed that 'Ran' is derived from the old Indo-European word *rani* meaning 'lady'). Ran is very much the flirtatious siren—of all the etins, female sea-giants are most likely to make eyes at humans, although to take them up on it can be disastrous. She is the maker of all sea-storms in the northern oceans.

In many ways, Ran acts out the darker and more destructive side of the sea-etin nature; unlike Aegir who comes across as friendly but might then turn on you, Ran makes no bones about being a ravager. She is beautiful, but her teeth are sharp and pointed and her fingers are clawed. When she smiles, your blood runs cold—or it ought to. Her hobby is collecting dead souls, with which she populates Aegirheim. While Aegir is both an "honorary" Aesir and an "honorary" Vanir, and tries to balance alliances with all of them, there is no question where Ran's alliances lie.

A folk-belief quoted in one of the Icelandic sagas is that if drowned people appeared at their own funeral feasts, it was a sign that Ran had given them a good welcome into her hall. In Fridhjof's Saga, it is said to have been a lucky thing to have gold on one's person if lost at sea, and the hero went so far to distribute small pieces of gold among his men when they were caught in a storm, so that they should not go empty-handed into Ran's hall if they were drowned. Ran's hospitality might extend for centuries, with the drowned souls feasting and partying and singing in her hall, but sooner or later the capricious Queen of the Sea tires of them, and sends them away. Where? Helheim, of course. She is, after all, Jotun through and through, and so would rather swell Hela's ranks than those of the Aesir gods her husband so faithfully feeds and waters.

On the other hand, dropping gold over the side of a ship and saying a prayer might well mollify her into granting you safe passage and good journeying. Those who were lucky at sea were said to be much loved by Ran, although this was granted to be an ambivalent blessing, as if she liked you enough, then it was only a matter of time before she brought you to be with her.

Invocation to Aegir and Ran

Lord and Lady of the Depths,
Keepers of the great flocks and herds
That float by the millions
Through glass-green waves,
Lady Ran of the ten-times-fingering weed,
Your hair spread throughout the worlds,
Lord Aegir of the great currents
And the waves that keep the ship afloat,

Generous in your bounty,
Capricious in your favor,
Brewer of ale for gods and lost souls,
Keep us safe as we pass over your realm
In life, in dreams, and in mystery.

The Nine Undines

Their names are a litany of the powers of the Ocean: Kolga the Cold One, and Duva the Hidden One are the eldest, twins in age and both reserved. Blodughadda, the Blood-Haired and bloodthirsty, is next in age. Then there is big-bellied Bara, and Bylgja of the Breaker; then another pair of twins—the terrible Hronn of the Whirlpool and the anguished, wailing Hevring. Then comes Unn, the Undine of the Tides; and Himinglava, the Fair-Weather Undine, is the youngest and most fickle of the lot.

— "Heimdall's Birth", Jotun legend

The nine daughters of Aegir and Ran are a sisterly lot, in that they stick together and nothing pries them apart. Although they might take lovers, the idea of any lover coming between their primary sisterly bond is ludicrous. In fact, if one wishes to become lovers with one of them (especially the younger, prettier ones like Unn or Himinglava), the unfortunate suitor is often required to be lovers with others of them as well (especially the more gruesome ones such as Hronn or Hevring or Blodughadda) in order to prove his sincerity. Those who are not up to the challenge are summarily discarded. The truth is that an affair with any of the Nine Sisters has a small chance of ending in death for any would-be lover, which one ought to keep in mind. Hurting any one of them will not only bring down the wrath of the other eight, it will also bring the fatal wrath of Aegir and Ran onto you; they are protective of their lovely, vicious offspring and will not allow them to be trifled with. They all like blood offerings; a drop put into the ocean or into salt water will do.

I met the Nine Sisters while visiting nine beaches on the coast between Cape Cod and central Maine. I was studying the elements, and Water was the one that I had the hardest time grasping. I asked for their aid, and they helped me to understand nine Mysteries of water. In the process, I learned something about the Ladies themselves.

When they visited me in the surf—only after I pricked my finger and bled into the water for them—I was struck with how unlike the folkloric beautiful mermaids of stories and cartoons they were. Their fingers were clawed and their teeth long and sharp; their shoulders were muscled and their faces somehow oddly shaped, with strange tilted eyes that changed colors with the sea. Some wore rough necklaces and earrings of shells and bone shards. The first that I met, Blodughadda (whose name means Blood-Haired), had long red hair and a shark's tail and fin; she was the mistress of blood mysteries, and the rivers that empty into the sea, the capillary system of the world.

There are two sets of twins among the Nine Sisters, and the eldest of the lot are Kolga (Cold One) and Duva (Hidden One). Kolga is white-haired and pale-skinned and is the mistress of the icy Arctic waters and the ice floes; her power is Cold. Frost-thurse blood is strong in her. Duva is the keeper of islands, sea mists, and hidden treasure, and rarely shows her face behind her blond hair.

The second set of twins are the terrible Hronn and Hevring; Hronn (Sucking Wave) is hideous and eel-tailed (and the only one of the sisters to have short hair, fair and pale), and is the mistress of the Whirlpool, and all vertical currents. Her power is Fear, and she is called upon to bring strength in the midst of terror. Hevring (Heaving Wave) is decorated with strands of jellyfish, has long black hair, and is usually weeping. She is the mistress of the sea's surface currents, and her power is Sorrow.

Bylgja (Breaker) is associated with seals and wave-horses, and the shore currents that drag swimmers out to sea; her hair is seal-brown and her power is the force of the tide. Unn (Billow) is the mistress of the rhythm of the tides; she wears her light brown hair in many tiny braids woven with shells, and wears many ropes of shells for counting on. She rules the sea's relationship to the sky, and seabirds are her pets. Her power is the use of the tides for moving in time; she has a strong relationship with Mani, the Moon God.

Bara (Big Wave) is a truly giant-sized mermaid, huge and fat, and usually carrying a club with which she strikes the land. Her hair is long and dark, and she laughs often. Her tail is that of a whale's, and her power is the ocean's erosion of the land. Himinglava (Sun Shining Through) is the fair-weather mermaid, the youngest and fairest of the lot, dolphin-tailed, chestnut-haired and fickle, the bringer of sunshine through the storm.

Eldir and Fimafeng

Eldir, whose name means "Fire-Kindler", is Aegir's butler and majordomo. He is a sea-etin, but is usually seen for some reason either in humanlike form or in the shape of a magnificent green-black cockerel. He welcomes and seats people, and breaks up impending fights, rudeness, and anything that might ruin the frith of the hall. He never forgets a face or a name, although he may attempt to turn you away if he thinks that you might cause trouble. Aegir has a great deal of respect for this fussy etin, and will generally take his word on most things, so appealing higher may not help you.

Aegir's other servant, Fimafeng, is younger and more cheerful. His name means "quick service" or 'handy service", and he knows where everything is and where to find it. He is not shocked by any request, and is a good guide around Aegirheim, as one can ask him embarrassing questions and he will be better able to provide the answers than etiquette-conscious Eldir.

The Lights Greater
And Lesser:
The Sky-Etins

e tend to forget that in the Norse cosmology, the entities that personify the Sun, Moon, Day and Night are also etins. They are not considered a genetic tribe of Jotnar unto themselves; they are giants who have been set to do a particular job from which they almost never get a break. They have sacrificed themselves, as it were, to bring light and darkness to the Nine Worlds. As such, they are close-knit and are culturally a tribe unto themselves.

Before the Aesir set up their day-and-night technology, the three ancient worlds were lit by the pale greenish light of the tree, and the glowing fires of Muspellheim. This gave a permanent twilight to Niflheim and the underworld. After the flood, Jotunheim was formed, and as it was closer to Muspellheim it got more light, a dull orange glow seeping through the world-barrier. When the Aesir set up Asgard, they put together a system whereby the Sun and Moon roll through the sky of each world on a set path. Each planetary-keeper rides in a chariot, and each has a herald before them to clear the way, who rides on a horse.

The gods of the Sun and Moon are Sunna and Mani, respectively. They were originally the children of a giant named Mundilfari, who was known as the Turner of Time. They were snatched up by the Aesir to forever ride the sky in turn. They tend to be fairly close to the Aesir and get along with them well, with the exception of Hati and Skoll, who do not consider themselves part of the Sky-Etin clan, being Iron Wood to the core. When the Sky-Etins marry, it is usually to fire-etins, with the exception of the ancient frost-thurse Nott, who has taken many lovers of many races.

Mundilfari

Mundilfari, or Mundilfoeri, was known as the "Turner Of Time", and was said to be able to manipulate time with great skill, a talent know to only a few giants before or since. His children were said to have been snatched by the Aesir to be the Sun and Moon because of their great beauty, but it is more likely that they were taken because of his bloodlines in them; although Sunna and Mani cannot turn time like their father, they have inherited a talent for sensing the paths of time, and knowing where paths of time and probability diverge. Obviously, this is a useful talent for people who are in charge of the daily timekeeping.

Besides Sunna and Mani, we know of a third child of Mundilfoeri— their sister Sinthgunt, whose name appears next to Sunna in an old Germanic charm. We know little more about Mundilfari, except that he may not be still alive.

Sunna

Sunna is tall, golden, and beautiful, and has been called All-Bright, Everglow, and Fair Wheel. Her personality is impulsive and fiery, almost childlike in her innocence and enthusiasm. She is married to a fire-giant, one of the sons of Surt, whose name is Glow. Since her job never stops, he generally visits her in the chariot. (One assumes that she gets the day off occasionally.) He cares for their young daughter, who is being groomed to take over Sunna's dangerous job should something happen to her (such as Ragnarok).

Sunna charges across the sky every day with wild abandon, never swerving from her path in the sheer love of chariot-driving. Her Sun Chariot is drawn by two golden horses, Allsvinn (All-Swift), and Arvaker

(Early-Waker), who pull the sun behind them. Its heat would be too much for them, except that Odin created a talisman called the Isarnkol, which hangs above their shoulders on the double yoke and constantly spreads cool mists, protecting them from heatstroke.

Sunna: Forgotten Goddess of the Sun
by Sophie Oberlander

> I hail Sunna, glorious in Her power.
> It is Her life-giving warmth
> That nourishes and sustains us.
> I give praise to this radiant Goddess.
> I celebrate Her glorious strength.
> Without Her loving touch,
> Our fields would wither.
> Without Her gentle care,
> Our world would be bleak and black.
> I will praise Her gifts,
> More beautiful than amber,
> More precious than gold.
> Hail, Sunna, life-giver and protector! [1]

As a Goddess, we underestimate the Sun. In many pantheons, the sun is embodied as a God, so this is somewhat understandable, but that paradigm does not hold true for all cultures. In the Northern tradition most especially, the healing, life-giving power of the Sun is personified by the Goddess Sunna (also called Sol or even Sigil, a name which links Her power to that of Victory in battle and indeed in all worthy endeavors). To those who lived in the cold and often harsh climate of Northern Europe before the conveniences of modern technology, the Sun's power was paramount for survival. A poor harvest might have immense negative impact on the community and despite our common stereotype of the Vikings as rapacious raiders, most were farmers, dependent on the vagaries of Mother Nature and the blessings of Sunna for their well-being. It is odd then, that as we remember and reconstruct the spiritual traditions of our forebears, that we should pay so little homage to such a fundamentally important Deity.

Surprisingly, even amongst modern Heathens, Sunna plays little role in daily worship. Perhaps it is simply that She has no fanciful tales to augment Her devotion. Perhaps like the purloined letter of Poe fame, Her presence is simply so obvious as to be easily overlooked. She's only mentioned once in Heathen lore after all, in the Second Merseburg Charm, a healing Charm found in a 10th century Old High German manuscript that celebrates Woden's power as healer. Many scholars such as Rudolf Simek even interpret this scant mention of Sunna as simply literary convention, an allusion to the healing power of the sun.[2]

The Sun embodied as "Sol" fares a bit better. She is mentioned as one of the Asynjur in several Eddic lays, most notably in the Gylfaginning, part of the "Prose Edda." Here we are told that there was once a man named Mundilfari and he had two children who were so beautiful, that he dared to name them after the Sun and the Moon (Sol and Mani respectively). The Gods punished him for his hubris by taking the children up and setting them in service to the actual celestial bodies for which they had been named. The human Sol and Mani forever drive the carts bearing the actual Sun and Moon (of the same names) and by this the hours of the day are set and maintained. We're also told that two giants, so hating the order that the Gods imposed upon creation, transformed themselves into hungry wolves and they constantly chase the celestial carts. At Ragnarok, the end of the ordered age, they will capture and devour the actual Sun and Moon plunging the world into darkness. [3]

The loss of the Sun and Moon is one of only a handful of traumatic events said to herald or occur at Ragnarok. So technically, Sunna's absence has immense eschatological import. She is one of the foundational pillars of an ordered, healthy, hale and whole universe, world and society. In the Germanic languages, the words 'whole', 'hale' and 'holy' are all connected-essentially, one cannot exist without the other. The Sun therefore, makes the world holy, and by doing so defines the 'inangarð,' the sacred enclosure of a healthy community. Given that the Gods themselves were often called the "Reginn" or "the Ordered Powers" and that order and structure was a defining characteristic of wholeness and that which was 'halig', or holy, we can see that the Sun is a very important Goddess indeed!

To understand the true power of the Sun to the Norse mind, we must go back further than the Viking age, which given the unfettered onslaught of Christianity across Europe was, in fact, the twilight of the ancestral religion. To truly understand the intrinsic devotion to the Sun, we must look at Bronze Age worship. Simek notes that there are numerous rock carvings glorifying the Sun[4] and one of the earliest images of devotion portray the Sun not as a Deity but as a sphere drawn by a horse.[5] The Roman historian Tacitus also notes an affinity for Sun-worship amongst the Germanic tribes whose practices he records in "Germania" and here, in chapter 10, we see again the image of the Sun being drawn forth by horses. Many of these images of the horse-drawn sun-cart date back prior to 600 BCE.

Branston also draws an interesting parallel between the ancient image of the sun disk and the protective qualities of a shield,[6] leaving one to speculate on the possibility that to the ancient Germanic mind, the Sun was the world's shield in the ongoing battle against chaos, disorder, and against that which was un-halig and thus both unholy and unhealthy. Thus Sol might be invoked as a protective Deity, to ward one against harm and disease. She becomes then not only the mighty emblem of fertility and life, but also of safety, security and strength.

Even well into modern times, the Sun-wheel remains a very powerful religious symbol throughout the world, not only amongst the Norse. Variations of it are found amongst Native Americans, Japanese, and even Tibetan religious art. In fact, had Adolf Hitler not corrupted and misused this symbol so grievously in the form of the swastika, it might well have become the most commonly worn religious symbol amongst Heathens today. As it is, however most are wary of reclaiming the sun wheel, even in its most abstract form, and few Heathens that I know are comfortable wearing it for obvious reasons. We may know the actual origin and power of the symbol, but it has been so corrupted in the modern psyche as to possibly be unredeemable.[7]

Be that as it may, for thousands of years before the upstart Bavarian psychotic became obsessed with it, the sun wheel functioned as a potent symbol of the Sun's Divine power. It represented the might of Sol to manifest in our lives, to bring healing, abundance, fertility of land (most especially the harvest) and of the body. Though we may not have tangible, physical evidence of the other Gods on a day to day basis, the passage of the Sun across the heavens was easily viewable by our ancestors and Her gifts immediately apparent.

Many of the holy tides, the holidays celebrated within both Heathenry and Neo-Paganism, revolve around the yearly cycle of the Sun and Her control of the earthly seasons. To peoples such as the Germans and Scandinavians who spent the winter months largely sequestered inside with their extended family, the return of the longer days of spring and summer must have proved welcome relief after the tedious and frugal months of winter.

Today, we may not be bound to the cycles of the seasons in the same way that our ancestors were, but we can still benefit from a certain mindfulness of the Sun's cycles. Most of us live busy, harried lives made all the busier by the supposed convenience of modern technology. The rhythm of our days is still largely governed by Sunna's cycle across the heavens: we rise in the morning, work throughout the day and seek our rest as She disappears into the Western horizon. Without Her life-giving light and warmth, the earth would be a barren, froze, lifeless rock. Technology enables us to forget about Her for a time, but when all is said and done, we are still dependent on Her for nourishment. Modern science has even proven that some people will suffer physically, mentally and emotionally if they do not receive enough of Her life-giving rays.[8] In our rush through our work day, many of us who ignore the rhythm She sets for us end up overworked, over-stressed and ill.

Sunna is our Pace-setter. She orders our days just as She did for our ancestors. She is our defender, teaching us how to maintain health and well-being even in the midst of industry and endeavor. Pausing as we go throughout our day: upon rising, at Her zenith at noon, and at sunset to thank Her for Her blessings, to reach out and bask in the awareness of Her presence, is a powerful yet simple means of connecting to this oft overlooked Goddess. Looking to Her to be our guide as we strive to maintain a healthy work-life balance is a subtle way of nourishing spiritual awareness in the sturm and drang of our daily, often numbingly mundane lives. That after all, is one of Her greatest lessons: nourishing a sense of the holy both within and without. Sunna teaches us to create the holy in our lives by managing our time wisely, mindfully and well.

[1]Exploring the Northern Tradition" by Galina Krasskova, New Page Books, 2005. P. 116.

[2]Dictionary of Northern Mythology," by Rudolf Simek, D.S. Brewer Press, 2000 p. 303.

[3]But following Ragnarok, there will be an age of rebirth and we find that the Moon and the Sun were not devoured before they had each had a child, also a celestial body which would in the new age, replace them on their daily journey across the heavens, thus restoring light and ordered time to the worlds.

[4]Simek p. 297.

[5]"Gods of the North," by Brian Branston, Thames and Hudson, 1980, p. 69.

[6] Branston, p. 69.

[7]I do know several Heathens who wear an early Bronze Age version of this symbol that bears little conscious resemblance to the swastika and therefore does not hold the same negative connotations to the modern mind. This may be a nice way to reclaim this sacred symbol.

[8]SAD - Seasonal Affective Disorder

Sunna-Rise

by Michaela Macha

Long lay the languid shadows of night
Over the landscape lulled into sleep;
Blue darkness holds the fields in fast slumber,
Silent the meadows, deserted the woods.

Mound-wights rise to roam among hillocks,
Moonshine bleaches the bones of the trees,
Haunting screeches—perhaps an owl hunting;
No time for the living this hour of ghosts.

But hark—what is heard, softly at first,
A sound from eastwards filling the ear?
A murmur, a grumble, a distant rumble
Soon swelling and surging, a thundering tide—

Árvarkr's hooves! Swift-footed hurries
The stallion of Sunna, herald of dawn,
Drawing the Splendorous One in Her chariot,
To Heimdall's children most welcome of sights.

Fast wheels Her wain, faster run wights
Home to their barrow and hide from the blaze;
Shadows flee hastily, crouch under boulders;
Soon the sky brightens at Sunna's fair smile.

Earth wakes to life, stirring in wonder,
Sleep-fetters loosen; flung is the froth
Of Alsviðr's muzzle as dew on the meadows;
Eyes and doors open, flowers unfold.

Gladly now hail the hearts of all humans
The glorious Goddess in fiery guise;
Her golden rays caressing the faces
As warm as Her laughter filling the sky.

Mani

Mani, the Moon God, is quieter and more reflective; he has been known to wander off course in order to watch over people and is especially fond of the humans of Midgard. One of his major tales has him rescuing children and taking them to Asgard. He is unmarried, as far as we know, and his herald is Nott, or Night, who rides a black horse.

Mani is calmer and more thoughtful than his sister. He has a compassionate heart, and is struck by seeing those in need, especially children who are being abused, and he is often prayed to in order to protect specific children. He is known to have rescued two children, Bil and Hjuki, snatching them up from the earth and sending them to live in Asgard. (Their names seem to be the foundation of the "Jack and Jill" rhyme.) He is also a god of calendars, mathematics, and other rational thought that requires counting and numbers. He plays a flute as he walks, and is especially revered by the Dark Alfar and the Duergar. Those who work with Mani say that his moon-cart is pulled not by horses, but by large dogs, and sometimes he simply walks, being a patron of travelers and walkers in general.

Revering The Moon God
by Sophie Oberlander

Over the past few years, I've come to develop a certain relationship with the God of the Moon, Mani. To modern Heathens, Mani doesn't seem to hold pride of place in regular worship, which I think is unfortunate. I also doubt that it was the same to our ancestors, for Mani, who I always conceive of as Sunna's brother, is very important from an eschatological standpoint. Not only is the sun swallowed at Ragnarok, but so is the moon. This leads to a crumbling and collapse of cosmic order. This is particularly important in Mani's case, for the moon governs cosmological rhythm. He is all about flow and time and rhythm. Because of Their strong association with cycles and time, deities of the moon were often Goddesses, for the moon controls the tides, which in turn influences the cycles of the female body. Not so with the Norse, however. In a beautiful example of harmonious juxtaposition, the Sun's vital projective force is female and the Moon, generally believed to symbolize intuitive receptivity and rhythmic awareness, is male.

I find this particularly fitting, as there is definitely a sensual aspect to Mani's nature. I also believe He has the power to pull us immediately out of temporal time/space and place us in that liminal state of being/place of being wherein magic is at its most potent. If He chooses to share it, He possesses immense wisdom in all things magical. He's a shaman's friend in this way, with the ability to keep us all balanced—reasonably so—during journey work, and possibly even during shaman-sickness. He's usually more than willing, if asked, to offer useful advice and guidance on such matters. He also possesses the ability to cleanse one of psychic miasma and taint. He can also ease one's access to the Hall of Records, again, if approached rightly.

Not much is written about Mani in the lore. He's essentially only named as the personification of the moon. He is responsible for guiding the body of the moon in its celestial passage and determines its waxing and waning. In many respects, He is the subtle reflection of Sunna's more immediately dynamic power. His presence is gentle whereas Hers is bold. Perhaps Mani's seeming affection for humans can be accounted for by the fact that two humans are said to be special to him: a girl named Bil and a boy named Hjuki. Most lore sources indicate that He abducted them, but I prefer the interpretation offered by House of Mundilfari elder Manny Olds: that he adopted them, rescuing them from a cruel father. (http://www.mundilfari.org/manifesto.htm) This casts a completely different, and far more compassionate light (if one will pardon the inevitable pun) on this particular Deity.

Many who work with Mani have also noted His particular affinity for numbers. Not being at all gifted in mathematics, I myself have not experienced this particular facet of His nature, but I do not doubt it. Given His impact on tides, ley lines, time, etc. this is not at all surprising. I would also suspect a certain affinity with maps and navigational tools of all sorts. This might make Him an appropriate and willing Deity to call upon during those times so aptly named by Christian mystics as "the dark night of the soul." He has the capacity to show us the way forward out of that darkness. He and His sister may also be called upon for safe travel and in any rites that mark passages. This is an especially important function in that we as a religion are just now beginning to develop/revive rites of passage for our young people. Initiatory rites, man- and woman-making rites, even rituals that involve fertility (marriages, baby blessings) are perfect venues in which to honor Mani. Mani in such a capacity would be ensuring the strength and cohesiveness of the tribe/community, for such rituals have great psychological import and can be immensely folk-binding. They help create and define place and function for each person within the tribe. This in turn creates psychic and spiritual continuity so important for smooth growth.

Women, of course, have a particularly intimate connection to Mani through the rhythm of their menstrual cycles, which, as noted above, are ultimately governed by the power of the moon. Through this connection, Mani can be said to govern the rhythms of fertility, conception and contraception. There is also a tangential connection between this God and certain aspects of herbalism, in that certain plants and herbs were traditionally gathered only by moonlight during specific phases of the moon. This was considered necessary to ensure the medicinal efficacy of the herbs. I've found him personally to be a very approachable Deity. He seems to like watching over and communicating with humans and generally has an easy-going nature, though there is also a certain mystery about Him.

In popular folklore, the moon is often associated with various states of madness (lunacy). Lunatics, in some cultures, were considered touched by the Gods. Mystics, shamans, poets, in the eyes of society may each at times exhibit the signs and symptoms of madness. There's a wonderful line in "The Power of Myth" by Joseph Campbell wherein he says essentially that the mystic swims in the same waters in which the lunatic drowns. (*My paraphrase.*) The type of ecstatic inspiration, which comes not from analytical study but from heart-felt, intuitive experience may perhaps also be seen as something smiled upon by the moon.

Since Mani and His kin govern time and cycles, they may also have some connection to recordkeeping and genealogy. Having been set in the heavens in such close proximity to humanity from the earliest age, He and His sister have witnessed the entire flow of human history. Therefore, Mani's day (Monday) is a good day to honor the ancestors, especially those whose names we do not know, for honoring night and day, sun and moon is, in effect, honoring our beginning.

Watcher

by Elizabeth Vongvisith

O Mani, who dreams behind
the moon's fair and addled face,
bemused and musing, over great seas
and stolid earth and the sky's burnished ceiling,
tell me about what you've seen while
roaming back and forth across the heavens.

You turn and turn and turn again,
crossing and recrossing, and still
you wander and gaze in silence,
circling, as a man gently considers
a problem incarnate before him.
Teach me about simple observance,
that quiet watching without
the anxious self-centeredness of opinion,
you who sees the world from the top of night.

And if you should pause in your journey,
even only briefly, look my way and smile,
Mani of the slow, deep wisdom,
for I'll be looking up at you
from down below, here where I am rooted
to the things I cannot bear to leave behind.

Daeg

Ahead of Sunna, as a herald, travels Daeg, or Day, a sky-etin who rides the red-bay horse Skinfaxi. The horse's mane sheds light as it goes. Daeg is the son of Nott by Delling, an Alfar lord who heads up an important House, and whose named means "Dawn". Delling and Nott were together only for a short time, but their son is one of the few Jotun-Alfar hybrids that we know of. Apparently the general taboo against (and shame of) Alfar crossing with Jotnar was offset by the fact that Nott is one of the sky-etins, entrusted with a crucial job by the Aesir, and that their son Daeg would be the herald of the Day.

Tall as a giant and beautiful as an elf, with hair of red-gold and eyes like the noon sky, Daeg combines the best of both races. While he has no wife that we know of, being too busy for such a thing, he takes lovers from many races, like his diversity-loving mother. Many are the folk of the Jotnar, Vanir, Aesir, and even some Alfar who have succumbed to his glowing smile. If there is someone whom he loves, however, it is Sunna, who is married to another and not interested in mixing romance with a co-worker.

Invocation to Daeg

Hail to the Master of the Day!
Golden and bright, you rise before the Sun,
The mists seek refuge before your burning smile
And the morning wafts flesh-pink
Over the standing corn.
We greet your coming with opening eyes
And open arms that stretch to honor you.
Skinfaxi's rider, glowing behind the horizon
And then bringing that glow
Through a thousand clouds,
May your coming always be joy
In our eyes and in our hearts.

Nott

Nott, whose name means merely "night", is Mani's herald, riding a black horse named Hrimfaxi. The dew drips off of Hrimfaxi's bit as he passes over the worlds. She is the granddaughter of Bergelmir the First Chief via his son Norfi, the famous giant architect who designed Asgard, Thrymheim, and the hall of Utgard-Loki. Her first husband (of three) was a Jotun named Nagifari, and their son was named Aud. By her second husband, Annar, a water-giant, she bore Jord, the mother of Thor. Her third husband, Delling, a red Alfar, gave her the son Daeg, who would be chosen god of the Day. Nott herself is a very old giantess, one of the oldest from before the flood, which she survived by being in the realm of the Dead at the time. It is rumored that she also had an affair with the old Vanir-god Frodi, and bore him Njord the sailor-god before leaving him with the infant boy. Nott is not known for being maternal; she tends to be a wanderer, leaving her various children to be raised by their fathers.

On the other hand, Nott is very much the wise old woman; although she is somewhat distant from most people's concerns, she can be helpful— when she chooses—for those who are searching for lost facts in the dark, especially about the past. She will casually drop a bit of her collected wisdom as she passes, like a star falling from her skirt. You may have a better chance at that if you are young and handsome and male, and you flirt with the old lady and remind her that she is beautiful and desirable—not that she needs reminding, but it's a gift she likes. Be warned, though; she make take you up on it.

Invocation to Nott

Hail to Nott, Old Woman of the Night,
The hem of your black robe twinkles
With the multitudinous stars as you go,
And we watch, and marvel at the Mysteries
You flaunt each night in your passing.
Hail, Hrimfaxi's rider, dewdrops sparkling
On your dark bridle, nourishing the Earth.
Hag of the Night, Sacred Elder,
Silver-haired like the clouds across the Moon,
Mother of Day, Mother of Earth,
Mother of the Sea-Lover whose ships breast the horizon,
Lover of Jotun, Alf, and Van, and any
Whose upturned face in the moonlight
You find lovely in your old, old eyes.
Bless us, Nott, with fine sleeping
And may your dark horse ride gently in our dreams.

Sacred Shapeshifters: The Iron Wood

he strangest subgroup of the Jotunheim etins must, of course, be the Iron Wood clans. To understand them, one must first understand the odd nature of the Iron Wood itself. The Jotunfolk call it the Heart Of Jotunheim, with the wider meaning that it is the heart of Jotun nature itself, its most sacred place.

There certainly seems to be something weird about the Iron Wood, something *unheimlich*, as the Germans would describe it; eerie, uncanny. It has been described as being somehow magically "radioactive". Some strong force emanates from it, and all the Jotnar born there are gods, or strangely deformed, or both. Hela was born there—her mother, Angrboda, is the Hag of the Iron Wood. (*Hag* should be read like its related word *hagia*, wisdom; she is the tribal wisewoman of the Nine Clans of the Iron Wood.) Angrboda's other children were born there as well, the great Serpent and the wolf-children, Hati, Skoll, and the terrible Fenris.

Iron Wood Jotnar are the most clannish of all; they rarely marry out of their nine clans, unless there is a shortage of babies, usually caused by too many deformities in the population. Other Jotun treat them with a strange reverence mixed with a little fear; we must remember that most of their Gods come out of the Iron Wood. In general, Jotnar of the Iron Wood are a strange-looking lot. Although all Jotunkind are skilled shapeshifters, the Iron Wood clans often spend so much time in animal or half-animal form that it is sometimes known as the Wood of Werewolves, some lycanthropes, such as Fenris, may even become permanently shapeshifted into animal form.

Another telling indication of Iron Wood Clan blood is that the flesh is "loose", as they call it; it means that they shapeshift so often and are so little tied to any one form that it is impossible to tell what their "original" form was, and indeed many forget it before they are out of childhood. Iron Wood Jotnar are shorter than other varieties, not much more than large-human size and sometimes shorter (with exceptions, like the nine-foot Farbauti). Many are deformed, or hairy and pelted (or even scaled or feathered), or hermaphroditic, or horned and hooved, or just strange-looking in some odd way. In fact, it is said among other Jotnar that being ambiguously gendered in any way is a sign of Iron Wood Clan bloodlines; witness the sex-shifting Loki and the hermaphroditic Snake. Of all the different kinds of Jotnar, the ones most likely to be named "trolls" are those of certain clans of Jarnvidur, especially the Hound-Beetle tribe. Some are vampiric and drink blood, or life-force. ("Primary", or hereditary, psychic vampirism is a trait that can be passed on to human bloodlines.)

Keep in mind that in the Iron Wood, to be strange-looking physically is not a bad thing. The effects of the magical radioactivity are such that the Jarnvidur folk have had to develop a culture where there is no concept of the "right" or "wrong" way for bodies to be, so long as one's malformities are not life-threatening or prevent one from functioning or enjoying life. Iron Wood Jotnar are raised to compensate for each others' physical differences and difficulties—a dwarfed troll will be put on the shoulders of a tall giant to see properly at a moot; someone with long legs will automatically look to carry someone with short legs if running is necessary; the weak of body are defended (especially since those who are weaker of body are very often stronger of magical powers) and the standard of beauty tends to be more about personal charisma than physical shape. While the weak of body are usually well cared for, the weak of will tend to be ruthlessly culled out.

Strangely enough, they are well-disposed toward any human who can deal with their hazing with goodwill and remain friendly. Hazing generally takes two forms. They may challenge you (which if you're dealing with lycanthropes is a matter of jumping you from the bushes) and expect you to take it for the pack-order rough-and-tumble that it is, either by submitting graciously or by putting up a good fight until they let go, at which point you make a friendly overture.

The other hazing method is to send their most ugly and deformed folk to get close to you, and then watch your reaction. The Iron Wood folk are well aware that those outside their wood do not share this cultural blindness to a physical ideal. What we humans need to keep in mind is that to an Iron Wood Clan Jotun, to be physically bizarre is not a bad thing. It is a badge of tribal pride, a mark of their bloodlines, the same ones that brought forth Gods. If you are clearly made visibly uncomfortable by their shape, they will lose respect for you. To accept them without comment, flinch, or other negative reaction will gain points. If you flinch, or show any disgust or pity or distaste, you fail. If you respond with friendship, you pass the test and they can be quite friendly, if still a bit rough in their way of showing it.

In turn, however, once they accept you, it will be warts and all. Once you've made positive contact, the Iron Wood can be a good space for people who don't carry socially acceptable shapes themselves to hang out. If you yourself are deformed or disabled, physically or mentally, they will not see you as damaged or abnormal; you are just what you are, specific only to yourself. Since they have a higher-than-normal rate of ambiguously sexed births (and, correspondingly, the most relaxed and normalized attitude towards shapeshifting between genders), those with gender issues may find a haven here, especially if they are working towards shapeshifting their own bodies in some way. There are many healers in the Iron Wood who specialize in helping the kind of deformities associated with Iron Wood bloodlines, including those in humans.

Iron Wood Clan folk are superb hunters, and can teach the art of skillfully tracking prey, including on an astral level. There are nine clan/tribes in the Wood; their totems are Wolf (thus all the werewolves in the forest), Serpent, Hyena, Lightning, Ghost Deer, Cave Bear, Knife

River, Blood-Alder, and Hound-Beetle. Each of the tribes has a chief—Farbauti, Loki's father, is chief of the Lightning tribe—and Angrboda, leader of the Wolf clan, is currently chief of chiefs, unchallenged since she beat out Farbauti for the position. There is a great deal of intermarrying in the Iron Wood—they are not monogamous by any means—and most Iron Wood Jotnar have the blood of many if not all of the Nine Clans in them.

The folk of the different tribes do have different gifts, although there is so much mixing and matching that only half of any given tribe is likely to have the classic gifts and appearance of that tribe. But, in general, the Wolf tribe does have the most werewolves and weredogs, and the Cave Bear tribe is full of werebears and tend to be large and shaggy. The Lightning tribe carries the strongest fire-etin blood, as well as a good deal of fiery red hair (which is actually unlike pure fire-etins, as they tend to be dark and swarthy). Serpent-clan are often weresnakes—Jormundgand was proof positive of some Serpent-clan in Angrboda's bloodline—and specialize in poisons; some can poison with a mere touch, although they can often also create poisons with their blood that are strong medicines and fight disease; they are as likely to be healers as assassins. Hyena-clan folk are carrion-eaters and carry a good deal of psychic vampirism in their lines. (Both Serpent-clan and Hyena-clan are known for having a high number of hermaphroditic offspring.) The Ghost Deer clan are great hunters, and work with the Dead and the Ancestors; the priests who oversee funerals are usually Ghost Deer clan members. Knife River clan folk are largely fisherfolk and know a lot of freshwater magic, as well as being the best carvers and toolmakers. Blood-Alder clan folk have a lot of healers, herbalists, midwives, and some folk who seem to be able to shape themselves into trees and bushes. They do the most sex magic, although it is a very ordeal-oriented variety. Hound-Beetle clan, named for the carrion beetle much loved by Hela (*Nicrophorus* species), live in the high ground of the Iron Wood, where it slopes up the mountains, and are the most generally troll-like; they have a strong affinity for insects and small vermin.

The clans do fight amongst each other—the epic fighting between the Lightning and Wolf clans over the position of Chief of Chiefs went on for nearly two decades—but they will quickly drop personal grudges and gang up together against an outside threat. If any member of a tribe chooses to boycott an inter-clan war due to personal reasons, that position is respected by both sides, although they cannot then help protect their own clan. Clan chiefs are not able to boycott; if they wish to stop a war, they have to stop their whole tribe from fighting or else resign. Generally, though, inter-clan wars start up quickly and are over just as quickly, and next year might see them just as friendly as if it never happened.

There are also animals in the Iron Wood who are more sentient than animals ought to be, although if you ask them, they will deny being Jotnar. It may be that the Jotun weres have crossed bloodlines with some animals and given them more intelligence, but no one speaks much of that. Just remember that anything you hunt might look like an animal, but it might be able to beat you at chess if it wanted to.

Meat is an acceptable offering for anyone you meet in the Iron Wood. They are also very fond of sweets, as they don't get much of that. If you bring them drink, don't bother with mead or beer; like the folk of Utgard, when they want to drink, they want the hard stuff. Strongly flavored liqueurs are your best bet. Small toys, strangely enough, are highly valued, especially if they are figures of bizarrely-shaped creatures.

Cannibalism is strong in the Iron Wood—not that it is missing anywhere else among Jotunkind—and that goes especially for funerary cannibalism. It is not unusual for a troll who has fallen in battle to expect that he will be cooked and eaten by his kin, who by doing so return his body to his clan, where it belongs. Older etins are stewed up in giant cauldrons to soften the meat, and cooked with savory herbs. If an Iron Wood etin is burned or buried, it means that they died of illness. To be invited to a funeral feast is an honor. If you can't stomach it, find an extremely polite and very solid excuse.

Angrboda

Angrboda is known as the Hag of the Iron Wood of Jotunheim. In the lore, she is generally only known through her marriage to Loki, and the fact that she is the mother of several of his children. She is almost always seen as a tall, muscular giantess with reddish hair—"hair the color of dried blood", as one seeker said—and is passionate, violent, bloodthirsty, and very wise about much old lore. In order to understand her (modernly insulting) title of Hag of the Iron Wood, you can compare the word Hag to the word Hagia, or wisewoman. She is the leader of the Wolf Clan, and also the Chief of Chiefs of the Nine Clans of the Iron Wood by right of many battles won, and she is a fierce warrior-woman and werewolf-shapeshifter as well as wisewoman, priestess, sorceress, seer. As the single most important person in the Iron Wood, she is aware of everything that goes on inside of its borders. However, like most Iron Wood Clan folk, she does not generally leave her forest or interfere in outside Nine-Worlds activities.

The Mother of Wolves is very choosy about who she will work with. If she doesn't like you for whatever reason, she will reject you, often violently. She has even less patience with emotional weaklings than most other Jotnar—to her, the weak of spirit who refuse to struggle get exposed at birth. However, if you are a strong and competent person who is having a rough time, she can be surprisingly sympathetic. To her, weakness is not about bodily problems, but about will; she doesn't care if you are crippled, so long as you continue to fight and keep going. She has a soft spot for the deformed and bizarre who rise above the world that attempts to drag them down. She is a Mother Goddess in her own way, but her mothering is very wolflike—fiercely protective of her own, but not above growling and biting when they do something stupid. She is skilled in the magic of the hunt, prophecy and divination, shapeshifting, and Jotun sex magic from a female perspective. For an offering, start with blood.

Although she is generally thought of as Loki's wife, in the hierarchy of the Iron Wood, Loki is Angrboda's consort, not the other way around. However, the two have not cohabited in a long time; Loki decided at some point to leave the Iron Wood and go on walkabout, and this led to his becoming involved with Odin and the Aesir, and moving in with Sigyn in Asgard. Angrboda was not pleased with the situation, but she knows enough to understand that she cannot control Loki, and she is proud and independent and likely has a few other lesser consorts in the background as well. She often wears men's clothing and is rarely seen in skirts; as a war-leader of her people, she usually goes armed.

Angrboda's marriage to Loki produced three children—Hela, who became the goddess of Death; Jormundgand the enormous Serpent; and Fenris the Great Wolf-Destroyer. While she was unhappy with his second marriage to Sigyn, it was not because of jealousy—Jotnar often take multiple spouses and share their time between them—but because she saw Loki's marriage to an Aesir woman as a betrayal of his blood and tribe.

There are conflicting accounts, in the lore, about who the mother of Fenris's children Hati and Skoll might be. In some accounts she is an unnamed giantess of the Jarnvidur; in others, she is his own mother Angrboda. Whether this incestuous affair took place is unknown, and may always be a mystery.

Angrboda

by Abby Helasdottir

"Thrice burned, thrice reborn,
Often laid low, she lives yet."

In Rökkr cosmology, the giantess Angrboda appears with a complexity that rivals even that of her daughter, Hela. Like Hela, she appears as mother, maiden, and crone, and also shares with her many of the same symbols.

Angrboda is remembered best by the Norse saga in her role as the Hag of the Iron Wood, the giantess with whom Loki would sometimes reside.

She gave birth to Hela, Iormungand, and Fenrir, and later even bore the lupine children of Fenrir: Hati and Skoll. In this respect, Angrboda, although described as a hag or crone, appears in the role of a mother goddess. She is the mother of almost the entire Rökkr pantheon.

The expansive nature of Angrboda is exemplified by her element, Ice. It is ice that has carved and created much of this world, over the aeons that it imperceptibly moves. A vivid reflection of this is found in the Irish creatrix-hag-winter goddess, Cailleach Beara, who was responsible for the carving of mountains and hills, and the creation and moving of monoliths. Like Angrboda, the Cailleach is thrice-born in her sisters, Cailleach Borus and Cailleach Corca Duibhn, and can eternally renew her youth.

The vast progeny of Angrboda is a mythic memory of her manifestation as that creative Feminine force that underlies the creation, and the continuance of the Norse cosmos. It is typified by Angrboda's element of Ice, and first appears in the opening moment of cosmic creation. The vast vaginal void of Ginnungagap, out of which the cosmos emerged, is the womb of the Feminine, rimmed by the vulva of the Dark Goddess; an image repeated in Hindu cosmology by Kali's primordial womb of Chaos. This imagery is most aptly represented in the lewd Sheila-na-gyg carvings found throughout the British Isles and Ireland, in which an ugly female figure, smiling licentiously, holds her vagina wide open with both hands. The derivation of the name is given variously as "hag" or "giant" (the word "gyg" being the Norse name for "giantess", according to goddess-scholar Dorothy Myers), both of which apply suitably to Angrboda, as both giantess and hag.

Another important British trace of Angrboda is in the low-lying Dane Hills of Lecheister, where she appears as the hag known as Black Annis; who has also borne the names of Blue Annis, Black Anna, Black Anny, Black Agnes, and Cat Anna. Her dwelling was a cave (called Black Anna's, or Black Annis's Bower) she is said to have clawed out of the sandstone rock using nothing but her long, and very sharp, nails. At the mouth of the cave grew an oak tree in which Black Annis would hide, waiting to pounce on unsuspecting children. These she carried off into her cave, sucked them dry of blood, and ate their flesh, before draping the flayed skins of her victims out to dry on the oak's branches. She wore a skirt sewn from the skins of her human prey. In a warning similar to that about Frau Holle in Germany, children were told that if they were naughty, or out after dark, to "watch out or Annis'll get you". Like Angrboda and Hela, Black Annis was said to have the face of the death goddess, being hideous and blue.

While the derivation of the name is not certain, the identification of these Leicester hills as the Dane Hills reveals the reason why Black Annis can be identified with the Scandinavian Angrboda. This connection has been identified by other writers, who have shown that in Denmark, this same figure was Angrboda, Anna of the Angles, and was also known by the name Yngona. The name Yngona references the Ingwaz rune, which is the runic equivalent of the vaginal vesica pisces design.

As Black Annis, Angrboda is shown much the same way as she is in the Norse myths: the mother who is also a killer. The gruesome reputation given to Black Annis can be better understood by seeing it as a vision of the Neolithic death goddess. Her long nails and sharp teeth are reminiscent of the death goddess in her bird forms such as raven and vulture, who devours the body following death.

In the east she was seated, that aged old woman, in Iarnvidr
And there she nourished the posterity of Fenrir;
He will be the most formidable of all, he
Who, under the form of a monster, will swallow up the moon.

— Völuspá

A Call to Angrboda

by Elizabeth Vongvisith

O hail to you, Chieftain of the Iron Wood folk;
Yours is the rulership kept strong with your will.

O hail to you, mother who gave birth to Death;
Yours is the spear that never errs in flight.

O hail to you, wrathful one, maker of sorrows;
Yours is the furious rage that gives no quarter.

O hail to you, mother of wolf and serpent;
Yours is the love shown in strength and firmness.

O hail to you, defender of Jarnvidr;
Yours is the courage that does not doubt itself.

O hail to you, wise Hag of the holy forest;
Yours is the knowledge that is ancient and depthless.

O hail to you, sorceress-queen reborn by magic;
Yours is the heart that can never be destroyed.

Angurboda's Song

by J. Freyson, Urdabrunnr Kindred

I am anger bored by the crying of a people
Who for the taste of freedom never fought.
I am anger bored by the weakness of a people
Who for the source of their own power never sought.
I am anger bored by the amnesia of a people
So quickly forgetting the lessons time has cruelly taught.
I am anger bored by my invoking as a Savior
During events which only stupidity hath wrought.

I am no chest of freely offered jewels,
No mere convenient tool
To guide you to the magic of the elusive wishing well.
I am no wiping of a tear,
No dissolving of all your fears,
No halting of thy own creation of the coveted Hell.

I am a sword drenched in blood,
The secret wriggling in the mud
Of thy own existence stripped of all its paltry shadows.
I am the etching of the runes,
The sacred space in which they are strewn
Bestowing wisdom on how to best conquer thy foes.

I am anger bored into the mind punctured with memories
Of the forced exodus from sacred lands into the raging sea.
I am anger bored into the heart stabbed a thousand times
With swords of wickedness shedding sacrificial blood
    which feedeth not the tree.
I am anger bored into the soul shattered by the power
Of my shrieking hideous wail in the midst of my agony.

I am anger bored like nails through the cross of the suffering spirit,
Penetrating the superficial body.

I am rage burning under the skin,
The iron chain of duty binding the kin,
The crimson flow from the child staining the mother's breast.
I am the great splitting of the yew,
The runes of wisdom which from the wound flew,
The dark jewel at the end of the wanderer's quest.

I am a holy temple dissolving in the flames,
One amongst the ten thousand names,
A well of tears fast running dry.
I am the old one cloaked in the shawl,
The hairline fracture in the impenetrable wall
The forewarner that the Dark Age is nigh
By and by.

I am anger borne aloft as a mighty shield held by hands
Burnished by endless days under the blazoning sun.
I am anger borne aloft as a mighty blade which to the hilt
Through the hearts of cowards I demand thee run.
I am anger borne aloft as a shining beacon of Truth's pure light
From which all of the Unnameable must fearfully shun.
I am anger borne aloft as the rolling voice of wisdom
Thundering in thy ears lest My will not be done.

I am the brunt of the oncoming storm,
Fury's power taking pure form,
The web of justice from which there is absolutely no escape.
I am the birthing brick of Warriors true
All of their lineage the enemy slew
The forgotten Earth Mother enduring the endless rape.

I am bearer of all things accursed,
The bitter brew when for your becoming you thirst
Bardic tales keeping alive the sacred mission of faith.
I am the fruit you dare not eat,
The serpent in the garden beneath thy feet.
Of the seven days of creation, I was the defiant eighth.

I am Angurboda, now and forever,
The creases of time upon my face hide not my battle scars.
I am Angurboda, now and forever,
Look for wisdom deep within the abyss
     instead of longingly at the stars.
I am Angurboda, now and forever,
Release thyself from thine own prison
     where fear comprises all the bars.
I am Angurboda, now and forever,
For once dare look deep inside thy own ancestral jars.

I am Age's withering hand,
The essence of all magical lands,
The supplier of the threads from which the Nornir weave.
I am the searing heat of the phoenix fire,
The burning flame of spiritual desire
The first truth that will be the last you believe.

I am the love which is often scorned,
The undying heart from which it is torn
Lover and apprentice to the God Loki.
I am the nourishment you must heed
The taste which causeth you not to feed
But if you wish to survive, you must eat of me
Completely.

Ritual for Angrboda's Blot
19th day of Blutmonath (November 19)
Pagan Book of Hours, Order of the Horae

Color: Black
Element: Fire
Altar: On a black cloth set a vase of bare oak branches with the dried leaves still attached, three lit red candles, a horn of mead, figurines of wolves, a wooden heart burned to ashes, and an iron knife.
Offerings: Ashes smeared on the face.
A promise to see ugliness with new eyes.
Daily Meal: Coarse dark bread. Mushrooms. Red meat.

Invocation to Angrboda

Hail, Hag of the Iron Wood!
From thy womb came
The Lady of Death,
Dark mistress of the shades;
The wolf of destruction,
The serpent all-encompassing.
Strong one who stands alone,
Who defends her children
No matter how ugly they might be,
Who defends her spouse
Even when all others revile him,
Who would die for her loved ones
Even when they are imperfect.
Your children exiled or imprisoned,
Yet the tide of death and destruction
Was not slowed an inch.
Hail, Lady whose heart
Was burned to ash by those
Who would not look upon ugliness
Lest they see in it a dark mirror
Of their own bright souls.

Chant: Angrboda Angrboda
Hag of the Iron Wood
Mother of Wolves
Defend Your Pack
With fire and steel and blood.

(All step forth and take a handful of ashes from the burned heart and smear it on their faces. The horn of mead is passed around and the remainder poured out as a libation. The candles are put out, the iron knife is laid on the floor, and all step over it as they leave.)

Farbauti

Chief of the Lightning Clan of the Iron Wood, Farbauti is a God of thunder and lightning similar to Thor—and like Thor, he is tall, broad, strong, and hot-tempered. There are differences between them, though. Farbauti, whose name means Hard-Striker or Cruel-Striker, is all Jotun-blooded, and when he smites people it is with more than lightning. Among other things, Farbauti is a disease-bringer, and a deity whose weapon is illness, senility, and the difficulties of old age. More about his appearance and manner can be found in his Lesson.

Farbauti is called "the Hard Striker" and most people "romantically" assume this is an allusion to the power of lightening, but I believe this is incorrect. What hits hardest of all is that which deals the ignominious wound: old age, insecurity, loss of sentience. He strikes hard, brutally so and where one least expects. He is not quick to attack, but once He sets His mind on an enemy He is like the plague of locusts that sweeps over the field leaving nothing in its wake but barren ground. Eventually, Farbauti confronts us all in one way or another, with the understanding that there are some battles, some challenges, we shall never win and in comparison to the loss that His hard strikes bring, dying is easy. He deals the blows from which one cannot recover. And He expects us to endure... that is one of His lessons, endurance in the face of shattering hardship.

What I do know is that while I could happily serve Farbauti, it would not bring out the better parts of my nature. He speaks gleefully of striking one's enemies sterile, blighting crops, causing illness and injury to those that have brought harm—and this is in a good mood! However, He is in no way evil as some Heathens would automatically assume. He simply is. His gifts are those of warcraft, siegecraft, and he governs lawful attacks. It is lawful, if not pleasant, in this Universe, to be stricken with disease and old age. I have found Him to be a staunch ally, warm, witty and very protective.

—Tamara Crawford

Prayer to Farbauti

by Tamara Crawford

Lord of Destruction, I hail You,
Lawful wrath and devastation,
Your enemies fall before You
As we shall fall in time,
With Your blessings.
Mighty Warrior, bold in battle,
I praise You.
Defender of Your people,
Weapons-wise, I bow my head before You.
You arouse fury in Your enemies
And in secret lay them low.
You are like the plague of locusts
That lays waste to all the fields,
Or the infirmity that slays our beasts of burden.
Your touch rouses the mind to madness,
Distorting Muninn's gifts.
You do not permit Your foes
Even the sanctuary of their own thoughts.
You are passionate, Lord, and fierce,
Strong and cunning and wise.
Your fury puts to flight the aggressor,
Consuming them in fire.
I honor You, Farbauti,
Father of Loki, swift Sky-Traveller,
Best of Warriors, Battle-scarred and ready.
Gird and guide me, Fierce Warrior,
May my steps to You be sure.
Hail, Farbauti.

Shadow Gods: The Rökkr

ökkr—the word was coined by Abby Helasdottir to describe the Jotnir, the Gods of the Jotunfolk. Their existence as deities is hotly debated in many northern-tradition communities. Some see them as merely giants who are "lesser" than the Aesir in status (even Hela, the awesome force of Death itself, whom the Aesir cannot force or wheedle); Some see them as legitimate deities, but ones who are evil or too dangerous for humans to worship or work with. (This attitude is often transparently a carryover of an individual's Christian upbringing, which sensitizes them to assuming that the universe is cosmically divided into good and evil, and they cast the Rökkr as some sort of stand-ins for Satan.) Some point out that even if these are the Gods of the Jotnar, there is scanty evidence that actual humans worshiped them in historical times.

So why are there suddenly hordes of people to whom these dark gods are speaking? As discussed in the first chapter, there is a good deal of speculation (and a growing amount of scholarship) exploring the idea that the Jotnar, and by extension the Rökkr, were the deities of an older, perhaps pre-Indo-European Scandinavian culture that was overrun by the widely spaced waves of the Indo-Europeans, symbolized by the Vanir and the Aesir. This gives rise to the speculation that the Rökkr are indeed the ancestral deities for some of us; just those of ancestors who go a lot further back.

Another theory is that there is more Jotun blood in the modern humans of this world than in former times (see the chapter on the problem of Jotun bloodlines) and that it is perfectly normal for the Gods of those nonhuman ancestors to be contacting and working with their descendants in this world. Considering that much of that bloodline-mingling seems to be other than accidental—and, indeed, may be orchestrated by the Gods in question—it makes a great deal of sense that they are calling their children to awake.

At any rate, whether some northern-tradition groups like it or not, the Rökkr gods are gathering a following... and most of those people are not interested in being cast as the equivalent of Norse Satanists, or willing to be some kind of eternal opponent. When those of us who follow the Rökkr gods mention this fact and get the Asatru equivalent of someone doing the warding-off-the-evil-eye gesture and backing away, we tend to roll our eyes. We are aware of the complexities of divine politics, and we feel that the situation is not so black-and-white as some would make it out to be.

It is true that the Rökkr gods are dark, in the sense that their powers deal with the death-and-destruction end of the natural cycle, but this is just as much a part of the sacredness of life as birthing and creativity. In the past decades, a similar issue reverberated through the Neo-Pagan demographic; those who were drawn to work with dark deities such as Kali, Hecate, Hades, Persephone, and Cerridwen had to defend themselves against the aesthetic biases (masquerading as spiritual considerations) of followers of more socially-attractive deities. The "undemonization" of the Dark Gods in that demographic is proceeding effectively; the idea of the "rotting" end of the cycle being sacred (and perhaps even beautiful in its own way) is much more widespread and has made its way into more ordinary group ritual. We expect that this will eventually proceed likewise in the northern-tradition demographics.

The Rökkr gods are generally accepted to be Loki, Angrboda (who is covered in the chapter on the Iron Wood that she rules), Hela, Fenris, Jormundgand, Surt and Sinmora. Some would add Nidhogg the dragon,

Mordgud, Mengloth, Utgard-Loki, and Hyndla; Sigyn, although an Aesir, is usually included in this pantheon due to her defecting from her people in favor of her husband. Which Jotnar are to be given "divine" status? Some would say that it should be the ones that the other Jotnar swear by, in which case only the first group would count. Others would say that it should be expanded to include any that we modern humans might propitiate, in which case the span would be much wider. I personally like the comment made by one spamadhr who donated material to these books: "If it's bigger, older, and wiser than I'll ever be, I treat it as a deity. That's never failed me."

The Meaning Of Rökkr
by Abby Helasdottir

Rökkr means twilight. Ragnarok is thus the twilight of the gods, a meaning that is implicit in the German translation *Gotterdammerung*. In this instance, the twilight represents the fading of the power of the gods of Asgard, as they give way for the return of the older Rökkr pantheon. Although the Rökkr pantheon can be seen as representing the night which overwhelms the Æsir gods, they are more accurately manifested as the spirits of the twilight itself. It is at twilight that the black body of the night goddess rises into the sky, and the Rökkr, who are astral beings, can be seen, marked out across her form as the stars and constellations.

The point of twilight (as well as its twin, the dawn; both phases being implied by the word *dammerung*) is the time when the world is most alive: when nocturnal creatures awake to a new night, and diurnal animals experience one final burst of energy before retiring for another night. This is the period of the daily thinning of the veils, when the world of night, for only a few seconds, exists simultaneously with the world of day. It is at this time that the light of both the Golden Sun and the Midnight Sun can be momentarily glimpsed, and it is because of this supranatural light that twilight and dawn are the times when colours appear at their most vibrant, and their most numinous.

Twilight is, thus, the time of meeting between the worlds, be they the worlds of night and day, chthonic and celestial, causal and acausal, or life and death. It is this twilight realm, which partakes of both worlds, and is a part of both but simultaneously of neither, that is the province of the hagazussa (hedge-sitter). Hagazussa is both a title of Hela in her crone aspect, from which we get the word hag, and one of the names given to the followers of the dark goddess. The hedge was used, from Neolithic times up to the recent past, to protect and define settlements, and the hedge-sitter was someone who had one foot in the safety and reality of everyday life and the other in the spirit realm. Hagazussa is the root of the modern German word hexe (witch), and is thematically the same as Tunrida (fence-rider).

The priority given to the twilight was not limited to the hagazussa, but was also a pivotal feature of the pagan world view. In contrast to our modern perception of diurnal time, where days begin at dawn, pagan Europeans saw the day ending with the sunset and beginning with the twilight; the night coming before the day. This fundamentally different way of viewing the world is the reason for the emphasis on eves in pagan festivals. Festivals appear to begin the night before because the nights are the beginning of the festival day.

Rökkr means shadow. Ragnarok is, therefore, the going into the shadow of the gods. Yet again, although the Rökkr can be seen as the darkness that consumes the gods of Asgard, they are more accurately seen as the shadow: causal emanations of the acausal darkness. Only by looking into the shadow is it possible to glimpse the black enormity of the darkness that is the Universe.

The shadow is the soul. It is the visible evidence of what exists within. To the Egyptians, one of the seven souls of a human being was the *khaibut* (the shadow that is the image of the self, often seen in reflections). This was echoed in the classical world, where the soul was the *umbra* (shade), which travelled to the Land of Shades upon death. The Rökkr form of this Land of Shadows is Helheim, Hel's country in Niflheim. The word Nifl is practically another form of Rökkr, having the multi-layered meanings of clouds, obscurity, mist, fog, and darkness (appearing as the Old High German *nebul*, Old Saxon *nebal*, German *nebel*).

It is no accident that Nifl has the same meaning as the Greek name Nephele, as both represent the dark, shadow of Hela and Hera respectively. This strain of goddesses can be found in Egypt in dark Nephthys, the wife of Set (whose Rökkr equivalent is Surt), and the goddess of the underworld and the sunset. In Semetic legend, also, the fallen angels, the Nephilim, were the children of the pre-Mosaic goddess Nephesch, who was referred to as the Soul of the World, and was twinned with the light Shekinah. Children like the Nephilim also belong to Nifl-Hela, and are called the Niflungar, more familiar as the Nibelungs.

Rökkr means darkness. It is the darkness that is implicit in the twilight and the shadow. It is only in the darkness of Hela and the Rökkr that we can hope to remove every illusion that surrounds us, and come face to face with the everything that is nothing, and the nothing that is everything. The Rökkr darkness is the ultimate experience of the abyss of Ginnungagap, in which all potential, all matter, all Wyrd, is contained in a simultaneously expansive and concentrated state. To journey into Ginnungagap is to return to the cosmic womb and its nurturing darkness, because it is from the dark womb of the goddess that all life flowed, just as individual lives all emerge from the darkness of individual wombs. With the end of life, these individual lives again return to the darkness of the goddess: the earth.

Darkness underpins our reality. It is not simply something that can be acknowledged and then forgotten, as psychology would have us believe, because it is all around us. Consider that what we interpret as day or light is only the temporary obscurement of darkness. It is darkness that is the natural, eternal state, whereas light (be it a flame, or a star) can only hope to mask the darkness for a time before its life is extinguished. We are really surrounded by darkness all the time, and only our eyes (reacting to light) fail to see this. When we acknowledge this darkness, we realize that we exist permanently within the womb of the goddess, within the void of Ginnungagap, but it is only at night, or in the realm of deep space, that she is unveiled to us.

The only light that exists in the darkness is the unimaginable light of darkness (as the void contains all things as one). This dark light is presaged in the light of twilight, the shadowlight, where two worlds combine under the twin rays of the black and gold suns. The shadowlight is the spark of the soul (the shadow), which the Niflungar seek to awaken within the goddess of the Cloud of Unknowing.

I have searched in the darkness, being silent in the great lonely stillness of the dark. So I became an angakoq, through visions and dreams, and encounters with flying spirits.

—*Najagneg, Eskimo shaman*

Loki

Probably the most infamous Jotun of all is Loki. While I could write about him extensively, I would rather have him spoken of by those who work directly with him. As the most famous (or infamous) Jotun in history, he practically requires a section all to himself. He is the central figure in the Rökkr pantheon, a position which is ironically echoed in Afro-Caribbean mythos as well—in those faiths, the trickster figure Eshu or Ellegua or Papa Legba appears as the central figure of the pantheon, and he is also witty, morally ambivalent, and occasionally androgynous.

Loki is also the most popular of the Jotun gods, partly because his madcap nature appeals to a lot of people, and partly because he is very gregarious and willing to talk to a lot of folks. He has more devotees than any other Jotun deity, and indeed the number of Loki-folk has increased dramatically in the past decade—not generally from the northern-tradition demographic, but from outside it. Loki will talk to anyone, regardless of their race, religion, or ethnic group; it is not uncommon—and unfortunately leads to a good deal of ill will—that someone will find (or be found by) Loki first, and then come wandering into Heathen circles because "he's a Norse god, right?" Often, their welcome may be chilly, or even downright hostile.

In modern-day reconstructed Heathenry, Loki is a problematic God. The problem in dealing with Loki is something avoided by those Heathens who have reconstructed their practices from Anglo-Saxon sources, because the God does not appear in those sources. For all other Heathens, he is regarded in the following three ways:

1) As the highest villain, and a great abomination against society and the others Gods in Asgard. He should not be honored or even spoken of (especially during holy rites).

2) With a wary respect, only afforded as a means of insurance against either Loki or Odin's wrath since Loki is Odin's oath-brother,

and it is rude to honor the one and not the other. This wariness also comes from Heathens not knowing clearly how to treat this God, so they err on the side of caution somewhere in the middle between the two extremes.

3) Greatly honored and loved. For those few who honor and love Loki, and use not their devotion of him as an excuse for improper behavior, they love Him whole-heartedly—although Heathens who view him in this regard clearly acknowledge that He is a difficult God to work with, because He will not allow them to stagnate, but rather will prod them to new growths and understandings.

—Casey Woods

However, Loki has more stories in Norse lore than almost any other deity. It seems that even in Christian times, the lure of telling adventure tales starring the plucky, witty trickster was irresistible. In one story, Thor's hammer is stolen by Thrym, the High King of Jotunheim, and Loki convinces Thor to dress up as the love goddess Freyja as a ploy to recover it. In another story, Loki is himself taken prisoner by Thjassi, who demands that he help kidnap Iduna and her apples in return for his release. Loki does so, but then manages to rescue her again. He turns into a mare in order to lure away the stallion Svadilfari, thus relieving the Aesir of their need to pay for the rebuilding of the walls of Asgard. Indeed, Loki's tales of saving the day are scattered throughout the other entries in this book, so I will not relate them all here in detail yet again. But the fact that you cannot get through a book of Northern-tradition tales—including this one— without mention of him—is telling.

In the Faroese ballad *Lokka táttur*, Loki is presented in an even more positive light. When a giant wins a match with a peasant, he demands the peasant's son as payment. The desperate father calls upon Odin and later Høenir to hide his son. But though Odin turns the boy into a seed of wheat in a field and Hønir transforms him into a feather on one of the swans in a flock, neither can hide him from the giant's bloody wrath. Finally Loki arrives to sets matters aright. He tells the peasant to build a boathouse and to put iron bars on the windows. Then

Loki goes out fishing with the boy; after catching a halibut, he transforms the lad into a fish egg and hides him amid the halibut's roe, then returns the halibut to the ocean. When the giant comes seeking the boy, Loki goes out fishing with him. The giant catches the halibut and counts each egg in the roe. The boy becomes frightened, and his egg rolls away. Loki then takes the boy back to shore with the giant in hot pursuit. As the boy runs into the boathouse the giant tries to follow, but gets trapped in the iron bars. Loki then cuts the giant to pieces and returns the boy to his parents, whereupon the peasant's wife embraces both of them.

Once again we see the triumvirate of Odin, Høenir and Loki, and once again we see that Loki is the one who can make things aright in the hour of greatest need. Where even Odin had failed, Loki was able to succeed.

—Kevin Filan

The tale that stands out the most, however, is the ambivalent story of Baldur's death. Baldur, the beautiful solar son of Odin and Frigga, dreams that he is to die. Ths is not surprising, considering that golden deities are sacrificial ones; Frey, the Golden One of the Vanir, is ritually slain and brought back to life every year. Baldur, however, was frightened of his destiny, and his loving mother decided to protect him from it. She went to every plant and animal and made them swear never to harm him, but skipped the mistletoe plant as it seemed so small and harmless. The gods then made a sport of hurling things at Baldur, throwing spears and darts at him to watch them fall at his feet without damage.

Then, suddenly, Loki stepped in with a dart made of mistletoe. He convinced Baldur's blind brother Hoder to join in the game, saying that he will guide his hand. Hoder threw, the dart struck Baldur, and the bright god fell dead. In shock, the Aesir began weeping and mourning, and Baldur's wife, Nanna, killed herself in grief. They began to build an enormous funeral boat to take their bodies. At the funeral, the boat proves so large that even Thor cannot move it, but suddenly a mysterious giantess arrives, calling herself Hyrrokin. Sneering, she shoves the boat out to sea and vanishes. There is some evidence that Hyrrokin is actually Angrboda, Loki's wife, come to make sure that Baldur's body is sent to the fire and the waves.

Loki, meanwhile, had fled, but returned to the Gods in one great final scene. Calling out every one of the Aesir, he revealed their sins and hypocrisies, all the ways in which they had cheated, lied, and generally did not live up to their own standards. (*I may do all of these things and more,* runs his implication, *but at least I am honest about it.*) He also openly admitted to being Baldur's slayer. Enraged by his words—and it is unclear whether they were more enraged by Baldur's murder or by having their flaws held up to the light—the Aesir pursued him like a pack of hounds.

Loki retreated to a deserted area of Midgard, near a waterfall called Franang's Falls. Here he had earlier built himself a small cabin, and he knocked four windows in the walls so that he could see anyone coming for him from any direction. Eventually, however, the Aesir found him and came for him. Changing into a salmon, he slipped into the falls to hide. The furious Thor put a net into the falls and weighted it with stones so that the salmon could not swim under it, and Loki was caught. After a struggle, he resumed his human form.

Thor, and several of the other Aesir, begged to be allowed to kill Loki, or begged that Odin should do it himself. They were amazed at Odin's seeming unwillingness to execute his son's murderer. In the midst of the ruckus, Loki's sons, Narvi and Vali—the younger one barely out of childhood, the elder barely a young man—stepped forth to attempt to defend their father and wrest him from Thor. At this, Odin cast a spell on Vali to turn him into a slavering wolf, and set him on Narvi, killing him. As Sigyn screamed, the Aesir ripped out the intestines of the dead boy and bound Loki with them, putting a magic on the dead flesh so that it would be firm as any chain. Thus bound, they cast him into a deep cave in the earth.

The giantess Skadi, still deeply enraged over the way that Loki had broken her heart, took a poisonous snake and hung it over his bound form, so that it continually dripped poison onto him. Sigyn stayed faithfully, catching the venom in a bowl, but from time to time she had to empty it and during that time he writhed and screamed in pain. When the earth shook, they said that it was Loki struggling in his bonds.

Currently there is a great deal of argument among those dedicated to Loki as to whether he is still bound under the earth, or whether he has broken free, or whether he is mostly free but some part of him is still bound. As Loki himself tells contradictory tales, we may not be sure for some time.

Almost every society has been forced to create two ethical systems—an ideal one and a practical one. Pre-Christian Northern Europe was no exception. They had a warrior code of ethics which placed a high premium on honor and honesty: without that, their civilization would soon have descended into anarchy...and yet because they lived in a harsh and often violent world, they were sometimes forced to do dishonorable things to survive.

Loki's treachery is more often than not reserved for the enemies of Asgard. He tricks Thrym into returning Thor's hammer; he steals Idun and her apples of youth from Thiatsi, and ensures the continuing survival of the dwellers in Asgard. For these things he is tolerated, if not loved. Time and again he saves the gods—but his very presence reminds them of their ungodlike behavior. When Tyr looks down at his missing hand, he remembers how he betrayed Fenris Lokison; when Odin rides Sleipnir he remembers how he and his fellow gods betrayed a giant so that Asgard might be protected. Loki brings Asgard some of its most precious treasures, but often he brings them at the price of honor.

Calling on Loki—or behaving in Loki-worthy ways—is not something which is done lightly. Accordingly, Loki appears to be a deity who is called upon only when all other avenues have failed. He is called upon not when the individual's life is in danger, but when the clan is in danger. He is the survival instinct which is more primeval than any cultural norms. If there were no wall around Asgard, it would soon have fallen to the giants... and honoring their bargain would have meant dishonoring Freyja in what would have amounted to a god-sanctioned rape. In the surviving legends, Loki does not appear to be a god of chaos (despite what some "Norse Discordians" may think). Rather, he is the god of order—but of order preserved at all costs. He is not immoral so much as amoral: in Nietzschean terms, he is the Will to Power, which seeks to triumph and does not concern itself with constructs like good and evil.

—Kevin Filan

About Loki
by Elizabeth Vongvisith,
spirit-worker & mortal -wife of Loki

Loki generally appears as a male, tall, good-looking and of moderate to slender build. He has often been seen as having green eyes and hair ranging from blood-red to a sort of orange-blond. He tends to be somewhat androgynous-looking no matter how he's dressed, though it must be remembered that he is able to assume any form he wishes, particularly if he thinks it'll help him get what he wants. He is also very charismatic, a smooth talker and a good listener, intelligent and persuasive, and he usually gets the better of everyone else in debate, flyting or verbal conflict of any sort. He can be engagingly childlike and is often very funny, even at his own expense. There is much about Loki that is admirable, but the reasons he is so widely mistrusted are because he is so very charming and skilled at persuasion, and because the things he does and says are not always in keeping with others' notions of honor or right conduct.

Loki's fire-giant blood is very evident in his personality, which is sometimes extreme and not always consistent. He is quite temperamental and can act impulsively. He is a master at wielding insults that cut to the bone, if you happen to catch him in the wrong mood. He can utter tender words of devotion one minute and hurl cruel insults the next, yet be perfectly sincere about both. Despite his temper, Loki rarely holds grudges, but when he does, he's a vicious, spiteful enemy, able to patiently wait to serve up his revenge ice-cold. His behavior often seems unpredictable and illogical to others not accustomed to seeing things from his point of view. Nevertheless, he inspires fervent loyalty in many people, even while incurring violent dislike from others. At the same time, Loki's loyalty only goes as far as his friends; with others, he's not always terribly concerned about being nice or fair. If you're not already a friend of Loki's and you have business with him, be aware that he may gleefully treat you as a plaything (and he is rough on his toys), or at best, he might be sarcastic and careless about your feelings or your comfort.

Because his primary weapon is speech, Loki more than anybody else understands the real power of words, as skilled as he might be at finding loopholes in them. He is not easily fooled or outsmarted, and you attempt to match wits with Laufey's son at your own peril—though if you do manage to get around him, he'll most likely have more respect for you rather than be angry. Loki adores pranks and jokes, though they may not seem so funny when you are the butt of them. He appreciates wit and clever speech in others, and while he'll most likely get the better of you in any challenge or agreement, he is not one to resist having a bit of fun in the meantime—which is another reason Loki is so distrusted. He has a way of making people forget why they're there in the first place.

And further along those lines, Loki is an accomplished seducer, with the pleasing talent of making one feel as if there is no one else he desires more. He likes to flirt and may even make sexual advances toward you, and he is not picky about your gender, your preferences, or whether or not you're already attached. Loki is difficult to resist, sometimes overwhelmingly so, but to him it's all in good fun. He won't be offended if you decline, and he considers the game of courtship quite as much fun as its hoped-for conclusion. He especially likes it if you rise to the occasion and banter with him with the obvious attitude that you aren't about to be taken in by his charm, but are willing to play the game anyway.

Loki is quite interested in mortal folk; there are a number of Heathens, Neo-Pagans and others who count themselves as his, and who say that it was he, not they, who made the first overtures of friendship. He seems to be the most gregarious of all the Jotnar, and perhaps of all the Aesir as well, as far as hanging around with human beings is concerned. Indeed, despite his reputation, Loki has allies in many places, most of whom are well aware of his character and inclined to treat him with varying degrees of wariness, no matter how long and well they have known him. Being a friend of Loki's can sometimes be aggravating, and even his closest companions may quarrel violently with him, but he generally tries to help his friends, and is capable of showing great kindness and care to them when he is moved to do so.

Loki is a sorcerer and has made it his business to learn magic from many different folk, sometimes without their knowledge. If you ask him nicely and give him some particularly delightful gift, he may instruct you in the finer points of shape-shifting, or teach you the ways of Jotun sorcery with its emphases on blood and other elemental magics. He might share the runelore he learned from Odin, or Freyja's seidr-craft. He is also knowledgeable about sex magic and may even offer to give you some (ahem) hands-on training with that, either through someone horsing him or directly. He can also help you with anything to do with word-magic, spoken, written or even sung. If you need it (and most people do) there is no better teacher than Loki to help you understand the importance of minding what you say and to whom. He will also teach you the value of keeping one's word no matter how difficult it might be — which can be a painful lesson. He has a particular soft spot for shamans and spirit-workers, as such people live on the fringes of society and their life's work often entails the regular crossing and disturbance of boundaries, something Loki himself is very familiar with. Those who have been called to this line of work might find Loki a surprisingly sympathetic and helpful, if sometimes annoying, ally.

Loki is not generally found in any one place in the Nine Worlds all the time, though he spends more time in Jotunheim than anywhere else. Trying to go to Asgard in search of Loki is not advisable (for a number of reasons) unless he specifically tells you to meet him there. There is some dissent as to whether or not Loki is still actually bound in his cavern; the experience of many Lokeans and spirit-workers suggests that if he is, it has not hampered his ability to move about the Nine Worlds as he wills, in some form or another. At any rate, since he is pretty hard to pin down, you'll need to ask him to come to you before you go out looking for him, unless, of course, you are bidden to meet him somewhere in particular.

Loki cannot be "invoked" and will not be summoned—or at least, there are none in the mortal world who can rightfully order him around. Certain Asatruar should take note: politely asking for some of his time and attention is more likely to win a response than if you approach him with an attitude of hostility because he is the "enemy of the gods." This is a mistake for which you will pay, sooner or later. Although Loki was banished by the Aesir and suffered a terrible punishment which left its mark on him in more ways than merely physically, he did not lose all of his cunning, power and dangerousness, and this should be kept in mind when dealing with him.

True to his often contradictory nature, Loki appreciates forthrightness and honesty in others, and if you need something from him, he will help you more readily if you just ask instead of trying to manipulate or second-guess him. However, Loki will expect something from you in return, and you would do better to have a boon or gift ready to offer rather than let him set the terms. If you don't, Loki might amuse himself by demanding something merely ridiculous or trivial...or he may insist on a favor or a sacrifice which you will deeply regret. He'll always seek whatever advantages he can gain from any sort of agreement, so it's probably better to go into it with something to offer than to be at his mercy, so to speak.

As for what to give Loki, his favorite things seem to be strong liquor, small toys and candy. Fireworks or anything that makes a loud ruckus (or a mess) is also appreciated, especially if it's something childish and amusing such as a wind-up sparking toy. Loki also appreciates handmade items, such as carvings or artwork, needlework or foods made from scratch, particularly things like cakes and pies. He also likes well-composed poetry, songs or stories, written just for him and spoken or sung aloud. Like his daughter Hela, Loki has a good deal of consideration for people without much money; he will not demand anything you truly cannot afford, so if cheap beer is all you can get, he won't insist on 30 year old single-malt Scotch. (If you happen to be wealthy, on the other hand, he'll cheerfully insist that you get that expensive bottle for him, since after all, you can easily afford it.) He will seldom turn down anything outright, though he may not be particularly gracious about it.

Loki the Trickster
by Abby Helasdottir

The sexuality of Loki is a true expression of his freedom, unhampered as he is by moral paradigms, and also expresses his gender paradox, in that he is inextricably bound to the Feminine, to the dark goddess, both literally, and symbolically. Loki bears the surname Laufeyson, a reference to his mother, not his father, illustrating wherein his power lies, in the Feminine. It also adds weight to the idea that Loki was part of a previous, matricentric culture where descent was matrilineal. Loki is a central part of the mysteries of the Dark Goddess, and as such there is a method to his madness, an order to his chaos. While his actions often seem sporadic and unplanned, they are in fact an expression of the Wyrd of the Goddess.

As Hela, his daughter, manifests as the dark left-hand soul of nature and the cosmos, so Loki is its light, right-hand side. He is the child who is not afraid to dream, or to create the dreams of others; he is the irresponsibility without which the world, and the Æsir, are stagnant and reflective. He is the innocence that is unafraid to point out that the emperor has no clothes, or perhaps, more to the point, that Odin likes women's clothes. He is laughter, the snigger in the corner, the witty aside, the remark that stings, but also induces discovery. He shows both the Gods, and humankind, that we cannot afford to take ourselves too seriously all of the time. Loki teaches us that the difference between cosmic and comic is just one letter.

Loki is fiercely proud and self-assured. None amongst the Æsir, Vanir, or Jotun can compare to his self-possession; if vanity were a crime, Loki would be guilty. Essentially Loki's nature in this respect is Faustian/Luciferian/Promethean; he is the man who would, and will, be god. Coming of pure Jotun stock, he worked his way up to achieving the god-hood of the Æsir, the divinity that, for some, is offered by the world of Asgard.

His is the fierce spirit of Homo-Galactica. If one were to rename that divine spark, inherent in humankind, that desire to reach the stars, one could call it Lokian. As the possessor of this divine spark, Loki also imparts it to those others who would be gods. Loki is the Light-Bearer, the god who ignites the divinity inherent within all beings, shaking the sullied mind into action. Like his aquatic child, Iormungand, Loki embodies a universal archetype found throughout many cultures of the world. He lives, in fact, several archetypes. He is the Bound Giant, like the Greek Prometheus, or the Hebrew Azazel; a Trickster like the Southwest Indian Coyote, and the Greek Hermes; the Shapeshifter of the Celtic Taliesin; and the Light-bearer of Lucifer, Lugh, and Prometheus. He is the closest, of all the Rökkr, to humanity because of his humanity; more than any of the other gods his characteristics are inherently, and obviously, human.

Loki's cross-cultural archetypal forms help provide a deeper understanding of those aspects of him that are merely hinted at in our myths. Prometheus is a Titan, the elder race like the Nordic Jotuns; although the relationship between him and Zeus is far more vociferous than that of Loki and Odin, he was similarly bound as a punishment. Beyond the obvious European trickster archetypes of Hermes and Pan, Loki's cultural cousins are most prominent in the mythology of North America. Here the trickster has even persisted in the modern figure of Br'er Rabbit. Across the continent, the trickster appears under a myriad of names: Raven, Blue Jay, Coyote, Rabbit, Mink, Great Rabbit, Nanabush, Glooskap, and Spider.

The characteristics of the trickster are consistent wherever he appears. He is always a bungler; his recklessness often results in the loss of life and he frequently never learns from his mistakes, although there is always a great truth revealed in his naiveté. Like Loki and his sexual foolery with Thor's goat, the American trickster figures are often connected with sexual vulgarity. In one story, Great Hare told his anus to watch some cooking food while he slept, but when he awoke the food was gone, so Great Hare punished his anus by burning it with a fiery brand. As a result, his intestines fell out, and Great Hare had to sew his anus back together with a length of string, which is why the anus has its wrinkled shape. Often, as in this case, the trickster is left to perform those peculiar jobs that the other gods consider to be beneath them. But he is beyond such self-consciousness, because he is fully aware that every task in the cosmos must be performed for it to function and continue.

Loki's trickster aspect also makes him one of the most recognisable, or perceivable, northern deities. He will often manifest himself in vicious, although inevitably innocuous, mishaps, such as making a computer crash when he is the subject being written about. Likewise, naming someone or something after Loki may ultimately prove detrimental. However, as with all Rökkr deities, the risk or threat that Loki poses are more apparent for those who are not of him. Loki never stops his trickery, but for those who are aware of him, and one with him, it is often in more of a friendly, well-natured way, with a glint shining in his eyes.

The myriad of aspects possessed by Loki are listed as kennings in the Skaldskaparmal. He is called: Son of Farbauti and Laufey, of Nal, brother of Byleist and Helblindi, father of Vanargand (Fenrir) and of Iormungand, and Hel's and Narvi's and Vali's relative and father, brother, comrade and table-companion of Odin and the Æsir, Geirrod's visitor and casket ornament, thief of goats and of Brisingamen and Iduna's apples, mother of Sleipnir, husband of Sigyn, enemy of the gods, Sif's hair-harmer, maker of mischief, the cunning As, accuser and trickster of the gods, contriver of Baldr's death, the bound one, and wrangler with Heimdall and Skadi.

Loki is also the god of lightning, the god of the southern or auster wind, and the god of transformations. He has several favoured animal forms: the salmon, the fly, and the falcon, but his most applicable form is the spider. Not only is the spider one of the totem animals associated with Native American tricksters, but it is also an animal with a strong connection to the goddess. Significantly, an ancient Swedish word for spider, *lockke*, suggests a linguistic origin for Loki's name.

Loki

by Fuensanta Plaza

Sudden, unpredictable change. Why do these words sound ominous? Why do we automatically assume, "change for the worse?" Change means birth, life, sudden joy, as well as death, illness, and destruction. Without change, life becomes death, movement is frozen into immobility, joy turns complacent. Loki is the god of change (and yes, He is a god). He is the unpredictable one, ever-changing, ever-shimmering, the joker in the pack. He is the god of laughter, and the god of miracles. He is wildfire, and beauty; he is also danger and destruction from which—always—new life will emerge. He is the god of hope. In seemingly desperate situations, when we see no way out, it is Loki we seek, whether we know it or not. It is Loki who will shift the situation and change it so that a solution pops out from the new situation like a seed from a pod. Without Loki, the gods are static, frozen into immobility. Their ways become set. Try to imagine the gods' life without Loki. Omit him from all the stories. Watch these stories shrivel and lose life.

It is amazing that we, as heathens, should confuse danger with evil. It is amazing that we should pay lip service to bold Northern folk, and be ourselves afraid of danger. It is amazing that we negate the qualities that make our religions strong. If we want flawless gods, we have come to the wrong place. If we want perfection, we need to look toward Christianity (and incidentally live with the problem of why one perfect god would choose to create the shit we live in). Our gods are not all-powerful, nor are they perfect. They are like us, only more so. We have been told by vague post-Christian sources to mistrust Loki as a devil figure, and we have obligingly complied. Why? Because Loki is a Trickster, and could trick us? So could Odin. So could Freya. It is easier to dump all our fears on one scapegoat god, but all gods are dangerous, whether we want it or not. No god should be lightly invoked.

Loki's role in Ragnarok? Who is to tell? Freya Aswynn, to whose book I owe much of my spiritual life, says of the gods that they evolve along with their worshippers. Who can tell what Loki is like today? Unlike Christianity, in which the main figure is static—and for good reason, being dead—the Heathen gods are alive. They have had many adventures since they were last written about and of those adventures, we know nothing. We insist on safely relegating them to the past, but they have a life in the present. The Gods have changed. Within our Wyrd, we have a certain range of free will. Within orlog, the world too, has a certain range of free will: "as above, so below, as without, so within, as the universe, so the soul…" And the outcome of the gods is as uncertain as our own.

Guidelines for invoking Loki are useless: Loki does not take kindly to guidelines—maybe not even to this one! The most I can do is describe my own connection with him. In a situation in which six people were involved, all with conflicting interests, one particular evening when I was tired of hurting, I lit a fire, put a cluster of zinkite opposite the fire, and the Dagaz rune between the two, and said to Loki, "Any trickster can solve a situation so someone wins and someone loses. If you are indeed the god of surprises, surprise everyone by proving them wrong. Fix it so everyone wins. This I will do in return: I shall wear the Dagaz rune, your rune, always. I shall honor you every time I light a flame, candle or fire. I shall bear witness to your kindness. This is my need-fire. In my need, I challenge you, and I know you can help. Now prove it."

That night, I suddenly woke up, because my covers were thrown off my body, and I was being pulled briskly downward by my ankles. I felt a huge, fierce joy had swept into the room. Essentially, the presence was emanating two things: it was glad to be called, to be freed from constraint—and it was testing me. The only thing I could do was repeat firmly, "the good of all and the free will of all." The tugging did not cease until I added "or not at all." The experience was both terrifying and wonderful: it was extremely dangerous, yet I have never felt so safe. The situation was solved, in true Loki fashion. The joke was on everyone and nobody got hurt; all fell into place.

I invoke Loki often, now. I never forget he can be dangerous. I accept the danger. I do not expect him to solve situations my way. Loki will solve them his way. At first I would invoke him as the catalyst, only reminding him that any bungler can harm, but only a true artist can heal. Now, I am no longer stupidly arrogant enough to remind him of anything. His will be done.

Four sentences bring a direct connection to Loki as to any other god: "Please." "Thank you." "Oops, sorry!" and the most important one of all, "I love you." I also call on his wife Sigyn, She of the staying power. Ever wondered what she saw in him to marry him? Constancy needs change. In that union, in that apparent contradiction, all of living is contained. In between the worlds Loki moves, god of paradox, guardian of the fragile balance between life and death, night and day, light and dark, creation and destruction.

Courting the Trickster
by Sophie Oberlander

I am always amused by the reactions I get when it becomes known that I am dedicated in part to Loki. (I am primarily bound to Odin, but the Old Man seldom evokes such a strained response.) No other God or Goddess seems to inspire quite the same degree of discomfort, or in some cases outright hostility, as Odin's blood brother. It often saddens me to see how Loki is approached for invariably the methods fall into one of two categories: either he is spoken of in jesting terms, and His name evoked to allow for expiation of any number of foolish acts, or He is regarded with suspicion, hostility and no small degree of fear. But Loki is far more than the sum of lore, and like any Trickster resists such neat, if derogatory compartmentalization.

The fact that Loki is a trickster is certainly not up for debate. It is His role, nature and function that are often misunderstood. The word 'fool' is often applied to trickster figures such as Loki, though it does not carry quite the same connotation as one might think. In the medieval period, the fool was often the only member of the court who could speak painful truths to the king without facing possible execution. As such, the fool as an archetype is a figure unhindered by societal constraints. He is not a safe or comfortable figure, and He has a disconcerting tendency to alter all rules and mores to fit His own desires. However, one must explore exactly what the ultimate goal of any Trickster's actions is.

While it is true that Loki (or indeed any deity that chooses the role of Trickster) can create a state of extreme discomfort and annoyance, I would posit that if He shows up, there is always a reason for His presence. What may on the surface appear to be totally uncontrolled chaos can then be regarded as coldly calculated strategy, with the Trickster as the vehicle of truth.

Loki is the enemy of entropy and complaisance, and He fights these with a vengeance. He is the enemy of a heart without passion, devoid of devotion. He can be wrenchingly cruel to His children, but in hindsight it is never 'cruelty' but rather the firmness of a parent to an erring child. And therein lies the secret to His motivation (as irritating as that may be to those of us who would choose to believe that we are beholden to no one): He forces us into accepting the full weight of our wyrd, into opening to the myriad ways in which the Gods may inspire us, to actively claiming our own potential and the responsibility that comes with it. He can be a bastard, it's true (and I say this loving Him dearly) but He's a bastard with a purpose.

I won't say that my relationship with Loki has always been easy, but I will admit that it was through Him, more than any other, that I came to define the spiritual journey as a process of falling in love with God. I was very fortunate in the early stages of my growth as both a Heathen and a priest. I started out dedicated to Loki, and over the years it was He who first led me to Odin. I knew the stories, of course, but put little stock in lore. There is a great temptation, especially in reconstructionist religions like Heathenry, to cling to lore, to hold to it as sacred gospel, using it to define and compartmentalize one's spiritual world. The spiritual journey, however cannot and will not be safely delineated in such a fashion (yet another lesson from my beloved Trickster), and when lore alone defines that journey our souls wither in their shells. Many people hold to lore staunchly because they are afraid to hold to God, afraid of the implications of Gods that aren't neat cardboard stereotypes or archetypes but living, loving, passionately manifesting beings. Lore is important only when one knows how to interpret it; otherwise it is a useless crutch and worse-than-useless blockage to the spiritual experience—all the more so when one cannot move beyond its literal interpretation. The Gods cannot be and are not defined by words dead on a page, but reveal Their wisdom to eyes trained in the exploration of the patterns and rhythm of Divine Being and Wyrd.

Having come to this conclusion early on as a result of my own personal experiences with Odin, I was not bound by any preconceptions regarding His brother's nature and was able to allow my relationship with Loki to develop naturally. And develop it most certainly did! Loki shows us that the Gods are real. They are alive, living, passionate and dangerous. Their existence is not bound about by the pages of the Eddas like withered flowers pressed into a book. They have the power to move in our world and in our hearts and bring transformation—whether we are ready for it or not.

Loki has caused me more fear and discomfort than any other God that I have ever honored, called or worked with and I thank Him for it. He has forced me to stretch the boundaries of my understanding to the breaking point and beyond, gently (and sometimes not so gently) pointing out areas where I fall short, especially in my faith, troth and trust. Then in His own inimitable way, He began to teach me. His presence is a constantly palpable thing in my life. Having observed Loki's actions within our own Kindred, I've come to realize that He acts as a catalyst and facilitator of personal growth. And with that growth may come the inevitable growing pains.

The Trickster is not an easy one to face or to accept, and not only because boundaries are irrelevant to Him. He forces us to examine in minute detail our own shadows, egos and facades. He is a powerfully kinetic instrument of truth revealing what is meaningless and unhealthy in a way that is utterly pure, odd though it may be to associate purity with Loki. The inherent difficulty in this is the element of sacrifice integral to His nature. Interestingly enough, for all that the Trickster may challenge us in facing our own masks, that very role of 'trickster' is but a mask that He himself dons. What lies beneath that varies: intense grief and pain, compassion, ecstasy.

I would definitely call Loki a God of ecstatic union. In my shamanic-work, I have had experiences of witnessing Loki standing at the foot of the Tree weeping as Odin hung, and certainly I've had hints that there is more to Their relationship than is ever recorded in lore. More than anything else, Loki is a God that demands, at least of his women, utter surrender to passionate union. He can be playful, raunchy, crude, sarcastic (and my GODS He is never silent—I've had running conversations with Him throughout my day and His commentary on mortal nonsense is stimulating to say the least!), tender (eliciting a vulnerability that I would have denied I was capable of), fiercely protective, and coldly compelling. But one thing that I have never in ten years of working with Him seen Him be is cruel for cruelty's sake. I was once told by Sigyn that to truly understand Loki's nature, one must see and understand Him as He is with Her—not something most Heathens bother to do.

Perhaps the key to understanding Loki is striving to see through His eyes, for I'm certain that the Gods' perception of our wyrd is quite different and far more encompassing that our own could ever be. I would never hesitate to suggest that a student talk to Loki, and that is one of the secrets to truly bonding with one's Gods: simple conversation, just as one would converse with a loved one in person. I've found Him to be one of the easiest Gods to contact, to feel intimately and directly—getting Him to go away is a totally different story, though! One of the greatest gifts that Loki has given me was introducing me to His bride Sigyn, and that has opened up a completely unexpected door in my spirituality. Experiencing the Gods on such a personal and direct level certainly takes nothing away from Their Divine nature; rather it enhances our own connection and understanding of it.

One area in which Loki's influence on me has been profound is my role as teacher and spiritual counselor within my kindred. A Wiccan acquaintance once, after seeing me in action, speculated that my totem animal must be a pit-bull! As Loki does not move within a person's comfort zone, so through Him have I as gythia been taught to rip away a student's comfort zone so that they may approach their kindred, Gods, and life from a position of truth and clarity not based on egotism, fear or conformity. This can often be harsh, but the results are definite and undeniable. Of course, I also have a tendency to make extremely off-color and/or rude comments at unexpected times, which is a less complimentary offshoot of being devoted to Him.

Basically, Loki stirs things up, having little interest in maintaining the spiritual status quo. There is a line in "Dreams of Isis" by Normandi Ellis: "Despite our best efforts to remain the same, we shall all be changed." And that is Loki in action.

Loki: Mother of Witches
by Mordant Carnival

Loki's sex-changing nature has been expounded upon by folklorists and devotees alike. It's a fascinating subject for academic study and a very good focus for those meditating upon the God in a spiritual context. The story of his birthing Sleipnir while transformed into a mare is well-known, as are those tantalising lines in the Lokasenna where His blood-brother Odin refers to another incident in which Loki has played a female role. Here Loki is described as having spent eight winters in some underground location, either milking cows or—depending on the translator—being milked, lactating. The closing lines of the same stanza accuse Loki of giving birth (some translators have rejected these as spurious, however).

It should be made very clear that this piece does not try to challenge Loki's maleness—it's not the argument that He is 'really' a Goddess, simply that He contains within His nature a maternal aspect and that in this aspect He could be seen as a maternal figure in relation to magical practioners.

From the Lesser Völuspá...

The wolf did Loki sire on Angrboda,
And Sleipnir he bore to Svadilfari;
The worst piece of witchcraft seemed the one
Sprung from the brother of Byleist then.
A heart ate Loki—in the embers it lay,
And half-cooked found he the woman's heart-
With child from the woman Lopt soon was,
And thence among men came every troll-woman.
  [emphasis mine]

The phrase rendered here as 'troll-woman' is an interesting one. It appears that it's a translation of the word *flagð*, a word which is also translated as ogress, giantess, witch, she-wolf. This strongly suggests female energy, then; wild female energy, of a fierce, fearsome, devouring nature, but could also be seen as metaphorically referring to monsters and witches in general.

Compare this passage from the Völuspá...

The war I remember, the first in the world,
When the gods with spears had smitten Gullveig,
And in the hall of Hár had burned her,
Three times burned, and three times born,
Oft and again, yet ever she lives.
Heid they named her
When she came to the house,
The wide-seeing witch,
In magic wise;
She performed seið where she could,
Worked seið in a trance,
To evil women
She was always a joy.

So one the one hand we're told that the witch lives and goes around teaching her scary magics to people (especially those evil women), whereas on the other it's suggested that Loki has devoured her heart and given birth from it. We needn't necessarily see the two interpretations as mutually exclusive, because we're in the realms of myth here where there's more than one way to skin a cat. We can see the witch as having survived by being reborn from Loki... one could almost say that the Balesmith himself has become her, temporarily, in the way that a possessed person "becomes" a God... And the brood of flagð? Those who have learned her wicked ways, perhaps.

And if all this sounds a bit darker than you usually like your Dark Arts, remember who's telling you this. All due respect to Snorri, but he's a Christian—not likely to be on board with the practice of magic or female emancipation either. There are older, deeper currents here; things obscured by time and faith and politics.

Gullveig says: follow the money. When your God wants women in their place, a woman out of her place becomes the very Devil. (And as for those seið-men...!) The negative character attributed to this brood of flagð in the verses above may well be an interpolation informed by these attitudes.

I find that approaching Loki in this way is a very powerful way of honouring Him. Even something as simple as amending devotions to include a phrase acknowledging this—"Mother of Witches", for instance—can add depth and richness to interactions with Him. Scratch Loki and he bleeds Babalon? Just a thought.

Trickster

by Sophie Oberlander

I never sought You.
Those places deep within my heart
Were far too burned and scarred
To let You in, hard like misshapen stone.
Or so I thought. But I gave much
The first time I hung on that Tree.
Not enough, by far, but just enough
To shatter that wall of stone
The barest fragment breaking free.
I heard Your whisper, but turned aside my face...
You could not be speaking to me.
I felt Your gentle touch cradling my wounded spirit
As You cradled Odin,
His body bloodied, His spirit on fire beneath that Tree
Long before I climbed its branches.

Was it through Your laughter that You taught me to love You?
Or through the tenderness of Your caress?
I have seen a face of You that few bother to see.
I have felt Your burning passion,
Gentle and tender beneath the Tree.
Brother, Lover, Friend,
No image of God quite prepared me for You.
You eased away my terror with Your wicked cavorting,
Making a broken child laugh by playing the fool.
I have seen Sigyn's quiet contentment,
And the love behind Your games.
I no longer understand the trepidation
In which others call Your name.

I have seen Your other face too,
When You took me to Your daughter's realm.
I have seen You, locked in ecstasy
Summoning up Her wards and wights for me.
My heart's stone did not so much break
As melt beneath Your flame.
I have tasted Your rage, Your fury at my hurt,
Reveled in the darkest glee
With which You opened the gates of Niflheim to defend me.
No one told me how much You cherish Your children.
I have seen You, Trickster, weeping in anguish
Every one of Your childrens' wounds piercing Your heart.

And I have seen You in battle, Odin's equal,
Though Yours a far darker art.

I have heard Your song,
Far sweeter than I ever knew it could be,
As You took my hand, and led me from that Tree.
It is Your stories I cherish most,
As we walk Bifrost bridge,
Dancing patterns amongst the stars.
You placed my hands upon the web,
And taught me songs to weave.
As I hung for Asgard, through You,
For Hella's realm I reached.

I know how You are feared,
Or mocked, or thought long bound.
But I know too, it was Your hand
Guiding me through my darkest despair and pain.
And how can I fear Your deepest love,
When it is the freedom of my heart I've gained?
Loki, now it is Your burning that I seek.
Let us mingle songs beneath the Tree,
For I adore the flame You have ignited in me.

To Loki
by Elizabeth Vongsvisith

Hail to my lord,
Burning brand of Jotunheim.
Laufey's son, Scar-lip,
Mother of Sleipnir, Wolf's-sire,

flickering flame of Ásgarð,
Hail to you,
Sky-traveler, Giants'-son,
father of Hela and Jormungand.

Hail to you, Shapeshifter,
Always surprising
Bringer of unforeseen gifts,
Bringer of endings

skilled thief and magician,
with your sly, bold ways;
bringer of changes,
and new beginnings.

Hail, my beloved,
Dazzling, daring,
Your speech stings the unwary
Your cunning cuts deep

who speaks brazen truths.
delightful Fool and Trickster,
like shards of shattered mirror.
as a drawn and deadly sword.

Hail to you, Flame-hair,
Beloved husband of Sigyn,
Þorr's friend and companion,
Brilliant, bright-eyed,

Ás-consort of Angrboða,
Oðinn's true blood-brother,
lover of goddesses and giants,
too beautiful to resist.

Hail to you, ever-defiant
Wielding your own wyrd,
Mindful of your honor,
Enduring the world's scorn

Breaker-of-Worlds,
faithful to your sworn word,
with honor accorded by few,
until the Nine Worlds' end.

Hail Loki, lightning-born
Fire of my heart,
Swift-footed Elder Kin,
Dark as the deep forest standing

child of the Iron Wood.
fire of my soul's hearth,
bright as burning stars,
fearsome in shadow.

Hail Loki, Laufey's son,
Burning brand of Jötunheim.
Clever stealer of treasures,
Ever changing the world,

flickering flame of Ásgarð,
Hail to you,
wild Father-of-Monsters,
now and forever.

Loki's Day
11th day of Lithemonath (June 11)
Pagan Book of Hours, Order of the Horae

Color: Red
Element: Fire
Altar: Upon a red cloth place three red candles, a stone with the rune Os carved into it, the figure of a mare, the figure of a bird, two small round stones, and a chain.
Offerings: Examine yourself for how you manipulate others, even for their own good, or with truthful means. Be ruthless with yourself.
Daily Meal: Hot, spicy food.

Invocation to Loki

> Laufey's Son,
> Trickster of the far north,
> Delicate spawn of giants,
> Wheedler and coaxer with the secret agenda,
> Liar who speaks the truth others will not hear,
> We call you, two-faced one whose soul burns bright,
> And invite you to be critical of our souls.
> You love to make us break our vows,
> When those vows are made heedlessly.
> You love to catch us in our own hypocrisies
> And puncture our bubbles of pride.
> Nothing is safe from you, no emotion
> Is sacrosanct from your prodding.
> What do we really think, you ask?
> What are we not saying? You know,
> And your shifty eyes catch ours,
> Your crafty smile slips across your face,
> And we blush in shame, knowing
> That you have read our foolish fumblings
> With the truth. For the truth is a flame that burns,
> You tell us. Do not pretend to eat fire
> If you are not willing to suffer the consequences,
> Which is to be cast out by others.
> Only when we are clear-eyed and humble
> Will your gaze toward us be free of slyness.
> Loki, Spirit of Truth and Lies,
> Burn us with the measure of our own words.

Sigyn

Sigyn is Loki's second wife, and the only member of the (possibly) Aesir race that we celebrate here. (Most folks consider Sigyn to have been born among the Aesir, although her actual origins are not mentioned in the lore.) That is because Sigyn is one of the few Aesir to marry a Jotun and stay with him, and the only one to defect entirely, rejecting her own people when they murdered her son and bound her husband with his intestines. When Loki was cast beneath the earth, she stayed with him in defiance of her people, holding a bowl to catch the serpent's corrosive poison. Only when she had to turn aside to empty the bowl did Loki writhe in pain.

There are two sides to Sigyn, as the folk who work with her often say. The first is the child bride, given to Loki for his new position as blood brother of Odin when he came to Asgard. Shy, innocent, almost childlike, this aspect of Sigyn is celebrated in Sophie Oberlander's essay below. Her other aspect is also discussed; both are sides of this little-known Goddess of the open heart and unconditional love.

Sigyn: Loki's Gentle Bride

by Galina Krasskova

I had been a priest of Odin and friend to Loki for many years before I ever encountered Sigyn. Up until that point, I had never had a particularly strong or close relationship with any of the Norse Goddesses, so it was a delightful surprise to find myself being strongly drawn to Sigyn, the wife of Loki—all the more so since She is unlike any other Goddess I have ever loved. Now, there's almost nothing about Sigyn in the lore. She's mentioned three times, in every instance referenced as the wife of Loki who remains with Him when He is bound, dutifully holding a bowl to capture the poison of the serpent, which Skadi hung above Loki as added torture. It is also noted that She has two sons by Loki: Narvi and Vali, the former of which is killed when Loki is bound.

Sadly, she often stands in the shadows of the more popular Asynjur like Freya or Frigga. I have seen Her dismissed as everything from a dutiful doormat to the epitome of the abused wife. Very, very rarely, however, have I ever encountered anyone who has had any type of interaction with this Goddess and I can well understand why: Loki is very protective of His bride. I myself have refused to hail Her in symbel halls where Loki is unwelcome. She, more than any other Deity I have ever encountered, evokes a protectiveness in those who know Her that one does not often associate with a God. Of all the things that I have been privileged to learn in my spiritual life, this I know with utter surety: Loki loves Sigyn as He loves no other and She alone holds the key to His heart.

Needless to say, I never expected to fall in love with such an amazingly gentle Goddess. Sigyn initially chose to come to me as a gentle, shy child bride. I had never dreamed that a Deity would choose the appearance of a young person! It was completely beyond my experience, but I have always believed in allowing the Gods to define the nature of Their interactions with us and so I welcomed Her. How could I not? She was, if it is not hubris to say so, utterly adorable! I was completely charmed by Her innocence, Her playfulness, Her gentle nature. I, who prided myself on being the implacable warrior, was well and truly brought to my devotional knees. Over the next few months, as I began developing a relationship with this Goddess, I found myself often frustrated by the lack of concrete information on Her, for I'm sure the manner in which She has chosen to reveal Herself to me may not be how She comes to every single person. Not only was there little to nothing in lore, but no one in the Heathen community that I had ever met or corresponded with honored Her.

Thankfully, this has since changed and I've discovered a small number of Sigyn's folk out there, but at the time, I felt as though I was the only one. Questions about Her background remain, however. For instance, I'd love to know who Her parents are, whether She's Vanir or Aesir or elf, for instance. I've often had the UPG that She was a foundling, fostered with Njord and His family, a small, waiflike thing that captured Loki's heart the moment He saw Her. A close friend, devoted to both Sigyn and Loki believes conversely that She must be Jotun, for had Loki married outside of His own race, surely even the Eddas would have noted it. She has a beautiful name for this Goddess she adores: Lady of the Staying Power, for She experiences Sigyn not as a child but as a grown woman, a source of immense security and strength for Loki.

Sigyn comes to me as such a gentle, shy, almost childlike Goddess. The lessons that She brings have been no less transformative then say, Loki's or Odin's, but She is gentle and playful about it. Personally, I see Her as a Goddess of love and devotion. She has taught me so much about my own heart, how to see the beauty and divinity in the smallest thing, and how to play...not something that I ever really did before. Most importantly, She has taught me the value of loving without fear and the strength in gentleness. Anger has been my besetting challenge for most of my life and after passing through years and years of less than subtle lessoning from the various warrior Goddesses, I've found to my surprise that Sigyn has brought an understanding that hopefully will lead to mastery and balance. I no longer see showing gentleness as a weakness or denigrate my own childlike wonder, which since I was a child myself I have long hidden away as a thing to scorn.

There is a strength in Her and, when She shows Herself as Loki's wife in the cave, a grief that often moves me to tears. Yet at the same time, She possesses an elfin inquisitiveness, unguarded sweetness and deep compassion that has allowed Her to open my heart as no other could. Perhaps because She comes in such an unassuming manner, She has the capacity to wheedle into places long barred even to the touch of the Gods. She soothes and I have found Her a willing haven when the call of duty becomes particularly painful.

She is so sweet, I just cannot come up with another term! There is simply no pretense about Her. When Loki first introduced me to Her, one of the first things I did to honor Sigyn was to set up an altar to Her, just for Her. Needless to say, it turned out to be completely unlike any other altar that I have: there are pretty things on it, stones like rose quartz that I never work with, toys...She had me buying Her dolls and stuffed animals! I hate to fall into psychobabble, but I think Sigyn is a Goddess that will help us to heal our "inner child". It's difficult to fight the impulse to nurture Her. Not only do I buy Her toys, but other people with whom I worship have taken to bringing gifts for Her altar, which I find incredibly moving. Sigyn has collected a nice little basket of toys and goodies all Her own. I've come to truly believe that She is the Goddess of the inner child and will heal heart-wounds within us if given half a chance. In Her child persona, She is whimsical and tends to "inflict" that attitude on those who love Her! I don't claim in any way to know how She comes to others, but for me, this is the form She has taken, though once I did see an incredibly fierce aspect of Her, when a child was in danger and She was easily as fierce as Kali Ma, though there was an intense sadness and grief throughout the entire experience.

I suppose I also see Her as a Goddess of neglected children. The best way that I know how to put it is this: Sigyn gathers broken things to Her breast. Her laughter is delightful and She is utterly devoted to Loki. She always seems so very vulnerable to me, a little girl who likes Her toys, likes to laugh, wants to be loved and Loki does love Her dearly. Through UPG, I've come to believe that He must have known Her for years before Their courtship began and I wonder about those years, stories left out of the lore of a time when the Gods were vulnerable and waiting in love.

I must admit, it moves my heart how tender and protective Loki is with His young bride. I knew Him for over two years before He chose to introduce me to Her. And she is so shy, so unbelievably shy. I find myself feeling very, very protective of Her, as if She were a little girl placed into my care. So not only has meeting Sigyn introduced me to another Goddess, one that is healing my heart in ways I never imagined possible; but I have seen quite a different aspect of Loki from what is commonly expected: a loving, tender consort/protector. Sigyn has taught me to open myself and embrace the Gods with the innocence and acceptance of a child. She too strips away the facades and walls and blockages within, but She does it so gently, so very gently that it is a sweet embrace. It seems to me as though even the other Gods relax and become more unguarded when in Her presence and this has granted me yet another immense gift, that of seeing another side to those Gods, like Odin and Loki, that I love. Her words on the matter: even the Gods need comfort sometimes.

Insofar as my offerings to Her go, I find that Sigyn, like many a child, likes fluffy, pretty things, things that inspire happiness and laughter. Flowers are always abundant on Her altar, especially pink roses. Hearts, in the case of my altar, fluorite, labradorite and rose quartz abound. She loves pearls and jewelry of all sorts, and stuffed animals ...especially rabbits, dragonflies and cows (an Audhumla thing, I think— there's a connection with Sigyn and Audumhla and primal creation that I've not been permitted to explore yet). I have a friend that watches Pokemon and certain sweet anime shows to amuse Her; I've even broken down and watched "Sound of Music" for Her just to hear Her giggle. For me, Her sacred herb is milk thistle though I find pretty much any healing herb appropriate. She also has me collecting keys, a symbol of a woman's authority in the home among the ancient Norse cultures. In fact, She insists that I wear a large, Victorian iron key at my waist at all tribal functions. I occasionally buy Her necklaces, beads: I see Her playing with beads, small, pretty boxes and the like.

There is no worse experience in the world for me than to know that Sigyn is upset. I know also that She is more than capable of coming to a person as a strong, independent Goddess in Her own right. It is simply that for me, this is what She has chosen. I've known other Sigyn's folk for whom it has been much the same. By honoring Her in this fashion, accepting Her choice of guises, I do not intend in any way to disrespect a Goddess whose name after all means "lady of victory." Sigyn is one of the most bright-hearted Goddesses I have ever worked with, and She teaches that to Her devotees. Her primary attributes are loyalty, devotion, love, happiness and an almost awe inspiring innocence. She is, above all else, a Goddess Who opens the heart.

Invocation to Sigyn

Gentle Goddess,
Teach me to play.
I've seen the joy You take
In the smallest thing of beauty.
Teach me gentleness,
the sweetness of Your song.
I want to sing, as You sing
When You know Loki is listening.
I wish to be among those nurtured
By Your tender hands,
A bright flower
Pruned by Your gentle fingers.
Teach me to love,
As You love:
Without condition.

(Invocation originally published in "Exploring The Northern Tradition" by Galina Krasskova, © 2005 New Page Books)

Sigyn's Courage

by Gudrun

Sigyn came to me during a dark time in my life, and brought comfort and strength, more than I could have expected. My first child was born prematurely, and was terribly ill. Even when I could bring her home from the hospital, she still needed a great deal of extra care, and she cried constantly and was always miserable. The pregnancy had been difficult for me as well, with a great many medical problems, and I was weak, ill, hypoglycemic from too much nursing, suffering from a terrible case of post-partum depression to the point of near-psychosis, and then forced through months of sleep-deprivation while caring for my child. My husband of the time commuted hours to his job, and was almost never home, and I was estranged from my blood family over their poor treatment of me, so I was all alone with my predicament. We had very little money, and no sitter in their right mind would have stayed with my sick infant anyway.

Night after night, I walked the floor with my sleepless, screaming child. Day after day, I fed her at my breast, only to watch her vomit up much of my milk from her underdeveloped gastro-intestinal tract that had been rushed too soon into digesting food. She could not digest formula at all, of any kind, so I was her only nourishment. Keeping her fed was a struggle. Keeping her happy seemed impossible. Some nights, when I could finally rock her, half-singing and half-weeping, into a state of restless sleep for a few hours, I would lie on the floor of her nursery, too exhausted to stagger into the bedroom and collapse, waiting with one ear open even in my sleep for her to begin crying again.

One night, I dreamed that I went into a house in the dark. It was a cheap prefab house, dusty and dirty as if no one had cleaned it in a long time, and I remember seeing empty cupboards open with no food in them. I placed my hands on my breasts, which were normally overflowing with milk, as the immense amount of often-wasted milk that I needed to produce to feed her was at least forthcoming as long as I ate constantly, desperately, often with her attached to my teat sucking out the nutrients as fast as I could put them in. In my dream, my breasts were flat and empty, and although I tried to tell myself that this was a dream, I had trouble believing it. I feared that when I woke up, there would be no more milk for my daughter, and she would die, even after all that I had fought to keep her alive.

In the middle of the dusty kitchen, sitting on the floor, was a thin, worn woman in an old shift. Her hair was dry and tangled, hanging to her shoulders, and her face was lined with despair, her eyes glazed over. She rocked back and forth, murmuring to herself. I knelt on the floor next to her and reached out to her, slowly. She looked up, suddenly, and seized my hands. Her eyes met mine, locked onto me, took me with her.

For that moment I was transported into a hideous place. Screams echoed off the stone walls of the underground cavern, screams so harrowing that I wanted to cover my ears. The sight of a rough wooden bowl, burnt in the middle and worn away at the edges, filled with a clear liquid that smoked, gave off fumes that stung my eyes. Sharp stones under my feet as I stumbled to the far side of the cave, blurred vision from fumes and tears, throwing the contents of the bowl against the wall with the eaten-away stone. Then a stumble to the other side of the dark space—must not lose that bowl!—to rinse it in the trickling water, fill it with the brackish stream, then back to the bound figure, to rinse off the poison, dodge the bites of the swinging snake, soothe and comfort and heal the wounds with my tears. Again and again and again, without ending. I would have called it hellish, that place, except that I know that Hel had nothing to do with this place of torment.

I wept with her. I spilled out my pain to her, wordlessly, through choking sobs. I was empty, except for that pain. *How could this happen to me? I did everything that I was supposed to do. I was a good wife. I got pregnant, like I was told that I ought to. All I wanted was the happy mother-child experience, like they write about in all the earthy-crunchy magazines—the mother in the long peasant skirt, smiling, nursing her babe and feeling right with the world, healthy and fulfilled and becoming one with the essence of the Earth Mother. All I wanted was that peaceful home and family, and here I am in a place of torment, through no fault of my own! I have no family now, no kin to aid me. I do not deserve this! I have done nothing wrong!*

I understand, she said to me. *I understand. I understand.* She rocked me, and I rocked her; we rocked together on that hard, dirty floor. *There will be enough,* she said. *You can see it through, and believe that there will be an ending. I believe. I believe that I am strong enough to come to that end.*

"But you did this for love," I whispered, my voice hollow and echoing in the too-silent room. "I don't know if I love her. All I feel is empty. I look at my child and I feel empty. I don't know if I can do this without love."

"There is not only love in this," she said. "There is also Right Doing. The Gods may create a place of torment for you, out of spite or merely indifference, but there is comfort in the Right Doing. Once you have started, you must go on, for who would you be if you abandoned it, after having begun?"

"I don't know if I can take it," I said in a low voice. My arms crossed over my empty breasts. "I don't know how much more I can give."

She reached out both her hands, gently, and placed them on my breasts, and said, "There will be enough to see it through." And, suddenly, there was that rush of pain and the letting-down, and I was full of milk again. I started half-awake; my daughter was crying again and the sound had triggered my breasts to let down and I staggered out of bed, back to my daily grind. As I took my screaming, writhing child from her cradle, I heard the last echo of Sigyn's voice in my mind. "My name means victory," she said.

"Victory," I whispered, as I stuffed the nipple in my child's mouth and held her, hard. The screams were stopped, for the moment. "Victory."

Sigyn's Song

by Galina Krasskova

Scorned they call me.
They tried to keep me away.
My heart lies bound,
Tortured for the truth he spoke.
We knew long ago what would be.
At his birth I knew
They would take my son from me.
I was a child myself, to be given such a choice.
Yet I gave willingly—
My memories, my pain, my rage
Gathered in the alabaster jar I cherish.
They tried to keep me away—final sacrilege,
As if I would ever deny my heart—
To drag me from his side
When the serpent holding all the fury of Midgard was tied.
They tried.
But how could I leave?
I looked into his eyes.
I looked as he was bound by their fear,
By their shame,
By their bitter, bitter pain.
I saw the grief. I saw the disappointment
That it had come to this, and I saw the love.
They never did believe how much he loved,
And in loving, still chose to do what no other would do.
All he ever did came from love,
And a truth, a law so steel bright strong
It could never be ignored.
Even we serve the law of the Tree.

I looked into his wounded eyes,
And as my son's flesh was wrapped about his,
I saw his anguish. How could I leave?
For the first time, I defied them.
I picked up the mask that my husband
Had so willingly worn for them,
I held it before me in my heart
And showed them the mirror of blade-sharp truth it hid.
For the first time I screamed—
I shrieked through the Tree.
Oathbreakers all, what he spoke was the truth.
What he spoke was the poison

Reflected back to its source.
For the first time I shrieked, and bloodied
By what was left of my son,
I gathered, becoming stone, the shreds of my pain.
I sat by his side daring them to tear me away.
They could forget, they could desecrate,
But not I.
I stroked his straining cheek,
Lips bleeding through bitter silence,
I twined my hand in his. And I captured his pain.
Not a cry did he utter, not a tear did he shed,
His eyes locked on mine.

And we, each soul torn apart,
Through Ragnarok we will live.
We feel. We bleed.
The poison searing my hands
As I shield my heart's face
Is nothing compared to the grief that we see.
They never saw what gift we bore.
How can there be hope to give
When they have tossed it carelessly into a pit of venom?
I will stay by his side.
He would not leave me in my pain.
I will be healer to all, Mother of all,
For I may be the only one left
To heal the gods from their games.

Hela

Hel, or Hela, the Goddess of the Underworld, is the eldest child of Angrboda and Loki. She is also the Goddess of Death in the cosmology of the Nine Worlds, and the Keeper of the Underworld. She is one of the most powerful—some might say *the* most powerful—of all the Jotun deities.

Long ago, before the dismemberment of Ymir and the creation of Midgard and Asgard, the underworld was named Jormungrund. It was populated by the dead souls of Jotnar, and some live ones as well—Jotnar are particularly good at traveling to the Deathlands. As far as we can tell, it was looked after by a goddess named Hel, but she was not the Hel who lives there today. Both the name and the job title seem to be something that is passed on. Apparently someone needs to take on the important (and fairly powerful) job of looking after the Dead, and someone is chosen from one of the races when the last Hel retires.

Jotun legend has it that when the old Hel died, the Dead roamed the Nine Worlds for seven years, as there was no one to keep them in check. Every race hoped to have one of its members chosen for this crucial task, which would create an unlimited power-base for whoever was allied with Death, if Death could be persuaded to side with its native race. Collective breaths were held across the Nine Worlds... and then Angrboda, the Hagia of the Iron Wood, had a daughter by her consort, the infamous Loki. When the girl-etin was barely walking, it is said, she took on her shapeshifting form, and it was that of a rotting corpse. This was the signal that she was the inheritor of the name and the title, and she was immediately named Hel, or Hela in the Jotun-tongue (the Alfar call her Leikin), and raised to claim the rulership of the Land of the Dead.

Various rumors went around that Loki and Angrboda had done dark magic to make sure that their child would be the Death Goddess; other rumors said that they had merely foreseen that it would be so, and married in order to bring it about. Whether it came about by chance or planning, it was a great disappointment to the other races, who had hoped to pull the

Deathlands out of the control of Jotun hands. Odin promptly put a "banishing-spell" on the tiny Hela, which basically banned her from ever entering Asgard, and indeed she has never set foot there.

When Hela came of age, she took over Jormundgrund and entirely recreated it, renaming it Helheim. Instead of caves and dankness, she opened it to the black sky and planted orchards, and grass grew over the stony burial mounds. She built the castle Elvidnir and swore that no matter how many the Dead, she would find a way to feed them all, if only sparingly. She redesigned Helheim in such a way as to bring maximum peacefulness to those who reside in it; instead of dank caves, it is a subtly ever-changing tapestry of hills and fields and colorful autumn woods.

Since then, she has dutifully tended to her Dead, about whom she feels fiercely protective. She looks down on necromancy and other forms of magic used to "bother the Dead", although she will allow seidhr-workers and others who respect her boundaries to enter a special area close to Hel's Gate, and speak with what Dead wish to come to them. It is not enough to say that Helheim is ruled by Hela. Her touch is stamped on every part of it. There is no place in that world that she is not aware of, and that world is huge. Most people don't get beyond the "tourist" area past the Gate, so they have no idea of the scale of it. Helheim is the biggest of all the Nine Worlds. It has to be, to hold the legions of the Dead. Its enormous area is held by the cosmic "rootball" of Yggdrasil, like a great disc around its base.

Hela is extremely protective of her dead folk, and She does not appreciate people bothering them unduly. As such, Helheim is strictly guarded. No one sneaks in, any more than they could sneak in to Asgard. (Odin managed it once in order to forcibly conjure up the Volva and compel her to answer questions, but never since.) If you have an appointment to speak with them, She will send whichever dead souls are willing to talk into the area that, for lack of a better term, I refer to as the "tourist area". The rest of Helheim is off limits except to those who live there, and those who work for Hela and have some sort of mark on them to prove it, or those who have been invited there by Her.

Hela sometimes stays at Elvidnir, or she may be out elsewhere in Her land on business. Like all wights of Jotun blood, she is a shapechanger, although her shapeshifting is almost always worked on several variations of her half-rotted form. Hela is probably one of the most physically grotesque of the Death Goddesses; it seems important to Her to push the literality of Death into people's faces. She has been seen as half beautiful woman and half rotting corpse, or half skeleton. Sometimes that division is above and below the waist; more often it is bilateral down the middle. Sometimes she appears as a woman with long pale hair whose whole body slowly moves visually through the process from whole to rotten to skeletal, over and over. Occasionally She has also appeared as a young pale girl with white hair and skin, smelling of rot. (In fact, the rot smell is always present with her, and it is a good way to know that you are actually speaking with Hela. The general coldness of the atmosphere around her is another tip-off. Unlike other deities whose presence is like a strong light, hers is more like a black hole.)

Part of her insistence on keeping these forms rather than a "normal", unrotted form is to force the understanding of Death onto people. She does not hold with any kind of denial around Death; She requires that it be seen and respected as the natural process that it is, and not euphemized or buried or prettied up. If she holds out a hand for you to take, it will be her skeletal one. This is a test. Remember that she was born in the Iron Wood, where showing your acceptance of the physical deformities of others is part of how you show respect and friendship. Take her rotting, skeletal hand (which, as some people have reported, feels exactly like a dead limb except that it moves) and kiss it. If you can't bear to do such a thing, you have no business being in her country. It is said that she only offers her living hand to the Dead, so you should be grateful for small favors.

Hela is tall, generally clad only in a long, simple robe of black or grey, and does not stand on ceremony. She has been described by several people as having a low, quiet "whiskey-and-cigarettes" voice, and she moves slowly and sometimes with a limp (that skeletal foot!) Her great stillness is one of the things that people notice about her. When she sits, she may move her hands some to gesture, but very little else; psychically she is like a great pool of black stillness. Every move is made with graceful, ghostly slowness. It is said that she moves fast only when she is angry, and then you're in too much trouble to notice.

In the northern tradition, it is often possible to bargain with one's deities, or to tease or cajole them, or otherwise play with rules-lawyering and trying to talk around them. Sometimes it even works. Odin and Loki are notable for being open to this kind of activity. On the other end of the spectrum, Hela is totally implacable. When she gives an order to you, nothing you can say will make her change her mind. If you persist in defying her, she will hurt you in some way that is perfectly designed with your personal misery in mind, and will be impossible for you to resist. She shows no sadism or glee in your pain; she just does it as coldly and impersonally as she does so many other things. No one says *No* like a death deity, and Hela's *No* seems to have actual weight to it; you feel crushed by it. There is no fighting her and no bargaining; she will continue to coldly say *No* long after you have no more fight left in you. This is a goddess who can make all the Aesir back down; remember this before you face off with her.

Generally, however, her coldly implacable side is only brought out when someone either A) clearly and knowingly breaks her rules, or B) asks for her aid and advice and then refuses to do what she tells them must be done. If you can avoid these two errors, you won't see it, but it is always there, just beneath the surface of her serene and compassionate demeanor. Many of the folk who have worked with Hela speak admirably of that detached, noninvasive transpersonal compassion, telling of how it gave them a safe space in which to heal themselves.

Hela has a deep wisdom and a great deal of objective perspective; she sees far and wide and studies the threads of Wyrd with an intense focus. She is capable of far-seeing planning on a long-range scale that leaves other, more self-focused deities (not to mention humans) in the dust. If you ask her for advice, you can guarantee that it will be designed with the greatest amount of long-term good in mind, although it may require a good deal of short-term pain and sacrifice. If you need help in extremity, and she feels that it is appropriate, she will give it. If she feels that giving you aid would interfere in your *orlog*, no plea in any world will change her mind. She will not aid anyone in going against the natural order, even a deity; one remembers how even Frigga did not win against her when it came to Baldur's death.

Some folk have felt themselves called to her Underworld and, once there, were informed that she had invited them down as a way to begin a death-and-rebirth period in their lives. If this is the case for you, forget trying to get out of it. This is not Hela's malice or even whimsy; she has neither. Consider it a heads-up that your life is going to fall apart and need to be rebuilt from scratch, and humbly accept whatever advice she may have as to how you can best survive this.

Offerings: Hela likes dried, well-preserved flowers, especially dried roses. She also likes blood, as do all the Death deities. What the Dead themselves seem to like more than anything else is music—instrumental and/or singing, and perhaps poetry read aloud to them. Second to entertainment, offerings of food and drink are traditional.

Working With Hela
by Lydia Helasdottir

You need to know that Hela's definitely lovable. I mean I am completely in love with her. Romantically, obsessively, madly. And also, that she is pitiless, and that's a good thing.

I met her first when I was very young, but I didn't know that it was her, and then I met her properly when I was 19 or so. I was having hunger stuff come up, wanting to rend and predate on people, and that was getting a little bit out of control; I was alienating the people around me. She came like a blast of cold wind and she made all my bones rattle, literally. It was as if I was just a skeleton and this cold wind went right through me, making me rattle. I formally became hers—or rather, I realized that I had been for a long time—her servant and ministrix, at that moment. That's ministrix, as in a minister in a church, and also in terms of a diplomat—her representative in the world, as it were. That part happened somewhat later on, when I became actually capable of understanding what that meant, without getting big-headed about it.

The kinds of jobs that I do for her? I do the classic ministering to dying people, obviously. Recently we were with someone who was dying, and had to force him to stay in his body until his son got there, so that he could say some things that were needed. She's had me learn martial arts. She made me learn runes as well, so that I could understand the processes of Death better. I also guide people into, through, and out the other end of fearful and traumatic experiences, if She thinks that it's good for their personal evolution. That's my greatest job.

One also needs to know that She is Everywhere. I find that she does tend to listen to people, especially when they are in despair, and they can come to sit at her kitchen table and ask her advice, if they do it in a non-egotistical, "yes, I realize that I'm talking to Death" sort of way. The answers that she gives aren't ever what you thought you were going to hear, and they are never comforting. You can't expect comforting from her at all; whether you go there as a priestess of hers, or someone who is requesting help, or just one of her workers, there is never any comfort.

She never lies, ever—and she never makes you guess. If she's pissed off at you, she will tell you exactly what she's pissed off about, and what you need to fix. So you can't ask her questions that you aren't prepared for straight answers to. "Oh, I'm kind of not sure if this current boyfriend is good for my spiritual evolution or not..." "He isn't. Get rid of him." "What! But... but..." "No. Get rid of him." But she will answer questions of those who ask, as long as they are not frivolous.

That's another thing about her. No cheating, no lying, ever. No slacking. Don't promise her anything that you won't be able to do. I have a problem with that. I'm always wanting to promise her things that will make me a better person, but she turns me down, because she knows I can't come through on them. She says, "No. Just do what I tell you." Seriously, if you fail, then you broke a deal with Death, and there are bad consequences for that.

Hela doesn't ask for much in the way of tribute. She's not one of those deities who are incessantly clamoring for offerings and doo-dahs and "You must put fifteen pomegranates on the altar by tomorrow or else I'll kill you". She doesn't seem to be all that interested in that stuff. She likes jewelry, burned things, utensils like spoons and knives, but you have to be willing to give them up and leave them on her altar, or maybe even bury them in the ground or throw them in a river. She likes tea, for some reason. She's not so much into food offerings. But most of all, she likes fear and pain and awe, and if you can generate those states and offer them to her, she likes that better than anything else you can offer her. If you can really get into one of your phobias and then offer that up, that will get her attention. But it has to be real.

She wears many different things. To me, she doesn't always show up as the traditional half-and-half. It's much more dynamic. You look at her skin and it sort of morphs from living to pale to ulcerous, and then you see the bits under the skin. It morphs over her body the whole time. Sometimes she will show up in full-on domme gear with spiky boots. I've seen her in very royal eggplant-colored velvet formal gowns. I've seen her in grey veils, I've seen her in a dress of glass splinters. I've seen her in dresses made of razor blades—a bit like the River Slith, only it's a dress. I occasionally see her in matte-grey scale armor.

I sometimes meet her in her kitchen, sometimes in her orchard. She seems to take me to her orchard when she wants me to do some healing on someone who is very sick, and she wants me to draw out whatever is making them sick. Then they will either heal or let the natural dying process happen...but I never know which one it's going to be. So I can't make my living as a healer, because I can't guarantee a reliable result in terms of getting better.

Besides, the Hela healing modality is harsh, and sometimes it will happen that I will painfully rip something out from them and give it to Her; She will always take that from me. Usually it's easy, but sometimes it happens that it literally gets stuck inside me and I can't give it to her. When that happens, I have to go have a full-on fear-of-Death experience to open the gate properly, and that usually means getting a good martial artist to do a neck-breaking move on me. I'll sit in a meditative position, and they'll creep up behind me with the full intention of killing me, and get me in some kind of neck-lock where my neck could be broken. This is because the meat puppet recognizes the killing intent, the movement, and the fear-of-Death kicks in at that moment, and the Gate opens and She can take the bad stuff out. But that's rare—it's happened maybe three our four times in all the years I've been doing this.

If something gets stuck, it usually means that it is so toxic that the natural quarantine process in me closes down on it, and She has to be so present in my body to get it out that I have to be at that moment of fear-of-Death. One of the really horrendous things I've experiences are these little larvae that hang around hospices, where people go to die. I don't know what they're called, but they live on the souls of people whose lives have been prolonged beyond what they should be, so that Hela has not been able to take them. The medicine and the doctors have kept them alive, and they don't want to be alive. This particular type of despair gets fed on by these creatures, and it is horrible, and whenever you get a session with someone who works in a hospice, they tend to be crawling with them, and it makes them very ill. Once the person has finally died, the little worm-things either jump onto the next person who's in that state, or they jump onto the hospice staff. So I'm Hela's Pest Control.

That is a very intimate encounter with her, because my body believes that it's going to die, and it means that she can be very present. But it doesn't last very long, because you realize that you're not going to die after all; the assassin didn't make the move. If you do a choking or sleeper hold, you can prolong the experience a little bit. If you take herbs that are traditionally used for euthanasia, but in a smaller dose, almost a homeopathic dose, and preferably things that don't damage your liver, you can do the same thing. But that's very dangerous. If you're going to be doing that, you want to stick with the Atropa family. None of that works as well as the actual real assault from behind, but you have to work with a really good martial artist who knows how to do full killing intent without actually carrying it out.

That was really interesting, the first time that I had to do that—"You want me to do what!" But please understand that this came after I'd been working for her a very long time, and that's not for everyone. Hela has really specific jobs for each of the people that she works with. My job is to be her messenger and diplomatic envoy, able to hang out with lots of different kinds of people without looking noticeably out of place. I'm not one of her more socially jeopardized, weird-looking employees. Boardroom, Hell's Angels, I don't care. But the cost of that is that I have to do her stuff everywhere. I don't get to do it only at pagan renfests, or even in friendly environments where it could be understood. I have to do it at people who have no clue about anything.

When she's nearby, my eyes go flat and turn grey or black, and my voice changes. I have to manifest that, even in a room full of executives while I'm making a sales pitch. So I've been hers openly for sixteen years now, full-on, but I'm always learning new things, going to higher levels. She's only been allowing me to work with sacred plants for about two years now, for instance, after a decade of not being allowed to use any drugs at all.

It's hard to make Hela pissed off, but when she is, she's pissed off really big and for a long time, and it's hard to placate her. The first thing is not to ask frivolous questions. Have a good reason to talk to her. When I come to her asking for help, she asks me if I've thought about it, and what the options and consequences might be. She interrogates me on that, and if she thinks that I've done all I can to figure it out, she will answer. Don't expect her to party. Her dad's a partier, but she's not. I find that an easy way to help other people talk to her is to actually go down their ancestor line, and associate with their dead ancestors, and find out about them, figure out what they were like before they died. Because they are actually in the realm of the Dead, or at least they've passed through it—most people aren't going to Valhalla these days—she knows them. To go that way seems to make a useful bridge. Go and tend the graves of your ancestors. That starts the process.

Second, put your house in order. Get into living—at least for a little while, if you can't do it permanently—as if this was your last day. It helps you to prioritize what you want to talk to her about. Talk to your ancestors, or at least show them some respect and honor them as the reason that you are on this planet now. These things seem to facilitate the communication with her. And then I would advocate for people to do some kind of divination about whether the time is right to talk to her. Then take at least three days before talking to her. One day should be for purification; at least take purifying baths. Take a second day to clean out your room and set up an altar with things related to dead stuff. Then take a day to think about her, and to live as if it was your last day. I wouldn't go any quicker than that for your first meeting.

Utiseta, sitting out, works well for talking to her. You can sit on barrow mounds, if you're in a part of the world that has them around. So does going under the cloak. You can spend a day being silent, being veiled, or not making certain gestures, such as not lifting your arms higher than your sternum. Mindfulness through temporary behavioral constraints. I have a cousin who had her hand tattooed on his shoulder, because she often comes up behind people and grips their left shoulder. I've seen Hela as a spot in the woods that was just darker than everything else in the dark. She's very dense; there's no graduated force-field energy at all.

She has absolutely no compunctions about hurting people, but it's never done out of malice. There is no malice in Hela. She's very professional and cold, almost clinical. "If we do not now excise and debride this wound, it will become septic. So we're going to hold you down and do it. Get ready to have your road rash scrubbed with a wire brush." There's no mercy, and no anesthetic. I got to experience a dislocated kneecap for about an hour and a half, and it was just the worst pain ever. They got me to the clinic and pumped me full of morphine, and it didn't work. Nothing helped, because this was a pain experience that She decided I needed to have.

Going through pain ordeals is harsh, but it does make you less fearful. Going through a pain ordeal makes everything else look smaller in comparison. She's really good at relativising. You're bitching and moaning, and she says, "Would you like me to do this instead?" and she holds out some horror show that she could easily inflict on you. Pain is one of her tools, as is fear. They do have a pretty good antidepressant function, though, which is something that you learn from her. If you are just crushingly depressed, which I get sometimes, you can offer that whole feeling to her. You can wrap it up and put a bow on it and say, "This is all I can do; it's all I have to give right now, sorry." She seems to like that for whatever reason.

But that also makes you capable of removing fear and pain in other people. You have to have "been there" to such a more extreme extent than the person you're trying to help that you can help them find the way out. So one of the things that she has me do is that I can do—or that she does through me—is to guide people who are in various states of mental dysfunction back to a normal place. This works because I've been through most of them.

Hela's relationship with Fenrir is unusual as well; very incestuous. Her relationship with Jormundgand is more distant and existential, because It is so inhuman. But her relationship with Fenrir is intimate, and extremely poignant. It just makes me cry, because Fenrir has a kind of tragedy about him that is just heartbreaking, and she keeps having to go do what is necessary to feed him, again and again. No one else feeds him. Hela and her people, and what they receive and inflict on others, is how he gets fed. And it keeps the world alive.

I've made the transition in the past two years where I am no longer doing Hela's work, I am being Hela's work. It's a weird linguistic subtlety, but it's an important difference. I can't switch it on and off— "Now I'm working for Hela, now I'm not"—but helping to feed Fenrir has helped me with that. I find people who are willing to accept physical torment, and indeed who dig it, and I dedicate that pain to Fenrir, to feed him, by Hela's hand. Those kinds of things require so much trust, and so much courage on both sides. It works best with someone who can manifest Fenrir himself, because then I can do things that I'm not willing to do to someone who is just a human being.

Hela cares about mad people, and cruel people, and sadistic people, and problem children in general. Like Shiva and Kali, whose people are untouchables and lepers and beggars, she is the patron of the socially unacceptable It's all about acknowledging, respecting, and eventually loving and integrating the monster inside. I know that if I was not working for her, I would be dead or in prison by now. I've got some pretty monstrous properties that are well chained, but it's not enough to chain them. They have to be put to work and worn out daily, or they'll just gnaw at the chains, and either keep you awake with the nasty clanking noise, or wear through them at some point.

But the flip side to that is that she accepts every part of you, even the most rancid, horrible, twisted, shameful, impossible to look at parts. She is about redeeming the unredeemable. It's a paradox, because at the same time that I speak of how horrid my inner demons are, I know that by making them work for her, I am nourishing and helping people through the physical manifestation of her presence around them. I can see it; there's evidence for it. And it doesn't at all contradict the fact that I am absolutely, irredeemably horrendous. Both of those things are true. People seem to do well and flourish from my work, and yet I am a monster. Eventually I had to come to terms with the fact that it is both. She's never told me that I have to "heal" my inner monster; that's not the point, and probably impossible anyway. But she shows me how it can be made useful. That's the core of Hela's mystery: the things about her appearance that are the most grotesque are the holiest.

Hela's Hand

by Gudrun

She comes to me in the dark, always from behind. No matter where I am facing, I hear Her voice behind me, feel that bone hand clamp down on my shoulder. While She exerts little pressure, I always feel like sagging under the weight of it. Sometimes her hand burns, sometimes it is freezing cold. Sometimes I am not sure that I can tell the difference.

Unlike other Gods, She is quiet. Her aura is like a black hole, drawing you in, not a showy glow of divinity. She speaks plainly, with no verbal frills like her father Loki. Sometimes She says only a few words... but they will be the exact words that are needed, whether or not you like them. Her voice echoes, somehow, even in close quarters.

Hela is found in silence, in dust, in the workings of insects, especially those who eat rotting flesh. She is found in carrion eaters and maggots—I watched a science-channel special on the "new" use of maggots to help clean the wounds of people with gangrene; apparently their bodily fluids are sterile and they eat only the bad flesh, then turn to flies and fly away. This is Hela, meticulously cleaning out the garbage; She does not need to be beautiful in order to do this. She is also found in necrotic bacteria, those tiny spirits that turn a dead corpse slowly into earth.

We think of life as clean and rotting as messy, ugly, chaotic, but the actual scientific truth is far different. Life is chaos, opening up and recombining in many different almost-random ways. The Gods of Life are profligate and wasteful, spawning a million so that a handful might survive, but the Gods of Death waste nothing at all. Rot is the neat, precise, predictable disassembly of the once-living into their component parts, so that life can continue its profligacy.

We turn away from rot, yet how many of us have rot within us? Rotting parts of heart and soul, things that fester in the dark of our personal basements. All these things belong to Her, and She reserves the right to open us up and claim them whenever She sees fit, even if we squall and cling to them. But She is nothing if not careful. She is precise, perfect; Her stroke is delicate as a scalpel—and hurts as much.

Hela's Rune is Ear, the Grave. Yet its figure is no great hole like a grave; instead it is the singletree, the scaffold upon which a carcass is butchered. That is the way She does her job—we are stretched upon the scaffold for her to work on. We are dead carcasses, being slaughtered; our flesh will feed and bring life to others. These days, the Dead are filled with chemicals and sealed in tiny boxes, not allowed to rot. Hela will not stand for this. To prevent a body from its destiny of becoming one with the elements is blasphemy, and evil. It is said that a soul cannot move on in peace to another life until its body is rotted; these days, souls move on while their last flesh still grimaces horribly in its pristine package, and what kind of trouble does this wreak on our souls? Go to the flames, go to the ocean, Hela says—go anywhere but there, although becoming one with the wonderful Earth is best.

I have seen Her holding the ghosts of dead babes in Her arms, rocking them and singing to them. She has no children of Her own that we know of, but all the Dead are Her children. If She wants to hold them, She has blue-faced babes aplenty, pale children to comfort, and elders to tend lovingly. She feeds the Dead, and whatever the jealous stories may say, no one goes hungry at Hela's table. It is named Hunger because that is what the Dead come to slake; every morsel they eat brings them further from their living life and pulls them towards the Void, where She will decide whether they will go on or stay.

There is a well in an inner courtyard of Elvidnir; I have seen it, though I dare not touch the waters within. They are blacker than night, and when I saw it I knew that this was Ginnungagap, Nun, the primal Void. Of all the Gods, only Hela and Surt do not fear Ginnungagap, and only Hela can reach into it, across it, through it with a human soul in her hand, and find for it a home. It was She who placed me into this body, and it is Her that I will serve while I live in this flesh.

Hymn to Hela
by Elizabeth Vongvisith

Below the dry desert, below the driftwood
Cast by cresting waves, below the humus and rot,
Below the grave and abattoir, below the gates of the charnel-house,
Lies the Lady's serene land, lies Helheim, largest of the Nine Worlds.

Under a gentle gray sky, under a vacant sun and moon,
Under silence and severity, under Her firm, flesh-stripped hand,
Under the wide crown of the Tree and under the waters of Niflheim,
There is the hall of forever, there is the final hearth and home.

And in the body's bone scaffold, in the heart's ambient chambers,
Through tendon and gristle, through the brain-pan and chest cavity,
Among the ever-dividing cells, among the veins and corpuscles,
Heed you Her voice, hear Her speak in every exhalation:

I am your death and what lies after,
     And I have drawn the borders of your life.
I am your most patient friend, and I am your most implacable foe.
I am the mistress of the dead, and I am the guardian of the living.
I am the secret way home, yet I know from where you first came.

Hail to the underworld goddess, hail to Helheim's ruler,
Daughter of the mighty Hag, hail, Angrboda's pride,
Hail the Trickster's child, born of the flame-haired firebrand,
Baldur's jailor and protector, Mordgud's friend and companion.

Hail the ancestors' mistress; hail the Keeper of the Dead!
You are the gallows and the axe; hail, Lady of endings!
Hail to the One who rules below, mighty in her inevitability.
You are the labyrinth's center. Hail, Hela Half-Rotted!

The Seven Faces of Hela

(An Astrological Hel-Poem by Abby Helasdottir)

LUNA:
I am the horn within Nal,
Which pours forth the waters of Gjall.
Dancers swirl around the navel that is my earth.
My skeletal face is lost and found
in the shadows of the moon
My heart is the hole of the labyrinth.
The labyrinth is the whole of my heart.
The spider's web is cast
as the sun shining on water
Turn, turn, turn.

VENUS:
I am the water that encompasses all,
And the life that flows through time.
In my eyes,
Life is but one single drop
Of water, cast upon my ocean.
Come sail your ships upon me,
And see that in me,
Are all things.
Four streams flow,
And all life they encompass.
Flow, flow, flow.

MERCURY:

Maker the modir.

I spoke and brought forth life.

Words etched upon a lattice,

I am the language of thoughts and birds.

Crystalline in the mind,

Mercurial in the dark.

I am the soul of poets,

The lover of dawn,

and the wolfen brood.

Rune, rune, rune.

SOL:

Svarte Sol er landa ljome,

I am the light of all worlds.

The black behind the gold

In disks thrown up from the void am I seen,

And in them is the void glimpsed

From the centre to the edge,

My form appears,

Shot through with the black light of Hel,

Stars unto infinity.

Eternity under the star.

Turn, turn, turn.

JUPITER:

Trees and leaves and birds of fire.

Mine are the arms that spread

Through all nine worlds.

The pulse of life runs through me,

As I run through it.

From heaven to Hel

From Hel to heaven

Of and within both worlds.

In icy blue am I made queen.

In the cold blue eternity of all that is me.

In one seed is every tree.

And in wyrd is everything.

Grow, grow, grow.

MARS:
Blood alone.
I am the blood of the sword,
And the blood of the womb.
Into me enter all souls,
Carried on the blackened beaks of carrion crows.
My ribs are the bones of the world,
Bones as purest crystal,
The colour of spirit.
When flesh decays away,
Only I remain,
Grim-faced inviting.
Mother of the dead,
Mother of the living.
With all life drowning in my blood.
Drown, drown, drown.

SATURN:
The base is connected to the crown.
The link is as an eight.
I am to be found beyond the eyes of humankind
And in the magisterial spread of the heavens.
Equations; calculations; theories,
All fail when faced with my enormity.
I am the unseen order of chaos.
I am the quickening of the soul.
The dragon, coiled round my tree,
Like the charge from base to crown,
All colours, all senses, all lives,
All thoughts.
The link is as an eight.

me and Hel
by Raven Kaldera

(I went through a terrible and wonderful transition and shamanic rebirth some years ago. This first poem, dedicated to Hel, the goddess who owns me, is about that period of time...sort of my version of How I Found Goddess And What She Did To Me When I Found Her.*)*

Death sits in your kitchen chair
across the table wrapped in darkness.
You cannot see under Her
robes to the bones and the screaming and
it is just as well. Her finger flicks in derision.
I have not come for your body.
You relax, a mistake. *I have*
come for your soul.
Much worse. You tremble. *Write,*
She says, pointing to paper
and pencil. *Write all the things*
about which you are ambivalent.
The things you love and hate both. Those which
snap you by reflex into old patterns. Write.

You write, you
weep. Like a mother wondering
which of her delinquent sons
will go to jail forever. Lover, child,
career, friends, causes.
Pieces of flesh. You
set down the pencil. *One,*
She says. *You may keep one*
as a keepsake. All others must go.

It is the bones and the screaming
now, inside you. You consider
offering Her your body, instead.
Would you die for these ambivalences?
Which of your fingers will you cut off,
which of your children will you present
with a sacred case of survivor guilt?
You wish to Hel it was
Her consort sitting there; He might
urge this on you, scowl and
stand tapping His foot, for years, even,
but He would not grab you by the scruff and
pull you through the gate
ready or not here we come. He is the
Voice that Urges, She is the Force
That Compels. She has no patience.
You will not be permitted
the luxury of confusion and fretting.
One, She says. *All others must
Go. And when they go, they will be
Gone. This is the Real Thing.
There is no Do Over, no Only Joking.*

You are allowed three seconds
then you must drop the weight.
For the gate through which you must
pass is no great portal
it is as tight as the neck of Her womb and
there is no room for heavy luggage.
You must be ready to fly. *For you see,*
She says, and it is the last
explanation you will get,
all else must be taken on faith,

Someday you will stumble onto the rocky road
that is your true path
and the fall would have killed you
if you hadn't been traveling light.

I Am Hel (A Song of Solace)
by Michaela Macha

Tune: "Skarazula Marazula" 15th century, better known from "Ballo in Fa
Dieses Minore" (Angelo Branduardi).

I am Hel the Dark One, and I will get you all.
Every man and woman must come into my hall,
The young ones and the old ones, and I will not let you go,
Even if all the worlds should weep for you.

I am Hel the Beautiful, be greeted and come in.
Enjoy my hospitality together with your kin.
Your ancestors are sitting next to Balder in the light,
I bid you welcome—I am Hel the Bright.

We greet you, our lady and mistress of eternity,
You will unite us with the ones who went before;
With our friends and families we keep forever company,
And we shall sing till sorrow is no more.

Hela's Day
10ᵗʰ day of Haymonath (July 10)
Pagan Book of Hours, Order of the Horae

Colors: Black and White
Elements: Earth and Air
Altar: Upon black cloth to the right place four black candles, a skull, bones, a pot of earth, a pile of withered leaves, and a gravestone. Upon white cloth to the left place four white candles, incense, an ivory chalice of mead, a crystal sphere, and a bunch of dried roses. Veil the windows.
Offerings: Blood. Pain. Difficulty. Toil. An arduous task that will take all you have to give, and will benefit the generations yet to come.
Daily Meal: Meat stew and bread.

Invocation to Hela

> Hail to Hel
> Queen of Helheim
> Wisest of Wights
> Keeper of Secrets
> Keeper of the hopes for tomorrow
> Guardian of Souls
> Implacable one of the frozen realm
> Half the face of beauty
> Half the face of Death.
> You who feed the dead
> At your meager table
> Where everyone gets their fair share,
> You who care not
> About wealth or status,
> About fame or fortune,
> Who cares for the peasant
> Equally with the ruler,
> Teach us that Death is the great leveller
> And that we need have no pride
> When we reach your halls.
> Lady who takes away
> Yet holds always promise,
> Teach us to praise loss and death
> And the passing of all things,
> For from this flux
> We know your blessings flow.

Walking the Labyrinth: A Devotion to Hela
by Elizabeth Vongvisith

Though it is nowhere found in the lore, some modern devotees of Hela attribute the labyrinth as one of Her symbols. This is a devotional exercise in honor of the Keeper of the Dead, representing a journey (real or symbolic) to Helheim, the land of the dead which is Her kingdom. You can do this devotional to symbolize a "death and rebirth" in your life, or simply to show reverence for Hela.

First, you will need to find a labyrinth near you, one which you can physically walk around in. Granted, this may be problematic if no such thing exists within a reasonable distance from your home. Also, many indoor labyrinths are within churches where some people may not feel comfortable, though usually no one will question your presence if you visit the labyrinth during regular hours. If you'd like to make an indoor one yourself, you can obtain a large dropcloth or tarp and paint a labyrinth big enough for you to walk around in comfortably (this method makes it portable as well). You may even consider making a permanent labyrinth on your property if you intend to do this exercise regularly.

If you can't make a suitable labyrinth and there isn't one close to where you live, I suggest finding a picture – any labyrinth, whether of the Minoan style or based on the medieval Chartres model, will work. (A labyrinth is not the same as a maze. Labyrinths have only one possible path; to leave the center, you simply retrace the way you took to get in.) Print or photocopy the image at a size large enough for you to trace with your finger and do this devotional as a sitting meditation instead.

Having found or made your labyrinth, choose an offering for Hela, the Keeper of the Dead. This could be anything, but it should have some connection to the purpose of your walk. If you aren't sure what to bring, I suggest red wine or dead, dried roses. Ideally, you'll leave your offering at the center of the labyrinth, but if this is not possible, choose a place where you can take it after the devotional is finished. If you maintain a permanent shrine or altar for Hela, you can leave your offering there afterwards.

Bring your offering with you to the labyrinth and stand at its opening. If you are using a picture, sit comfortably in a quiet place and place the image of the labyrinth before you. Say a prayer to Hela, in your own words or using the following:

> *Keeper of the Dead,*
> *I approach You with reverence,*
> *Mistress of Helheim.*
> *I come to You with devotion,*
> *Hela Half-Rotted,*
> *I walk this path to draw nearer to You.*
> *Hail Loki's daughter,*
> *Lady of the land of the dead.*

Step into the labyrinth and began to travel its circuits, or else trace with your finger the coils of the design. Don't be in a hurry; take your time. You may wish to repeat an appropriate chant or prayer over and over, or you may choose to walk in total silence. It is also worthwhile to meditate on the nature of death and your feelings about it, on Hela and the things She might have to teach you, or all of these.

When you reach the center of the labyrinth, stop. You have come to a place of stillness, the border of Helheim where the world of the living meets the world of the dead. Stand or sit quietly, centering yourself. Repeat your prayer or otherwise make a greeting to Hela, Keeper of the Dead, and wait for a response. It may not be verbal; it may simply be a feeling or a physical sensation, like a slight chill. She may even speak to you or otherwise make Her presence felt. Hela is implacable and her presence can be unnerving, but she is also very wise and capable of much compassion and kindness. She does not lie, and her counsel, though it may be difficult for you to hear, is always good.

When you feel it's appropriate to do so, make your offering to Her there, if possible, with any appropriate words of thanks. Then retrace your steps. If you were unable to make an offering in the labyrinth's center or you are using a picture, upon exiting, immediately go to whatever place you've picked out previously to leave the offering with your thanks.

The first time I did this devotional exercise, at a beautiful outdoor labyrinth in Woodland Park, Colorado, I was met halfway in by Garm, Hela's hound, who accompanied me to the center of the labyrinth. Walking inward seemed to take a very long time, as if I was indeed journeying to the land of the dead. When I arrived at the center, Hela was waiting for me. I spent what I thought was another long period talking to Her, then after giving Her my offering, I left. Coming out of the labyrinth, by contrast, seemed only to take a few minutes. Later, my friend told me that while she waited for me in a nearby parking lot, I was only absent for maybe ten minutes at most.

It is possible that you may experience something similar, which can be disorienting. Even if you don't, however, this exercise can have emotionally profound effects that may take some time to get used to. Don't be afraid, but don't do it frivolously, either. In the end, the spirit in which you undertake it is what really matters. Hela will accept your devotion if it is given with reverence, love and respect.

(Raven's Note: While we do not know to whom they were dedicated, the Norse people did use labyrinths — the ones generally referred to in modern days as "Cretan-style", with eight or nine circles. There are over 600 old stone labyrinths on Scandinavian shores that exist to this day; in the Middle Ages, although their religious meanings had been lost, sailors and fishermen walked them in order to ask to be spared on their journeys, and other folk walked them to ask for help when a loved one was in peril. The most famous Scandinavian labyrinth is on the isle of Gotland.

If you want to build yourself a labyrinth, understand that in order for it to be magically effective, it must center on the cross of two major ley lines. Ley lines come in two sorts: positive, which push energy upwards, and negative, which pull them downwards. Any two ley lines crossing will create the right field for a labyrinth, but different types will act differently. The ideal is one positive and one negative, but two positives will help travel "upwards" – to Asgard, for instance – whereas mine is built on the cross of two negative ley lines and the center drops down straight to Helheim when it is activated. It's easier to dowse negative ley lines because underground water follows them. I once saw a picture of an old Scandinavian labyrinth – and next to it was a pump, set into the ground!)

Fenris

There are few of the Rökkr more demonized than Fenris, or Fenrir, second child of Loki and Angrboda, and few that fall easier into that category. Angrboda was the Mother of Wolves; as leader of the Wolf Clan of the Iron Wood, the majority of her children were werewolf-giants. However, her eldest son by Loki was larger, fiercer, and wilder than all the rest. He grew so huge that it was said that when he opened his mouth, his jaws reached to heaven and earth. He was kidnapped by the Aesir and given to Tyr to raise, in the hopes that it would tame him, but the separation apparently made things worse. When he reached adulthood, he began to go on killing sprees, devouring everything in his path, and he was large and strong enough that no chain could hold him. (The Aesir tried, first with a magical chain called Laeding and then with one called Dromi, but he broke each in turn.)

Then the Aesir hired the Duergar to forge a chain out of gold melted with six impossible things (the roots of a mountain, the beard of a woman, the footfall of a cat, the breath of a fish, the nerves of a bear, the spittle of a bird), and chained him. The story of how he was chained is told in Kevin Filan's essay on Fenris below, but suffice it to say that he now dwells in a cave under a mountain on Lyngvi's Island in Lake Amsvartnir in Niflheim. There he waits, broods, and occasionally flings himself against the chain and the blade holding him, and waits for the day when he can break loose and wreak his revenge.

Easy to demonize, yes... and it would be folly to do so. Fenris is a deity, not a demon; like all the Gods—and all the Rökkr Gods—he is the embodiment of a sacred truth. The mystery of Fenris is not an easy or uncomplicated or straightforward thing. People who are still instinctively dividing up the world into good or bad as whether it causes them pain or inconvenience are not ready for his mystery.

Fenris is, in many ways, Jotun essence taken to its furthest point, its ultimate uncompromised end. This means understanding that when we say that the Jotnar are, by nature, part of nature... that means also that they partake of the entirety of nature and not just the euphemized happy bits that we like to pretend are what nature "really is". Every part of nature is dangerous and not terribly disposed to privilege humans over any other part. The sea eats people, the fire lays waste to countrysides, the ice storm freezes you, the earth will receive your corpse and fill it with maggots. Our planet whirls around a sun that will burn out, in a galaxy that will wind down and disintegrate before it can explode again into life.

To understand these things as not only "not negative" but as awesome, mind-bending, even beautiful—that's how we understand Jotun nature. It's terrifying, yes—and there is also a good and benevolent side, but you don't get only that aimed at you, ever. It's about accepting the whole package without this secret fingers-crossed idea that if they just like you enough, the forces of nature will make a special exception for you. And that doesn't work.

Although the Fate incurred by Fenrir may be unavoidable and unchangeable, it does not necessarily mean defeat or resignation. One of the great lessons of the Rökkr is that this life is nothing, that there is no integral meaning to it, and that it can all so easily be consumed by Fenrir. The purpose of living, then, is to realize this truth, and then to build one's own worth and meaning from existence.

—Abby Helasdottir

To see Fenris is to see a magnificent creature who must be chained, or he'll eat the world. It's seeing the grandeur of a hurricane, an earthquake, a solar flare, and knowing that this too is the hand of the divine... and at the same time knowing that they will do terrible harm. Fenris is what he is, entirely and fully, and he will not compromise himself to be anything else for anyone else... even if he must be bound. Are there things about your nature that you would rather be imprisoned than have to compromise? If not, then perhaps you might not understand Fenris. He embodies our ambivalence toward the Universe, which sees us as expendable flecks of dust... and the only way to get around that is to see from a higher perspective, one that can appreciate the divinity of ambivalences.

Loki and Angrboda both love their children immensely, and that includes Fenris. They miss him, and are sad for him, and weep that he must be chained. At the same time, they didn't stop it from happening—even Angrboda the Mother of Monsters, who would go to the wall for her children—because they knew it was necessary.

The lake's water on the northern side of the island was pinked by the two streams of blood that trickled over the rocks and into the surf. I followed the streams down into a cave, which took me in pathwalking terms to the western boundary of my property, where there are huge fallen stones. In the cave, in the dim light, I saw him, huge and chained. A wolf bigger than a horse, a sword thrust through his muzzle and pinning him to the ground. Bound with glittery chain no thicker than a necklace. His yellow eyes slitted in the dark, and I heard his voice in my mind.

I wanted you to see me this way, he said to me. I could come to you unbound, with the small part of me that is allowed to walk loose, so long as I wreak no destruction. But I wanted you to see this, because I knew you would understand.

I knelt on the great flat stone beside him and wept. Yes, I understand, you who are one of the greatest creations of the Iron Wood. I understand both the hunger and the necessity. I reached out and just barely touched his pelt, near his shoulder. I knew that if he were free he'd eat me, no matter that I would willingly be his friend, and that those chains were what allowed

me that small touch. It was his nature, and part of mine. I remembered
that Joshua had said something very similar about me once.

I had not brought any offering for him, so I let my tears drip onto him.
It was all I could think of to do. We spoke for a short while, and then I
washed my hands in the streams of blood and left. The air was very bright
and cold outside, and the mists had cleared for the moment. Lake
Amsvartnir sparkled in the sunlight, and my own world seemed very far
away.

—*Raven's Pathwalking Journal*

This is something else that I've seen happen, as well as experiencing it myself: Those who look the Great Bound Wolf in the eye and fully see him, completely know him, always weep. To truly understand both the magnificence and the sorrow that is Fenris is to be swept up in that sorrow, if only for a few moments. I honor my own ambivalences, as I honor the ambivalence of his existence. Not everything is easy, black and white, and anyone who tries to see him in either light has missed the point.

Fenris is what he is. He would rather die than be other than what he is. He is frightening, yes. But it was valuable to me to see him, to speak with him, to hear his wisdom—and yes, it is wisdom—about the dark places in the soul. He is an expert on that. For those of us with Jotun blood, and the attendant anger-management issues it may bring (especially those of us with the predator-hunger within us), we can find great value in working with Fenris, and not just as an object lesson in self-control. To come to terms with this kind of inner Beast necessitates seeing it as not entirely negative, even if it must be chained. To deal with it in a healthy way requires learning to love it for what it is, and that means learning to see its magnificence. To weep for Fenris, to revere and honor him, gives us a place to stand with regard to honoring this part of ourselves.

Wolves were an important and ambivalent symbol in the lives of Europeans as well. The wolf was universally feared and loathed by the average peasant, whose experience with them was the predator that threatened their flocks and perhaps, in a lean year, even the peasants themselves and their children. On the other hand, the warrior classes saw the wolf in terms of power, fierceness, and bonding to a pack; many of them were predators themselves, and ironically appreciated the wolf for just that ambivalent nature. Whether the peasants were their pack or their prey would vary from situation to situation, and on some level they understood this well.

On the other hand, a lone wolf was a problem. The word for outlaw in northern Europe was "wolf's head", referring to the bounty on the severed heads of lone wolves who became a problem to settled villages and needed to be exterminated. In many ways, Fenris is the ultimate lone wolf figure; he is kidnapped by the Aesir as a puppy and torn from what would have been his tribe and family. Rather than eventually accept them as his pack, he runs wild and wreaks mayhem, a story that is a warning on many levels.

The mythological wolf is not merely bound to the archetype of Fenris, or only to Norse cosmology. Studying other wolf-mythos helps us to understand the crucial place of the demonized Fenris in our own. Abby Helasdottir writes:

The scene of Fenrir threatening cosmic stability was represented in the northern skies by the constellation of the Greater Wolf's Jaw; a stellar array comprised of stars from the constellations of Cygnus, Pegasus, and Andromeda. This constellation gapes menacingly towards the pole star, with the twin tails of the Milky Way appearing as the two rivers of saliva and blood, Wil and Wan, which flowed from Fenrir's mouth. This idea of a cosmic wolf is not limited to Rökkr cosmology, and appears across Europe and Asia, and even in the Americas. In the myths of the Slavic and Baltic regions, a wolf that would eventually destroy the world was chained to the centre of the heavens, the Pole Star, by the Zorya, the triple-aspect goddess of fate known by a number of various names throughout Eastern Europe. The wolf would eventually be released from its iron chain to do the will of the Goddess and consume the world. This wolf was symbolized by the constellation of Ursa Minor; because the star Polaris is the tail of Ursa

Minor, it depicts the tail of the Slavic wolf, attached to the hub of the heavens.

This lupine connection to Ursa Minor, and the continuation of cosmic order, is further compounded by the philosophy of a Greek sect, the Cynics, founded by Antisthenes (a pupil of Socrates) and his follower, the sage Diogenes of Sinope. The Cynics regarded themselves as the watchdogs of the goddess, their name coming from the Greek word *kynikos*, meaning dog-like ones. They would observe the Polaris star, which they knew as Kynos Oura (The Dog's Tail), and believed that when the star began to move from its home (ergo: when the dog was unleashed) the end of the world would be imminent. That Ursa Minor was the cynosure (literally, the centre of attraction) for the Cynics, makes an interesting reference to the Cretan stellar goddess Cynosura, from which the word derives, whose constellation was likewise Ursa Minor. Similarly, in the mythology of the Kirghiz, the seven stars of Ursa Major were visualized as a group of guards who watched over the two brightest stars of Ursa Minor, who were represented by two horses, running from a cosmic wolf. The day when the two horses are finally killed by the wolf is the day the world ends.

The concept of a cosmic wolf was essential to the expansion of the Mongolian Empire, because they believed they descended from the azure-blue wolf Eternal Blue Heaven, who represented the vault of the sky. This divine ancestry provided a mandate for Genghis Khan's empire, and for this reason, the Mongols referred to themselves as Blue Mongols. The Mongols are related to older Turkic-speaking peoples, who also featured the tradition of an azure sky wolf, and their shamanism is similar to forms in the American continents (and Rökkr shamanism) where the wolf is seen as well. In Cheyenne magick, for example, the ancestral wolf was seen as the star of Aldebaran, while his consort, a white wolf, was represented by Sirius.

As discussed in the first chapter of this book, there is a strange polarity between Baldur and Fenris. Each is a sacrificed god in his own way. The Aesir seize and sacrifice the Rökkr god who is "the darkest of the dark", the most unbridled expression of the destructive end of Jotun nature, in order that civilization might survive. In return, the Rökkr gods Loki and Hela arrange to sacrifice and seize Baldur, the god who might be termed "the brightest of the bright", the ultimate expression of Aesir glory... in order that civilization might survive, after Ragnarok, where he will be the ruler. Each is held hostage to the future, one to bring about the end and one to renew a beginning. Just as the exchange of hostages with the Vanir— Njord, Frey and Freyja in exchange for the ill-fated Mimir and Hoenir— inextricably binds them to the Aesir, so this exchange of hostages binds them to the Jotnar and their Rökkr gods.

The Mystery of Fenris and Tyr
by Kevin Filan

In Jotunheim, the children say "The Hag of the Iron Wood had three children, and the daughter was Death, the son was Destruction, and the third encircled the world." This is the story of the son, and his binding in Niflheim, and of the cost of that binding.

Today we know very little about Tyr. Other than a few scraps of lore, a rune, and the myth of the binding of Fenris, most of his legends and tales have been forgotten. Yet we know that once he was among the most important of the deities. The heathens named one of the days of their week after him, and Tacitus tells us that he was very important among the Goths and many of the Germanic tribes they encountered. The Romans equated Tyr with their warrior god Mars, which tells us that he was a very powerful and widely honored deity indeed. We also know from Tacitus that Tyr was occasionally given human sacrifice. But we also know that some tribes gave great honor to a deity whom the Romans identified with Mercury—a wandering runemaster and magician whom we know better as Odin.

Some linguists believe that the word "Tiu" or "Tyr" comes from the same root as the Sanskrit "Dayus" or the Latin "Deus"—the chief god. Before Odin was ruler of the Aesir, they surmise, Tyr was the leader. Others point out that Tyr was closely connected to the "Thing," the place where people came together to discuss ideas. If he was ruler of the Thing, it would only be reasonable to surmise that he was at one time the master of order at the assemblies of the gods.

We also know that Tyr was known for his honesty. The Old English Rune Poem equates Tyr with Polaris, the Pole Star, and states:

Honor's a star that holds very true
With ones elevated. Always on course
Through darkest of dark-times and never the noble deceives.

And so this is not only the story of how Fenrir was bound: it is also the story of how Odin claimed the rulership which was once held by Tyr.

After the Aesir had cast Jormungand into the sea and sent Hela to Helheim, they brought Fenrir to Asgard to be raised among them. They knew the Norns had spoken. They knew that if Fenrir were allowed to run free he would finally devour the world. But just as men often try to escape their destiny, so the gods sometimes try to thwart their omens. They knew the proud pup would grow into a mighty beast, and hoped that maybe they could domesticate Fenrir and make a guardian of him.

And so Tyr took the young Fenrir in and raised him. Of all the Aesir, Tyr understood how to subdue savagery. The blood of Jotunheim ran pure through his veins—he was the child of the frost giant Hymir. Tyr knew better than anyone what it took to hold passions in check, and he did everything he could to teach this to Fenrir.

Anyone who has ever had a dog knows the emotional bond which arises between canines and their keepers. Tyr was known for being loyal and fearless; he loved his kin and his tribe and protected them against any who would harm them. How could he not love Fenrir? As pack predators, the wolf encompasses all of these traits... and Fenrir was the mightiest of wolves, the quintessence of wolfhood. Some say that Tyr was the only Aesir brave enough to feed the mighty wolf. I believe that Tyr loved Fenrir because he understood him—and vice versa.

But as Fenrir grew it became clear that the prophecies were not to be denied. And so the gods tried to bind him, but the mighty wolf broke every chain they laid upon him. At last the gods sent Skirnir, the one who brought Frey his wife Gerda, to the dwarves. They had called on their usual intercessor between the dwarves and Aesir, but this time Loki refused to help. He knew as well as anybody—and better than most—that Fenrir had to be bound, but that didn't mean that he was going to play any role in the betrayal of his son.

The dwarves answered Skirnir's challenge. They made a chain from the sound of a cat's footfall, the beard of a woman, the roots of a mountain, bear's sinews, fish's breath, and bird's spittle. They named this chain Gleipnir—"Deceiver."

The Aesir challenged Fenrir to break Gleipnir, but Fenrir was no fool: he knew there was magic to the chain. And so he said that he would do so only if one of the gods would place his right hand in Fenrir's muzzle as a pledge to free him if he failed to break the chain. In Germanic culture, your right hand was used to swear an oath, and oaths were very serious business indeed. There were few insults more deadly than "oathbreaker" and few crimes more base than breaking an oath. It was not fear of Fenrir that stopped the gods from offering their hands; it was fear of dishonor. For a long second the assembly of gods stood silent. Finally Tyr, the leader of the Aesir-Thing, the one who loved Fenrir best, the one whose very word was oath, stepped up and placed his hand in Fenrir's muzzle. He was honorable, yes; among the Nine Worlds you would find none more honorable than Tyr. But he was also lord and chieftain over gods and men, and sworn to protect their realms. Fenrir, who loved Tyr and trusted him, allowed the other gods to lay Deceiver upon him. And so Fenrir was bound, and so Tyr sacrificed his hand—and his word, and his honor—to do what had to be done.

Snorri Sturluson says all the gods but Tyr laughed as Fenris struggled against Deceiver. He should have said that Tyr wept for the friend he loved, and for the burden which had been laid upon them both.

In a small clan, the rulership of Tyr works best. When everyone knows they can trust the absolute honor of their leader, when everyone knows that their leader will never lie to them, they can function as a powerful and effective unit. But in a larger clan, sometimes it becomes necessary to do things which aren't "honorable." Machiavellian manipulations and unspoken nastiness are required on occasion; double- and even multiple-dealing may be called for if the ruler's people face danger. Tyr could not understand that. He was an straightforward god, not a cunning one. He was no wily strategist like Odin. And Odin knew that, and knew that the gods needed a leader capable of both honor and cunning. Some say Odin did what had to be done for gods and men. Others say that Odin coveted Tyr's position as ruler and plotted to overthrow him. Perhaps both are right, perhaps both are wrong. On this neither the One-Eyed nor the One-Handed God will say yea or nay.

And so Odin gifted Tyr with Fenrir and told him that he was the only one with the strength to care for the great beast. And Tyr, who had long admired the mighty wolves who follow Odin, accepted the gift gladly. He knew that Odin did not lie: he knew that no one else in Asgard or Vanaheim could be alpha to Fenrir. And Tyr took the wolfling as gift and loved him as Fenris grew to love him.

After Tyr was unhanded his power waned. He had followed his greater oath; he had protected his people even at the cost of his own defeat and his personal dishonour, even at the cost of pain to the wolf he loved as his own child, but in betraying Fenrir something had broken inside him. And so little by little power passed to the tree-hung one, just as Odin had foreseen. In time Tyr was almost forgotten and Odin was hailed as the All-Father who commanded the gods.

They say that Tyr still visits Fenrir and brings him the treats he loved when they walked together unbound. He sits by the side of his mighty wolf and strokes his fur and together they weep for the things that must be. And Fenrir knows that Odin was the mastermind behind this, and so he has sworn that on the day of Ragnarok he will be the one who brings Odin death. Fenrir has sworn this not only for the binding which Odin brought upon him, but because of the suffering which Odin brought to the master he loved and loves still.

For myself, I say only that the ways of gods are not the ways of man, and their truths are not mine to understand.

A Moment With Fenrir
by Elizabeth Vongvisith

I had been a Northern-Tradition spirit-worker for a couple of years, but I had not encountered Fenrir until I witnessed two spirit-possessions by this son of Loki and Angrboda within the space of a few days. It wasn't until then that I began to understand the great Wolf and appreciate both his power and the wisdom of those who bound him.

When Fenrir was horsed by a man who had been chained up for the purpose, I saw him clearly. It was as if my Sight telescoped out between the worlds, through and past the man horsing him and into the realm where Fenrir is chained. I could see a great brindled wolf, yellow of eye and sharp of fang, teeth bared and every muscle and sinew tense with unimaginable, tortured strength. During the next few minutes, I saw what Sky-Treader's most terrible offspring really is…and that was surprisingly difficult to endure.

At first I was overcome with a strong desire to run away, but though I took one or two steps back, I found myself unable to move further. Fenrir's enormous rage overwhelmed me, even bound and controlled as he was. And while some of his rage is directed at those who fettered him thus, much of it is simply the savage desire to tear apart whoever and whatever stands in his path, the ecstasy of dealing out pain and death. I understood right away that were he given the chance, Fenrir would most likely devour me without a second thought. I doubt it would matter that I am not his enemy, that I am beloved of Loki his father, or that I also serve his sister, Hela. The knowledge was sobering, because while I had held it in my head for some time before that, this was the first time I had felt it with my heart.

It's a humbling thing to really know for the first time that for all your imagined gifts, "higher purpose" and self-importance, you are merely meat to be flayed from your bones before being swallowed in pieces. Those who believe that the beings of the Nine Worlds are all at their disposal or command would do well to avoid contact with Fenrir lest their illusions be very painfully stripped away—though that might just be the best thing for them. There is no mortal alive who can subdue Fenrir or calm his fury if he were to break his chain. To see him is to know, totally and completely, that there is no turning the Powers That Be on and off at will, despite what humans like to tell themselves. "Nature red in tooth and claw" doesn't even come close to describing him.

For all Fenrir's wildness, though, he has a shrewd mind that knows full well why he is there and why he was chained, though he deeply resents it. He has given himself over to bloodlust, yet he is willing to bide his time, to wait patiently until the day comes when he can once more run amok and have his revenge on those who bound him. And because of all this, there is a sort of strange dignity about Fenrir, a majesty that utterly belies his reputation as a mere indiscriminating beast. That realization broke my terror apart and allowed it to give way to a sudden pain that pierced me to the core and literally took my breath away. I tried once more to tear myself away from the scene and leave, and again I found that I could not.

In those moments, though it was painful, I began to understand the Mystery of the great wolf, bound until the end of the Nine Worlds. I stood there distraught, weeping as Fenrir's snarls and growls came to my ears from both this world and the other, and all the time I remained aware that were he not chained, he could easily kill those of us within his reach. I watched as Fenrir was quieted by a divine hand and gradually put to sleep, to dream things I'm not certain I want to know about. When it was over and the man horsing him slowly sat up, dazed and himself again, in my mind's eye I could still see Fenrir, restless in his slumber in a world far away. In the wake of his departure, I experienced a rush of mingled and confusing emotions — relief, sadness, anger, sympathy and a profound respect too — the kind of respect I'd have for an erupting volcano. I can appreciate it and even love it, but I have no illusions that either my appreciation or my love will protect me from its hot magma and choking ash.

To know and understand Fenrir is to know and understand that destruction sometimes comes for no purpose other than destruction itself, and that this is as much a part of a functioning universe as life, love and rebirth. Ragnarok or no, I fear there will be no happy ending to Fenrir's story — but I likewise suspect that it doesn't matter to him either way. He is what he is and neither cares to appear otherwise, nor tries to. He is unapologetic in his lusts, a hunter and a killer without conscience or shame. Fenrir is the mightiest of sorrows, chaos uncontrollable — bound for the present, but never truly tamed, and his Mystery is that this is both tragedy and cause for reverence.

Hymn to Fenrir
by Elizabeth Vongvisith

Hail Loki's wolf-son, mightiest of sorrows,
who would devour all, light and dark,
with gleaming razors and hot breath,
a never-ending feast of spilled blood,
shining guts, torn and rent flesh
there at the threshold of madness.

Hail, child of the Witch Queen,
wildest son of the Iron Wood,
blood-tinged, red-eyed, pain-driven beast
bound fast and wyrd-wrapped in rage,
as tears roil around you in a great salt sea
there on the underside of the subconscious.

Hail to you who are chaos uncontrollable,
without compromise, without shame,
fear's ending and love's devourer,
biding your time until time's end,
silent in shadows, merciless in patience,
there at the borders of the underworld.

Hail to Fenrir, he who exists
at the terminus of the senses,
waiting, waiting for the worlds to crumble,
for the rejoicing in destruction
and the shattered spear and sword,
there at the ending of all things.

To My Beloved Brother From Hela
by Lydia

Brother, I must wake you once more from your fitful peace,
To feed and torment you lest the world fall still.
I gaze upon your terrible form and I feel my heart breaking,
I hear your rasping breath and I see my blade rushing,
For I must do this to you again and again,
Washing the world in the blood of our sins.
You rise up towering in fear and rage,
Always the chain and the sword and the foam—
Your sister is here, it's me—
I cannot release you, nor let you be.
You drink deeply from my eyes and from my veins,
And I must feast upon you too;
Must have your pain and your tears and your howls
Lest we both starve...
And the world come to a sullen and dusty end.

Fenris Unleashed
by Michaela Macha

"Nine nights only your own will bound you
to the World's Tree, you treacherous God,
while I wore a chain that I chose not, forever:
With cruel fetter my freedom you took!"

"Too vicious were you to willfully roam:
Greater your hunger than Geri's and Freki's,
greedier than ravens, you gorged ever more;
that's why we tied you, tail, legs and jaw."

"Was in nine realms no room for a wolf-pup?
Of choice you bereft me to change in my ways.
My trust you betrayed—Tyr most of all,
Who'd fed me and cared like a father for me.

"All of you lost your honor that day;
stronger was I, but still you tricked me:
Cunning magic you cowards employed—
Tyr you let pay for the promise you broke.

"Eternity's enmity is what I owe you.
Raving my greed now, grown with the years:
Not quite enough are the nine worlds to feed me,
hardly they'll suffice my hunger to slake."

"I stand against you to strike you back,
though well I know what wyrd is mine:
That I will fall with all my Einherjar,
whose lives I've taken, that life might survive.

"With bitter sacrifice bought I the wisdom
for many a day this doom to delay;
hope I have kindled, none kept for myself:
Two mortals survive in the wood of the Tree.

"Short is your victory: Vali, my son,
will rip your jaws and rule a new world.
Come, let us end it! Ages we've waited,
we who were old when the worlds were still young."

For The Wolf
by Corbie Petulengro

Wolf, you grin at me through the window
Like my inner wolf self
Not the noble totem in china
and plastic beside my bed
But the wild, rending, jaws that threaten
to tear apart all that I love...
You would have me see my own children as prey,
leave their tiny bodies bloodied at the doorstep,
rip the throat of the love that shares my bed,
run howling for the night...
Wolf, I must close the window, bury
my head for love of them
or love of you will destroy us all,
yet if I deny you live in me
You will have the right to tear out my tongue
for my lies.

Bindings: A Poem For Inner And Outer Fenris

The Hag of the Iron Wood had three children,
And the daughter was death,
The son was destruction,
And the third encircled the world.

It is cold in Niflheim, in your cell
Beneath the stone, where you hate me
Redly in your dreams. I am your prey, again and again,
Not out of love but rage, for what I have done to you.
Yet better you take my dreamself,
However deep the wounds,
Than ravage another. I will not hide behind those I love
When the Great Wolf comes; take me, bite off my hand,
Limit and cripple me,
Make me bleed and weep,
Make me remember, every day after,
When I reach instinctively and fall ever short,
The price of my honor,
And still it will be worth the price.

Mountain's roots.

Your feet are chained, predator of the sun,
With the chain made of six impossible things
That you may not run free in the world
And drink slaughter. I know what you would do.
Your lies cannot convince me that you would
Ever be harmless. Nor would you fight for the good.
There is no way around this trap.
You threaten me with terrible things,
Should I shut the door on your cage,

But I will not be moved by threats. The worst you can do
Is hurt me, and should you be free,
That would come of its own at any rate.
At the bottom of the mountains are the caves
Where dwell black things, evil that never sees the light,
The place where you hide from your mess,
And leave me to the binding of wounds
And tearful recriminations. There I chain you,
And there let you lie on damp stone
Beside the echoing trickle of underground rivers.
I will bring you food and drink, what meager stuff I can,
Heavy with the drugs of fantasy and dream,
And you will not die, but only sleep
And chase the sun in dreams. It is kinder this way.

Beard of a gentle woman.

Your phallus is bound, son of the fire,
Most male in a family of slippery genders.
All penetration is good to you,
Cock ramming home into screaming hole,
Teeth slicing through skin,
Tongue gouging into arteries,
Muzzle ripping into the softness of a curving belly.
They are all to be taken, save you
Who never yield yourself up in that way.
You have no color vision, wolf-child,
All is black or white, and you are black,
And that is that. I will not let you forget
The wound, the castration, the inescapable fact
That there is more than man in this body,
Whether you would have it so or not. I bind you
With the symbols of the third, your sister-brother,

Who lies like your coils of chain around the world.
Lust will not stir you. It is kinder this way.

Spittle of a bird.

Your jaws are bound with sleep, you whose teeth
Would rend and tear the very sun.
I sit with raven's spittle in my hair
And sing a croaking song, one that will lull you
Perhaps imperfectly, but well enough for now.
Like the soft music that whines everlastingly
From the radio on the prison's death row,
Soothing each angry man to sullen apathy,
I will sing to drown out your growls
And remind you that I have not forgotten you,
Even if you must be bound. It is kinder this way.

Footfall of a cat.

Your howl is bound, singer whose voice
Turns the blood to ice, freezes the prey
Where it stands unblinking, paralyzed.
Silence rules outside your cell; your whimpers
Will not be heard by others.
Nor will your terrible words of seduction,
Your razor-sharp tongue that cuts and lashes.
You will not lure in any others
To crouch and reach timidly between the bars.
They have no key to let you out anyway,
And their finger-bones are not yours to gnaw on,
Like smug trophies in the back of your cell.
Nor will you hear their voices through these walls,
But only velvet stillness. Nothing will
Disturb your sleep. It is kinder this way.

Breath of a fish.

Your sniffing nose is bound,
Hunter, tracker, chaser of prey;
For when you are free, none escapes its keenness.
You run the trail close behind,
They can hear your panting, the pounding tread
Of your sharp-nailed paws, and their breath
Catches in their throats. Only water,
River or stream, breath of the fish that swim therein,
Can foul your tracking, foil your lethal purpose,
Make you howl in confused rage at the riverbank.
So I surround you with the river of my tears
That you might not be waked from your sleep
And go springing at the bars, only to fall
Choking on the cold stone. It is kinder this way.

Nerves of a bear.

Your endless strength is bound,
Your tireless seeking of new throats to catch.
There is but one thing greater than the Rökkr warrior,
Snarling beast of the pack,
Jotun blood in your veins turned to werewolf,
And that is Odhinn's bears of rage
Who go into battle impervious to pain and wounds.
So must I be impervious to your cries
And never touch the door. You will make certain
That I share that pain, whether I will or no,
But it must never sway me
Lest I come to pity, and in your world
Pity is rewarded only with death.
For I too love you, Wolf—how could I not?

And it tears my heart to bind you,
But there is no other choice. The bars must be strong
And close together, and you must rest,
Close your wild golden eyes,
And not dwell too much on the reality
Of your prison. It is kinder this way...

...at least for you, if not for me.

*(For Fenris must be chained
Or Chaos will be King.)*

Ritual for Fenris's Day
2nd day of Wolfmonath (January 2)
Pagan Book of Hours, Order of the Horae

Color: Black
Element: Fire
Altar: Upon a cloth of black light a flaming brazier, and drape many
        lengths of fine chain across the table. Place there also the figure of a
        wolf howling, and a chalice of animal's blood.
Offerings: Blood.
Daily Meal: Red meat.

Invocation to Fenris

First speaker:
        The Hag of the Iron Wood had three children,
        And the daughter was Death,
        The son was Destruction,
        And the third encircled the World.
Second speaker:
        I call you, Great Wolf,
        But not to waking.
        Sleep sound in your chains,
        Sleep gently in your torment,
        I would not recall you
        To knowledge of your pain.
        I call you in your dreams,
        I call you in my dreams,
        May we run together
        In a world golden and fiery
        Where a hundred suns
        Blaze together in the sky
        Like berries ripe for picking
        Like rabbits to be chased.
        May my wild self run with you there
        And learn some measure of freedom.
Third speaker:
        We all wear chains of our own binding,
        Lest we do harm to others,
        And within each of us stirs that which hates them
        And desires all freedom.
        Speak of him, that he may know you love him also,
        Even though he must be chained!

*(All speak in turn of their inner beast, and why he is worthy of love,
even though he must be chained. Pour the blood out as a libation.)*

Jormundgand

The third child of Loki and Angrboda spilled forth from the wolf-priestess's womb like a scaly waterfall, in the shape of a giant serpent. Sometimes it happened that way, in the Iron Wood, the place where magic leaked from the very ground underfoot. Many giants were born werecreatures, with animal forms, but some were born so animal that they never took a humanoid form to begin with. Usually they were dogs or wolves; Hela's loyal guardian Garm was one of these, as was Fenris, Loki and Angrboda's first child, but the last time such a one as the Great Snake was born, it was Nidhogg the Dragon, child of unknown frost-giants in Niflheim.

Angrboda fed the greeny-blue snake-child as best she could on scraps of meat, and laid it to rest at night in a great cauldron, which it quickly outgrew and had to be moved to a pond, and then a lake. By the time she was killed by the Aesir, the Snake was outgrowing its lake and was the wonder of the Iron Wood. It was not so much that it could use magic as that it *was* magic, a living conduit of power. Spells done in its presence were triply strong, and it was quickly growing large enough to devour anything in its path. When Odin and his band kidnapped it, they flung it into the ocean, and Odin bespelled it to stay there. Its length is stretched around the diameter of Midgard, its living flesh a carrier of Odin's protective warding-spell, whether it will or no. Its presence protects the fragile humans living there.

Jormundgand—which means simply "World-Serpent", as the creature has no name as such—is like no other creature in the Nine Worlds, including any other Jotun. It was created from the magic of the Iron Wood acting on the combined bloodlines of Loki and Angrboda, two of the most powerful Jotnar the Iron Wood itself ever brought forth. Of all the Jotnar that I've dealt with, the Big Snake is the one that I think is most easy to misunderstand. It is an incredibly alien creature. Touching its nature is very strange. It is hermaphroditic—not terribly unusual for the Iron Wood—although it tends to "feel" to the person contacting it like whatever their gender is. It doesn't speak in words, or any kind of a language that we would consider a language, but it does speak, somehow. I can't explain that—it boggles my mind to try—but the one time when I shared a body with the Snake (which seems to have no name; as it is unique, it doesn't feel like it needs one, it is simply "I") it felt as though all the verbal parts of my brain were being shoved aside and disconnected. It took an hour before I could properly speak, after that.

Those of us who work with Loki's family tend to doubt that the Snake claims anyone, not the way that Loki or Hela (or Odin or Thor, for that matter) do. I think it will attempt communication with specific people, and they may mistake that. If they say that the Snake talked to them in words, or in human thought-concepts, that's generally when I doubt them. However, it is possible that the human mind "translated" the concepts into words without realizing that this is what was happening.

Iormundgand the World-Serpent
by Abby Helasdottir

Iormungand is the aquatic child of Loki and Angrboda, and, in a distinct contrast to her parents and siblings, her form is serpentine and monstrous. Iormungand is the World Serpent who lies in the sea surrounding Midgard, her tall gripped in her own mouth. According to Æsir-centric mythology, Odin had cast the serpent into the world sea, in an attempt to soften and postpone the inevitable blow of Ragnarok; likewise, Loki was bound beneath the Earth, while Fenrir was chained in the Gulf of Black Grief. But beyond this superficial tale is a figure who represents an emanation of the great goddess herself.

In both traditional and contemporary Norse literature, the Midgard serpent is known by a number of names, with some of the most frequent ones being Jormungandr, Jormungand, Midgardsormr, and Iormungand. She is also known under a number of kennings, such as The Encircler of all Lands, Twisted Bay-Menacer, Holm-Fetter, Deadly-Cold Serpent, Stiff

Land-Rope, The Coiling Eel, The Sea Thread, Steep-Way's Ring, Coal-Fish of the Earth, Sea-Bed Fish, The Water-Soaked Earth Band, and Fiorgyn's Eel. The name Iormungand has the most significance for those wishing to utilize the World Serpent's energy and wyrd in magick; this is because the name has the same source from which the serpent's rune, Ior, also derives its name.

The image and symbolism of Iormungand is remarkably nearly universal. Assuming the more cosmopolitan name of Ouroboros, she is distributed throughout the world, in a vast number of cultures and belief systems, from Europe to Asia and even to Africa. In most instances the meaning remains the same, that of an eternal cyclic force, destructive in essence, but also essential as a part of nature's regenerative process. These fundamentals are also true of Iormungand, a reality that now even some practitioners of orthodox contemporary paganism have grudgingly admitted. A link between the goddess and the serpent can be traced well back into the Upper Paleolithic and Neolithic periods. Significantly, images of the snake goddess from this period are often accompanied by coils, zig-zags, and meanders; all symbols of water. Consequently, in mythology, the world serpent is invariably associated with water.

Beyond Northern cosmology, the principle appearance of the Ouroboros symbol is in Gnosticism. The venom of the World Serpent, and the Serpent herself, are symbols of the universal solvent, or the elixir of life that "passes through all things", the unchanging law that connects all parts of existence and creation. This role of the bridge between all realities is expressed in one alchemical manuscript which depicts her body half-black, symbolising the earth and darkness, and half-white, representing heaven and light. A similar idea is seen in Orphic cosmology, where the World Serpent was Aeon, who lay coiled around the Cosmic Egg, and represented the life span of the universe. This myth has it origins in the cosmology of pre-Hellenic Greece, where the Cosmic Egg was the progeny of the goddess Eurynome and the wind serpent Ophion. Ophion coiled itself around the egg, until it cracked and all life emerged.

In Sumerian-Babylonian mythology, the mother of all life was Tiamat, the vast salt-water ocean, symbolized as a huge cosmic serpent. She joined with Apsu, the sweet-water ocean, and in so doing, brought into being the first stages of the cosmos. Ultimately, in a mirroring of the Norse myth of Thor's attempt to kill Iormungand, Tiamat was killed by the patriarchal sky-god Marduk. However, she is by no means dead or absent from our reality, because she is the foundation upon which we walk. An almost identical tale is told by the Aztecs of central America, in which the creatrix Cipactli existed before all creation as a monstrous alligator swimming through primordial chaos. Life and the cosmos was created when her body was divided, by two serpentine gods, her lower body falling to become the earth, and her upper body rising to become the heavens. Again as in Sumerian myth, Cipactli continues to live after her primeval death, and at night she can occasionally be heard crying and sobbing, wishing all life would die back into her. Similarly in the creation myth of the Chibcha of Colombia, Bachue, the primeval mother, originated in the waters of a huge lake, to which she, and her son, and lover, returned as dragons after the creation of the human race. Nu Kua, the creator goddess of ancient China, was also serpent-bodied, while the Incas perceived the earth as Mamapacha, a dragon goddess who lived within the mountains.

Iormungand also represents the cosmic force defined by science as entropy. Iormungand causes change, and in order to instigate this change, her nature is chaotic and disruptive. Because of this chaotic nature, Iormungand is an oft-times unstable and apparently malevolent force; as her presence throughout history illustrates. When great periods of instability arises, be it as war, revolution, or natural disasters, they illustrate Iormungand thrashing her tail upon the world shore. No matter how much people may try to ignore this kind of side of history, it is an essential part. Similarly, Iormungand, lying in the world ocean, not only causes change, but also maintains stability in encircling and protecting the world of Midgard. In the words of Benito Mussolini, "Blood alone moves the wheels of history", and so the blood that Iormungand spills enables time to move onwards, and the thrashing of her tail prevents the waters of humankind from ever growing stagnant. She ensures, as all the Rökkr do, that life is never predictable.

The necessity of Iormungand is shown in conventional Norse mythology by the very fact that the gods can never truly capture or bind the snake. In addition, Wyrd ensures that they can never do this, thwarting their attempts at controlling a cosmic force that is far greater than they are. The poem Hymiskvitha from the Poetic Edda tells the story of Thor's fishing trip with the giant Hymir. Using the head of the giant black bull Himinbrjoter (Sky-cleaver), Thor caught Iormungand on his line. But as he tried to drag the snake up from the waters of Midgard, the giant Hymir, in what was obviously an appreciation of Wyrd, cut the fishing line, allowing the serpent to escape and later fulfill her role at Ragnarok.

Hoped, yet the worm had fallen beneath the stroke;
But the wily child of Loke
Waits her turn of Ragnarok.

Iormungand is an expression of chaos; entropic, but still controlled. The Great Serpent is not the force of a mindless kind of anarchy, or nihilistic destruction, but rather yet another vital strand of reality in the labyrinth that forms the Web of Wyrd. Thor, in a macho act, was trying to destroy a vital part of Nature, and Nature herself, as manifested through Wyrd, would not allow such an act to occur. The gods are the products of nature, not vice versa, and as such they are subject to her laws, will, and Wyrd, in the same way that mortals are. When Thor did finally slay

Iormungand on the plain of Vigrid at Ragnarok, he too lost his life, proving that the removal of the force of the serpent incurs a disaster of far greater proportion than the serpent's continued existence provides. His attempt to catch Iormungand was not the first time the Snake had made a fool of him. When he and Loki travelled to the capital city of Jotunheim, he challenged the ruler in a strength test. He was told to lift the cat of the Jotun king, Utgard-Loki, but after much exertion he could only lift one paw; it transpired that the cat was really Iormungand.

The rune of Iormungand is Ior, from the Fourth Aett of the Anglo-Saxon Futhorc; it expresses many of the attributes of Iormungand, but also introduces other sides to the serpent's nature. In contrast to the destructive, and entropic, nature of Iormungand, Ior the rune has a beneficial and accessible aspect, and this is where the everyday magick of Iormungand has its source.

The magick of Iormungand and Ior is protective and binding in nature; this is expressed in Ivy (Hedera Helix) the plant associated with both the World Serpent, and the Ior rune. Like the serpent that it symbolizes, the ivy entwines itself around life, causing change by bringing death, and subsequently allowing new life to begin. Throughout this process, the Ivy remains evergreen (eternal) and constant, in an act of initial paradox, a plant of death, but also a plant of life.

Ivy displays the contrast within Iormungand by acting as a protector as well as assassin. When Ivy grows upon the outer walls of a house it protects the inhabitants from malicious magical attack, be it of a human source, as in a magician using the Nithsong, or a curse, or from a more supernatural being. The traditional carvings used on Scandinavian buildings evoke the protective powers of Iormungand and Ivy through serpentine and entwining designs, ensuring the safety of the inhabitants.

A more malicious aspect of Iormungand's magick is the use of Binding Magic, which invokes both aspects from the ivy's two sided nature. Defining malice, of course, depends on the practitioner's intent and their perception of what is personally right or wrong. Binding Magic in its various guises has a well-documented history. It was used in battles during the Viking age to render enemies helpless, and here it had a particular association with the Æsir god of battle, Odin. He was the patron of a particular kind of binding known as the Herfjottur or War-fetter, which would confuse an enemy, making them vulnerable to attack. As with the form of cursing known as the Nithsong, the Thurisaz and Isa runes were often used to enforce a binding. In most instances, the binding is only a psychic one which is applied in the same manner as a curse, but with a result equal to an actual physical binding on either the body, the mind, or even both.

Chant to Iormundgand

Ior Ior Iormundgand!
Serpent bound, wound around,
Holding all the world within your coils;
Serpent bound, wound around,
Turning through the ocean's shining waves;
Serpent bound, wound around,
Ring the world with power like a wall,
Serpent bound, wound around,
At the cost of your freedom Midgard's saved.
Ior Ior Iormundgand

Day of the Serpent
5ᵗʰ day of Solmonath (February 5)
Pagan Book of Hours, Order of the Horae

Colors: Malachite green, sea-blue, and silver
Element: Water
Altar: Set a cloth of sea-blue embroidered with a great serpent in malachite green and silver, and on it place a figure of the Midgard Serpent with its tail in its mouth. Around the room strew colored ribbons in a great circle. The ritual takes place within the circle.
Offerings: Cords or ribbons knotted into a circle.
Daily Meal: Eel. Fish and seafood. Seaweed. Salad. Cooked greens. Eggs.

Invocation to the Midgard Serpent

> Hail Iormundgand
> Child of the Trickster
> And the Hag of the Iron Wood,
> Brother and sister of Death,
> Neither male nor female
> But complete within yourself,
> Neither forward nor backward
> But eternally circling,
> Neither of the earth
> Nor apart from it
> But forever surrounding us
> In our Middle Land.
> Teach us, O Serpent,
> Of what it is to see the end
> And the beginning as one,
> To see all things
> In their place on the wheel,
> To live with the turning
> And not mistake it for a straight line
> Even when the horizon
> Is too far away
> For our weak eyes to find.

(All join hands and do a circle dance around the outside of the room, just inside the serpent boundary, chanting the Chant to Iormundgand.)

Hati and Skoll

When the Great Wolf, Fenris, began to run amuck, he first went back to the place where he was born. Tyr and the other Aesir had tried to keep him from going back to the Iron Wood, but one day he escaped and fled to his birthplace, and was reunited with his mother Angrboda, and his werewolf half-siblings. It is not known what happened to him there, save that when he left, his maddened devouring rage had begun in earnest, and a woman of the Jarnvidur had borne two wolf-pups, the very image of their father. In another account, the mother of Hati and Skoll was Angrboda herself, by Fenris her son, but we may never know the truth of this.

When Fenris was chained, Hati and Skoll were the only ones who came to defend him. Loki and Angrboda themselves did not interfere, knowing the necessity of the binding, but his young sons tumbled forth in a vain attempt to free their father. Instead, they were captured by the Aesir, and Odin put them to use, bespelling them as he had bespelled the Great Snake. Sunna and Mani had often been known to dawdle or change their course, which meant that the days and nights were not always dependable and on time. Mani was especially bad at this, as he liked to look down on what was happening, and the adventures played out below his feet enchanted and delayed him. There had been complaints about this from many mouths, and so Odin put the two wolves into the sky as a way to make the chariots run on time, as it were. Skoll was bespelled to chase Sunna's chariot as a dog herds sheep, keeping it to its path, and Hati (also known as Hati Hridvitisson, and Managarm) was similarly charged with herding Mani's dog-cart.

While they do not spend all of their time in the sky—when the Sun and Moon are on time and stick to their schedules, the wolves can run free on the earth below—if either sky-etin is late, they are lifted into the sky to do their job. Skoll is the quieter of the two, and says little; he does not love the involuntary nature of his job, although he gets some fun out of racing Sunna, but he is aware that it is a better deal than the one that befell his father. Hati is more outgoing and more moody; he veers from cheery mischief to wrath, and deeply resents the spell that pulls him so often to the sky. Both are aware that if Ragnarok comes, they will be able to chase and kill Sunna and Mani, and free themselves from Odin's spell, and they look forward to that day.

Wolf Song to Hati and Skoll

The sun-cart's wheels are ripe red fruit,
Let them sink on my teeth, run their juice on my tongue;
Let the chase I am set be a game that I play,
With laughter, with leaping, with wit may I run.

The moon-cart's wheels are pearly fruit,
Let them sink on my teeth, run their juice on my tongue;
Let the chase I am set be the prey I will hunt,
With knowing, with keening, like Death may I run.

Servants Of The Dark: Giants of Helheim

elheim, the lowest of the Nine Worlds, is the repository and home for the Dead of many races. Jotun souls go there when they die, as do humans of Midgard who are not collected by Freyja or Odin's valkyries. A very few number of Alfar souls go there, as a teind that is part of a bargain with Hela. And, it seems, so do some of the humans of our world.

The history of Helheim can be found in snippets and bits. There are some references to a third world, Jormundgrund, that came into being soon after Muspellheim and Niflheim; it is referred to as the underworld of the Giants. Even then, it was run by a goddess named Hel, although this was not Loki's daughter. It seems that the name is more of a job title, and it is passed on from one being to another over time. Whoever this elder Hel was, we do not know why she retired, or stepped down, or ceased to exist. We do have a bit of information that suggests that the frost-giant Mimir was her consort for a time, a fact that he will admit to when pressed. But for whatever reason, the elder Hel left, and then the mantle was passed to the newly born daughter of Loki and Angrboda.

The current Death Goddess promptly rebuilt the older Jormundgrund into the current Helheim. While most people think of Helheim as simply a section of Niflheim that has been carved off into a separate world, it is in fact the largest world of the Nine, coiling around the Tree like an immense ring, holding all the legions of Dead. The few live people who go there for spiritual reasons find it still and peaceful, with rolling hills and barrows, dark lakes, and a twilit sky. There are a few nasty places—Dead Man's Shore, which is littered with corpses; the Hall of Serpents, where poisonous snakes drip venom down onto evildoers; the silent Black Sea in which no life can be found. Hela's own palace, Elvidnir, is half beautiful mansion and half falling-down ruin; it is probably one of the largest halls in the Nine Worlds. She does take in the rare journeyer, but there are many dangers associated with going to Helheim.

For her staff, Hela seems to have largely chosen frost-giants from Niflheim, probably for their cold, implacable nature. Their job is to make sure that the right people get in, and the wrong people stay out. It is also their job to make sure that those living folk who are allowed in behave themselves, and they can be ruthless in their work. Every one of them is faultlessly loyal to Hela, or they wouldn't be there. They know that their jobs are considered some of the worst in the Nine Worlds, and they don't care. They are there because the jobs need doing. Hela is extremely protective of her dead folk, and takes care of them as best she can.

Many of the obstacles to entering Helheim were put there to keep would-be necromancers from constantly bothering dead souls for information. Odin even managed to steal in once and harass the soul of a dead giantess, the Volva, although Hela increased her security and he has not been able to manage that trick again. Mortal, god, or wight, no one so much as sneezes in that realm that she does not know about, and thus her staff needs to be supremely dedicated to their often thankless jobs, which, of course, they are.

However, if for whatever reason you manage to get permission to enter Helheim (or at least the parts of it that are not off-limits to you, which will only be a small area), it is good to have a positive relationship with the guardian wights. They have a great deal of wisdom collected through endless ages of aiding and shepherding dead souls; they know a lot about Darkness, and Depths, and many other things. Do not scorn them as allies and resources, even if their position frightens you. There are worse things than Death in the Universe.

Mordgud

Mordgud is the "maiden etin" who guards the main gate of Helheim. "Maiden etin", translated into Jotun terms, seems to refer to an unmarried female warrior, more the Amazon than the blushing human maid. It is akin to understanding the different Hellenic words for an unmarried woman; "kore" implied innocence and fragility while "pallas" implied something fiercer and more warriorlike. However, while Mordgud is a tall, muscular etin-woman who generally appears in shiny black armor, she is more than just a thug at the door.

Mordgud has also appeared as a skeletal figure (one of her illusions) or a forbidding dark shape with a loud voice. Her tower, built of the black shiny stone that seems to be so common in Helheim and Muspellheim, stands by the Gjallarbru bridge, on the far side; if you make it over the bridge, you then have to deal with her. Don't try to slip past her; she has had millennia of experience in discerning the dead from the living, and you won't be able to fool her for a second. She will stop you, and you must state your business. If you have no specific appointment, she might turn you away. At that point, you'd best go home and try to get through to Hela, her boss, and beg for an appointment. If you get no answer, you're probably out of luck and Her Ladyship doesn't want you visiting.

If Mordgud does let you by, she may demand that you leave something behind as a token of your good behavior. If she asks for this, you should immediately give her the most valuable thing that you are carrying, unless it is something to be delivered to Helheim. She is honorable and will give it back when you return past her watch, unless you misbehave yourself and incur Hela's wrath. Other reports say that she requires people to recite their ancestry, or at least their families, so be ready in case this comes up. If you don't know your ancestors, say so; don't make them up.

Some reports claim that Mordgud extracts a toll of blood from living people wishing to enter Helheim. At any rate, it is good common knowledge that one ought to give a token of blood whenever dealing with the deities of death—some won't even look at you unless blood is involved—and it's not surprising that Mordgud might demand some. Have a lancet on you just in case. Understand that leaving your blood with her is more than just an offering; it's leaving a bit of your energy behind so that you can be controlled should you act up.

> I've always experienced Mordgud as a Goddess who brings
> the awareness that wisdom need not always be beautiful to be
> true.
>
> —Tamara Crawford

Although her job is very much like Heimdall's—she does seem to be his "opposite number"—she is more than just a security guard. Mordgud has seen as great deal of death, and has shepherded many people from the realm of the living to the realm of the Dead, and she has deep knowledge and wisdom of such transitions. She is a psychopomp in her own right, and can be called on by those who feel stuck in their own dead places. She may not lead you out, if the time isn't right, but she might point out the way for you.

Mordgud is also a good ally for those whose spirit-work involves laying the ghosts of the restless Dead. She is skilled at setting up a channel for their transport, and very good at helping a confused spirit-worker determine the difference between an actual ghost-soul and a haunt-stain. She can also be useful for those who work in hospitals and hospice care, and have to watch souls leave their body in various states of pain and suffering, which can confuse the dead soul and make them a wandering ghost. Calling upon Mordgud when an imminent death is approaching can take them on the right road, rather than leaving them lost.

Mordgud's ancestry is unknown, and people don't generally ask her about it, but some interpret her as having frost-giant bloodlines, and some say fire-giant bloodlines. There is also a rumor that she is a daughter of Loki by some quick liaison with a random frost-giantess; this is solely the UPG of a few spirit-workers who have heard comments from Mordgud or

Loki, and noticed that Hela occasionally refers to Mordgud with terms that imply she is a younger sister.

Some folk honor Mordgud on Samhain Eve, the time when the veils between our world and Helheim are the thinnest, and thus an appropriate time for the goddess who keeps the boundary between living and dead. As the next day—November 1—is said to be Hela's birthday, it seems a good flow from one to the other.

My Encounter With Mordgud And What Came After

by Mordant Carnival

I'm sitting in the dark. The light from the VDU is the only light in the room as I begin to shut everything down for the night. I'm winding down for sleep, and my mind is wandering. I'm reflecting on my own doubt: my fear that none of the spirit-work I've been doing is real, that perhaps there are no guides or Gods but only the echo of my own thoughts inside a locked room of incipient madness. I reflect that I will never truly lose that doubt, only put it aside for a spell. It will be held at bay for as long as They speak to me, but will always creep back; it may be eroded over the years, but it will never be gone entirely. I reflect that perhaps this is not such a bad thing.

The voice is clear, sudden, a silent shout from that place in my being where they speak. There are words yet no words, images and colours. "Doubt? I am Doubt. Doubt is the bridge, and Doubt guards the bridge. Your Doubt is the span that connects you to Beyond; and all the hordes of Hel might be free in a moment, if they had no Doubt. I am Mordgud!"

She's on me suddenly, strong as anything I've ever encountered. I am overshadowed and somehow I know that full possession is imminent. I hit the floor, knowing that if I don't sit I may fall. I don't fight Her—I know enough not to fight, that this will only make the possessory state more extreme. Instead I try to stay calm and explain to Her that the body She's trying to possess is overtired, and that there is nobody in the dwelling for Her to speak with (except my partner, who is sleeping and who I don't want disturbed). She seems puzzled, as if She was expecting to find me in a communal dwelling, or at least attended by someone who could witness Her message. For a long moment I wait, trying not to struggle, not to panic and attempt to throw Her off, while the questing spirit seems to raid my sensorium to confirm what I've said. I promise that if She'll only hold off I'll find a way to communicate with Her another time. I also remind Her that I don't know Her—that I should really be allowed to confirm Her identity before I let Her take my body for a spin. At first I don't think She's going to leave, but slowly She withdraws.

I walk weakly through to the bedroom and lie down. She hovers at the edge of my consciousness, speaking softly, until sleep takes me down.

The next day I investigate Mordgud online. I confirm what I'd already suspected: aside from Her name and a job description, Mordgud's lore is lost. I check in with Hela, and with my patron, Loki. Hela says little, but in my mind I feel a sense of calm agreement. I think She'd be very angry to find someone impersonating Her servant, so I take this as confirmation. Loki makes some vague, ribald claim in respect of Mordgud. I don't know if I am to take it that Mordgud is one of His lovers or a product of one of his many liaisons, but He confirms that my visitor was who She said She was.

I work some on my Hela icon, which seems to have taken on a life of its own and will probably never be finished. I add a wire and lace poppet to represent Mordgud, and make it known that I'm okay to work with Her. I'm still not happy with the idea of possessory work, but I'm coming to terms with the fact that it will be required of me at some point.

For the next couple of days, I feel Her around a lot. I've been skiving on my trance-work again, and now She takes charge. The sensations of impending trance are familiar; normally I can put this work off for a few hours or even days, but I've been stalling Them for too long. They let me make it as far as the bed before knocking me out and sending me to Hel.

I meet Mordgud on the bridge. Heimdall's opposite number, she guards the way to (and from) the lands of the Dead. I perceive Her as a very tall, muscular woman. She is wearing boots but otherwise appears unclothed. Patterns of light and dark cover Her body, including two rows of mandala-like tattoos on Her torso. At the time I wonder why a guard would go unarmoured, but later it is revealed to me that Mordgud is Her own armour: defence is part of Her being.

Because I'm there at Her instigation rather than as a trespasser, She is not unfriendly. She tries to slip an arm about my waist as we walk; I stiffen at the contact. She laughs and lets me go, joshing a little. She uses a term I'm not familiar with, and later cannot recall; the meaning was something like "newfangled", but carrying connotations of prudishness. It's clear that Mordgud views my reserve as an unhealthy modern trait, one which She'd like to see excised. She leads me over the bridge to the far shore, then heads back to Her post. (The rest is another story.)

Since then, She has become one of the strongest presences in my spirit-work. What is She like? Profoundly powerful, awe-inspiring. As a personality, She is no less powerful and magnificent than many of those Gods whose lore has survived and who are more popular as recipients of modern worship. I'm increasingly of the opinion that She, or one of the earlier beings that has fed into Her, was the subject of considerable reverence at some point. Despite (or perhaps because of) Her role as a guard, She has a loving side, protective and compassionate.

She's with me a lot, usually in the evenings after the sun has gone down. (In heathen times, this would be the beginning of a new day. For the purposes of my magicoreligious work I treat days as beginning and ending at sunset rather than midnight.) Working with Her has affected my ancestor work fairly dramatically, with my ancestor harrow becoming one of the 'noisiest' in my household. Most of my work with Her so far has focused on spending more time with and generally making a fuss of my Dead.

She generates a lot of physical movement: if I allow it, She will direct me through a few stretching exercises and then trigger periods of ecstatic dancing, during which I receive messages and direction in respect of ritual kit to be created and practices that it might profit me to undertake. I've come to feel that She would be a great ally to have when learning martial arts or yoga, practices involving the body. She is a great one for suddenly grabbing you in the middle of an exercise, or pushing or pulling your body into what She evidently regards as the proper configuration: "What are you doing?" She seems to say. "That's not right—let me show you!" I'm learning that resisting her involvement is more trouble than it's worth.

Although She is a forceful and insistent being, there is a certain element of playfulness about Her. I've rapidly come to hold Mordgud in very high regard, and I look forward to continuing my work with Her in future.

Invocation to Mordgud

Hail, Mordgud, Gatekeeper of the Dark Road,
Helvegr's watchwoman, never sleeping,
Your dark eyes watch always the oncoming road
For the lost soul who must be rescued,
Wandering in the dark with no hope
Of being gathered to Hela's peaceful breast.
Hail, Right Hand of Hel,
Warrior who protects the Way
From those who would plunder
The wisdom of the slumbering Dead,
From those who would raid
The secrets of the Underworld,
From those who would wreak their doom
In foolishness before their time,

All these you turn away with upraised hand,
Though fools may not understand
The kindness that you do them.
Hail, Guardian of Hel's Gate,
Whose eyes see the Dead, in all their forms,
Weeping, sleeping, bewildered and fearful,
Laughing with open arms,
All are ushered through your Gate
With your exquisite compassion and comfort
For you leave none behind.
By the Dark Road of Stars, we hail you!
By the roaring river Gjoll, we hail you!
By the gold-roofed bridge, we hail you!
By the passage of knives, we hail you!
Mistress of the Knife's Way,
Mistress of the Black Tower,
Mistress of the Last Spear,
We hail you, Lady of the Last Gate,
And may you welcome us in our hour of need.

Garm

Garm, Hela's enormous dog-guard, lives in the cave Gnipahellir. He is an eight-foot-tall black hound with glowing eyes. It is important not to underestimate Garm. While he may act like a big dog—vicious and dangerous or friendly depending on who you are—it's an act. There is as much intelligence in Garm as in any other of Helheim's guards. He is a Jotun who is always in dog-form, but he is no dumb beast. Garm seems to be on a general patrol around the borders of Helheim, meaning that he could be anywhere at any point. More often than not, however, he will be lending support to Mordgud at the main Gate. Garm will probably decide if you should enter based on a sniff or two. Don't ask us what he's sniffing for; we don't know.

If Garm goes off on you, howling and roaring and growling and menacing you, he's probably giving you a chance to back off and leave. Take it. If he really intends to kill you immediately, he will just do it. Garm can move frighteningly fast, and you will be eaten before you realize what's happened. One way to appease him is to bring him a gift of meat, or bread baked with blood (these were traditionally called Helcakes and put into graves for the purpose of placating Garm); he might accept these and let you through, but then again he may decide that your intent is wrong, and then no offering will sway him.

Garm is vigilantly loyal to Hela; he is her hound and her servant. As a weredog, he likely has links to the Iron Wood. It is said that he is a friend to Fenris, and that this is why when Ragnarok comes he will slay Tyr, even if it means his death.

Invocation to Garm

Hound of Hel
Harrier of Hordes
May you look kindly upon our footsteps.
Black Brother
Baying at the Gate
May you look kindly upon our footsteps.
Scenter, Sniffer,
Great Guardian,
May you look kindly upon our footsteps.

Recipe for Garm's Helcakes

½ cup sour bread starter (which is ½ cup milk mixed   with
⅓ cup rye flour, left at room temperature for two days
until it has a slightly sour flavor)
2 cups animal blood
2 tablespoons honey
3 ½ cups rye flour
3 ½ cups oat flour
¼ cup warm water
2 teaspoons salt
4 tablespoons active dry yeast (2 packages)

Turn the sour bread starter into a large mixing bowl and stir in the blood
and honey. Dissolve the yeast in the warm water and stir gently into the
mixture. Add 1 cup of the flour, stir in, cover and let rise for an hour.
Slowly knead in the salt and the remaining flour until you have a stiff
dough. Cover and let rise again; punch down the risen mixture; let rise
again; then shape into small rolls and let rise once more. Mark Hel's Rune
(Ear) on each of them with a knife. Bake in a moderately hot oven (about
375 degrees) until done.

Other Guardians of the Helheim Gates:
Bigvoer, Listvoer, Ari, and Hrimgrimnir

Bigvoer and Listvoer are a pair of etin-women who are often placed on guard to one or more of the Gates, especially the inner Gate. Sometimes they appear with Mordgud; sometimes she may send visitors on to their Gate. Like her, they may require a token left with them until you return. If you leave clothing, they may wear it until you return. They appear as a pair of elderly, cackling hags, but do not underestimate their strength. They are sorceresses and can deal with you quickly. Be polite and even a bit obsequious to them; this will make them laugh and make them better disposed to you.

Another gate-guard is Ari, a frost-giant whose favorite form is that of a great shrieking eagle. He loves to frighten the approaching rows of Dead by swooping down on them, but unless they stray from the road he does not actually harm anyone. According to the Voluspa, if Ragnarok comes, Ari will leave his perch—which is a craggy mountain that forms part of the Na-gates, or Corpse-gates—and mingle his song with the hordes' shield-song as the giants go marching on the Aesir.

Yet another gate-entrance is guarded by Hrimgrimnir, a very tall frost-giant. He tends to blend into the stonework and only come out if he thinks that you don't belong. Of all the gate-guardians, Hrimgrimnir is probably the most unpleasant. In *Skirnirsmol* it is suggested that one of the punishments for dead women cursed by the Gods is to be a slave of Hrimgrimnir; the implications are that he forces himself on whatever females he can find. As far as we can tell, this is not something that he does while on duty as a gate-guard, but it is possible that his off-duty practices in Helheim are fairly unsavory.

Hrimgrimnir may well be left over from the previous Jormundgrund regime; something about him speaks of the Time Before The Flood. He is huge and pale, with bluish-white skin that appears somewhat moldy. His long greyish hair and beard are laden with lichens and mold, and his eyes are cold and unresponsive. He speaks little, and mostly grunts, but when roused he can speak—and roar—just fine, and his strength is what you would expect from a large frost-thurse. He is not above assaulting perceived vandals, and cheerfully breaking them into pieces and eating them.

The Thief At The Hidden Gates
by Corbie Petulengro

And would you go under the ground
Through the center of the labyrinth, through the hole
Gaping like a dark cunt in the earth,
Sneaking in the back way?
Do you think that you will find a land
Of summer and mirth, first thing? No—
First is the crawling, the passage that narrows
Until you are on your hands and knees,
Breathing the dust, suffocating in the dank earth,
You spit and cough and cry and think
That this was not what you wanted, no, not this—
And then you turn back, saying, This must
Be wrong; I was mistaken,
I will find another way.
But there is no other way,
And that includes the way back. You go round
In circles, wearing out your knees and lungs
And the only way is forward
But you will not take that way, no,
Not until you are so far gone that Death
Is imminent and there is nothing to lose.
Then you can move forward.

And would you challenge the guardians
When you come to their gates? You were clever,
You would not approach the front door
Like the knight riding up to the dragon
With lance cocked, expecting death or glory.
The brave knight, waving his vulnerability,
Waving his trust, ready to be plucked
Like a bright flower—how pathetic,
You think. I need not be such a fool
Nor lay myself wide open.
No, you were clever, you would
Go in the back way and hope
No one's eyes would pick you out,
One shadow in the darkness,
One worm in the soil,
But you did not know what it was to be a shadow, a worm,
And now you are finding that out.
Intimately. When the roof rises
And you can stand again, go from worm to man,
You weep your gratitude only to find
That the gate ahead is blocked
By eyes that find you as surely
As the hen's beady stare at the rising worm.

Will it be the old hags, the women
Who cackle and ridicule you,
Pluck at your clothes, steal your shoes,
Wear your precious things in a mockery of your hopes?
Will it be the eagle, shrieking, buffeting
Your ears as you cower, unable to speak,
And where would your fine speech get you here?
Will it be the thumping tread of the giant, his hand
Enveloping your spindly form, breath cold
As icy winds, crumbling moss spread over his

Grey hair and face? Rot sweeps from his mouth,
And the chill breezes, and you are caught.
What will you say, you who wanted to rape
The Underworld of its treasures?

Will you live there, locked in a box,
Glass-covered, weeping, beating at the frosty window,
Shown off with a sign carved in runes:
Here is the fool, the thief, the arrogant one,
The wanderer who wanders no more.
Some part of you will live there, cold and bitter,
Unless you are willing to face the Presence at the center.
Grovel before Her, beg forgiveness,
Know that there will be no forgiveness, and beg mercy,
Know that there will be no mercy, and beg a lessoning,
And once it is granted, swallow it down whole.
Be assured, it will choke you.
Be assured, it will poison you.
Be assured, it will change you,
As Death is the great changer,
Be assured, you will go forth from that place
Far different from the bright thief who entered,
And all the things that made you think
This would be a good idea,
This would be an easy ride,
This would be an adventure to brag about—
All those things that shaped you
Will have no more meaning for you.
Are you ready to go down
And lose all your reasons for going?
Be assured, from one who has trodden those paths,
If you could see yourself, vomited forth gasping
From the dark hole in the earth,

Corpse-pale, rot-smelling, wild-haired,
With wild eyes that see your worldly life
And slide away from it, perhaps your footsteps
Would slow at the edge of that hole,
Perhaps the massive loom of the front gate
Would seem, in contrast, not so foolish
As your foolish soul once believed.

Ganglati

Ganglati is Hela's personal maid, the chatelaine/housekeeper of Elvidnir. She is huge and ponderous and moves very slowly and with a limp, but still manages to get a whole lot done. Like all of the giants of Helheim, she is slow to warm up to anyone, tends not to make friends with those who don't come around regularly, and the best way to get on her good side is extreme courtesy and the occasional small gift (which she may seem to ignore until you are gone). If you ever intend to stay in Elvidnir, though, it's best to get on her good side. Things like a soft bed with no vermin and an uninterrupted night's rest are rather dependent on her good graces.

One thing that Ganglati will do is to judge you on how well you treat servants. If you are uncomfortable with being served, and try to tell her that she shouldn't wait on you (which is simply you disrespecting her job, and getting in the way of her doing it properly) she will think you a fool. If you are arrogant and condescending towards her because she is just a fat, slow, limping serving maid, she will say nothing, but will find ways to make your stay in Helheim utterly miserable in many tiny, nasty ways. As with all of Hela's staff, appealing to the boss will make no difference; she is generally aware of what they are doing and if it happens, it's because she has allowed it to, and either doesn't care or thinks that they are within their rights to dish out a lesson.

Nidhogg

Yggdrasil, the great World Tree, has its roots in the lowest worlds—Niflheim and Helheim. Its most obvious third protruding root is found, huge and dark, at the great well Hvergelmir in Niflheim. Hvergelmir means "Boiling Cauldron", and all the rivers of the Nine Worlds flow from its churning depths. Next to it lies the third root of the Tree, drawing nourishment from the Well, so huge that it runs off the boundary of Niflheim and into Helheim; the Wall of Helheim incorporates it like it would a small mountain. The dragon Nidhogg, a thirty-foot multicolored wingless earth-dragon, crawls back and forth over that wall to gnaw at the great root on both sides of the border.

When not coiled around the lowest root of the World Tree, Nidhogg crosses the wall into Helheim and visits Dead Man's Shore. This is a place where the sun never shines, and the dark waters of Helheim's ocean stretch out between the worlds. Corpses and the shed skins of serpents litter the shore. Nidhogg comes down periodically in her task as carrion-remover and eats the corpses. Many fear her because of her job, but she is an important part of the cycle. Like Hela who is intimately connected with the life-phase of rotting, Nidhogg represents the next part of the cycle, when the rot feeds life. Whether it is carrion-eaters or the earth itself, nothing grows unless something dies and rots to feed it.

This is a lesson that modern Westerners have a hard time with. We are taught to hide and ignore all aspects of natural waste. Fecal material is flushed away to contaminate our water supply rather than to be returned to the earth which can better handle it. Menstrual blood is hidden shamefully and not spoken of. Crawling insects are considered disgusting and foul, especially those who clean up corpses. The terminally ill, with all their smells and wastes, are secreted away in hospitals where no one has to look at them. Few have worked intimately with a compost heap, watching food waste slowly rot into rich, black soil filled with worms and other life. In the fantasy world that modern Western society has created, all waste—and as a corollary, anything that is aesthetically unpleasing—is flushed away and vaporized, and we never have to worry about it again. Nidhogg, as the ultimate carrion-eater, has other lessons for us.

When you meet her at Dead Man's Shore, Nidhogg is sometimes followed by her brood of serpent-children, whose names include Goin, Moin, Grabak, Grafvollud, Ofnir, and Svafnir. They cluster around Nastrond, the Hall of Serpents, but will not attack anyone outside of that hall, on Hela's orders. They might come at you and try to knock you off your feet, however, or squirm around your ankles in an attempt to disconcert you. Do not show fear; address them individually in a polite and conversational voice, as if they were human beings offering to shake your hand rather than great serpents coiling around your ankles. They will respect your courage and courtesy (especially the latter) and may even speak to you. The Hel-serpents talk in hissing whispers; human speech is not easy for them and they rarely bother with it, so if they talk to you, you can consider yourself honored.

The serpent surrounding the base of the Tree is not unique to Northern cosmology; in Babylonia the huluppu tree grows with a dragon at the base and an eagle at the top, and the dark goddess Lilith in the middle. The cosmic tree cannot exist without all its functions, and Nidhogg performs an important function—that of removing dead wood and stimulating new growth. By gnawing away the dying root-parts of the Tree, Nidhogg stimulates new branches and leaves in the rest of the Tree, and new root matter. Like Tanin'iver, the blind dragon at the base of the dark goddess Lilith's huluppu tree, Nidhogg performs her unthanked task without complaint. If we are to be able to appreciate all parts of the cycle, we must understand and appreciate her duty as well.

Nidhogg
by Abby Helasdottir

Deep within the earth, in the misty nætherworld of Niflheim, lies the great dragon Nidhogg. It lies coiled around the well of Hvergelmir, from which all the waters in the world flow, and chews on the roots of the World Tree, so that the Tree constantly dies and is reborn. The dragon's attention wavers only when it stops to gorge itself upon the corporeal remains of the dead—for its name means *corpse-swallower*, or the *lower one*—and to hear the pronouncements of Wyrd when the volva speaks.

Nidhogg is the chthonic counterpart of the aquatic serpent Iormungand, but unlike the Snake, and all preceding Rökkr beings, the origins of Nidhogg are totally obscure. The dragon, like the World Tree on which it chews, appears to have arisen out of Wyrd itself, having no creation, no creator, suggesting at least that they both began their existence so remotely in the past that they have gone beyond the need for any explanation. Certainly, Nidhogg's nature is so incomprehensible, so chaotic, that it is simply beyond any such definition.   Nidhogg is represented by the traditional constellation of Draconis as it winds its way around the North Pole, just as Nidhogg is coiled around the axis of the world tree.

In classical astral mythology, Draconis represented the dragon Ladon, the guardian of the Hesperidean golden apples. Ladon lay coiled around the tree of immortality which bore the apples in the western garden of the goddess, just as the serpent imparted wisdom from a tree in the biblical garden of Eden. A sense of this can be glimpsed in the way that the dragon is also entwined around the polar constellation of The Lady's Wagon (Ursa Minor), representing the goddess in her maternal aspect. The dragon constellation is circumpolar, meaning that it never sets above 30 degrees latitude, suggesting the eternal nature of the great dragon.

Nidhogg is in continual, and torrid, communication with an eagle that sits amongst the highest branches of the World Tree. Ratatosk (Branch-Borer) the squirrel runs up and down, back and forth, along the tree, exchanging insults and gossip between the dragon and the eagle, hoping to stir up trouble between the two. Ratatosk plays the same role as Loki does amongst the gods, causing trouble between powerful forces, but, at the same time, communicating between Hel and heaven, and thus assisting the flow of Wyrd.

Although Nidhogg's continual chewing upon the roots of the World Tree will eventually shake it to its core at Ragnarok, as is its intention, and although it is a force of absolute chaos, the dragon still performs a pivotal role in Northern, and Rökkr magic. The dragon is an embodiment and expression of the geomantic energies that run throughout the earth, and in particular along ley-lines, and at the sacred megalithic sites that populate western and northern Europe. These earth energies are often regarded as dragon energies, because like the dragon, their power is forceful, almost unknowable, and resides deep within the earth and in stones. One of the most famous of such places is the so-called Saint Michael's line, which runs directly through a number of dragon-related sites in lower England.

These energies are known as *wouivre* (a Celtic name for earth energy/spirit), and although related to Nidhogg, they are the serpentine energies of the Goddess in Her draconian manifestation. The *wouivre* are akin to the eastern concept of the Kundalini, which is raised up through the body, altering personal patterns of energy, matter, and spirit. The figure of the labyrinth, as an actual, physical design, mirrors the subterranean or acausal fields of dragon labyrinthine energy that exist within the earth. The process of travelling around a microcosmic labyrinth in a meditative state evokes the macrocosmic energies and induces a change of consciousness, and perception. To invoke the *wouivre* through the walking of a labyrinth, the labyrinth used need not be a traditional, or established one, although the years of existence will induce a greater sense of the

Eternal. Wherever a new labyrinth is laid out, the *wouivre* are drawn towards it, and the *ond* and Wyrd of the site will be both increased and enriched.

The vast axis of the World Tree is a macrocosmic representation of the human spine. So just as Nidhogg, gnawing on the roots of the tree, sends its energies reverberating throughout the the trunk and branches and to every berry and seed, so too when *wouivre* energies are awaken at the base of the spine, they rise up through the body and impact throughout it.

Nidhogg's Blot
15th day of Blutmonath
Pagan Book of Hours, Order of the Horae

Color: Black
Element: Earth
Altar: On a black cloth set several bare tree branches in an earthenware
       vase, a horn of mead, and the figure of a dragon.
Offerings: Pieces of wood with names of missed duties scratched on them.
Daily Meal: Tree fruit such as apples or pears or cherries or peaches.

Invocation to Nidhogg

> At the base of the great World Tree
> Dwells a black dragon
> Whose name is Nidhogg,
> Whose sole task is gnawing
> At the roots of Yggdrasil.
> As quickly as it gnaws away,
> New growth comes forth
> In a never-ceasing spiral.
> At the base of each soul
> Dwells a black dragon
> Whose name is Conscience,
> Whose sole job is gnawing
> On our blithe thoughtlessness.
> As it gnaws and forces us
> To do what should be done,
> It clears away our disorder
> And allows for new growth
> In the tangle of our lives.
> Teach us, gnawer at the roots,
> How to listen and decide.

Chant: Roots of the Tree,
      Hidden, mysterious,
      Reveal them to me,
      Dragon of Earth.

(Each person shall snap a twig from the branches on the altar and take it with them, laying it under their pillow to remember Nidhogg and their own consciences. The mead is passed around and shared, and the remainder poured out as a libation to Nidhogg.)

Tales of the Giants

he following stories were told to those who work with the Jotunfolk, by the Jotunfolk themselves. Many of them show a different side to the Aesir-centered stories of the Edda; one admirer of the stories has referred to them as "Eddas Through The Looking-Glass". Again, it was difficult for us to decide which of the stories we were given should be listed here. Many were heartfelt and wonderful; our agonizing choice ended up being that we would not use stories that dramatically contradicted existing lore. Small contradictions, especially where the existing lore contradicted itself, were fine. Things entirely outside of existing lore were fair game.

As with any situation where there are opposing sides, there are two—often painfully different—views on each situation. These are stories from the point of view of the Giantfolk themselves, as told to their various human amanuenses. In these stories, they live as more than just shadowy enemies of the Aesir, but as actual races of beings with their own passions and hopes and dreams. Readers will also find some of the Aesir themselves in these stories, because these races intermarried and interbred and befriended each other, and are generally far more intertwined than anyone cares to admit.

Read on, and discover the World of the Tree, in all its glory!

Laufey's Son

(as told by Hela to Raven)

n the beginning, there were the frost giants of Niflheim and the fire giants of Muspellheim, and when the great flood came, many were washed away. Some found safety on a piece of Ymir's body that congealed into a new world, and they named it Jotunheim—the new home of the giants. Some say that it was formed of Ymir's spine and shoulders, for it formed itself into a land of great and imposing mountains, trees that nearly reached the sky, huge and fierce animals that roamed the dark forests, and lightning storms that split the sky.

The surviving Jotnar found it welcoming, and they married each other and produced many new Jotnar—the mountain-etins, the woods-etins, the sea-etins. Some settled high in the cold northern mountains, or the western mountains by the ocean, or the islands, or the eastern rain forests, or the southern woodlands. And in one place in the south of Jotunheim, they settled in a strange forest. Its trees were shorter and harder than anywhere else in the world, and they bore strange fruit. Magic leaked from the very earth; the place reeked of it, and tainted everything that was born there. The etin-folk named it the Iron Wood, and they recognized it as the sacred heart of Jotunheim, the wellspring of its magic. Werewolves and werecreatures were born there, and beings strange and twisted, but their deformities were considered a sacred thing. For a twisted troll to say that he had the blood of the Iron Wood was to replace scorn with reverence in the eyes of the onlookers. Magic ran strong in the blood of the Iron Wood folk; seers and galdr-folk came forth from that place, to marry and spread their bloodlines through all the etin-folk.

The folk of the Iron Wood divided themselves into nine clans, and each elected a chieftain. There was much fighting as to who would be Chief of Chiefs, however, and many were slain in the battles, and the blood soaked into the earth. Finally the fighting came down to two clan chiefs, both of whom swore that they would defeat the other and win the leadership of the Nine Clans.

One was Farbauti, whose name means Cruel-Striker, and whose clan was Lightning. He was tall and strong and broad as the side of a mountain, and belched fire from his mouth. Fire-giant blood ran strong in his veins. The other was the young chieftess of the Wolf clan, a powerful witch with the lineage of the Volva in her. She was tall and strong and had hair the color of dried blood, and she could see into the future and prophesy. And she saw that she would be Chief of Chiefs, and set out to make that prophecy come true.

And it came to pass that Farbauti went from the Iron Wood and came to the western mountains, and thence to the ocean, and he wandered in a boat among the many islands off the coast of Jotunheim, some so close to the world's border that one could almost see Vanaheim in the distance. And it was there that he met a beautiful giantess named Laufey, the Lady of the Leafy Isle. She had earth-goddess blood in her, old and ancient as Jord, and she shone like silver in the moonlight, and Farbauti could think of nothing but her from the moment that he saw her.

It is said in the lore that he struck her with a lightning-bolt, and thus was their son born. The truth of the matter is that love and desire for him did indeed strike her like lightning, and the fruit of that love and desire was that she swelled with child. Yet she had not gone but three months before her womb began to burn, as if a brand flamed there, and it caused her great pain. Farbauti feared for her, and wished her to return with him, for there were healers in the Iron Wood who understood the nature of its bloodlines. She agreed to travel with him back to the Iron Wood, although she sorely missed her leafy isle, but she understood that their son must claim his right to the chieftainship, should it come to Farbauti's death. Her husband built for her a cottage out of stone, and guarded it, for he feared that the wolf-chieftess might strike at her.

He was right in this thinking, for the wolf-chieftess heard of Laufey and her swelling belly, and the Sight came on her, and she saw as in a hazy dream that this son of Farbauti's might someday master her. So she called upon her brothers and sisters, and in wolf's hame they set upon the cottage, where Laufey lay within moaning in pain, for her time was almost upon her.

Great was the duel between Farbauti and the wolf-chieftess, and many scars they left upon each other, but in the confusion Laufey slipped from the house and fled as fast as an etin-woman laboring could run. She fled the Iron Wood, but the wolf-giants came after her, sniffing out her trail. She fled from Jotunheim itself, and crossed the world-border into Midgard, yet still they followed her, and the howling froze the blood of the Midgard humans who heard the chase. She fled into the Myrkwood, so fast that the fierce tribes who lived there could not catch her, but the wolves followed. And so it was that she came to where the trees of the Myrkwood were charred and blackened, and saw the burning waste of Muspellheim beyond. And she knew somehow that the burning in her womb had brought her here, to the burning land.

As she stepped foot into Muspellheim, Surt the Black came forth with his men-at-arms, and challenged her. "What seek you here, island woman?" he growled.

"I seek sanctuary, in the name of the father of my child, Farbauti, who is descended from your sons," she gasped out. "For his enemy is hot on my heels, and this child pleads to be born."

"What will you give me, island woman," Surt asked, "if I shelter you from all harm until there is no more harm to come? What will you give for your protection?"

Laufey held out her hands, and showed that she had nothing on her save her shift. "I come empty-handed into your kingdom, my Lord Surt," she said, "and I have nothing to offer. What would you have of me?"

"Empty-handed, perhaps, but full-bellied," Surt said. "Give me the treasure that you carry. Let me be godfather and second father to your child, and I will give you both sanctuary, for as long as you wish."

Laufey hesitated, for she did not wish to betray Farbauti, but the wolves were howling in the distance and her womb burned so that she could no longer stand or walk, and she finally gave in and agreed. Surt bore her to his castle, and the wolves were stymied, and howled many days along the border of Muspellheim, but they did not dare enter, for Surt was too powerful in his own kingdom, and the very land would rise up against them and burn them to death, and so Laufey and her son were saved.

Surt's palace is hewn from black glassy rock, and his hall has many fireplaces around it, big enough to cook an ox and still have room to turn the spit. And it was in the largest of these that Laufey lay down in the coals, and she lifted her skirts and spread her legs, and a burning brand came forth from her womb. Surt took tongs of iron and drew the brand from her body, and as he did so it became an infant boy with hair the color of flame. And so was born Laufey's son.

Laufey sent to her husband, telling him that he had a son, and pleading to return. But Farbauti was still at war, and felt that it was too dangerous for his wife and child, and he bade her bide with Surt until it was safe. But the years passed, and it was still not safe enough in Farbauti's mind, and all Laufey's pleading had no effect on his fear. Laufey burned first with desire for her absent husband, then with resentment, then with anger. Meanwhile, Surt the Black raised her son like his own, and showed him the mysteries of fire, and the fire-blood in his veins.

When Laufey's son was thirteen years of age, and was going from child to youth, Farbauti sent to Laufey and told her that it was over, and the wolf-chieftess had won. He had agreed to a truce, for she was more powerful than he, and she had been elected the Hagia, the Wise Woman and Chief of Chiefs of the Nine Clans. In return for giving her the title, he bade her promise not to harm his wife and son. So Laufey made ready to go, but before they left a seer of Muspellheim came forth at Surt's bidding and prophesied for Laufey's son.

The seer looked deep into the red-haired youth's sharp green eyes, and she gasped, and said, "You shall have no home, wanderer, save the road itself, and that road will be hard for you, and yet all places on the road shall be your home. You shall have freedom greater than any other, yet be bound by your own choosing. You shall be dearly loved and terribly hated, and little understood. Your name shall be more well known outside the Nine Worlds than any other name in the Nine Worlds save two, and one shall be your blood brother and the other spring forth from your loins." And with this prophecy, they left for the Iron Wood and came to Farbauti at last.

Farbauti made ready to welcome Laufey back, but she spoke forth in anger, and said, "You would not let me share your danger, but only your safety, and I say that this is not love. For I would have died by your side, yet you ordered me apart. So I will not live here with you, but will go up into the mountains that look down upon your forest, and there I will build a home and live. You may visit me when you will, but I will not live with you." And Farbauti wept for the first time, but there was no moving Laufey, for her feet were planted like the earth.

So Farbauti turned to his son, and said, "Will you go with your mother, then, or will you stay here with me, your father?"

Laufey's son was silent a long while, which was surprising to those who knew his quick tongue, but finally he said, "You are the father of my blood, but you were not there when I needed you as a child. Surt the Black cared for me then, and which is more important: the father who gave me his blood, or the father who gave me his time? I cannot choose, and so I will not. I will live with you, Chief of the Lightning Tribe, until I am a man, but I will be known henceforth only as Laufey's Son." And Farbauti accepted this, although with heavy heart.

Laufey spoke forth, and asked, "Will you bring our son to the council of the Clans, and see him welcomed into the Nine?" But Farbauti would not go forth where the wolf-chieftess held court, and he would not see his son welcomed with her hands, which was not all pride, for he still feared that she would break her word and kill his son. Laufey laughed and said, "Seers have spoken for our son, and they did not see him dying before his time, so I will take courage and go before the wolf-chieftess and demand our son's heritage." And a council was called, and she brought her son before them, and Farbauti watched from the trees lest there be foul play.

When the wolf-chieftess heard, she was sore in her heart, for she remembered the dream wherein it was whispered that Farbauti's son might one day master her, and she did indeed contemplate killing him in spite of her word. And with this in mind, she hid a knife in her skirts, even though the deed seemed evil to her. Yet when Laufey and her son came to the clearing where the Council stood, and she faced the youth across the fire, with his flame-red hair and his sharp green eyes and his three-cornered smile, the vision came on her again, and she saw it more clearly this time.

And she saw that someday, not far off, when Laufey's son came to manhood, he would come to her and would indeed master her, but that mastery would be Love. He would become her consort, and he would be the father of all of her children, and she would love and desire him above all others, and sometimes hate him as well. And she saw also that he would be her greatest joy and her greatest sorrow, and that he would be the eventual cause of her death, and her rebirth. And she saw also what the seer of Muspellheim saw, that he would wander forever, and be loved and hated, and come to both fame and infamy. And she would have wept, but she was too proud; and she would have screamed at the trick that the Norns had played her, but she saw the wyrd that must be, and that it was her orlog to take part in this path. The knife fell from her stiff fingers, to bury itself unseen in the earth.

So Angrboda did the only thing that she could do. She stepped forward, in all her regalia of the Hagia of the Iron Wood, and she welcomed him into the tribe, saying, "Laufey's son, child of the lineage of Farbauti, you are welcome into the Nine Clans of the Iron Wood, the sacred heart of Jotunheim. We are your family, and we will guard you, and succor you, as long as you live among us. May none who hear me ever say otherwise!" And she threw back her head and howled, and there was sorrow in the howling, and all wondered to hear it, but they all joined in as well, and with one great howl Loki was swept onto the path that would be his life.

Loki and Sigyn's First Meeting

(as told to Sophie Oberlander)

am no teller of tales, no great Bard of Bragi's get. My inspiration comes from Woden alone… but every so often, another God will whisper in my ear for a time. I, with my small talent, record these things as faithfully as hands and heart will allow, but I am an imperfect tool and my words are often weak for the task at hand. I beg indulgence now as I recount the tale that Loki has chosen to tell. It is what I have been given and what I am permitted to share. He has left parts of the story out and glossed over others. Suffice it to say, Sigyn is his treasure and what he shares, he does so with her consent.

This story begins before Loki came to make a home in Asgard. Oh, he and Odin had been blood-brothers for some time and he often visited the All-Father, even assisting him from time to time, running errands and carrying important messages. No one was as swift or cunning as the flame-haired sky-traveler after all, and Odin often trusted him with secret duties. Loki was observant and sly and quick to note those secret things others would keep hidden from the All-Father, and these he also carried back to his blood-brother. The work appealed to him for a time, though it did not earn him any true place in the halls of the Aesir. Suffice it to say that despite his dealings for and friendship with Odin, Loki did not often stay in Asgard for any great length of time. Aside from his bond with Odin, there was little to keep him there. It was after the great war, when the hostage price had been paid and some of the Vanir had come to live on the Aesir's odal lands that this tale came to pass.

Njord, sacral king of this bright tribe, had bartered himself and the lives of his children and future grandchildren for peace with the Aesir. He came to live among them as a hostage, though his kingship was never in question and he was given rank and respect among his new folk. He built a great hall by the ocean, and filled it with plants and herbs and finely crafted things from the land of his birth. Here his children dwelt until they too built halls of their own. He was a peaceful man, though no less a king for it, and exile from Vanaheim seemed a small price to pay for an enduring peace. He was respected and well liked amongst the Aesir and many often came to his home to learn the skills of the Vanir—herbcraft, witchcraft, peacecraft and other things best saved for other tales. His children thrived in their new home and he was, more or less, content.

It was not easy, however, ruling a tribe in abstentia, particularly one as passionate as the Vanir, even with the aid of his consort Nerthus who did the ruling at home. Negotiations and political intrigue did not cease with the treaties of peace, and often he and Odin sat in counsel, two kings debating governance of their folk. Messengers went often between their two halls, long after fragile, woven peace became firm reality. It was in such a function that Loki first set foot in that bright and shining sanctuary. Years after his Wyrd had well unfolded, as he was telling this tale to me, he mused that had he known what would happen, upon entering Njord's home, he'd have gone there sooner!

Odin had entrusted Loki with documents pertaining to some rather delicate trade negotiations with the Vanir. He was to carry them to Njord and await the other leader's reply. It was a simple enough task, but one that piqued Loki's interest. He'd never been inside the Vanic King's home and had heard tales of its beauty. Vanic architecture tended to be wide and spacious, light and organic in contrast to the more elaborate structures of the Aesir. The Sky-Traveller had an eye for beauty of all kinds and looked upon this particular task as an adventure, a chance to feed that aesthetic desire. Arriving in the hostage-king's lands, it was as if he had left Asgard altogether. The hall was best approached along a stretch of beach and the smell of the sea, the salty air, the crying of the gulls and the chill of the water which permeated every breath was a welcome change from the often stultifying rigor of Asgard's halls. Further, the Vanir bore Loki no particular ill will; they had not the ages-old hostility with the Jotun tribes that so poisoned many interactions with the Aesir. He was often treated hospitably in their halls, and this day was no different. He was shown into an expansive indoor garden and told, with courtesy and apologies, that it would be a bit of time before Njord could see him. He turned down the offer of food or drink and decided instead to wander beneath the skylight, exploring the unfamiliar plants and flowers.

Loki walked amongst the plants, hearing a fountain somewhere in the background, slowly feeling himself relax. He could understand why folk tended to gather at this hall. It was a peaceful, relaxing place and he thought it beneficial that this man had come to the Aesir. He had just lifted his nose from some glorious crimson flower when he heard a squeak and saw a small form ducking behind a bright, flowering bush. Curious as only the god of mischief could be, he decided to investigate. There was a small, upturned basket of sewing on the ground and a few scattered flowers. Grinning, Loki crept around behind the bush only to see the figure darting off again. Laughing, he set up chase. "I won't hurt you, little one. Why don't you come out?"

"No." It was a small, feminine voice from somewhere behind a row of flowering shrubs.

Loki chuckled. "Please? I am all alone here and have no one to talk to." He sat down cross-legged on a rock and waited, sensing that if he was patient, and did not startle her, this little stranger would come to him.

Eventually, two little eyes peeked out from behind a fruit tree. He smiled at her and beckoned, trying to look harmless. Hesitantly she came out in full view and Loki smiled, a genuine smile, at the little girl standing before him. He says later that he felt dizzy and stunned and realized later that she'd captured his heart with that first, shy glance, but he did not realize it right away. With a little bit of encouragement, the girl approached him, looking at him with wide, worried eyes. She was slender, pale and seemed very delicate, though pretty. He wondered what she was doing there—she very obviously wasn't Vanir; she had not the abundant, vital power that flowed like green-gold blood through every Vanic man and woman he'd thus far met. She faced him, twisting a bit of her apron in her hands.

"My name is Loki. I am visiting here on business. I like your garden." He smiled gently. The girl returned the smile somewhat hesitantly and shifted nervously but crept a little closer.

"I didn't mean to intrude," he assured her. "I didn't know anyone was here." He moved over and beckoned for her to sit, but she just blinked up at him owlishly. Finally he asked her name.

"Sigyn. I live here," she told him softly.

"In the garden?" he asked with innocent eyes, wanting to see her smile again.

"No!" the girl giggled. "I got rooms upstairs. But this is my favorite place."

He nodded solemnly, "I can see why. It is beautiful." He produced a bright purple flower from his sleeve with a flourish and held it out to her. Her eyes widened and she squealed with delight, fingering every petal gently; it wasn't a flower she was familiar with. "How did you do that?" she whispered in awe, creeping closer.

Loki grinned. "Magic," he said, and beckoned for her to sit again. This time she did, curling her legs up under her, attention half on the flower and half on the strange man at her side. By the time Njord himself came into the garden to greet his visitor, Sigyn was giggling happily by Loki's side, the two of them wrapped in conversation. He watched them for a few minutes, pleased to see the little girl looking so happy. Eventually though, he cleared his throat to announce his presence. Loki looked up surprised and a little sheepish, Sigyn squealed again and ran to Njord's side, hugging him and then dragging him over to meet her new friend, babbling in the Vanic dialect. Loki was utterly charmed and it showed on his face, causing the elder man some difficulty in suppressing the grin that threatened. "I see you've met my foster-daughter." He smiled indulgently at the girl.

Loki could not stop smiling. "She was kind enough to keep me company."

"He gave me a flower," she told the sea-king.

"That was very kind of him, and it is your favorite color too." He stroked the girl's hair gently. "But I'm afraid I must steal him away now. We have business to discuss. I shall bring him back later," he promised her, exchanging a bit of a smile with his Jotun guest.

The girl looked disappointed but nodded, waving goodbye to her new friend, who returned the gesture, a small smile playing at his lips.

Their business was concluded amiably enough, drinks were shared, and eventually he did get to see Sigyn again, if only to bid her goodbye. Over the next few weeks, his mind kept coming back to the child, flitting like a ghost through the Vanic king's gardens. He began using any excuse he could to visit, both business and simple social calls. It didn't do much for the Vanic ruler's salons to have Odin's Jotun blood-brother show up unannounced, but then Loki didn't care overmuch for those salons. He spent his time in the garden or on the beach, entertaining Sigyn, spending only as much time as was necessary with the others. Njord was always hospitable, if a bit smug as he watched the two of them together. (Had Loki thought about it, he might have questioned that smug look—after all, prophecy ran strong in Vanic lines.) He took to bringing her simple gifts, pretty things that he knew would make her smile. She was obviously well loved and well taken care of in Njord's hall—other goddesses, particularly Frigga, Eir, and Iduna visited and doted on her—but she was very shy and he couldn't quite place the source of the sadness that clung to her like a strange miasma. He asked Odin about her, but his blood-brother only got a rather sad look in his eyes and told him that was a question for Njord.

It was almost a year later that he finally questioned Njord about her. He'd visited again, on business this time, and acceded to the man's request to remain in his private counsel chamber. When Njord turned to face him, it was as a man and father, not as a king and ruler of his people. "You love her," he said simply. Before Loki, stunned and a little worried, could protest, Njord continued, "And you're curious about her."

It was all Loki could do to nod, "I don't intend her harm!" he protested immediately, used to being suspected of the worst by many of the Aesir. Njord simply waved him away,

"I know that. I see it, in the threads. You could no more harm her than I could." He sighed heavily and came to sit opposite the slender Jotun man. "But you're curious about her origin." The sea-king offered him a drink and settled back, eyes dark. "My son found her a few years ago, not long after this hall had been built. She couldn't have been more than four or five years old, a bruised, hungry, disheveled thing, crying in the forest. Ingvi found her when he was out walking. She tried to run from him at first but was too scared and too weak to get very far, and he has a way with children. He calmed her and brought her to me." He smiled a little, a smile tinged with pain. "We don't know where she comes from... I suspect she's..." he hesitated searching for a term in the Aesir language that would not be derogatory "forgive me, a half breed." He inclined his head to Loki. "I've always suspected the child born of an Aesir and Jotun union," His mouth tightened "and abandoned as a result. She's delicate...and too gentle to thrive amongst the Jotnar, and yet if she is indeed part Jotun, would not necessarily be welcomed by some of the more insular Aesir." He snorted. "I don't know. I could be wrong. She could not tell us. What we do know is that she was mistreated and abandoned."

"I asked her once where she was from and it made her cry." Loki whispered, looking stricken.

Njord nodded, "It was a year before the nightmares stopped. She remained very fearful. She's made a home here and I do consider her my own. She knows that." He said softly. "But some wounds are hard to heal." He sipped his drink slowly, eyes on the fire that crackled and danced in the stone hearth. "The women are kind to her, but...treat her as something of a pet. I do not think they truly see her worth save a few like Frigga or Idunna. I know she has captured your heart." He locked eyes with Loki. "These Aesir, they betroth young. I...cannot do that. It is not our way."

"I would not have asked," Loki said quietly. "She is too young." He looked away. "I would not have asked you until she was much, much older."

"It is written in the threads." Njord smiled. "Be her friend. She needs that. When she is older, we shall speak on other things. She has already informed me that she is going to marry you." He grinned outright at the stunned look on the sky-traveller's face; it took a lot to throw Odin's blood-brother off balance. He did not think it untoward to allow himself the pleasure of knowing he'd finally managed it. (According to Loki, in private, Njord has never let him forget it either, something Sigyn giggles over).

Njord was quiet for a time, "One more thing," he said slowly. "I know you have a wife in Jotunheim." He held up a hand to forestall Loki's explanation. "When she is old enough, you must tell her everything. I will not have her coming to you blind." Loki nodded, recalling again that Vanic ways were as different from the Aesir as the Aesir were from the Jotnar. "And build your hall in Asgard. She needs stability... I do not think she could tolerate being moved about." He rose and Loki rose with him, walking to the door. "My daughter is wiser than she seems on the surface."

"I know." Loki smiled, all the masks falling aside for a moment. "That is both a strength and a sorrow to her." He inclined his head, offering thanks to the man, leaving with lighter heart than before. He could only imagine how the meeting would have gone had it been with someone else.

Within a few years, it became clear to all that Odin's flame-haired blood brother was courting the young foster daughter of Njord. It aroused no little consternation among some of the more traditionally-minded of the Aesir, though Njord protected the girl from all of that. He obviously did not mind that his foster daughter was going to wed a Jotun, and he only became angry once, when one of the men accused him of child-selling—insinuating that allowing Sigyn to wed Loki was the equivalent of sending the child into slavery. The shild paid for that insult padded Sigyn's wedding chest and put an end to such open accusations. Njord's rage had been as great and as cold as the ocean depths and few wished to see him thus angered again. It was clear though, that no one understood the love between the two, and many assumed wrongly that Loki had used some Jotun witchery to win her affections... to what end, they did not wish to speculate.

Loki never returned from his many travels without some small gift for Sigyn, and he even built his hall on the outskirts of Asgard, a gift to his bride on their wedding day. He found out, on that day, that she'd kept that first purple flower he'd given her. They wed when she was fifteen, though that is a tale for another to tell.

Andvari's Bride

(as told by Loki to Elizabeth Vongvisith)

or many years, Loki and the foster-child of Njord had loved one another, but Njord decreed that they could not marry until he deemed her ready. Finally, when Sigyn's fifteenth summer approached, Njord gave Loki his blessing, and Loki went straightaway to Sigyn and asked her to be his wife. She agreed with much love and enthusiasm, and a date was set within half a year for their wedding feast.

Before that happy day, however, Loki greatly wished to obtain a wedding-gift for his young bride, something lovely and rare which would make her think of him each time she looked upon it. Sigyn loved jewels, more with a child's delight than with any trace of greed, and Loki decided to have made for her a gift which would show all who dwelt in Asgard the extent of his love, for though they would not marry according to Jotun custom, as he had married Angrboda, Loki would have his new wife bear his Lightning Clan totem anyway. So he decided to commission from the Duergar an arm-ring for his young bride. Thus Loki bade Sigyn farewell, telling her that he would return before long, and he took himself off to Svartalfheim to seek a smith who was capable of creating what he had in mind.

He went to Nidavellir, the great city of the dwarves, and wandered the streets until he came to a tavern full of Duergar. They regarded him with suspicion and curiosity, for though the Duergar have many travelers in their land and welcomed visitors (especially those with fat purses), some of them already knew who Loki was, for his reputation preceded him. No one would answer his inquiries until at last he began to jest and tell stories nearly as winningly as Bragi himself, and began buying rounds for the company. Then the dwarves, who were very fond of tales of far-off lands (and drink) warmed to him and clamored for more. Loki was not averse to being the center of attention, even in the midst of a serious errand, and he had supplied himself well with gold from the coffers and strongboxes of various households in Asgard (which, certainly, no one would begrudge him, as he was the blood-brother of Asgard's lord and soon to be married to one of their own) so the merrymaking went on long into the night, with drink, laughter and song.

During this evening of gaiety, one dwarf who sat in the corner of the tavern kept regarding Loki with an apprising gaze. Loki was not unaware of this, but as the hours passed and the dwarves' heady and very strong ale began to take effect, he dismissed it from his mind, and it was with a great deal of staggering that he left the tavern at sunrise, with the advice of the Duergar the only clear thing in his mind: *Go to the deepest cavern under Mount Clearspring, and find you there the door to Andvari's hall. He is the oldest and best of the gold-workers in this land.*

So Loki wandered off, none too steadily, and if behind him a furtive shadow slipped through the mountain-rooted land, gradually overtaking and then passing him entirely, he did not see. The Duergar ale was something he had never tasted before, and he had drunk rather too much of it. His vision was blurry, his head hurt and his stomach felt queasy, and he really wanted to lie down, or perhaps even to curl up and die, but the thought of Sigyn's face when she saw the arm-ring kept him moving one foot in front of the other, until finally he came to Mount Clearspring, where there lay a deep, clear and cold lake. Loki paused and peered into its waters at his own reflection; his hair was wildly messed up, his green eyes were dull and ringed with dark shadows, and he had the general look of one who has been run over by a cart. Nevertheless, after splashing some water on his face and making some attempts to improve his appearance,

Loki took a deep breath and only a little unsteadily bore himself to the door which led under the mountain and to Andvari's home.

He knocked, and the door was opened by one of the smith's many children, a half-grown dwarf whose beard was only just coming in. "Welcome, stranger," he said politely. "Who are you and what brings you to my father home?"

Loki said, somewhat faintly, "My name is Loki Laufeyson. I come from Asgard, seeking Andvari's skills in gold-working." He smiled in what he thought was a charming manner, and he was mostly correct, but the effect was rather spoiled by the alcoholic fumes which rolled off him as he stepped closer to the young dwarf standing in the open doorway. Andvari's son took a pointed step back and managed to refrain from waving a hand before his face. "Come in," he said, and held the door open for the strange and obviously intoxicated Jotun whose clothing bespoke wealth and position.

The young dwarf led Loki down a series of twisting corridors until they came to a large room right underneath the mountain's heart. Loki paused as his bleary eyes adjusted to the dim room. One wall was taken up entirely by a mighty forge. A great anvil stood in the center, and on the other walls, many metalworking tools were suspended, from the largest, heaviest mallets to the most delicate, tiny pinchers for setting jewels. And from the ceiling... Loki blinked and was momentarily startled enough to forget his throbbing head, for there were hung many fine rings and brooches, jewels set in elaborately worked settings, cups and drinking horns trimmed with gold, and silver-inlaid weapons and pieces of armor which gleamed in the bright firelight coming from the forge. *Truly, I have chosen well the one who can make what I want,* he thought, staring at the treasures overhead, which wavered slightly in his gaze.

Overcome with awe and liquor, Loki put a hand out on the door frame to steady himself. He did not see, at first, the form of the dwarf who had been eyeing him in the tavern, but when Loki caught sight of Andvari standing there, he smiled. "So, you yourself gave me the advice to seek you out. That was cleverly done." The dwarf only bowed, and taking a slightly wobbly step forward, Loki went on, "You already know who I am. I want to commission a piece of jewelry, an arm-ring for my wife-to-be, Sigyn Njord's daughter, and I want it to be a wonder of the Nine Worlds. I have the wealth of Asgard at my disposal and can pay you very well for this," he added.

He saw the old dwarf smile in a manner in which, frankly, Loki had never expected to see on the face of a Duergar. Andvari came closer so that he and Loki were standing face to face, or rather, face to chest. He leered at Loki up and down, from his feet to the ends of his bright hair. "And what *else* would you be willing to give me, son of Laufey, were I to say that I have wealth enough already, and that there are other things I would consider as fitting compensation for such an undertaking?"

Loki raised an eyebrow, then let his mouth curl into a lazy smile. "I would be willing to, ah, negotiate further," he said, and that was true. And after all, Sigyn need never know what he had done, exactly, to win her wedding-gift. He only hoped he was capable of rising to the occasion. There was a roaring in his ears, and the heat of the forge by now was growing intolerable, even for one with the blood of the fire-etins, especially if that one was as drunk as Loki. As much as for his own comfort as for effect, Loki unclasped his cloak and let it fall, then untied the lacing at the neck of his tunic and pulled it off over his head. He saw the old dwarf gaze greedily follow his movements, eyeing Loki's lean body, and thought smugly, *Yes, I am fair, and I am not above bargaining as the Vanadis bargained for what she wanted, if it comes to that.*

"Come and sit, friend, and let us discuss this further," said the dwarf, and indicated two chairs set close to the fire. "And I would pledge your health, and our bargain, and of course your soon-to-be marriage to the lady Sigyn," Andvari added. There was nothing for Loki to do but comply, and though his head was buzzing, he followed the dwarf to the place indicated. They sat, and Andvari leaned very close and set his hand on Loki's knee. Loki did not draw away, but sat grinning rather foolishly at the Duergar, wondering if he would pass out before Andvari led him to his bed.

"My wife died a few years ago, and my sons and I are alone, without the comfort of a lady in our household," Andvari was saying, but the Sky-treader was not really listening. Loki's dizziness increased, though he tried hard not to let it show. The dwarf gave him a horn positively brimming with ale, and at the sight and smell of it, Loki's stomach gave a great heave, but he managed the tiniest of sips. "That's no pledge," the dwarf admonished, and so Loki took a great gulp...and another, and another after that. "To marriage!" Andvari cried, and he heard his own voice echoing the sentiment. They drank some more. When the horns were empty, Loki was in a very bad way. He stood up, babbling incoherently as the dwarf nodded and answered him. Something was being said, something important, but he had lost all sense by then. He heard himself agreeing to some bargain, and it dimly penetrated his fogged brain that he was in no shape to be giving his word, let alone showing Andvari a fine time among the linens, but maybe that didn't matter. Andvari had taken his hand and was leading him away. The last thing he remembered was the dwarf's satisfied smile.

Loki awoke in a bed, though he was alone. His head ached and pounded. His tongue felt as if it was coated in fur. His stomach...without even opening his eyes, Loki rolled over and heaved over the edge of the bed. Someone was holding a chamber pot for him. When he finished, he looked up and saw a group of young Duergar, all boys, staring at him. The eldest one, the one who had opened Andvari's door for him, was the one holding the pot, which he hastily set down.

"Mother!" they all cried.

Loki stared at them without saying anything at all. *I do not remember giving birth to such a brood of Duergar*, he thought in confusion. *How long have I been asleep?* Then he noticed that his own clothes were gone and he was clad in a shift. His hair seemed to have lengthened, and looking down at himself, Loki saw...Oh. His voice had changed and was now pitched higher than before. He had apparently taken woman's form at some point during the preceding drunken night, but he knew he was now too exhausted and hung over to resume his own shape. *Well, so what?* he thought waspishly. Loki clutched the open neck of his shift together, more out of nervousness than modesty, and said, "Where is Andvari? Bring your father to me."

One of the young dwarf children scurried off, and in moments, Andvari appeared in the doorway of the small bedchamber where Loki had lain. "Ah, I see you are awake, my dear. Good." He came to the bedside and kissed Loki as lovingly as any husband kisses a wife. Loki did not move away; he merely stared at Andvari. "Children," he said, "leave your father and me alone for a moment."

The young dwarves filed out, glancing curiously at the two. Loki waited until the door had closed behind the last of them, then dropped his hands and said flatly, "Andvari, tell me. What is all this?" He gestured at the lady's clothing hanging on pegs on the wall, the table upon which rested a box of jewels and a bunch of keys, and his rather more prominent chest. Andvari smiled, and the smugness in it did not escape Loki.

"Don't you remember? You asked me to name my price. We discussed your terms—that I would craft for your new bride the fairest, most delicate golden arm-ring ever seen in the Nine Worlds, and in return, you would live as my wife for the duration of its making. And then you changed your shape into woman's form, and you and I took to your bedchamber here to seal the bargain." He sighed happily. "And so today I will begin work upon the arm-ring, and you will be mother to my sons and mistress of my household, Loki Laufey's son. Or ought that to be Laufey's daughter?" he chuckled.

Loki narrowed his eyes and clenched his fists among the dainty linen bedding, but he could think of no way to refute this, and no way to get out of the bargain since he did not, in fact, remember much of anything except that he had agreed quite enthusiastically to something and he realized that he must keep to his word. So Loki nodded slowly, and told Andvari, "Fine, then. Leave me now, so that I may dress and see to the needs of your...er...our sons." Andvari took his leave, and when the door shut, Loki sighed deeply, got out of the bed, and tried to decide which gown he should put on for that day.

For several long weeks, Loki lived as Andvari's wife in every way. He saw to the management of the household, which consisted of Andvari, his seven sons (some of whom were very small and little more than babies), and a few apprentices and servants. He cooked for the family. He spun wool and linen and wove them clothing. He bore the keys to Andvari's household and saw to the servants' duties. He brewed ale and collected honey from the hives on the mountainside, and he milked Andvari's cows and made butter and cheese. He slept with Andvari too and made no complaints, though he found all the work rather tedious (and Andvari rather tedious as well, after the first few nights). He did become fond of the gold-smith's young sons, and often found himself dreaming of the day when Sigyn would bear him children. But for now, the distaff and the spindle were Loki's lot.

The arm-ring was a true wonder, however, and well worth the price of having the youngest of Andvari's sons occasionally wetting himself (and Loki) whenever Loki held him on his lap, or being seen and pointed at by passing Duergar as he struggled down the mountainside in his skirts, carrying buckets of milk. First, Andvari took red, white and yellow gold and carefully, painstakingly hammered them into the finest strands, no thicker than spider webs. He then wove them into an intricate repeating pattern, the three crossed flaming arrows of Loki's Jotun clan, and placed fanciful knotwork all around it, all of which was painstaking work. If he dawdled a little more than necessary during this task, Loki did not mention it.

However, the day came when the arm-ring was soon to be finished, and Loki was very pleased with it, eagerly anticipating Sigyn's happiness when he presented it to her at their wedding. Andvari now did positively drag out the finishing of the arm-ring, for he was loath to have Loki leave, and he knew too his young sons would miss their "mother" when Loki had gone back to Asgard. But Andvari thought he knew of a way to keep Loki there under his mountain a while longer.

One day, Andvari called Loki into his forge and showed him that the arm-ring was done. It was truly magnificent, light and fragile-seeming, but strong—*like Sigyn herself,* Loki thought. He was so delighted that he threw his arms around Andvari and kissed him heartily, and did not miss the look the dwarf gave him as they parted. "Come, let us drink to the arm-ring's making, and to the conclusion of our bargain!" cried Andvari, and he called in his apprentices, servants and sons to join them in their merrymaking.

Loki soon found himself surrounded by many burly Duergar, and at once he guessed Andvari's plan, to intoxicate him again and force another promise and a lengthy stay, and to have his men prevent Loki leaving if he chose not to engage himself further. But Loki had prepared himself for this eventuality.

"I have just the thing, my husband," Loki simpered, and going to a storage-room, he came back with two large jugs of ale which he had brewed himself. The dwarves uncorked them and inhaled the fumes rising from within; it was indeed a fine batch, and as they tasted it and gazed upon Loki in his comely woman's form, many of them thought that the Jotun man had made a better wife than even a Duergar woman might have. They set to drinking, and though plied with cups, Loki did not get tipsy along with the rest. The ale was of a kind often brewed in Jotunheim, and while to Loki it was a commonplace drink which he was used to quaffing in great quantities, to the dwarves it was novel and fascinating, so they drank much more than they had planned. Soon they became inebriated, while Loki alone remained in command of his senses.

Finally, Andvari and his men were roaring and staggering about, sweating and cursing in the tremendous heat. Some of them looked as if they would soon come to blows, while others were weeping with their arms over each others' shoulders and vowing eternal brotherhood, and a few had collapsed and were snoring loudly on the floor. Loki hid his smile as Andvari came stumbling up to his "wife" and said, leering, "Now is the time when a man's thoughts turn from the pleasures of drink to those of the bedchamber."

Loki batted his eyelashes and said, "All right," and they left the crowd of drunken Duergar and went to Andvari's chamber. And Loki, reaching up and letting his long red hair fall free down his back, said, "I would ask you for one thing, my husband."

"What's that?" Andvari asked, reaching out to draw Loki closer to the bed.

"That you don't wake up," Loki said, in his own voice. He spoke a few words in the ancient Jotun tongue, and the old dwarf fell backwards on the bed, senseless...unharmed, surely, but not to awaken for a long time. Loki pulled off his gown and shift, having taken his man's form again, and put on his own clothes. He went to find Andvari's sons and bade them farewell, and though it grieved him to see their dismay at his leaving, he promised that he would not forget them. The eldest dwarf-lad in particular was quite upset, as he had come to admire his "mother" greatly, but Loki made him yet another promise. Then he went to the great forge where Andvari's men were still making merry, and shouting those same words he used in the bedchamber, he caused them to fall asleep where they sat (or sprawled, in some cases).

Loki took the finished arm-ring from Andvari's bench and wrapped it carefully, then hid it among his clothes. He hoped that Sigyn had not become alarmed at his long absence, but then she was already used to his frequent comings and goings by now. Surely if she was upset, she would forgive him when he returned to her and made her his wife at last. Loki smiled again as he left the mountain, and by the shores of the clear lake, he changed himself into a falcon and left Nidavellir, winging his way back to Asgard.

He returned not long before the wedding date. Sigyn *had* been worried—not that Loki had abandoned her, but that some misfortune had befallen him. It was not the last time she would worry thus. However, she greeted Loki with the same loving affection she had always shown, and they were married within a few days time. When Loki produced the ring and placed it on her arm, everyone gasped at its wondrous beauty, and Sigyn's eyes filled with tears, for she knew that Loki, in having it marked with his clan totem, was naming her his wife among his own people as well as the Aesir, no matter what the Jotnar (or his first wife) might have thought.

At the wedding feast, Odin came up to Loki and remarked, "You have won for your bride a fair enough treasure to inspire envy among Freyja and her women, and many a covetous glance from others besides. How did you manage it? For you could not have—ahem—*borrowed* nearly enough gold to pay for this rare gift."

Loki only smiled and said, "My brother, all it took was a woman's touch."

The morning after Loki's departure, Andvari awoke with a pounding head, and he was sore vexed at Loki, but in time eventually he did find himself another wife of his own people, and was content, though the memory of his Jotun bride irritated him greatly, and he ever after swore loudly at the mere mention of Loki's name. And in later days, the Duergar said that Loki had instead snared Andvari in his net and forced from him his gold and so earned Andvari's curse.

Andvari's sons, though, found that Loki kept his word. To their father's immense displeasure, he came to visit and brought them fair gifts when each of them became men and married wives of their own. He also kept his other promise. When his bride bore a boy-child, Loki named him Narvi, after Andvari's eldest son, though Sigyn did not know the reason why until many years had passed, and then, as Loki intended when he told her this story, she laughed.

Angrboda's Children

(as told by Angrboda to Raven)

fter Angrboda and Loki first met, that fated day in the Iron Wood, they were apart for many years. Loki grew into manhood, living in the Lightning Tribe with his father, and often going to his mother's home in the mountains above the Iron Wood. Angrboda put the matter of Flame-Hair aside in her mind, like an ache in the foot that promises worse things to come, but that one has learned to ignore.

Then one day an etin-woman came to her for a seeing, saying that she was in love, and wished to see what would come of it. Her hair glowed orange like coals, and Angrboda could see at once that she was of Surt's kin, and asked of that.

"Yes, I am of Muspellheim's tribe," the etin-woman said, "but I have come to live with the Lightning Tribe. My name is Glut." She did not say the name of her beloved, and Angrboda read for her, and said that the affair could go many ways. She did see children, and this made Glut happy. But before she returned to her tribe, Glut spoke in longing of Angrboda's magic. "I have heard that you are skilled in the magic of the flesh," she said, "and I would fain learn these things to charm he whom I love."

"The things that I know," Angrboda said, "only a woman can teach another woman."

"Will you teach me, then?" Glut asked. "I will look to you as an older sister, and I will serve you as handmaiden for one turn of the moon, for these lessons." So Angrboda agreed, and Glut served her for one turn of the moon, and during that time learned the magic that women can work with their flesh.

And Angrboda came to love Glut, and consider her a younger sister, and when the time came for her to return she said, "Surely the one that you desire will come to you now. When you marry him, I will stand with you, my sister."

Glut embraced her and said, "I would have you by me, but if I win this man, his father will not have you at the wedding, for he is Loki, Farbauti's son. But perhaps if I can bend the son's heart, I can bend the father's." And she kissed Angrboda, not seeing that the wolf-chieftess stood as stone, and went back to the Lightning Tribe.

Many sleepless hours, and then many sleepless nights, had Angrboda in her bed of furs and skins. She raged, and wept, and cursed Glut, and Loki, and the Norns, and the world. Finally she ran out of tears and curses, though not out of rage, and she said, "This is not meet for a chieftess and Hagia. I am no child, to be heart-torn over a man who barely knows my name. A chief must be generous to others, and a Hagia must be above these things. Glut is a fine girl, and she is of Muspellheim, where he spent his youth. Doubtless she is the right woman for him. And perhaps if I see them married then my Wyrd might change, and I shall be rid of this thorn in my heart."

She put the matter away again, for she was strong-willed and could swallow any tears, and tried her best to think no more about it until Glut came to her door one day, and said, "My sister, I have won him! And it is all due to your magics. I have you to thank for this joy."

Angrboda turned her spine to steel and chained her tongue, and said only, "My sister, you will be married then! My blessings; I hope all goes well for you."

"I have spoken to Loki, and he will ask his father to allow you at the wedding," Glut said. "But I have no family here, as my mother and grandmother are dead, and my great-grandfather Logi lives in Utgard, a long way away. You are as a sister to me; will you speak for me of marriage?"

"I will do this," said Angrboda. "As you have come to me and asked this, I will do it." And though the words were like iron weights on her chest, she went to the Lightning Tribe and to Farbauti's house, when the Chief was not home, and spoke to his red-haired son. And though it pained her, she forced herself to look into his green eyes, for she was proud and would not show this youth her pain. "My sister Glut tells me that you wish to marry her," she said to him. "Will you treat her with the highest love and respect, and care for the children that I have foreseen coming into the world between you two?"

Loki bowed an ironic bow to her, and said, "Of course I shall treat her well, Wolf-Chieftess. Like a princess of Muspellheim will she live. All our children shall eat the finest mushrooms and the breasts of thrushes. I shall gather them all myself with my own hands."

Angrboda set her jaw. "I am looking out for my younger sister, as she has asked," she said, "and youths like you should not mock their elders."

Loki's green eyes glittered at her, and his three-cornered smile grew lewd. "I am not so young as all that," he said, "and you are not so old as all that either, wolf-chieftess." Those sharp green eyes swept up and down her muscular body, not stripping her naked, merely appreciating. Angrboda dug her nails so hard into her own palm that she felt blood pooling among her fingers.

"Treat her well," she said roughly, "or I shall make you so miserable that you will wish I had just killed you and had it over with."

He stepped back, then, like a man who has gone to laughingly pet a dog only to see it growl and show its teeth. "As you will, wolf-chieftess," he said. "I can see that you love your sister well."

She gave him one sharp nod, and then left him. When he and Glut were married on the next new moon, she stood next to Glut and witnessed the cutting and binding of their hands, and if she did not smile, most thought her fierceness was because she did not approve of Laufey's son. None could have known that she was praying that this bond would free her from the wyrd that she had seen.

She expected, then, to be able to wipe him from her thoughts, and she would almost have managed save that he kept coming by with messages from Glut. His Muspellheim wife missed her adopted elder sister, and wished her to visit, especially now that she was swelling with child. *Good,* Angrboda thought. *Bear his children, and free me from my premonitions.* But she did not visit, for she thought that to see them together would make her weep. Glut finally came herself, round and red as a setting sun, and Angrboda did indeed weep when she saw her, but she shed her tears into Glut's hair as Glut wept as well, and passed them off as joy in seeing her. To be fair, that was not entirely untrue. "Does he treat you well, my sister?" the wolf-chieftess begged her.

"He treats me well enough when he is home," Glut said, "but he is gone more often than he is about these days, and I am lonely. I fear that he is growing tired of me."

Angrboda's jaw clenched. "Should I speak to him?" she asked calmly.

"Oh, no, my sister; he is difficult enough to pin down. I think it is simply that I want more time from him than he wishes from me, or from a marriage. I fear that he is bored with me, and the more I try to grasp him, the more he flutters out of reach."

"Sometimes," Angrboda said, "one needs to hold more lightly." While she wanted to be angry with Loki, for Glut's sake, she felt kinship with him in this. "Those with wild spirits do not do well pinned down," she tried to explain, but her words fell lamely from her mouth.

Months later, Glut gave birth to twin girls, whom she named Eisa and Einmyria. "After my grandmother, Glut Logisdottir, who named her daughters similarly," she told Angrboda. The children's father nearly missed the birth, being away on his wanders, but managed to arrive at the last moment and see them born.

A season after the birth of the twins, Glut came to Angrboda's house again, with a babe on her back and another in one arm, and a large bag of her belongings on the other arm. "I am leaving my husband," she declared. "Will you allow me to stay with you, my sister?"

"Make yourself at home," said Angrboda. "What has the bastard done?"

Glut came into the wolf-chieftess's hall and settled one sleeping babe, and began to nurse the other. "I am certain that he no longer loves me," she said. "He does not come to my bed any more, and no longer tells me wonderful things. He has been gone a whole month, so I left." Her bright head drooped. "I thought that I could keep him with the skills that you taught me, but he fled anyhow. I think that his heart is already given to another."

Angrboda's eyes burned with rage and she bolted from her hall in wolf-form, determined to find Loki and beat him senseless for his callousness. Huntress that she was, it was only a matter of hours before she tracked him down, dallying and fishing in the River Slith. He saw her bounding through the woods toward him—she did not bother to hide her wrath—and stood. "I knew that you would find me, when you heard Glut's complaint," he said.

The wolf-chieftess changed to woman-form and struck him, hard enough to knock him down and leave a mark. "How dare you cast her off like that?" she hissed.

The flame-haired youth scrambled on all fours, trying not to fall into the river of knives. "We do not suit each other, Glut and I. She clings too much, and I am no stay-at-home. It is better this way."

Angrboda's balled fist snapped open into a clawed hand. "After she bore your children, after you swore that you would treat her well?"

Loki stared up at her from the riverbank where he had fallen, with his sharp green eyes. He made no move to defend himself. "After you wrapped her up and gave her to me like a gift, wolf-chieftess? She was a fine gift, yes...but not the one I wanted."

"What then?" she panted, her eyes blazing. For just a moment, as she stared at him, the barriers fell from his eyes and she saw behind his mocking smile—his youth, his apprehension, and his desire. She saw herself through his eyes—*so solemn, does she never smile? But there is that fire behind her eyes. Nothing stands in her way. Any other woman I could run over, but not her. She is a cold red lily with steel knives for petals, a sleek and beautiful beast with deadly fangs. I wonder if I could make her smile. I need to make her smile—but all I do merely angers her! My charm falls as nothing at her feet. No, I know that she would settle for no compliments, no charms, no words even. Nothing less than my soul. And I long to give that to her...but I am so afraid. I am so afraid that I cannot even speak of it. I cannot speak, and that is something that I will not have—*

"Then speak," she whispered through lips as dry as a parched gully. "Tell me, or—" *I beat you black and blue, I run you through with my blade, I—*"I will go from here, and never speak to you again," she said. The words fell like stones, and when he realized that she had read his thoughts, the doors behind his eyes slammed shut, and then his gaze fell...and then rose again, and he forced the barriers back down.

"I want you," he whispered back. "It is you that I want." *When you are near me, I see nothing else. I can think of nothing else. You are like a hot fire that takes my breath away. I have wanted you from the first day I saw you.* "And I do not know why," Loki whispered.

She stood, poised, like a blade about to fall. *I do.* It reverberated unspoken in the air between them. *I could tell him what I feel,* she thought. *No. To the four winds with words. Words are his toy. Bodies are mine.* And with a growl, like the predator that she was, she fell on him.

Her nails dug into his back at the same time that her mouth met his. It was a kiss with teeth. He gasped into her mouth, and then rose to the challenge, and after that it was all teeth and nails and fur appearing and vanishing and mixed howls and shrieks that gave way to panting, and more panting, and then many, many small cries. They did not let go of each other until Sunna had long vanished behind the horizon.

When they returned together to Angrboda's hall, Glut was waiting for them. She took one look at both their faces and smiled impishly. "Good," she said. "Now I will not have to watch you both sit about and pine for each other. It is a pity that I had to be married before I realized what was going on, but at least I have two beautiful babes out of this mess. Now, sister, shall I stand with you while you marry my former husband?"

Angrboda was startled, and flushed red with embarrassment, but Loki only laughed. "You shall indeed, beautiful Glut," he said. "Although I expect my father will be so angry that he will set a dozen trees on fire with his wrath. He is not quick to lose a grudge...and neither is my fierce wolf-woman here."

"It is true," Angrboda said quietly. "I do not think that your father will ever forgive me for what I have done to him in the past. It will be difficult to have such bitterness between family members."

Loki shrugged. "Perhaps in a few hundred years he will get over it. In the meantime, there is nothing that he can do. We are to be married, you and I, and you know it. It is our Wyrd, and if Father wishes to complain, he can take it up with the Nornir."

So Loki and Angrboda were wedded, in front of all the Iron Wood, save indeed Farbauti who was wrathful, as they expected, and would not come to see his son pledged to his enemy. Their blood was shared and a great feast was given which lasted for four days and nights. For many years their love was like a great flame that burned between them; sometimes it erupted into anger, for they were both fiery and passionate, and sometimes they even came to blows, but always the intensity drew them back together into Angrboda's bed. Now that he had left his father's house once and for all, Loki kept no hall in the Iron Wood, but only shared that of the Chief of Chiefs. All the tribes treated Laufey's Son with the respect due to the consort of the Hagia, and at first this pleased him, but after a time it sometimes rankled to be honored for his marriage position rather than his own deeds, and he resolved silently to gain his own fame, however he could.

At first they were together every day, for years. Loki learned much from Angrboda about magic, of the flesh and the earth and the river, and of many other things, although he had not her gift for seeing. In turn, Angrboda learned much from Laufey's son, about song and words, about moving from world to world, for in all matters of movement he excelled. It was from him that she learned to take the form of a bird and fly, although she did it less gracefully than he, and at greater cost. All this time, she let him come and go as he pleased, for she had promised herself that she would never chain him or cling to him. Yet as time passed he was gone more frequently, sometimes for months at a time, and she played with Glut's children and thought of him often.

Then the day came when Loki did not return for half a year, and when he came back he told of his meeting with Odin, and how they had exchanged blood and become brothers. The hackles rose on Angrboda's neck, as a wolf's will when she scents danger, and she said, "I foresee no good in this, unless you exploit it before it exploits you."

"Odin has invited me to live in Asgard," Loki said. "Surely I can be of some use there, if only eyes and ears."

"Be of use to Odin, you mean," she said bluntly. "Go if you must, but guard your quick tongue, or else I see you coming to grief." So Loki began to spend half his time in Asgard, and half in Jotunheim. Yet as the years wore on, his time in golden Asgard grew longer, and his time in Jotunheim grew shorter. Angrboda said nothing, for she had sworn that she would not try to pinion his wings, but she missed him sorely at times, and tried many ways to forget him when he was gone. The years turned into decades, and she never knew when she might see him in her doorway, or how many months he might be away from her. Finally, when he returned home one day but was so preoccupied that he could hardly pay her any attention, she growled at him, "Have you come to love another, then, that your eyes are fogged with mists?"

Loki looked everywhere except her gaze, and said many things, and tried to put her off, but she finally got it out of him: that he had married his child bride Sigyn and built her a home in Asgard. The Witch-Queen was wrathful, for in order to take another wife or husband, it was custom to get the blessing of the first one, or disquiet would result. She demanded to see Sigyn, but Loki refused her, and they fought bitterly. He told her that the Aesir take but one spouse, and that she was counted merely a concubine in their eyes; that Sigyn was his real wife by their laws, as he had married her under their customs.

"Waving about swords and spears and spindles!" said Angrboda scornfully. "That is no wedding. There is no wedding without blood. Was there no other woman of your own tribe and people that you might wed?" His marrying without her knowledge she resented, but his marrying a woman of Asgard she feared, for it might split further the breach that was forming between Loki and his people. They warred about it all day, and then he fled; but to his credit he returned in the morning. For her part, she had been awake all night worrying that she might lose him entirely, and she welcomed him back warily, but with no more rage.

From then on, Loki was careful to spend half his time with one wife and half with the other, for he did not want Angrboda to come looking for him in Asgard; he sought to protect the gentle Sigyn from her whiplike tongue. Sigyn quickly swelled with child and bore him a son; when she went into her pains Loki was far away in Angrboda's arms, but sensed the suffering of his second wife. "Well, then, go to her," the Witch-Queen said, hearing his thoughts.

"Will you not be wrathful if I leave your arms to go to her bedside?" he asked her.

"No man is a man if he will not be with the woman he has swelled with child in her time of need," Angrboda said. "I would expect you to do the same for me, when my time comes. Perhaps she does not know how to respect another wife, poor foolish child, but I do, whether I like it or no. Now go." She flung him from her bed, and hid her head under the hides, so that he would not see her weep, for though they had lain together many times, no child swelled in her womb, and this was a grief of hers.

It came to pass that a quiet Death occurred, one which was spoken of in no lay or story, but affected the Nine Worlds nonetheless. It was the death of Hel, the old Queen of Jormundgrund, the Jotun underworld. Jormundgrund had long been partitioned off from Niflheim, and the old witch-queen Hela had presided over it since the Nine Worlds began. Indeed, no one knew from whence she had come or whose womb bore her, though there were those who said that she was the firstborn daughter from the loins of Surt. Perhaps her origins were known by Mimir, who had long been her consort under the earth before he went to Asgard, but he said nothing of his time with Hela, and would not speak of it, and still will not. No one marked her death but the Dead, and indeed no one knew where her soul went, but the doors of Jormundgrund closed, and admitted no more Dead.

The Dead Jotnar then began to wander the world, nesting in the trees and haunting the homes of the living, for the great Gate of the Underworld was shut fast against them. Angrboda did not fear ghosts, but their sad presence made her think of her empty womb, and she began to long for a child of Loki's seed, to give one of them life again. She had borne wolf-children before, to men of her clan and outside of it, but they were all grown and she wanted a babe to mother again, of the lineage of her beloved. So it was that she came to Loki with an idea of how they might conceive children together.

In the center of the Iron Wood, there lies a stone circle in a clearing, with many smaller stones set into the turf in a labyrinthine pattern. Around the border of the clearing lie scattered small houses, built by those who needed to partake of the magic of the heart of Jotunheim, for here the power was so strong that it seemed to ooze and drip off the very trees. Loki and Angrboda built another small hut together, and placed in it a bed of sheepskins, and there they lay together three times, and each time conceived a child.

The first birth was a hard one, and the midwives feared for Angrboda's life, yet finally she delivered up a baby girl. The child was pale and perfect, and never cried; even as she grew she spoke little, but in clear words from the start. Loki and Angrboda looked together into her eyes when she was born, and they did not immediately say what it was that they saw, but both then looked at each other with faces as pale as their newborn child's own face. "Her name is Hela," Loki said when he could finally speak.

"Folk will cry our hubris, if we name her thus," said Angrboda, "yet I believe that you are right, my husband."

"I have never cared before when they cried hubris," Loki said, looking upon his daughter with awe. "I care not now, and let them say what they will; the truth will come out before she is a woman."

The second birth was a son, a wolf-pup, but so huge a pup that Angrboda was in labor for days to expel him. She looked in his yellow eyes and said, "This one has the power, too, but it could turn many ways with him." But Loki only loved him, and played with him on the floor of their hall. At first Fenris was sometimes boy and sometimes wolf-pup, but as the time wore on he stayed more and more in wolf-form until he had near forgotten any other way. There were some folk of the Iron Wood who were like this, and even some Jotnar of other tribes who would forget themselves and became trees or stone permanently, so neither parent was surprised.

The third birth was the strangest yet. During the final months, Angrboda's belly heaved like rippling water, and all who saw it were dismayed. She would stroke it, and sing, and then it would calm down, but even Loki was concerned at what they had now brought forth. When only six months had passed, she was so swollen that even she began to fear for herself, and sent Loki winging across many miles of Jotunheim to Gymir's hall, where Gerda kept her great walled garden of herbs. Loki was lucky to find Gerda at home, and begged from her some herbs to bring on a woman's labor prematurely. The calm dark giantess smiled knowingly, and gave him a packet to dissolve in a potion, and he winged home to find his wife in her bed, moaning and weeping, her belly heaving like a storm at sea.

Yet when the herbs had been drunk and her womb opened, the actual birth was the easiest of all, for it only needed to open wide enough for the head of a snake. A great green serpent, as long as Loki's arm, fell from her womb in rippling coils onto the floor. All who were present gasped, and Loki himself could not speak. Yet the serpent, even in its infancy, glowed with power, and it was clear that this child was not a maker of magic, but a piece of magic itself, come to life. Angrboda commanded Loki to gather up the snake and place it in her arms. As he did so, she laughed and took it to her breast, and he shook his head in wonder at his witch-wife.

Loki wondered how a woman could raise a serpent-child, but Angrboda showed herself to be equal even to this. She could not nurse the Snake at her breast, so she chewed meat soft and fed it gently, cradled in her arms. She discovered that it had no language, yet was intelligent in its own way, and she sang to it constantly. The Serpent grew quickly, an inch or more each day, and followed its mother around slithering on the ground, and slept wrapped around her body. As the months passed, it spent its time more and more in water—the river, the lake, seeking larger and larger ponds. After three moons had passed it no longer needed any help in finding food, and Loki shook his head and said that it would need larger water soon, if only for the fish supply. Angrboda went to the water's edge daily and gave it meat, and stroked it, for she did not wish it to become so wild that it forgot the touch of affection.

Soon after the birth of the Snake, Hela was presented to the folk of two tribes—the Wolf tribe and the Lightning tribe. Yet when her mother led her forth from her hall, a small silent child, they did not expect to see the great crowd gathered. For all the tribes had heard of what Loki and the Chief of Chiefs had done, and had come to see their children. And as the child Hela turned her head, for a moment one side of her face was as a skull, and all murmured. The power that coursed through her was the power of Death itself, and they knew that Hela had been reborn. Death, and all its power, was still in Jotun hands, no matter how many others might covet it.

The other chiefs came forward and knelt before the child, and asked for her blessing; solemnly, she gave it. Even her grandfather Farbauti came forward and took her hand in his, and told her that he would protect her, body and soul. Then he vanished into the woods without a glance at Angrboda. Loki's pride was such that he looked as if he might burst. That night he put his arm around Hela, put the serpent-child across his lap, and took the pup Fenris under his other arm, and declared that his children would be more famous than any others in the Nine Worlds someday.

Yet the time came when Loki longed to return to Asgard again. Sigyn missed him, and so did their young sons. Angrboda sensed his desire, and she held stubbornly to her vow not to try and hold him, so when he said that he was going to be more in Asgard than in Jotunheim for a time, she said only, "Go, then. I am a fair enough mother; better parent than you, and I shall raise our children. Only keep a discreet tongue in your head, Flame-Hair, or you shall bring us all down. I would not have the Aesir know that we taken the power of the Wood and made gods between us, not until they are grown."

So Angrboda beseeched Loki to keep the knowledge of their children secret, and for a time Loki acceded to her wishes, but Odin was his blood brother and he was loath to keep such secrets from him. Besides, he wished Odin's wisdom on the matter, so finally he gave in. Both were deep in their cups, and Loki told of his three children and their strange births.

Odin's blood ran cold when he heard the tale. He remembered the prophecy of the Nornir, that one would come among them whose seed would sire both the most powerful witch in the world, and Odin's own destroyer. For as many years as he had known and loved Loki, he pushed the prophecy out of his mind, thinking that surely it could not refer to his blood brother. And, surely, Loki's descriptions were harmless enough—his daughter, Hela, was a strange child, but certainly no more of a danger then her powerful mother. The wolfling was large, but there were many large werewolves in the Iron Wood. The serpent was strange indeed, but could do little to attack Asgard. Yet, still, Odin's blood ran cold.

After Loki had left, Odin went up into Valaskjalf for a long time, refusing all nourishment for days. No one knew with what burden he was struggling, not even Frigga, yet all felt the weight of that struggle. When he finally came down, all he would say was, "The threads of Wyrd are tangled, and I cannot see through that tangle. Things could go many ways, and there is no set path before us."

"I could have told you that, my husband," Frigga said, seeress that she was, as she and her maidens plied him with food and Iduna's nectar. "Yet it is times like this that are the most powerful, as a single choice may force the threads."

"Powerful, yes," Odin said, "but most dangerous as well." Then he called together a council—not the Moot of the Aesir, but only a small, trusted group. Faithful Tyr came, and his sons Thor and Heimdall, and his wife Frigga, and they went behind closed doors to hear Odin tell what he had heard from Loki.

It is not known what was said in that council, for no others knew even that it was happening, but when they came out Odin gathered Tyr and Thor and a small band of their best warriors, and bade them be ready to arm and ride. Then he commanded that a festival-hall be built in Asgard, and tables made ready for a feast. When that was done, he sent a message to Angrboda, the Hag of the Iron Wood, and begged her to come to Asgard. It was to speak of her husband Loki, he said, and it was important. Loki was off on his travels at the time, and did not hear of it; nor did Odin speak to Sigyn, waiting faithfully at home, of this event.

In her turn, Angrboda received the message—delivered straight to her hall by Odin's two ravens—and sat for a long time by the fading coals of her hearthfire, pondering. Her guts told her that there was danger, but she could not decide for whom. *My husband has done something terrible this time,* she thought, *perhaps found a trouble that he cannot get himself out of, and they are calling me to help him. Am I called to rescue him, then? Surely his child-bride in Asgard cannot fight him out of trouble with fire and sword and magic, but I can.* And, finally, she rose and took on the form of a great crow, and flew to Asgard. She did not bring a war band, for she feared that they would never let her enter unless she came alone, so she resolved to rescue her beloved on her own, no matter what the price. Apprehension rose in her throat as she saw the white walls, for she remembered well the fate of Thjassi, but no one molested her as she entered. Upon her landing, Odin himself came forward, and welcomed her to Asgard, and bade her come and dine with him to discuss what must be done.

The Hag of the Iron Wood stepped carefully into the great banquet-hall, feeling very much the barbarian. A great feast was served, of which she ate little, waiting for Loki to be spoken of. *Perhaps he is imprisoned,* she thought. Finally she could wait no longer, and turned to Odin. "Where is my fool of a husband?" she asked. "Is that not why you have brought me here?"

"My business with you does indeed involve Loki," Odin said. "Give me a moment, and I will have this business brought to you, that you might advise me on it." And he stood, ready to leave the hall, and yet before he left he hesitated. He looked upon the tall, proud giantess in her cloak of furs, and he bowed before her respectfully, and Angrboda saw a sorrow in his demeanor. Then he left the hall, and she sat with furrowed brow, waiting.

He had been gone but a moment when she realized that with Odin's departure, all others in the hall had also gone, and she was alone. Sensing danger, she started to her feet and drew her blade—she had wondered why Odin had not insisted that she give up her sword—but there was no one to fight. Then, in a split second, the entire hall burst into flames. Fire ran down the tables as if oil had been poured over them, and the roof was an inferno in moments. Angrboda's long red hair was the first to catch, and she went up like a torch, screaming curses.

Odin and those trusted few who had come to the feast watched the hall burn, and heard Angrboda's screams. The fire-spell was a dangerous one, and cost Odin dear, but he dared not let her get to the door of the hall to fight. As they watched, the roof fell in, and they saw her figure like a torch, stumbling through the debris. Slowly, slowly, she peeled the flame from her blackened body, and fell to her hands and knees on the earth. They heard her mumbling magics, and saw that her skin was beginning to grow back, her charred flesh to heal. Amazed and chagrined, Odin threw a second fire-spell, and the flames attacked her once more. A second time she burned, and a second time she struggled to her feet and began to use her magics to survive. A third time he hurled the spell, though it cost him so dear that he nearly collapsed, and had to be held on his feet. This time, the giantess did not rise from the flames; they consumed her until nothing was left but a heap of ashes, with her charred heart in the middle.

Odin was brought, weak as a babe, to Frigga; she poured what power she could into him. "You should rest," she told him. "Only time will cure this."

"I cannot rest," he said. "There is no time. This is only the first part. You must give me enough life to carry out the next; I shall rest in your arms tonight." So Frigga poured all the love that she could give into his wasted form, and Odin grew strong enough to rise from his bed. Calling together his warband, they made their way to Jotunheim and the Iron

Wood as fast as they could fly. It was the first time that so many had made such a fast attack on Jotunheim; there was terrible danger, and Odin knew it. Yet still he trusted to his great luck to carry them through.

No one in the Iron Wood knew of Angrboda's fate, and they believed that she would be honored as a guest of the great Loki, who had spoken much of his blood-brotherhood with Odin, and his comradeship with the Aesir. It was also the case that no Asa had ever attacked the Iron Wood, for the magics of the Iron Wood were strong, and it was one of the sacred places of the Jotnar. Yet Odin had gathered together those among the Aesir and their allies who would dare to enter it, although there were not many of these. Some cried that the Iron Wood was a place of poison, and that it would taint their blood and make them bear twisted children, like unto the trolls that dwelt there. So it was with only a small band that Odin came into the wood, using every ounce of his magics to force the trees to allow them through.

Since it was the night of a great festival, the holiday that Angrboda had been loath to spend away from her tribe, the folk were full of liquor and food, and those that were not dead in drunken slumber were in their beds or the bushes making merry with each other. Odin's people stole into Angrboda's hall, and there they slew all they found in their beds asleep. They found Fenris, the wolf-child, and put him in a sack. The snake they found nowhere in the hall, but Odin found it swimming in the lake behind, and seized it likewise in a sack. Then they went to lay hands on Hela, who was but a child no higher than that of nine summers, and who stood watching them silently with old, old eyes.

When they reached for her, however, she lifted her hand, and lo it was made of bone and rotting flesh. And they flinched back and cried out, and she pointed her bony finger and cursed them all if they should touch her. "Death I am, and death I shall be to you if you lay hands on me, with diseases that no healer can cure nor your golden apples abate! Well I know that my mother walks the road to Jormundgrund, and this too is your doing, and there is no one to greet her at the gate!"

And Odin fell back, and even he did not dare to touch her, and he saw that his plan to control Death had came to nothing. "Go then and meet your mother at that gate, if you can, corpse-child," he said to her, "and as you will not come with us, you shall be banned from Asgard forever and never step your stinking foot into our fair land!" And, angered at being driven off by a mere child, but still fearing her with a deep revulsion in his belly, he fled with his men and their burdens, first setting fire to Angrboda's hall. The serpent they flung into the ocean around Midgard, and Odin wove a spell to protect Midgard by its living body, that it might always be a barrier of magic. The wolf-pup Fenris Odin brought back to Asgard and gave to Tyr to raise, hoping to turn Angrboda's child into an ally of the Aesir.

But Hela, fearing for her mother, began to make her first and last journey on foot to the Land of the Dead. Alone and unaided she left the burned hall and the Iron Wood that had been her home and crossed the River Slith, going downwards to Niflheim. Mile after mile she walked, for days and days, and with each mile closer to the Deathlands more of her became as a corpse, until she was limping painfully on one rotted leg. Yet still the corpse-child kept on until she came to the deserted road and the great dark gate, and there she waited for her mother's ghost, patient and silent in the snow and ice.

Yet the days drew on in that lonely place, and Angrboda did not come. For Loki had arrived at night, while Odin was looting his wife's house, and some took joy in telling him of the death of the Hag of the Iron Wood. He rushed to the hall, which was still roaring in flames, but he had not learned nothing from his foster-father Surt the Black. Leaping through the flames unharmed, he found Angrboda's burned body, which crumbled at his touch. All that was left was her ashen heart, still solid, so he placed it in his mouth and ate it, keeping it safe in his belly, and fled Asgard as fast as he could.

When he reached her hall, he found it plundered and burned, and her kinsmen dead, and his children gone. He screamed and raged, and the folk of the Iron Wood arose, and they all wept and raged with him. They would have marched on Asgard as they were, armed only with their fury and rude weapons, but Loki recovered himself enough to stop them. "There has been enough death for one night," he said. "Now it is time to undo at least one of them." And he drew forth Angrboda's ashen heart from his throat, and placed it on the hearth of the burned hall, and took a knife and let blood onto it from his arm, and every one of her kinsmen in the Wolf tribe came forward also and let their blood drip, so that the hearth ran with blood. As the sun rose and the word spread, Jotnar from the other tribes came as well, and may of them shed their blood for her life also, as Loki danced about the hearth and the Wolf tribe howled a strange song.

It is said that half the luck of the Iron Wood clans went into that spell, but that not a one of them ever regretted it. Even those who did not love the wolf-chieftess would rather have seen her alive than bear this insult from the Aesir, so even the trolls from the Hound-Beetle tribe came, and some of them shed blood for her—not for herself, they said, for the Wolf tribe had often fought with them, but because her daughter Hela was much beloved of them. And when the thunderstorm rose that night, Farbauti's son called lightning down to strike that bloodsoaked hearth, and Loki's spell came true. Angrboda rose again alive from the ashes of her heart.

"Where are my children?" was the first thing she asked him, with the rage of a mother wolf in her eyes. And Loki wept for the first time in front of her, and admitted that he did not know, and begged her forgiveness for all he had done that had brought this upon them. "If you had not gone to Asgard, if you had not turned your back on your tribe, the Aesir would never have known until they were grown," she said to him, and her words were as a razor blade. "If our children are dead, it may have been Odin's hand that held the knife to their throats, but it was yours that pushed his arm."

Loki swore that he would find his children, if they were alive, and avenge them if they were dead, and he fled her burned hall with such speed and wrath that the leaves were torn off the trees. Back to Asgard he flew, where Odin was seated in his chair at Valaskjalf. Odin could not see into the Iron Wood, but he could sense that great magic had been happening there, for the trees tossed like a sea during Ran's storm. Then he saw Loki in the form of a falcon, winging through the air to Asgard, and he came down from the tower as Loki arrived. Geri and Freki growled at him, but Odin quieted them with a word and waited to face his blood brother..

It is not known what happened there in the doorway of Valaskjalf, for Odin sent everyone away and spoke to Loki alone. Some say that they heard screaming, others sobbing, others only a grumbling silence that made their skin crawl. Some claim that Loki came within an inch of slaying his blood-brother, others say that Odin charmed him with words and talked him into submission, still others that Loki's rage was all a show to demand weregild. Afterwards, Loki would tell no one of what was spoken between them, not even Angrboda when she demanded and raged at him. But when he came forth from that courtyard, his face was like a smiling mask behind which empty darkness loomed. Some who saw him were relieved, but those who could see past his smile were terrified.

Loki knew, now, where Fenris and Jormundgand had been taken, and at least that they were safe. Hela Odin denied taking, so he searched for her everywhere, in falcon form or many others. It was not until he came upon the frost-thurses of Niflheim that he found one who had seen a half-rotted child limping through the snow towards the Road of Death, and he understood where his daughter had gone, and why.

Back he flew, downward and northward, though the cold wind battered at him and he was near exhausted. He found his daughter where he thought that he might find her, crouching in the snow near the great black Gate. Her pale hair was stiff with frost, and snow had fallen on her thin form, for she had not moved in days. As she turned her head, he saw that the side of her face was as a skull with rotted flesh hanging from it, and there was sorrow and compassion in his eyes as he approached her and called her name.

She turned her head, patiently. "So you are come, my father," she said. "I am waiting for Mother. They slew her; did you know? I felt her die."

Loki knelt in the snow and took his daughter in his arms. Her little body was cold as ice, and crackled with frost. "Yes," he said simply. "But she will not come down this road, dear one. I have brought her back to life. She waits for you in the Iron Wood. Her arms are open; they will heal your hurts. Come back now, my daughter. There is no need to wait here in Niflheim, in the cold. Come home."

Hela did not move, and Loki lifted her in his arms, but as he moved away from the Gate, there was a great rumbling sound. To his astonishment, the great Gate opened, and the ghosts of the Dead came pouring through. "My friends," Hela said, gesturing with her flesh hand. "They kept me company while I waited."

The spirits surrounded them like a cloud, frightened, angry, buzzing like flies. Hela hushed and calmed them from her position in her father's arms. "Do not fear," she said to him. "They will not harm you, so long as I am here." Then she slipped from his arms and stood in the snow, knee-deep. "I cannot go home, Father. If I go, the ghosts will come with me, and the Iron Wood will be vexed. I must stay here with them, and keep the gates open for all the wandering souls in the Nine Worlds."

Loki bowed his head, and fell to his knees next to his daughter. He tried to speak a few times, but no words would come, something that almost never happened to Flame-Hair. Finally he managed to say, "If this is what must be, then so be it. But you cannot stay here, in the cold and the snow, my child!"

The ghosts buzzed around them, and surrounded the half-rotted child, and seemed to push her towards the Gate. "I will not stay here in the snow, Father," she laughed, and it was rare to hear her laugh. That laughter bubbled forth as she moved through the Gate, accompanied by the great mist of ghosts, and as she passed the threshold the dim, dank grey land beyond began to bloom. It burst into springtime and greened into summer. The dead apple trees just inside the wall bloomed from flowers to ripe fruit. The leaves turned to autumn in a blaze of color, welcoming their new mistress, and then paused, just at the moment before they might fall to the ground. A few brightly colored scraps dropped to the ground before Her, as if offering themselves as a carpet for Her entrance.

Through his tears, Loki watched his daughter wave goodbye to him, a small dark figure against the background of sudden bright color. She was still laughing with joy as the Gate slowly swung shut.

When he returned to the Iron Wood, he found Angrboda staring into a fire built outside the wreckage of her burned hall. "At least she is safe from harm now," she said, not looking at him.

"More than safe," he breathed. "More than safe. She is where she is meant to be, although we shall miss her sorely." He dropped to his knees by the fire, exhausted. "I did not foresee any of this," he said. "Forgive me! Please forgive me."

Angrboda kept her eyes on the fire, not on him. "I may forgive you in time," she said, "but I do not know when that will be." There was no fire in her, only coldness, like a silent winter. "You may as well go back to Asgard," she said. "Go back to your child-bride, who will forgive you anything without even being asked. May she have luck enough to protect her children from the doom that lies between you and your blood-brother, since I had not enough to protect my own."

"What would you have of me?" he cried. "What can I do now?"

She was silent for a long moment. "Hela is safe," she said, "although I would have seen her to her coming of age with a mother's love; I fear that she shall grow cold, there among the Dead, and she so young. My serpent-child is bound in Odin's spell, and we have not the power to undo that. But I think that it will grow to love the ocean, and it is not that one I fear for the most. That one is our son. They know not how to raise a wolf-child, there in Asgard. Without the love and training that I can give him, I foresee endless grief for him."

"He is held hostage," Loki said. "As long as we have no more children together, make no more Gods between us, Odin will not harm him. And he is given into Tyr's hands, and Tyr at least is a man of honor; he will not slay a child for the deeds of his parents."

Angrboda turned to stare at him, then, and he could see the cold fire that gleamed in her eyes like steel being forged. "Then we will burn the hut in the center of the Iron Wood," she said, "but I tell you this: If any harm comes to my son, I will have vengeance on your blood brother and his whole family. I will take out my weregild in trade, a son for a son. Hela will help me...and so will you, no matter what price you must pay for that vengeance. Do you so swear to me, my husband, on the ashes of my heart and my hearth and my hall?"

Loki swallowed. "I do so swear," he said, although his heart sank with the words.

"Then go, and do as you will," she said, and her voice cracked, but she did not finally weep until the sound of his heels was long gone into the woods, and she was alone.

Loki went back to his hall in Asgard, and even Heimdall said nothing to him as he entered. He went straight to Sigyn's arms, but in the night he arose and went to the bed where their young sons lay, and caressed their brows in their sleep. *A son for a son,* the words echoed in his head, but he turned his thoughts terrified away from that path, and buried himself again in Sigyn's bed. Yet though he hummed a hundred songs, sleep eluded him still.

Far away in the Iron Wood, the Chief of Chiefs still sat, humming also, staring into the fire, sleepless and alone. She did not turn her thoughts away from the future. She had very little left to lose.

Gerda's Three Weddings

(as told by Gerda to Raven)

hen Gerda was only a young girl, just about to come to her womanhood—which comes early to etin-women—she went with her family to Vanaheim for the first time. Her father and mother had gone to Vanaheim before, as the Jotunfolk who dwelt near the coast often put their hands into the trading between Vanaheim and Jotunheim. Gerda had seen the wooden carts, heavily laden with casks and boxes of foodstuffs, come trundling over the rough roads carved by giant hands through the jagged mountains and immense trees. She had tasted the soft, fine grains, better than any grain that could be grown in her heavily forested world, and the good ale from Aegirheim brewed with Vanaheim barley, and the great cabbages like giant green flowers sprouting from the Vanaheim soil, more fertile than any other in the Nine Worlds.

But it was nothing like finally walking on that soil, to seeing another world. Vanaheim was the first world other than her own that she had seen, and they traveled across the sea to get there in a ship that made her clutch the bow and try hard to still her stomach. Her mother fed her honey brewed with spicy roots to ease her belly, but even so she remembered that first trip as little more than a misery. She envied her older brother Beli his easy, cheerful climbing about the deck, and his mocking of her cramped misery did little to help. When he tormented her for the final time, waving a half-rotted fish at her and jeering, she got up unsteadily on her feet and threw a heavy coil of rope at his head, which knocked him overboard. Then their father had to fish him out by grabbing the other end of the rope, and their mother slapped and scolded her, but Gymir was laughing. "Don't push our quiet little Gerda too far!" he roared proudly. "She may seem like a mushroom, but she has the soul of a tiger-cat under there!" But Gerda sulked and chewed on the end of her black braid of hair until the trip was over.

The first thing that she noticed about Vanaheim was how open the land was. "Where are all the trees?" she asked, used to the thick crowding forests of her home; here, the woods were short and small and further between, and much of the land was patterned like a great quilt in fields of golden wheat and barley and rye, the red of kale and the feathery green plumes of dill and fennel, the yellow of mustard-flowers and the blue of flax-blossoms. They stayed at Billing's great hall on the Jotunheim-facing coast, for he was the master of all trade between the two worlds, and much respected in both. And when the hot summer was at its peak, they went to watch the sacrifice of the Corn King.

It was the first time that she laid eyes upon Frey, the Golden Lord of Vanaheim. He came to his yearly duty, tall and golden and smiling. He rode down the dusty road on a great white horse, and the people called out, "Ing! Ing!" as he came. The small knot of watching Jotunfolk stood to the side, a small pool of silence in the cheering crowd, and Gerda stood in the center of it. She watched him dismount in the wheatfield, where all but the last sheaf was cut down. The sickle flashed in the hand of someone clad in ragged grey, and the sheaf was swiftly wrought into a wreath to place on Frey's golden hair.

Gerda's mother and father, and even her older brother, had seen this rite before, and they hardly flinched when the knife went in and the golden-haired god fell to the earth, his blood soaking into the stubble-clad field. There was a scramble to get the cup filled and passed around, so that as many as possible might drink. After all the cheering, it seemed as if there was dead silence in the air, as if every voice had died with the golden Vanir. Gerda did not wish to break the silence, so she waited until they had started down the road to Billing's hall before she said, "That was a shame, to kill him. He was a fine-looking man."

Her brother burst into jeering laughter, and even her mother chuckled. "That was Frey, one of the Lords of Vanaheim," her father told her, "and he dies in that way every year. If the ritual is done properly, he will be back to life by tomorrow night and walking about, good as new."

"Every year, father? But cannot another take his place sometimes?"

Her father shrugged and said that he did not claim to understand the way of the Vanir. "But this is what Frey was born to do, it is said. It is part of the secret of Vanir fertility. And now we should take our supper."

Gerda had one more question, but she did not ask it, because she did not think that either her father or her mother had the answer. So she tucked away into the box of unanswered questions in her head, which was a very full box because she was still quite young.

Many years later, when she was a grown woman and most of her questions had been answered, a messenger came to her father's hall in Jotunheim. Gerda had grown into a tall woman, pale-faced with long hair the color of the dark turned earth. She was still quiet, but even her brother had learned by then not to push her too far. Once he ruined a thing of hers and laughed at her when she demanded weregild, and she turned into a lean black leopard and leaped upon him, scratching his face with her claws. It took her father ten minutes and three different shapes to pull her off of him, and it took her mother a month to properly heal Beli's face. After that, Beli walked cautiously about his quiet sister, and did nothing to make her eyes flash red at him in the shadows.

Gymir's hall was surrounded by a wall of fire, that no enemies might enter, although of course it wavered and split aside when any member of his household approached it from the inside, or a friend approached it from the outside. Yet this stranger came rushing through the flames on a blood-red horse, and the horse seemed not to be touched by the flames. As the folk of Gymir's household piled outside, her brother came up beside her, his hand on his sword-hilt. "A rune-charmed horse," he said. "This man must be sent by someone of power."

Her father came up beside them. "Mayhap," he said, "but I am the lord here, and he must still do courtesy to me." And he called out to the man to speak his name, and his errand, or a hundred arrows would lodge themselves in his head.

Gerda did not know that Frey, the Golden One of Vanaheim, had climbed the steps to Odin's tower Valaskjalf, the throne in front of the great window that looked out upon nearly all things. He had gone there just weeks before in order to search for his sister Freya, who had long been missing, searching for her lost husband Odr. The great wolves at the foot of the stairs, Geri and Freki, growled at him but let him pass, for his errand was good, and indeed he saw his sister turning back toward Asgard and returning to her summer home.

But then, as he would tell her himself much later, the glass shifted and showed a hall in the middle of a ring of fire, in the snowy winter of Jotunheim. Frey blinked, for until this time nothing in Jotunheim had interested him much, but he did not look away. The door to the hall opened, and an etin-woman stepped out and looked up, and for a moment it was as if she had locked eyes with him.

She locked eyes with him for only a moment, but it was enough for him. Frey, the Golden One of Vanaheim, sat on Odin's throne like a statue, his heart seemingly stilled in his chest. All he could see was those dark eyes, and her frown of concentration. He watched the wintry sun glint off of her nearly-black hair in its tight, elaborate braids pulled sharply back from her pale face, saw her height and broad shoulders and ample figure and the way she held her head high. Nothing else existed for him to see in that moment. Then she called out to someone in a voice that he could not hear, and waved, and he realized that she had not seen him at all. Her glance had been for someone beyond the gaze of Odin's mirror. Then she stepped back into the hall and closed the door.

Frey could not move from the seat of the throne all day, though he knew that Odin would be wroth if he found him there. He sat with his breath harsh in his throat, waiting only for one more glimpse of the etin-woman. He got one, just as the Sun was sinking over Asgard and he knew that folk would come looking for him. Night had already fallen in Jotunheim, and she came outside with a basket over her arm, accompanied by two other etin-women. The other two laughed and talked gaily, but she only smiled with that same self-enclosed look about her. Frey studied every inch of her face, her profile, the movement of her hands as they helped brush back the snow from a small cellar and pull out roots to fill their baskets. He drank in the pale flash of her throat as she adjusted the mantle around her shoulders, the same dark-earth color as her hair. He watched her braids fall forward as she stooped, and his heart fluttered as they brushed against the snow near her knees. Then she went back into the hall with her maidens, and the door shut behind them, and though he sat for many more hours, all was dark within the great carved-tree hall and no one came forth.

Finally he left the tower, and wandered up and down the moonlit road as if in a trance. When dawn broke and Odin seemed to be busy elsewhere, he returned desperately to Valaskjalf in the hopes of seeing her again. Geri and Freki growled at him and would not let him pass, though he ordered them and pleaded with them, for they could sense his desperation and felt that his errand was not pure of heart. Weeping, he fled to his father's hall on the shores of Asgard, Noatun, the white curved building given to him by the Aesir for the time of his hostaging.

Njord saw his son's red-rimmed eyes and haunted glance, and brought him to sit before the fire at his fireplace, the mantel of which was the bow of a ship. "My son, what ails you?" he asked in concern.

"I have seen a maiden," said Frey, and then realized that he would have to tell of being in Valaskjalf. But this was his father, who would put him before the Aesir, and so he told of it. "You have been to Jotunheim with the traders, my father," he said. "Do you remember a hall, near the shore, carved from a single giant tree as the giants often do, and surrounded by a ring of fire? Do you remember a tall girl with hair the color of turned earth in braids to her knees, with eyes as dark as shadow, with skin pale as Niflheim snows?"

Njord was silent for a moment and then shook his head. "A hall in a ring of fire, yes, that is Gymir's place. He is an etin-lord of great power, my son, and if your heart is set on his daughter, I can think that it will only go ill for you. Forget her, my son. There are hundreds of women in Vanaheim who would willingly be your bride, or if you will not have your own kind, there are fair ones here in Asgard as well. But the etin-women are fierce, and I see that you would have to endure great loss for her."

Frey raised shadowed, sleepless eyes to his father's face. "And why should I, who go willingly to the blade every summer, fear loss? What is it that I must lose?"

Njord was silent again, and said, "Of all your possessions, what is most fine to you?"

The golden god's hand went to his sword. "This," he said. "For it was a gift from my mother and from you, and the last thing I received before coming here as a hostage."

"You may have to give it up," said Njord, "if you continue on this path."

Frey unbuckled his sword-belt without a pause and flung it on the floor. "Then I will give it up," he said. "It is only a sword. This is far greater."

Njord took up the sword from the floor, and placed it back in his son's hand. "When you took up this magical blade," he said, "you swore an oath that it would be the only sword that you would ever wield. If you give it up, you will have no sword again, ever, and you will be defenseless. Please, my son, think again."

Frey stared into his father's eyes for a long time, and then he spoke. "I cannot live without her," he said. Then he turned and rushed from Noatun, clutching the sword, and spent many hours pacing up and down the roads weeping. He would not speak to any who saw him, and they wondered, and were concerned, for the Golden One of Vanaheim was never seen in sorrow.

It throbbed in his head. Gymir's daughter. An etin-princess, child of a powerful lord. His friends had warned him about etin-women. They desired them, it was clear, but they also feared them—not as much as an Aesir might, but enough. One did not seduce an etin-woman; they came to you on their own terms or not at all, and one certainly did not try to take her unwilling, or you might find yourself beaten bloody or torn to bits. And indeed, there were hundreds of fair maidens of his own race who would gladly—and indeed already had—shared his bed and considered it an honor, and if this should not be enough, nearly any unmarried woman of the Aesir—and some who were married—would fall willingly to his charms. Why bother with a woman of the Jotnar, a barbarian who would scratch you as soon as look at you, and whose kin would likely do worse?

But Frey spent the rest of the week wandering up and down the road, as if he could not decide where to walk, as if it no longer mattered where his feet took him. His friends tried to distract him with the usual delights and comforts, but his eyes merely stared into the distance, seeing darker ones that locked with his. He did not speak, and hardly ate or drank; when he arrived in Asgard, he went straight to his room in his sister's house, and would not speak to anyone.

Over and over, he recalled what he had seen of her. He wondered why she wore a covering dress that reached from her neck to her ankles, instead of the tendency of most young etin-women to dress in furs and knives, showing off their tall, strong bodies. He wondered if it was modesty, or merely a strong sense of privacy; he wondered what it would be like to see that dress pooling around her ankles. He wondered what her voice sounded like, and how that pale skin would feel beneath the touch of his hand. As the Golden One of Vanaheim, he had lain with more women—and men—than he could easily recount, yet he somehow felt that if he could be with this woman, all the others would fade away by comparison.

He knew also that if he lay with her the one time, he would never wish to leave her... and that was not done. His own people would look askance at an etin-bride; the Aesir to whom he was pledged would be even more disapproving, and the Alfar even more than that. Etin-women were to lie with and then leave; one would then take a civilized wife who would follow you about respectably and faithfully keep your household and raise your children, including any that you happened to make with such side-trips. *You could lie with her, and then forget her,* he told himself, and then he laughed. *No, you will never forget her. And she deserves better than that.*

Getting up his courage, he sent a message to where Gymir held summer court on the coast of Vanaheim, but the message was refused at the gate, for Gymir did not want a Vanir courting his daughter. The messenger was turned away, and Gerda did not know. When the letter was delivered back into his hands unopened, Frey was plunged into a deep sorrow. He did not leave his rooms at Sessrumnir, and spent many hours lying on his bed and weeping. A cloud of grey seemed to engulf him, and his golden light was dimmed entirely.

Freya came back to Asgard at this time, and though many of the Aesir came to welcome her, with tears or heartening words, her brother was not among them. And she was downcast to see this, and asked about him, and was told that he had not come out of his room in many days. She asked in fear if he was ill, not wishing to lose yet another of her kin, but Loki said, "Ill, yes, with an illness that you know well, Lady of Love, and that only one thing can cure. He has lost his heart to some woman who will have him not, and he will not speak to any of us of it."

Freya came to him at once and cried out to see him red-eyed and tossing in his bed. "Who is this woman who has done this to you?" she cried. "Only tell me her name, my brother, and I shall place a bewitchment upon her so that she might fall helplessly in love with you, and then this will all be over!"

But Frey refused her gift. "I would win her on my own terms and hers, for if she loved me by the power of magic, I would always fear that it might fail, or that without it she would care nothing for me." And Freya wept and kissed his forehead, and though she nodded she did not speak, although it tore her heart to see her brother this way. But it was now her time to go back to Vanaheim for the winter, so she bade him to try and sleep, and left his side.

Finally Skirnir, an Alfar friend from his youth, the first who had befriended the lonely golden-haired youngster when he had first arrived in Asgard, stormed his room in Sessrumnir. "My friend, what has become of you!" he cried. "Whoever this maiden is, we will get her for you, unless she be wedded to another, and perhaps even then, for marriages have often been broken beneath the plow of a handsome god! Who is this woman, my friend? Tell me and we shall plan our attack!"

Frey hesitated, but the truth burned within him, and he yearned to tell someone. When Skirnir heard, he laughed uproariously, and said, "So the Golden One of the Vanir is in love with a barbarian etin-maiden! This is fun indeed! Do you actually intend to marry her, or do you merely mean to plow her furrow, Fertile One?"

"I would do both, if I might," Frey said, "and more than that still, but I cannot even speak to her. She is well guarded in her father's hall, and her father likes not my suit, and sends back my missives. If I go there myself next summer, I would be killed, and at any rate I cannot wait that long. I think that longing for her might kill me before then."

Skirnir shrugged. "I could go there," he said, "and I could take a message. No oath binds me here. Of course, I would be risking my life, but I think that I could get through Jotunheim and impress some barbarian lord and his daughter."

Frey drew in his breath. "Would you court her for me?" he asked. "Would you arrange a meeting? I will be forever in your debt."

"What would you give me," said Skirnir cannily, thinking of Frey's great wealth, "if I were to do this for you?"

"Anything," Frey replied. "My horse, my boar, my ship—what do you want?"

Skirnir's eyes fell to the magical sword at Frey's side. It had been forged by the Duergar for Nerthus of the Vanir to give as a gift to her son, and its hilt was wrought like golden wheat and its blade was inlaid with many runes. "Give me your sword," he said, "for I want something to use in my hand, to stay by my side."

Frey was silent at this, and his thoughts warred with one another. His father's words echoed in his ears, and he looked back and forth from Skirnir to the sword. Finally he said, "Ragnarok is far away, and may not ever come. This is now." And, he thought, if anyone had to hold his sword, at least it would be his friend Skirnir. He held out the sword to Skirnir and said, "Go to Jotunheim. Convince her for me."

And so it came to pass that Skirnir came bursting through Gymir's wall of fire, armed with Frey's magical sword and riding Frey's magical red horse, Blodighofi, who did not fear fire. He backed the horse to the door and made it kick with its hooves, striking loudly. "Do we let him in?" growled Beli to his father.

"He may be rude and a fool," said Gerda, "but by the rule of hospitality he is owed a drink. And aside from a mark on the door, by which you and your own friends have done worse, my brother, he has not attacked us." And she went calmly to the door and welcomed him.

Skirnir introduced himself and his errand, and when Gerda heard that missives had come and that she had not heard, she cast a disgruntled glance at her father. Skirnir opened his pouch and showed her the jewels that Frey had given him, and promised her more if she might marry his master, Lord Frey the Golden One of Vanaheim.

As she stood staring at the jewels, Gerda's heart skipped a beat in her chest. She remembered the tall fair-haired man whose throat had been cut, and how fine she had thought him. Then she hardened herself. Why did such a man not come before her himself? Why did he send some minion to bribe her with gold, as if she was a thrall to be purchased? "Take your gold and jewels to other maidens," she said. "The daughters of Jotunheim are not so easily bought."

Skirnir's face darkened, and he drew the sword from his belt and waved it around in the air. "Agree to marry Lord Frey or meet your doom!" he cried.

Gerda stood her ground. Behind Skirnir, two dozen etins had their blades half out of their sheaths, watching for the word from Gymir. She set her jaw and glared at him. "Threaten the daughters of men with your blade," she said, "but do not try to frighten a giant's daughter with such puny things."

Skirnir's face turned red with rage and he began to rant, cursing her with a long litany of deaths and disasters if she did not submit at once. She stared at him, wondering if he had gone mad. Then the sword flashed through the air, and accidentally struck a beam, and one of the lamps fell to the floor with a crash, and everyone ducked, cursing. "Shall I kill him now, Father?" hissed Beli, his eyes gleaming.

Gymir gritted his teeth visibly. "Not yet, my son. I have an idea." Then Gymir pulled his daughter aside and spoke to her where only her family could hear. "You are my child, and I will never force you to wed where you would not," he said, "but my business is often in Vanaheim, and a marriage to the Golden One might be advantageous. At least meet with him, speak to him, and if you find him hateful I shall shelter you from all harm."

"But this fool is in your hall now, my father!" she hissed. "What shall I do with him?"

"Pretend to be frightened," said her father, "and say that you will meet with his master. That will get him out of here before he sets the ceiling on fire and we must slay him for it."

Gerda sighed and shook her head, for she was not one for dissembling, but she awkwardly knelt before the ranting Skirnir and pleaded with him to stop, that she would meet Frey and discuss marriage with him. "Where?" Skirnir demanded.

She thought of asking to meet him in the Iron Wood, and bit her tongue, trying not to smile. Perhaps somewhere in Vanaheim was best, she thought. "In the Barri Woods," she said, remembering the thick stand of trees where she had played as a child while visiting the coast of the Vanir. That reminded her of the one time she had seen Frey, which had been his death. *Could I marry a man who dies by the knife every year?* she wondered. "In nine days," she added, giving herself time to think about it.

Gymir stood forth then. "We must discuss the bride-price," he said, and Gerda was reminded that her father was very much a merchant. Still, it might distract this raving messenger. "My daughter is no mere milkmaid, to be had for nothing," he said.

The sword wavered in the air, and dropped. Finding now no opposition to his demands, and faced with an etin-lord ready to haggle, he was no longer on sure territory. "What would you ask, my lord Gymir?"

"That sword," said Gerda, pointing to it. "If he wants me, he will give his sword to my family." It was one way to get it out of this lunatic's hands, she thought.

Skirnir looked dismayed. "But Lord Frey promised it to me for my service here—" he began, but Gymir cut him off.

"No, no, if he will have my greatest treasure, I will have his! Tell your lord that no other bride-price will do, and that if he wishes to bargain, his wedding will be much delayed," said Gymir. "And you may leave that sword here, in token of your good will."

Skirnir stared at the sword, and at Gymir, and perhaps it occurred to him that Frey was in such a state over Gerda that he would gladly give away the sword to this family of Jotnar rather than delay the wedding for weeks while they haggled over precious stones and bales of grain. "Very well," he said sourly, "I will leave it here, by your threshold. But none may touch it until she is delivered to their wedding night!" Then he stalked out of the hall and leaped onto the red horse to leave, and all the fists of Gymir's men relaxed on their sword hilts.

But Beli stood forth angrily and faced his father. "My father must value his daughters so little, that he would sell them so cheaply without a fight! Why did you not allow me to slay the rascal, and then we would have had the sword anyway!"

"With how many of my men dead?" Gymir pointed out. "And even if you did kill him, then we would have the Aesir and the Alfar down on us, and a war would begin. Now, I do not mind a war or two, but the spring shipments are ready to go across the water, and—"

"These are the words of a trader, not a warrior!" cried his son. "You have sold my sister for credit in Vanaheim!"

Gerda put a hand on his shoulder. "I but promised to meet him and speak of marriage," she said. "I can still reject him, or if it comes to marriage, I can divorce him if I like him not. I am sure that I can find ways to make him sorry that he fell in love with me." And she bared her sharp Jotun teeth, and Beli snorted and went to look for some ale.

When Skirnir thundered back over Bifrost, he found Frey waiting anxiously by the gatehouse, next to where Heimdall kept his watch. Frey ran up and seized his stirrup. "Tell me what happened," he said urgently. "Before you even get off my horse, tell me!"

Skirnir tossed him a grin. "She is yours," he said. "She will meet you in nine days in the Barri Woods to discuss the wedding with you."

Frey's face went from dark to light to dark again. "Nine days!" he moaned. "It will be nine days of agony. But at least she will see me!"

Skirnir dismounted and pulled him aside. "There is one problem," he said. "Her family asks for your sword. I told them that you had promised it to me, but they were adamant."

Frey rent his hair. "Then they must have it," he said finally. "I give you my horse, Skirnir, as a gift instead." Then he went to Odin, and flung himself on his knees, saying that there was a family matter in Vanaheim that he must see to, and giving his word that he would return as hostage in one turn of the Moon's path. Odin saw his reddened eyes, and though he did not guess at the cause, he released Frey to go home for one month.

She met him in the woods, in the darkness, so that she would not have to look into his eyes at first. He brought a torch, but she called down a gust of wind to blow it out. He saw her only as a tall figure in the shadows, waiting for him, and it seemed that he saw as well the flash of red eyes in the darkness, and the graceful shadow of a great cat. She stood alone, draped in her dark cloak the color of the turned earth, her hands clasped before her. "So you are the one who has gone to such trouble to woo me," she said. "My father likes not your messenger. Why did you not come yourself?"

"I was afraid, Lady," Frey replied, and his voice was soft.

"Afraid of my father? He might have spitted you on a pike, that is true," she said.

He shook his head. "I would walk through many pikes merely to speak to you. No, I was afraid that I would fall to my knees before you and beg you to marry me, and that would shame us all in front of your family. I could not trust myself, so I sent Skirnir."

She was silent for a while, a still figure in the darkness. "You would have done better to come yourself," she said finally.

"Skirnir says that your father asks my sword as a bride-price," he said.

Gerda lifted her head proudly. "I ask that price," she said, "in exchange for my pledge to you. It was no idea but mine. Am I not worth your finest possession?"

"If you will marry me, you will be my finest possession," replied Frey. "I will gladly give up my sword to you. I would give you anything I have. But I am bound by my hostage-vows to fight with the Aesir, and if Ragnarok comes, it may be used against me."

"Then we shall have to make sure that Ragnarok does not come," she returned. "But I warn you, I will not dwell in the lands of those who killed my kin."

Frey shook his head. "I cannot break my hostage-vows. My father and my sister and I swore them on terrible ancient powers. I must live in Asgard or Alfheim for two-thirds of the year, and only visit my home during the autumn."

She was silent for a moment. "Vanaheim is not so bad in the autumn," she said finally. "I could live with you there at that time. And for the rest, I could spend the springtime in Alfheim, though I like it not, and I expect that the Alfar will like me little as well."

"I am not without power in Alfheim," Frey said, smiling. "They will treat you well, or hear from me about it."

"But in the spring," Gerda said, "I will go home to my family's hall, and you must go make peace with your hostage-masters, and we will be apart. There is no hope for that. I will never go to Asgard." And Frey could see from the tilt of her chin that nothing could move her on this point, and so he agreed. It pained him to be caught between his oaths and her pride, but his love for her was great enough that being together for half the year was worth losing her for the other half.

She stood still again for a moment, as if she had not expected him to agree, as if she was only just realizing the full force and depth of his love for her, and she looked for a moment lost, like a girl who is unsure of what to say. Then he stepped close to her, and decided that the time had come to go beyond speaking, and he kissed her, and his golden aura enveloped her like the sun rising behind a dark standing stone. And soon her long cloak fell to the ground, and her dress pooled about her ankles, and they spent the night there together in the Barri Woods.

Just before dawn, as the sky was beginning to lighten, Gerda asked the one question that she had carried with her in her heart all these years. "What is it like, to die and return?" she asked him as they lay together under the trees.

"Cold," he said. "It is cold, and dark, and I walk the Hel-road, and every year the guardian says, 'Greetings, my lord. It is good to see you again.' And every year I am afraid that they will open the gate for me, but they always turn me back, and then I awaken to my body."

"Do you remember the pain after you awake?" she asked him.

"Always," he said, and kissed her.

When the sun rose, Gerda and Frey set sail in his magical ship to Jotunheim, where they landed on the shore near her father's hall, and Gerda took him to meet her family. Gymir looked upon the Vana-lord who would have his daughter's hand, and saw that he was scratched and bleeding, and smiling so brightly that he shone like the sun, and Gymir said, "I see that you have satisfied my daughter." And he laughed, and all his folk roared with laughter, but Frey laughed too just as loudly, and lifted his shirt to show his scratches, and this opened their hearts to him. Frey and Gerda pledged their troth there, in front of Gymir and Aurboda, and the wedding was planned for a fortnight hence.

But there was one among them who did not laugh, and who indeed sat scowling through the ceremony. Afterwards, Beli went to Gerda and pulled her aside, and told her, "You bring shame on all of us by marrying outside your people."

Gerda pulled away and said, "I do not live my life for you, my brother, and I shall marry whom I choose." And she went away from him.

As she walked away, he called after her, "He is now my life-enemy, sister who values not her own kin! If it comes to war, I will kill him!" But she did not look back or speak to him, and indeed it was years before she spoke to him again.

After a fortnight of preparing, Gerda and Frey came forth to be married. A thousand guests of her father's attended from all corners of Jotunheim, and some came even from Niflheim, and gruff Surt the Black and some of his many sons came from Muspellheim. There were cliff-giants from the mountains, and frost-giants with snow still in their beards, and wolf-folk from the Iron Wood, and many others. The skin of a great cave-bear, which was the totem of Gymir's family, was spread before them and they stood upon it. Their hands were cut with knives and bound together, and the blood shared between them. "And now you are our family," said Gymir, "strange as it may seem. May you both be happy together, or at least not too miserable." And all the Jotnar howled for them, loud enough to shake the rafters of the hall.

Then they mounted the ship yet again, and Frey took Gerda home to Vanaheim, where he brought her before his mother Nerthus. "This is my beloved," he said to her, "whom I have married according to the custom of her people, and I would have you welcome her as a daughter."

"According to the custom of her people, perhaps," said Nerthus, "but if you wish me to welcome her as my daughter, you must be married according to the customs of your own people as well. I will not see any marriage to my son the Golden One unless it is with the wheat-wreaths and the burning grain." So Frey and Gerda had a second wedding, and the Vanir came from far and wide to watch them, and his sister Freya came and embraced Gerda.

"I am overjoyed to see my brother so happy again," she said. "He has loved no one like this before, in all the days of his life. Indeed, we thought that no one could capture his heart! Yet here you are, and I do not have to fear for him any more. I will welcome you as my sister, if you will have me, daughter of Gymir."

Gerda wondered at this, and said, "Tell me, Love Goddess of the Vanir: Why did your brother choose me, when he could have had any woman of your people, or of the Aesir?"

Freya embraced her and said, "Love strikes where it will, and who knows this better than I? I do not begrudge him his marriage, though it be to golden Vanir or proud Aesir or fey Alfar-maid or bearded Duergar-woman, or yet to a tall and beautiful etin-bride. Love is love, and it is always good."

And on the morrow they were awoken by singing, and when they came forth from Nerthus's house, the Vanir crowned them with wreaths of wheat, and laid sheaves of wheat in their hands, and drew them forth singing into the winter fields where a great fire was burning, and their hands were bound together, and Gerda's braids were unbound and her long hair wrapped around Frey's shoulders. Bowls of grain were given to them to pour into the fire as an offering, and then gold rings were given to them to place on each others' fingers. They were taken to a bower made in a hollowed-out hayrick, and while they had a second wedding-night, the Vanir sang sweetly all around them.

The next morning, Frey said to his twice-wedded bride, "I fear that there must be a third wedding, for the folk of Asgard will not respect you as my wife unless we are married before them as well. And I will not have them say that you are some passing fancy that I will likely put aside when I am tired of you."

"But I have told you," Gerda said, "that I will never go to Asgard." And they parted in silence, with kisses and tears, and Frey went back to fulfill his oath, and Gerda returned to her family at Gymir's hall, where she sat silent in the wintry garden and stared at the withered herbs.

Her mother comforted her, and told her that many women went without their husbands; some were wed to sailors, or travelers, or men with other wives or families. It was not uncommon for giants to have more than one wife or husband, and to live apart. "Perhaps you should take a second husband, to comfort you when your golden lord is away," she suggested.

But Gerda shook her head. "I have seen no one I wish to wed," she said, and would say no more about it.

For himself, Frey was quieter than usual, and he did not join in the revelry of Asgard, and he was often seen to sigh to himself. But he took up again his duties and no longer lay weeping in his bed, and many of the folk of Asgard considered him cured of what had ailed him. However, gossip travels with a will of its own, and Skirnir's tongue was by no means discreet, so it was not long before all of Asgard knew that Frey had secretly married an etin-woman. So it was that Odin and Frigga called Frey forth to Gladsheim, and he came, knowing what it was they would ask.

It was Frigga who spoke first, as he knew that she would; marriage was her realm. "My lord Frey," she asked him, "we hear that you have wooed the daughter of an etin-lord. Tell us, do you intend to wed her, or is she merely a concubine you are visiting in Jotunheim?"

"I have already wed her, Lady," Frey said, "by the rituals of her people, and of mine. Gymir's daughter is my wife, and nothing shall change that."

At this a great clamor arose of many voices speaking at once. Some cried out against this union of Asa-sworn Van and Jotun lady; some cursed Frey for a fool; some said that at least there had been no wedding by their own customs, so it was no real wedding after all. One woman's mouth spoke forth that this was the known promiscuity of the Vanir, and that it had finally brought shame on them all.

At this, Freya stepped forth and chided the crowd. "Do you all scoff at the power of Love?" she demanded. "Love has done this, and I say that it is well done. There is little enough love in the world; do not condemn love that has sprung up unawares!" And saying this, she remembered her lost husband, and turned away in tears.

Frigga stood also, and held out her hands to both those who condemned and those who defended, and also those who stood silent. "Rather than letting this be a division between these worlds," she said, "let it be a bridge and a frithmaking between us." And Odin stood forth with his wife, and although some still muttered about the weak words of women, the clamor was silenced.

Odin turned to Frey. "We will welcome your bride, if she comes here," he said, "but as you are a sworn frith-guest of ours, you must marry her by our customs, in our city."

"That, my Lord Odin," said Frey, "will be entirely up to her."

The next day an Alfar lord and lady came to Frey, and they spoke formally to him. "Lord Frey, you were set to watch and guard us by the Aesir, and we have long respected you, for you are a good and honorable man. But now we hear that you would take a giantess to wife, and we ask you not to do this, for it would bring shame upon you."

"Who I marry is none of your concern," Frey said. "I love this woman, and she shall be my wife, etin or no."

"My Lord, we beg you," protested the Alfar lord, "do not bring this giantess as your consort into our land! Do not force this bloodthirsty barbarian upon us!"

Frey smiled, thinking of Gerda, and how she had licked his scratches. "I shall do that," he said. "I shall bring my bloodthirsty barbarian etin-bride into your realm, and you will treat her with courtesy and hospitality, because I am the Guardian of Alfheim and I say it will be so." And though they pleaded with him, he would not hear them. And so it was that their marriage was condemned by as many as welcomed it, and from that time on any who would wed against the desires of their family or clan, or against the laws of their people, could call upon Frey and Gerda to bless their union.

In the meanwhile, while Gerda sat at her father's home, her cousin Skadi came to Gymir's hall. Skadi was a whirl of white furs and stomping boots, shaking snow off of her hood and doffing her doeskin gloves. "Greetings, Lady of the Snows!" cried Aurboda. "What brings you to Gymir's hall?"

Skadi's eyes lit on Gerda. "First, to congratulate my cousin on her wedding. Forgive me that I did not attend, but I was still in mourning for my late father Thjazi. Second, to tell you that I am going to Asgard to demand weregild for his death, and I hope to enter with my cousin when she goes to her husband."

"I have told my husband that I will not set foot in Asgard," Gerda said. "And what does your father's weregild have to do with me?"

Skadi's dark eyes gleamed. "It has much to do with you, my cousin. Why will you not go to Asgard? Do you not realize what a chance this is for your people?"

Gerda frowned at her, but the frost-giantess continued. "Those Aesir never let my father have a place in their council, even after he married one of them and inherited her land after she died! But they may let us speak, if we are married to some of them, because the Aesir underestimate their womenfolk. You are Frey's wife; you might have a chance to get your people's voice heard there in the White World. Why do you pass up this chance?"

"But you are no one's wife, Skadi," said Aurboda. "What is your plan?"

Skadi smiled coolly. "Why, I shall go and claim the property of my father and stepmother, and I shall ask for weregild for my father's death. I shall appeal to Tyr, and I expect that he will say my request is fair. And as weregild, I shall ask One-Eye for a husband. The Aesir believe that womenfolk all need fathers and husbands to protect them, they will believe the request." She threw back her head and laughed, shaking snow everywhere.

"But then you will have to marry whoever Odin chooses," Gerda said. "My husband is kind and beautiful; what if yours is not?"

"Then I will divorce him after a reasonable time," Skadi said, "and by then my voice will be well established there. Besides, I hear that Frigga's youngest is most handsome, and perhaps I will get lucky." She rubbed her hands together. "Come with me, cousin; we shall be as sisters there, and keep each other company, I promise."

Gymir stepped forward and touched his daughter's shoulder. "I would not force you to leave my household," he said, "but Skadi speaks wisdom.

They would never let a warrior onto the council there who was not sworn to them, but you are a bride, and they would not see you as a warrior but as a wife; such are their ways. You could speak for your people."

So it was that Gerda dwelt on the matter for some days, and finally she agreed to go to Asgard, though her heart was heavy. And a message was sent to Frey, who rejoiced and began to make ready for their third wedding day.

But Skadi went ahead, in her snowy sleigh, armed with weapons and clad in her best snow-white furs, and railed for weregild at the gates of Asgard. And, as the tale goes, Odin allowed her to claim her inheritance of land, although no bloodline gave it to her, and he placed all the unmarried Aesir men in a circle around her. She allowed herself to be blindfolded, and was told that she must touch the feet of the men, and choose one only by their feet. So she chose the one that she felt had the best-formed feet, and lo and behold when the blindfold was removed she stared into the face of Njord the Vanir Lord of seafaring, the father of Gerda's husband Frey. And all the Aesir men breathed a sigh of relief, for they had feared to be forcibly married by Odin's word to the forbidding giantess. Skadi was a little disappointed that she had not chosen the beautiful Baldur, but Njord was a handsome man, and clearly kind of heart, so she was content enough with the way things had gone.

The next day, when Gerda came to Asgard, Frey kissed her in front of all of them, and said, "This is my beloved, and let no one speak against her." And Freya stood with them and spoke for them, and Frigga came forth to speak of frith and peacemaking and the sacredness of marriage vows, and finally Odin spoke forth and blessed their union, and no others spoke out publicly against them. And it came to pass that Gerda married Frey on the same day that Skadi married his father, and they placed their hands on Frigga's spindle and walked under Odin's spear, and there was feasting and dancing for days. Thrice-wedded, they went to their third wedding night as if it was their first.

Gerda tried to make herself at home in Asgard, and Freya gave her a walled courtyard at Sessrumnir to plant the cloistered herb gardens that she loved. Many of the Aesir were courteous to her, and came to value her, but though none dared mutter against her in her hearing, she heard many of them curse her kin, and her race, and speak ill of them. And Gerda was silent, for it was not her way to do battle in public over the words of others.

She finally spoke to her husband about it, but he bade her to ignore their hard words, and to remember that they were not speaking against her. Still, it ate at her heart, and she felt that an insult to her kin, or to her race, spoken in her presence, was indeed an insult to her. The months drew on, and she did not feel at home, and began to long for a place where she did not have to guard her tongue so. And after a long time of this, she discovered something that made her troubled heart weep, something she had forgotten until it came upon her.

So Gerda went to her husband and drew him into her walled garden, in the night while the stars shone down upon them. And she sat with him on the bench where they had sat many times before, and laid her hand upon his knee, and said to him: "There is life in my womb, heart of my heart. We have quickened us a child."

And Frey cried out in joy and would have embraced her, but she held him away from her and said, "I tell you this not as tidings of happiness, but of sorrow. For when our child comes of age, to whom shall he be forced to swear fealty? If battle should be called, what side will he be on? What geas shall be laid upon him before he is even born?"

Frey was silent, and then said, "As my father swore to be a hostage to the Aesir, so he swore also for his children, and their children and grandchildren. So I am hostage, and my sister Freya, though not our half-sisters who have other fathers. And Freya's daughters are also so bound, and so would be my children."

Gerda placed her hands over her womb in a gesture like an iron gate, and said, "I will not bear children to be hostages to anyone's whim. I will not give them life only to take away their freedom, especially as they have my blood in them, and will be scorned by many."

"Yet I cannot fulfill my oath otherwise," said Frey. "What would you have me do, my love? For this is your womb, and your decision. That is the way of the Vanir."

Then it was her turn to be silent, until finally she said, "If this is how it must be, then I will bear you no children at all. I will not have them torn between loyalties that they did not choose. I will still this life in my womb, and I will bear no more until there is peace between all our peoples."

Frey heaved a sigh. "That day may never come."

"Then I shall remain barren," said Gerda. And he embraced her in silence, and they both wept, but that night she gathered certain herbs from her garden and brewed them into a brew, and stilled the life within her womb. And so it came to pass that the Lord of Life, who gives such growth to the fields and flocks, has a barren marriage, and that Gerda turns often to her herbs to ensure that it is so, and that many women who need also to still the quickening life within them turn to her for aid and ease of passage.

And after having lived many years in Asgard, Gerda made ready to leave and go to her home in Jotunheim, for she did not feel that she could stay there any longer. She told her husband that she would meet him in his hall in Alfheim, and his home in Vanaheim when he was allowed to come home, and that he would always be welcome in her father's hall in Jotunheim. They wept again, and embraced, and parted, telling each other that their love would endure even such a yearly parting, and promising to see each other in the summer.

Gerda packed quietly, and would have left Asgard with no one knowing, yet Skadi got wind of it and came to her as she was clipping sprigs of herbs to take with her. "You would abandon me here in the White World, then, my cousin?" she asked.

"It grieves my heart sore," Gerda said, "but I must go. I cannot live among the killers of my kin and the haters of my race, though we both agreed to make this sacrifice. My sacrifice will be different, though."

"Then if you must go and leave me alone as the sole voice for Jotunheim," Skadi said to her, "I charge you with this: When our people come into councils, speak for me. Remind them why they sent me here, and why we work for peace against all odds. Be my voice, not that of your family. Do this for me, your cousin alone in the White World."

"Alone?" asked Gerda. "Is your husband, the father of my own beloved, not to your taste, my cousin?"

"His hall is not to my taste," said Skadi. "For the mewing of the gulls and the noise of the sea awakens me too early, and I stink of salt air. And he will not dwell far from the sea; my mountains make him long for the waters. He is a pleasant enough fellow, but we shall have to live apart for much of the year. So it seems, my sister, that we shall both be absent brides... but my place here is now assured, and my voice will speak for our race, if you will speak for me."

"I will do this," Gerda said to her, and they embraced, and Gerda went forth from Asgard and never returned. She kept her word, speaking for Skadi in the councils of Thrym, and she spent the winter with her family in the snow, and then went forth to Vanaheim in the summer, much as she had gone forth so long ago as a young maid, to see the Golden One die by the hand of the priestess of the Vanir, and to welcome him back to life with kisses when he arose again.

Winter's Fury

(as told by Skadi to Raven)

efore the Jotun goddess Skadi came to Asgard after her father's death to claim her inheritance and a husband, she was worshiped widely in Midgard among the humanfolk. She went often among them during the winter months, preferring to spend the summer months either in Niflheim or in the far northeastern reaches of Jotunheim, where it was snowy year-round. It was Skadi who first taught them the making of skis for the quick and snowshoes for the slow, of winter dogsleds and traps of many kinds, of tracking and recognizing spoor even in the bitter cold, and slowly they became winter hunters under her guidance. She taught a few of them, also, of the ways of the stars, and how to read their chill and gleaming knowledge.

Among the northerners of Midgard who lived more than half the year in snow and ice Skadi was much beloved, and also not a little feared. To gain her favor could mean the difference between surviving the bitterest winter in reasonable comfort, or seeing one's children perish of cold and starvation. They did not fool themselves into thinking that Skadi was a kindly mother goddess; she was a maiden of ice, a white wolf in the snow with blood on her breast, a spear of ice falling upon the unwary. They knew her nature, both cold and bloodthirsty, and they offered her sacrifices.

When the seers looked upon the signs of Nature in the autumn, and knew with sinking heart that this winter would be especially harsh, a young man was chosen among the handsomest of the village, and offered to Skadi as consort and sacrifice. He was sent naked to a bower built for them in the snow, there to await her pleasure, and she could take it as she wished. Then he was lashed to a tree, and his testicles tied to a buck livestock animal of some sort—goat or bull—and they were ripped from him. Whether he lived or died was up to Skadi and how well he had pleased her, but he would never share his seed with another woman again. His blood was caught in a vessel of carven stone and left on her altar, and she would have mercy on the village and send them plentiful game, and fewer snowstorms.

When Skadi came to Asgard, the Aesir were well aware of her reputation among the humanfolk of Midgard; they knew of the shrines built to her and the sacrifices made. She was a Goddess in her own right, and thus after a time they allowed her a voice at their Moot, once she was safely married off to Njord. Yet the marriage with Njord did not last, and while Skadi claimed the inheritance of her Aesir stepmother and dwelt in her castle in the few snowy mountains of Asgard, she often grew lonely in the strange golden land, so different from the places that she loved to roam. She could not go home as often as she chose, as there were decisions to be made and she was the only voice to speak for Jotunheim, and the burden of it weighed on her heart.

One other thing weighed on her heart as well. She was still married to Njord the hostage sea-king—for it was not the custom of the Vanir to divorce before the first year was up—yet she no longer lived with him, nor shared his bed. He had been a pleasant enough bedmate, but now she slept alone, and the huntress was not used to sleeping alone. At home, in the court of Thrym, Jotun men vied to share her bed, and offers of marriage had come thick and fast. But here it was different. The men of Asgard might admire her crisp beauty, her snow-pale skin and eyes the blue of a winter sky, and they might even bed her, but they would not take a giantess to wife, nor even treat her as more than a brief pleasure-tryst. Frey was entirely taken by her cousin Gerda, and she would not tread there out of respect, even were he interested, which he was not—his eyes were all for his own etin-bride, and Skadi begrudged them not. There were no Jotun men in Asgard save Tyr, who had an Aesir wife and an Aesir mistress... and Loki, who had been the cause of her father's death.

At first she would not speak to Loki, nor even look at him, though he plied her with fair words. She was no fool; she knew that her father's greed had been more than half the reason for his death in the guarding flames of Asgard—that and his foolishness, to attempt to fly into their citadel without permission—but she had loved her father in spite of his flaws, and it was a long time before her coldness towards Loki thawed in any way.

Yet, finally, she managed to speak to him, and to her surprise found him to be a fine listener—something that she would not have expected from the green-eyed wagtongue. In spite of her misgivings, she found herself telling him about her loneliness, her family, her empty bed. He simply nodded, and said, "It must be hard for you here, Lady, especially now that your cousin Gerda has gone back to her people."

"Aye, and though I do not blame her, there are times when I wish that I could do it myself. Yet I am here, and I have made the commitment; I will see it through. I would not turn tail like a hare so soon," she said.

"No one could ever accuse you of cowardice," Loki said, and it was the sort of compliment that a giant gave to a giantess, and in spite of herself Skadi glowed.

Soon after, Loki spoke to Odin about Skadi's sadness. The All-Father smiled and said, "Well, my brother, of all the people here you are the one who could best bring a smile to her face, if she were to forgive you your part in her father's death."

Loki's brow wrinkled. "Are you saying that you would have me court her for marriage, after her handfasting with Njord is over? I do not think that she would wish that; nor would I." For Loki's thoughts were ever on Sigyn, the child in Njord's household who was growing fast towards womanhood, though he spoke of this to no one save the sea-king,

Odin looked at him with sharp eyes that twinkled, and said, "No, my brother, I would not order you to marry the white she-wolf, for I know that your heart is elsewhere in my realm." And Loki started, for he thought that he had kept this secret well, but Odin merely smiled, and said, "Yet you could bring her some comfort, for a time, or at least pleasure. There is no harm in two meeting as equals in this way, as I did the beautiful Vanadis. Give her some comfort. We need her happy, for otherwise she might fill her castle with men from Thrym's court, and I would not have that here in my land."

Loki went away and thought about this, and decided that a roll in the furs with Skadi would not be so bad a thing, and besides he heard the implicit request in Odin's voice. "Of all the things that he has asked me to do, this is one of the most pleasant by far," he thought, not knowing that someday it would be one of the things he would most regret. Yet Skadi was hard to approach; she was still cold and distant, and he did not wish to count on words to win her.

One day Skadi came down to Gladsheim while all and sundry were in the yard, playing music and watching folk dance. She seated herself on a great chair and sat, glumly staring at the dancers as if they were hardly there at all. Loki looked over at her, and an idea flew into the trickster's head. Hurrying off to the barn, he grabbed a large buck goat by the horns and dragged him out.

A few minutes later, Skadi looked up to see Loki being dragged along by a furious buck goat. A rope was tied around his horns, and the other end was tied around Loki's testicles. He was screaming and waving his arms in a manner that suggested there was more acting going on than genuine pain, but it had the desired effect on the crowd. Roars of laughter broke out all around. Skadi stared openmouthed at him. Loki met her glance just for a second as the goat dragged him past her, and winked at her. She realized immediately that this was meant to be a reference to her sacred rites, although not a serious one. She sat there openmouthed, not sure whether or not to be offended, and then as the goat dragged Loki by again the rope strategically snapped, and he tumbled rear-first into her lap.

"Oh! Oh, my Lady, I am so sorry! Oh, that brute!" he cried with exaggerated pain, and then winked again and flashed her a smile. For a moment she stared at him, still dumbfounded, and then slowly she smiled. Everyone around saw that smile, and applauded.

He may have been mocking my sacred rites, she thought, *but I sense no malice or scorn in him. He is a trickster, so perhaps this is his way of asking. If so, it can mean only one thing... he is proposing to become my consort. Why else would he do this, in this manner? And it is true, as a Jotun and my equal he should not be unmanned, and it would be a fine way to pay his debt to me. As my consort, it would be a life lived for a life taken.*

She put her arms around him, and said, "I trust that the goat did not harm you, then?"

Again that flash of a smile. "I believe that I am still intact. However, perhaps some testing is in order."

Skadi inclined her head to him, still with that reserved, knowing smile. "I would be glad to aid you in your tests, Laufey's Son." *A man who wore only his mother's name,* she thought, *ought to do well following a powerful woman. And I am told that his other wife, the Hag of the Iron Wood, is a strong one as well, so if we can divide him properly between us, it will be fine.* He took her hand, and she rose and followed him, and together they went to his bed. There they stayed for three days, pausing only for food and drink and sleep, for Skadi was a woman of strong passions. And though by the end he was exhausted, Loki pleased her well.

Indeed, her heart opened to him, and she began to dream of love, and a bridal bed with a man who would, she was sure, accompany her wherever she chose to travel. For was not Flame-Hair a far traveller himself, born of her own mountainous land? No, it had been folly to think of marrying outside her own kind; she smiled at his heavy-lidded eyes and kissed him, tentatively. It was not a kiss of passion, but one of budding feelings. Skadi was slow to warm to love, and was not easy with effusiveness.

On the third day, as Skadi was dressing to go home to her hall, she asked him, "Shall we travel to the Iron Wood to speak to the Hagia, then?"

Loki, who was half asleep by the time, was startled awake. "What? Why?" he mumbled groggily. "What has Angrboda to do with this?"

Surprise showed in Skadi's eyes. "I would not tread on the hem of her garment; I would gain her permission to take you as my consort, as she is my senior in this. Besides, there are details that we women should work out together—children and inheritance and such—"

Loki sat bolt upright. "What are you talking about?" he asked, staring at her in bemusement. "Consort? What do you mean?"

The ice-giantess froze in mid-movement, and her boot tumbled out of her suddenly confused fingers. "You wooed me with my sacred rites—well, a version of them, anyway. Did you not mean to offer yourself as my consort?"

"By the Slith, no!" Loki cried, and then regretted his harshness as soon as it was out of his mouth. "I mean—I meant only that we should take our pleasure together; that was all. I have no intention of marrying—" The word "you" was swallowed before it left his lips. He fell back on the bed and closed his eyes. "No, no, you misunderstood, sweeting."

Skadi slowly rose from the matted pile of furs and sheepskins. "Then why did you come to me in the way that you did?" she asked. There was no expression on her face at all, and hardly any in her voice, and if he had been paying attention, Loki would have known that this was a very bad sign.

Instead, he yawned and shrugged. "I thought that it would get your attention."

Very slowly, and in a low voice, Skadi murmured, "You mocked and defiled my sacred rites merely in order to get me into your bed? You had no intention of following their meaning? You committed sacrilege for three nights of sport? Is this the truth, Flame-Hair?"

Loki looked up, beginning to realize that the woman standing over him had gone cold as a statue of ice. "I did not mean it as sacrilege," he began lamely, but suddenly her face was an inch away from his, and her wintry-blue eyes were gleaming with rage.

"How dare you!" she hissed. "How dare you treat me like some lesser girl to be used and discarded! I am not to be trifled with in this way! Do you realize what an offense you have created? A mortal would be dead by now!" Behind the rage, tiny burning coals of love were being snuffed out by a freezing blizzard. She wanted to weep, wanted to curse her own foolishness, but instead she struck him and fled his home, burying her hopes by the roadside.

Loki left his bed and looked for her, but did not find her, and he dared not go to her castle for fear that she might gut him like a fish. When he returned home, he found Njord standing by his doorway, half in shadow. "So, Loki," he said. "You would have not only my foster-child but my wife as well?"

The trickster's breath went entirely out of him in one whoosh. "Please accept my apologies, my Lord," he said. "I thought that you two were as good as divorced. Besides, this was a mistake that I do not intend to repeat."

"Then you will not be marrying her, when our year is up?" Njord asked.

"By stone and bone, no," Loki said in a tired voice. "I am already married to one she-wolf, I do not need another one. That is the last thing that I need."

"Good," said Njord, "for if you had taken Skadi, I would have refused you Sigyn. She is no match for that one."

"She only used you as a stepping-stone for her ambitions," Loki said suddenly, harshly.

Njord inclined his head. "I know," he said. "I did not mind being so used, as her intentions are honorable, and we have parted friends. And I intend we shall stay so. Your people need someone to speak for them here, Loki, and this is a job that you have not wished to take."

"My people!" Loki spat. "My people are who I choose to be with. I will not be told who to ally myself with, or who to impress!" He stopped, wondering at his own words; Njord merely looked at him for a moment, nodded inscrutably, and left.

Skadi, for her part, nursed her wounded heart in silence, and never spoke of it anyone. So it came to be that no one knew of it, although on that fatal day in Odin's hall after Baldur's death Loki did make a spiteful mention of their short-lived affair. But even if her heart was healed, her pride was not; she bitterly resented Loki's treatment of her sacred rites, and considered his actions an offense against her status. Soon after, when Sigyn grew old enough to marry and Loki wedded her in Asgard in front of all the Aesir, Skadi watched with cold eyes. *So you were not looking to wed, were you?* She left quietly before the ceremony was over, and said nothing.

Yet Skadi came to find out that more damage still was done to her than merely her heart and her pride. Loki was as much a God as she, and when he performed his mocking version of her sacred ritual, his deeds reverberated through the worlds and affected the deeds of mortals. It was not long afterwards that Skadi found the humanfolk of Midgard had decided to stop sacrificing the blood of their fine youths for her; surely, they reasoned, Skadi would like it better if their young men lived to hunt further in her name, and they began to make the ritual a mock-sacrifice rather than a real one. She was furious, and cursed them with bitter winters and no game for eleven years, but in the end she relented and took their bloodless offerings, deciding that the blame lay at Loki's door and not theirs.

So it was that by the time Loki was caught and bound by the Aesir, Skadi had a deep and burning fund of resentment against him. After the last of them had left the cave where he lay bound by the guts of his eldest son, she remained, gazing upon his furious face and the weeping visage of Sigyn, kneeling at his side. Drawing from her coat a venomous snake, she hung it from the stone-spears jutting downward form the cave-roof, and bade it stay there. "As you have made me suffer, so shall you suffer," she said, and left just as the venom was dripping from the serpent onto Loki's bound form. As the screams began, a picture flew into her head—Loki and the goat, and his false screams. "You shall suffer for me one way or another, blasphemer," she said, and did not look back once as she strode from the mountain's gaping maw.

The Tale Of Heimdall's Birth

(as told by the Nine Undines to Raven)

egir the Sea God lives under the waves in Aegirheim, off the coast of Vanaheim, where he holds his great feasts and does his brewing. Most modern folk like to think of him as the god of brewing, which is a slight on his great power; brewing is only a side hobby for him. Like Poseidon and Llyr, he is the ruler of the seas, and specifically the northern seas, clogged with ice and treacherous with storms. While Aegir likes to put on a jovial face, his wife Ran plays out the fickle and dangerous side of his nature for him. Her name means Robber, and she is the Thief of Ships, dragging the sailors down to death. Their ghosts are trapped in the hall of Aegir and Ran, entertaining the cold water-deities, until she tires of them and sends them on to Helheim.

The nine daughters of Aegir and Ran are known as the Nine Undines, or the Nine Waves. They take after their mother in temperament, mostly. They are said to be both beautiful and terrible, although beauty is always in the eye of the beholder. They are shapechangers, and can summon illusory forms that are lovely enough to make a sailor leap overboard in desire, although their true faces show with sharp teeth and claws and strange eyes the color of the sea. Their names are a litany of the powers of the Ocean: Kolga the Cold One, and Duva the Hidden One are the eldest, twins in age and both silent and reserved. Blodughadda, the Blood-Haired and bloodthirsty, is next in age. Then there is big-bellied Bara, and Bylgja of the Breaker; then another pair of twins—the terrible Hronn of the

Whirlpool and the anguished, wailing Hevring. Then comes Unn, the Undine of the Tides; and Himinglava, the Fair-Weather Undine, is the youngest and most fickle of the lot.

It is said that the Nine Maidens love each other more than any other, and that their alliance is unshakeable. They never quarrel, or if they do, no one sees it. So when one of them chose to lay with the canny Aesir god Odin, against the wishes of their father Aegir, the other eight covered it up. It is also said that Odin lay with all nine of them; if this is so, he must have been either very brave to lie with nine deadly, toothed, bloodthirsty mermaids, or else very drunk on their father's brew. Either way, it is certain that at least one sea-etin lay with Odin, and that she got with child by him.

When she made it known to her sisters that she was with child, they all circled her in protection, knowing that their father—and especially their equally bloodthirsty mother, who had no love for the One-Eyed One— would be furious. So they all made a pact that no one should know which of them had done the deed, not even their parents. They all went away, and hid for many months in caves in the darkest part of the sea bottom, where not even Aegir and Ran could find them. In time, the babe was born, and they brought him in their arms to Aegirheim, where they confessed to their angry parents what had been done, if not who.

Aegir demanded again and again to know which of them had done the deed, but the sisters were a solid wall and would not move, and not one of them could be turned against another. Ran threatened to hang them all by their hair from the bottom of the biggest iceberg, but still they would not reveal the babe's true mother. "Let him be known as the child of Odin and the Nine of us," they all said, "for it is as good as true."

Then Ran declared that regardless of which of her ungrateful daughters had whelped the pup, she would not have it raised in her home. Since the sisters had no real care for the child either, they agreed and set him afloat on a boat headed for the island of Vanaheim, hoping that the child would wash up there and be adopted by some kind parents. It had also occurred to them that the child's father might wish to know his son, and indeed Odin had been waiting to see what would happen. As soon as the babe's boat surfaced, he saw it from his throne at Valaskialf, and set out to intercept it.

Scooping the child from the water, he brought the golden babe straight to Frigga's apartments at Fensalir.

Frigga, who was used to dealing with her husband's various children by his affairs, saw that the babe was fair and finely formed, and named him Heimdall. She offered to raise him as her own, but Odin had another plan in mind. He wished a child of his to come to love the humanfolk of Midgard, helpless and hapless as they were, and he decided that this son would live two lives, one as a mortal man and one as a god. He took the foundling in his arms and placed him back in the boat, which he deposited on the ocean inside the girth of the Midgard Serpent. Little Heimdall floated to shore, where a poor fisherman rescued him and brought him home. There he was renamed Rig, and grew quickly as mortal children do, for a mortal seeming had been cast upon him by his father.

The golden child was raised by loving although poor mortals, but he always felt that there ought to be more to his life than this, and he yearned for something more than the fishing-boat and the pig-yard and the garden. If there was one thing that he feared, unreasonably, it was the sea. His foster parents put that down to his early abandonment on the little boat, and forgave it of him. Sometimes, while walking the beach, he would see the sunlight glinting off of what might be the head of a woman among the waves, and when he squinted closer he would see the flip of a tail as it vanished into the water, but nothing more, and he refused to go into the salt waves. If he had done so, he would have discovered that he could swim as well as a fish, but his strange fear held him back. So it was that his mothers watched him from afar, but never spoke to him, and he did not know his origin.

When he grew old enough to leave the seaside farm, he did so, and wandered all of Midgard. He lay with women of every class, from rich to poor, and sired many children, and this too was part of Odin's plan, to get his blood into as many of the folk of Midgard as possible, and thus enrich their bloodlines. Through time and glory and battle and many adventures, Rig was finally made a king in the prime of his life, and Odin who watched was proud of his son. Eventually he grew old and near to death, and on his deathbed, as his eyes were closed by the family who stood weeping about him, a great cloud of birds lowered themselves from the sky and took up his body, and all wondered in awe and amazement.

His body was carried to Asgard, where a small spark of life still remained in it, ready to be snuffed out. Odin restored him to youth and to his immortal self, the body of the youth who was born of the meeting of sea and sky, with eyes of a blue somewhere between the two. He rose in wonder from his bed to find himself in the land of the Gods, and himself one among them, and they cheered him, and called him by his true name of Heimdall. And so it was that he was given the job of gatekeeper of Asgard, and took up his destiny as Odin's son and prince.

Frigga took him to her breast and called him as her son, and he called her Mother. Yet eventually he asked of the story of his birth, and it was told to him. He cried out in anger, remembering the far-distant heads in the water, and his fear of the sea, and swore out against the cold women who had abandoned him to the waves, and he not even able to know which womb it was that bore him. So to this day Heimdall avoids the ocean, and keeps to his father's home in the sky, although he loves and protects the humanfolk of Midgard with a great passion. His heart is hardened against all those of Jotun blood for his anger with his mothers, and this sorrow and anger is one of the things he learned from his life as a mortal, along with his personal caring for them.

And if you ask the Nine Undines to this day, they will not say which of them bore him, but only that he once came from all their arms and was delivered up to his destiny, and as he had both a mortal mother who loved him and an Aesir mother who values him, what need has he of any of them? And then they are gone into the water with a splash and a flash of their tails, and no one can see, through the cold waters, whether any salt tears are shed for him, the child of the meeting of sea and sky. But every year on his birthday, a storm rises up at sea, and all will do well to keep to land on that day and avoid the uncertain mercies of the Nine Ladies of the wild ocean's miles.

Loki and Heimdall

(Elizabeth Vongvisith writes: "Some of this tale was told to me by Loki, and some of this came from Bragi. His storytelling skills far surpass my own, naturally, but I've tried my best to do credit to them.")

t is well known that Loki once stole the necklace of Freyja at Odin's behest. However, few now remember that a second time, Brisingamen was stolen by the Father of Strife, as he was later named among the Aesir, or that from this theft would spring forth one of the bitterest feuds in all the Nine Worlds.

Heimdall, Watchman and guardian of the gates of Asgard, and Loki, the sly and cunning son of Laufey, had never been friends. For his part, Heimdall despised Loki as one of the hated Jotun-kind, and resented Loki's constant movement in and out of Asgard without leave or knowledge of its watchman. None save Odin himself were supposed to come and go in secret. Yet when Heimdall demanded that Loki be prevented from going abroad and returning whenever he chose, Odin bade him to pay no heed—Loki would not bring the enemy etin-folk through some secret way into the gods' keep, nor would he betray them into the hands of the sons of Muspell. Whatever reasons Loki had were his own. Heimdall accepted the counsel of his father and lord, but his dislike of Loki did not abate.

Loki was well aware of Heimdall's distrust and hostility, and delighted in aggravating it. He also despised Heimdall for turning his back on his mother's blood, whereas Loki himself made no secret of his own origins. Impudently, he flaunted in Heimdall's face both his Jotun heritage and his ability to pass in and out of Asgard, just for the pleasure of making Heimdall (and others) angry. He also knew the son of the Nine Daughters had sworn to guard and defend the realm of the Aesir and all who resided therein, and that included himself. Furthermore, Loki was Odin's friend and blood-brother and out of respect for his father, Heimdall would lift no hand. So for a long, long time, the two were merely bickering rivals, who nonetheless stopped short of the drawing of swords or rattling of spears.

Loki again stole Brisingamen from Freyja's hall. It is not known exactly why, except perhaps that he knew Heimdall loved and honored the Vanadis above all the goddesses save Frigga, and he wished perhaps to dig the knife in a little deeper and jeer at the Watchman for his inability to keep Freyja's greatest treasure safe. Brisingamen was under lock and key in Freyja's bedroom when Freyja wore it not, and was further guarded by her folk. Also, Heimdall had made it his business to watch the doings of Loki very carefully while the latter dwelt in the gods' realm. However, Loki managed to accomplish his thievery anyway. None that were taken in by his schemes or blinded to his purpose would later admit to having let Loki get past them, but still, he managed to steal Freyja's golden necklace, and if you wish to know how Loki did it, you must ask the son of Laufey himself.

With the prize in hand, Loki fled Asgard, but he halted a little ways away from the wall surrounding the land, where Heimdall, scowling, could still see him. There he stood, taunting Heimdall and showing him the prize he had obtained, before changing himself into a falcon and fleeing, Brisingamen clutched in his claws. Immediately, Heimdall dropped his spear, changed himself into a second falcon, and pursued Loki, for it was also in his oath that he would guard the treasures of the gods from theft and mishandling, and by his action, Loki was now an outlaw in Heimdall's eyes.

The chase was long and difficult; it is not easy to catch Loki or to keep up with the swift Sky-traveler when he does not want to be found, but Heimdall never relented in his pursuit. He followed Loki wherever the other went. Day became night, night slowly rolled on toward day, which turned again into dark, and Heimdall still did not quit his chase, nor did Loki stop his flight. They passed far from Asgard, into and out of the worlds, where people looked up in astonishment at the two who flew so swiftly that no bowman could ready his arrow in time to fire even a warning shot as they passed overhead.

Finally, as the sun began to rise on the third day, Loki began to tire. He knew he could flee but little further, and then Heimdall would win the necklace back when he, Loki, was too exhausted to continue. He descended toward a narrow, lonely strip of rocky beach, where great cliffs reared up nearby and the waves crashed against the rocks, or swept toward the pebbled sand in arc after arc of dark, cold water. There he resumed his man-shape and turned to face his pursuer. Heimdall landed near him, also assuming his man's form. They were weaponless, but neither of them cared. Here, they both knew, things would come to a head, far from the watching eyes of Odin and the rest of the Aesir.

"Give me back the golden necklace of Freyja, and I shall allow you to depart this place unharmed," shouted Heimdall, "though this is not for your own sake, but for the sake of my father, Asgard's lord, whose blood-brother you are unworthy to be!"

Loki's eyes flashed, but he smiled fiercely. "Allow? You may 'allow' me nothing, Watchman. I took this from under your very gaze, from the hall of the Vanadis, from within Asgard's mighty walls, and you could not stop me! It is mine by right. Go whimpering and mewling back to your post!" he shot back, smirking.

"Then I shall take it!" Heimdall roared, and with that, he advanced on Loki, who, despite not sharing the other's size or strength, snarled like a wild cat and sprang to meet him.

The two of them fought viciously for many hours, wrestling and struggling with their bare hands. Loki changed himself into many beasts and birds, into a terrible frost-giant, into smoke and air, but always, Heimdall too shifted his form, though he was loath to, and kept calling for Loki to resume man's shape and fight in earnest. Finally, Loki resumed his own form, and Heimdall immediately pinned him to a rock. Darkness was falling. They had battled all the day, and though Loki had taken the worst of it and was injured, bloody and sore, he would not admit defeat. He knew that Heimdall would not kill him, lest he be named kin-slayer, but his heart now burned with a desire to overthrow Heimdall, who was equally determined to conquer Loki and win back Freyja's necklace.

"Give me Brisingamen," Heimdall said softly, "and I shall yet release you to go wherever you wish. But if you return to Asgard, I will do my best to keep you out."

Loki's eyes narrowed, then he spat in Heimdall's face. "I told you once before, no one 'lets' me do anything. I will go..." Loki burst into flames. Heimdall cried out and let go, and the flames darted across the beach, changing back into Loki's running form, his long legs carrying him swiftly to the dark, churning water, where he had before not dared to go, for fear of Heimdall's nine mothers, the daughters of Aegir and Ran.

"...wherever I wish!" Loki shouted, and changing himself into a seal, he made quickly for a isle of bare rock, little more than a sharp boulder sticking up out of the sea, some ways away.

Heimdall ran to the edge of the sea, then stopped, fists clenching. He gazed out at the nine women's heads, silently bobbing in the water far away, which had appeared almost as soon as he had alighted on the stony beach. His lips drew tight and his fair face turned darker and grimmer. He then turned his eyes to the seal, who had reached the rock and now heaved itself atop it, turning to watch Heimdall with glittering eyes that no real seal ever had. The nine wave-daughters did not move or speak. His heart burned with anger, and with hatred of Loki, at the thought of what the other had forced him to choose.

The seal barked once, and at that sound Heimdall gritted his teeth and strode into the water, taking seal's form and swimming straight toward the rock upon which Loki sat. The nine wave-daughters did nothing, but their heads turned to watch as Heimdall reached the stony outcropping and his seal's-shape clambered up to Loki.

They strove, biting and shoving at each other, until Loki dove off into the sea again. Heimdall followed him, swift and unerring as a dart. But Loki was nearing the end of his strength, and the wounds he had taken earlier were bleeding copiously into the dark sea. Still, for spite's sake, he would not give in. Finally, Heimdall chased Loki back toward the cliffs and managed to drive him forcefully up against the hard rocks. Loki's seal-shape vanished. His man's form floated, senseless, in the water. Heimdall returned to his own shape as well and dragged Loki back toward the beach. He found and took back Brisingamen from its hiding place among Loki's clothes, then he turned Flame-hair over and shook him until the other's eyes opened and fixed, vaguely but resentfully, upon Heimdall.

Heimdall opened his mouth to say something, but no words left his lips. They stared at each other for a few long moments. Heimdall felt his hands itch to wrap themselves around Loki's neck and finish him off, and the weight of nine pairs of eyes watching them, and for a moment he was filled with a wild rage. Then he snorted and cast Loki back down upon the sand. "Crawl home, if you can," he said in a low voice. Loki did not answer. Then he turned his back and walked away, ignoring the nine women in the water, changing into falcon-form as he strode. With a triumphant cry, he flew into the red-banded sky, wheeled once, and was gone toward Asgard with the dwarf-made gold glittering in the sunset. The nine daughters of Ran and Aegir turned to watch as he disappeared. Then they sank beneath the water and were gone.

Loki lay on the beach, trying to regain enough strength to go home, and it was not until long after dark that he managed to get up and return to Asgard. To his surprise, when he reached the gate, no one was there to stop him. He wondered what this meant, but was too weary and too wounded to care. He came again into Asgard, burning with shame, spite and resentment, and went straight to the hall he shared with Sigyn and their young sons.

But to his dismay, Sigyn was not there either. Loki adored his shy, childlike bride, and she was the only person in all of Asgard who trusted Loki completely. They shared a rare understanding. He knew she would never have left willingly, not when she was so anxiously awaiting his return. Loki wondered what had caused her to leave and felt alarmed, but he sank onto the doorstep of his house, too tired even to call for his sons, and he knew nothing but blackness for a while.

In the meantime, Heimdall, upon his return to Asgard, had called for an assembly of the gods. Sigyn had been summoned despite her protests, and sat at the back of the hall in its shadows, worried and afraid, for Loki had not yet returned home. When Heimdall told his story, Sigyn's hands twisted together. Her heart grieved for her husband's defeat, and her worry for him increased.

After hearing of Loki's theft, the battle between Heimdall and Loki, and Brisingamen's re-taking, the gods spoke loudly and at length. Something should be done, many of them said. Loki had gone too far, if the Watchman himself had been forced to leave his post because of him. Lately Loki's pranks had begun to take on a more malicious character; rumors were spreading and people were muttering, yet no one could say for certain why Loki's attitude of friendship toward the other Aesir had begun to alter. Sigyn knew, but she did not offer her opinion, and she knew too that no one would listen to her anyway.

Some called for Loki's banishment from Asgard. Freyja called for Loki to be brought to her so she could beat him with her bare hands. Idunna stood up and somewhat angrily reminded them that Loki had once caused the theft of both her apples and her own person, and no one had afterwards called for banishment or beatings. Tyr said that Loki should be brought before them all and asked to give his side of things before any action was taken. Some called out their agreement with this, others shook their heads and muttered darkly at the idea of allowing Loki a chance to use his weapon of words. No one spoke out in Loki's defense, however.

"He has not returned to Asgard yet, if indeed he will at all. I left him lying on that beach, nearly dead," Heimdall said contemptuously. Tears sparkled in Sigyn's eyes, but she still did not speak. The gods continued to argue. Finally Heimdall turned, and his keen sight perceived Sigyn where she sat. "There sits one who may answer for Loki and tell us why he came to do this thing," he said. Everyone turned to follow his gaze.

Sigyn was deathly pale. She swallowed hard. "Tell us what you know, lady," Freyja said politely, though she was still full of anger against Loki.

Sigyn said, "I knew naught of this. My husband does as he chooses, and sometimes does not seek my counsel beforehand. He did not tell me he planned this deed." Something in Sigyn's voice made many of her listeners feel a stab of pity for her; many of them yet wondered why she had ever agreed to marry Loki at all. They believed Loki had seduced his hapless bride, whose youth and naivete had made her an easy prey to his charm. They felt that Sigyn had remained with Loki merely out of fidelity to her marriage-oath. That Sigyn loved Loki passionately, and that she understood him better than any of them save Odin, never occurred to the gods.

"I say that he has wronged you as well. For you sit here alone to answer for his infamy, while he slinks off to some dark place to lick his wounds." Heimdall came toward her and Sigyn rose to meet him. He looked down at her grimly, yet not without compassion. "Cast him off, Sigyn. A marriage-oath made to one such as he is no binding thing. You do not deserve to share in your husband's guilt, nor carry the shame of his crimes. Renounce him and be welcome among us, your kinsmen and friends."

At these words, the atmosphere in the room shifted. The other gods murmured assent. Sigyn looked into Heimdall's proud, stern face and felt the eyes of many others on her. She knew they were asking her to choose. She bowed her head and would not speak, but in her heart, there was a growing anger.

Tired himself, injured, angry, and to his later regret, Heimdall said loudly and impatiently, "Lady, you must know that Loki has not shown you faith or troth. He is a bad husband—it is known that he keeps a concubine in the Iron Wood, whom he still visits when he leaves Asgard. You have been true to him, but he himself has known the embrace of many a woman within these walls and without, even after he took you to wife." At these words, several people exchanged uncomfortable looks. Sigyn closed her eyes. Heimdall didn't notice. He went on, with a sharp gesture, "He has acted with no thought of you or your sons! He does not care about his own family, his kinsmen and friends, nor for anything save trouble and strife. His word is false and his oaths are lies. Leave him! He deserves no comfort or succor from any in Asgard!" His voice rang inside the hall where they were gathered, and his face became wild. Others wondered at Heimdall's attitude, but called out their agreement, encouraging Sigyn to renounce her husband. Odin alone sat in silence, watching the scene through narrowed eyes.

Sigyn raised her head. She saw Heimdall's face, and the desire for private revenge there. She saw all their faces, and the desire for Loki's downfall in them too. Her own lovely face became hard, and her voice, normally so soft, made the hall fall quiet in an instant. "I tell you no," she said firmly. "No. I will not renounce my husband, he who has shown me love and comfort, the father of my sons, the joy of my heart. Yes," she continued, louder now, and growing angrier as she saw the skepticism written on others' faces, "he is. Loki loves me dearly, and he has remained faithful to me in his own way, though none of you will believe it. I promised him I would be his loyal wife until the day of my death. When he hears what you have asked of me and what I have answered, he will know I am his loyal wife still. I would have thought better of you, my friends and kin, than that you would ask this of me. The shame is your own, not mine. I have nothing more to say."

Sigyn turned her back on them and walked out of the hall in pride and defiance, but by the time she had come to her own home, she was weeping openly. She dried her tears as best she could, not wishing to alarm her children. At home, she found Loki lying weak and injured, with their young sons at his side. They had found their father unconscious and carried him to his bed, then had done their best to clean and bind his wounds, and they greeted their mother's arrival with relief, until they saw her face. Sigyn knelt beside the bed and took her husband's hand in her own. Loki opened his eyes and smiled weakly at her.

"Don't worry, beloved. It looks worse than it is," he said gently. Sigyn shook her head, unable to reply. Loki's sons had told him that their mother had been summoned to an assembly. His quick eyes searched Sigyn's face, and he frowned when he saw that she had been crying. "What did they say?" he asked sharply.

Sigyn told him all that had passed, and though Loki did not interrupt or take his eyes from her, a change came over him. The air around him grew heavy and hot, and began to crackle with sparks. Loki's expression darkened, then became terrible to behold. Sigyn faltered, and Narvi and

Vali gazed at their father nervously, but with an effort, Loki regained his self-control and his face became smooth. He smiled at his sons, then took his wife's face in his hands and kissed her. "I'm glad to be home. Now, let me rest," was all he would say to them.

But Loki's heart had been kindled into a burning hatred for Heimdall—not for his own pride, not because Heimdall had defeated him, but because of what he had tried to force from Sigyn, whom Loki loved more than anyone would believe. And though he would not know it for some time, Heimdall's hatred had likewise been awakened against him, because Loki had caused him to enter the domain of his mother and her sisters who had abandoned him, the sea which Heimdall hated more than anybody would believe. So was their mutual enmity begun, and so it was said by the seeress from whom Odin sought counsel that they would be the end of one another when Ragnarok came.

The Courting of Mengloth
(as told by Mengloth, and parts of it by Hela)

hat name she was given at birth, we shall never know, for she does not speak of it, but by the time she was old enough to sing, her love of jewels and fine necklaces prompted her family to call her Mengloth, which is Necklace-Glad. She was a fair child, with flaxen hair, but pale and sickly; her mother nursed her through illness after illness, despairing of bringing her to health like the younger brothers and sisters who had come after her. While they ran through the mountains to play and hunt, she would stare mournfully from the window of her bedchamber, which looked out through the rough stone caves of the mountains of northern Jotunheim.

A sickly child is alone much, for other children grow impatient, and small Jotnar especially. Her parents consoled her with special morsels and pretty trinkets, but they could not buy her health. Wisewomen were called to see her, but though each sang over her and fair stuffed her with herbs, she never grew entirely well. Old Hyndla herself came down to see the child, and announced that she had inherited weakness of bloodline, and that she would either die or be very important. Such strange pronouncements were not unusual for the odd old Bloodwalker, but her parents worried much over her.

But by this time, she was no longer alone so much, for little Mengloth had a secret that she told to no one. One night while she lay much fevered, her very spirit left her body, and her mother feared to lose her entirely. Her soul hovered in the air and then found itself borne on the wind, wafting like a weightless leaf. Then, the next thing she knew, she was riding along behind the eyes of someone else, staring up at the face of a tall, strikingly handsome man.

The eyes were blurred, for they were wet with tears. It was a boy-child, she realized, not much more than her own age, and he was crying. The man shook his handsome head and said in a fine mellifluous voice, "Sometimes I wonder how a child so clumsy could even be my son." Then he picked up the broken pieces of something—Mengloth could not see through the tears—and took them away. A pair of hands covered the eyes, and the sobbing continued in darkness.

Mengloth waited, uncertain, wanting to comfort the boy whose head she had landed in, but not knowing how. After a while, he fell asleep, and she found herself drifting back to her body. The fever had broken, and her mother rejoiced, but the thought of the boy haunted for some time. Eventually, being bored with her convalescence, she undertook to find him by putting herself in a trance—and find him she did. This time he was happier, laughing and playing with his older brother. The frail Mengloth found his wild, energetic antics wonderful; she had never played so hard herself.

From then on, whenever she was ill and confined, she visited the boy-child in her mind. Sometimes she saw things as he saw them, and sometimes she seemed to hover about him like a ghost, watching from the outside. The connection seemed entirely one-way, though—no matter how loud she called out to him, he never seemed to hear her. Sometimes, though, when she was hovering around him, he would pause and look oddly at where her consciousness hung in the air, and then shake his head and go on with his play.

Mengloth learned a great deal about him, though. She learned that his name was Svipdag, and that he was the son of the great star-hero Aurvandil, companion and friend of Thor, and the sorceress Groa. Svipdag's intimidating mother always frightened Mengloth, for whenever she came around, Mengloth feared that the sorceress might see her and do something. She would flee at the very sound of Groa's voice, and not return until Svipdag had run off again.

His relationship with his father was even more complex. Though it took her years to figure out, she came to realize that Svipdag idolized the great star-hero Aurvandil...and that he was a constant disappointment to his father. His older brother Thjalfi was already in service as a page to Thor, well on the way to being a hero himself, but Svipdag was poor hero material. He was forgetful, and dreamy, and could not hold a sword without tripping over his feet. His hands were clumsy with knives and crafts, and he would injure himself regularly. He was nearsighted as well, and would accidentally knock things about. He would sometimes trip over his tongue and stutter. Put to weed a field, he would wander away in the middle of it; put to watch sheep, they would all be lost in the woods while he played with stems of grass. In spite of this, he was cheerful and good-hearted, and laughed often, but it was clear that he would be neither warrior-hero nor craftsman nor skald, nor even a farmer...and his father knew it, and watched him often with an unhappy look on his face. Svipdag seemed not to notice it, but Mengloth saw it, and her heart bled for him.

As Mengloth grew older, her brothers and sisters found mates, one by one, but she resisted it. Somehow, after being in Svipdag's head, she could not imagine that a physical relationship could be more intimate than that, even though it was only one way. Instead, she apprenticed with the local healer, feeling that since she was so often ill, she ought at least to find out what could be done about it. After all, she told herself, my mother will not always be there to care for me, and so I must care for myself. In spite of her sickliness she grew giantess-tall and broad, clear signs of her mountain-etin blood. She felt herself to be plain and awkward, unlikely to gain the eye of those seeking beauty, and so she went about oblivious to many whose eyes followed her. If they had been asked, they would have spoken about the warm glow that emanated from her when she smiled, lighting her up from the inside, and making her almost beautiful in some indescribable way.

When Mengloth had learned all the healer knew, she went to another, and another. She found that she had the healing knack; her large hands were gentle and warm, and she had a gift for looking into the bodies of others and seeing their hurts and imbalances. She also discovered that the Jotun healers in different places had similar knowledge, but each possessed some skills or lore that was unknown to the others. Sometimes it had been learned from their teacher, and not always completely; some spoke of lost lore that had slipped through their fingers.

After a time, she made a decision: she would dedicate herself to collecting all the healing lore of the Jotnar that she could find, that it might not be lost to the vagaries of time and Death. To this end, her life became a series of apprenticeships that moved further and further afield from her home in the northern mountains, eventually taking her out of Jotunheim completely. She studied with hedge-witches in the western islands, and—for a week—with Ran beneath the waves, who taught her about dampness and moisture in the body. She studied with snow-frosted healers in the Niflheim caves, learning about teaching the body to bear up in the cold. She studied with troll-women in the Iron Wood, who knew a great deal about how to heal a deformed body and help it to compromise with the world, and also the healing uses of shapeshifting. She learned about bloodlines and their diseases from Hyndla, the Hag of the Northern Mountains; about herbs and their growing from Gerda, the daughter of her mother's old friend Aurboda. She studied with healers in the fiery land of Muspellheim, their hands soot-blackened with ash, for none knew better than they how to deal with burns and fevers. Eventually, she met and became friends with Sinmora, the Lady of Muspellheim, who taught her about healing with heat and the warm steam-room.

Her travels even took her down into the caves of Nidavellir, where she learned from a Duergar healer-man who excelled in setting bones and doing surgery. She then traveled westwards out of the lands of the Jotnar and into Vanaheim, where she studied with a Vanir healer who knew much about the nourishment of the body. It was there, in Vanaheim, that she met another fellow traveler far from her home, studying with the same teacher: an Asa woman named Eir, who was a handmaiden to Frigga, the queen of Asgard.

The two met eye to eye with the kind of excitement that comes only from knowing a kindred spirit. Within an hour of meeting, words were spilling from them about the many things that they had learned, about their passion for the arts of healing. They both moved quickly through the skills taught to them by the Vanir healer, but both delayed leaving for their homes immediately, because they were too busy sharing with each other. Day after day folk would smile to see the tall, broad, plain giantess and the short, slender, plain Asa woman animatedly discussing some bit of lore about livers or lungs, or whether the gland of light that lies behind the eyes is more developed in the Alfar than in other races, or some other such subject that no one else could decipher, or cared to.

All during this time of travel and learning, though, Mengloth still kept watching Svipdag. When she would fall into her bed, exhausted at night, she would touch his life gently once more before falling asleep. When she had a moment of peace during the day, she would go into trance and see where his life was leading. She watched him struggle to impress his father, to become a hero and a warrior, to do battle first with his fumbling hands and feet. She watched him try to learn the arts of weaponcraft until he wept with the frustration of it, saw the repressed laughter and pity in the eyes of the friends who reached out and tried to help him, saw him shove his mother away when she tried to comfort him. Rarely did more than a week or two pass without Mengloth seeing him, wanting more than ever to reach out and speak to him, to be more than a ghost that rode along. Even being his ghost, though, mended her loneliness somewhat.

Yet somehow she missed certain things, adventures that flew by while she had her head deep in her studies...or deep in her conversations with her new friend Eir. So it was that she was taken by surprise when she found him holding the hand of a pretty young island-giantess who was already showing with child, and them both standing before the intimidating Groa and her star-hero, telling them that they wished to be married. Mengloth felt as if she had been struck beneath the ribs with a great club. She watched, frozen, as Groa dropped the bones to read their omens. "Not good," the old giantess muttered, "but not so bad either, if you've already gone and done the deed and there's no helping it."

She did not stay to watch them be wedded, or—her mind shied away from it—the wedding night, even if the girl was too swollen with child by then to give much pleasure in bed. Instead, she went back to her apprenticeship with new intensity, nursing a wounded heart. She did not blame Svipdag—how could she, when he did not even know of her existence? She was too sensible a girl for that. *You could have gone to him before this,* a nagging voice in her head kept whispering. *You could have shown yourself to him, and perhaps you would be standing there now, in front of his mother and father.*

No, she gritted back; *how could I tell a young man that I have been spying on him since childhood, using him like a storybook that always tells a new tale, to salve my loneliness? Besides, what if he spurned me? That would be the far worse fate. No, let him have his young bride and his new family, and let me have my mission. It's better this way.*

So she buried herself in her studies, and for two years she did not look in on Svipdag, though there were nights when she wept into her pillow from missing him.

It was meeting Eir, the repository of all the healing knowledge of the Aesir—and by extension, much of the healing knowledge of the Alfar, under whom Eir had also studied—that Mengloth's resolve hardened. So much had been lost, had gone into the grave...surely there was a way to recover that, too? There was still one world that she had yet to plunder, and that one lay at the foot of the Tree, and was ruled with iron hand by a Goddess who did not like her Dead to be bothered. *If healing is the enemy of Death,* she thought to herself, *then I must face that enemy at the center of her domain, sooner or later, rather than merely facing it in the countenances of those I am trying to heal.* Yet Mengloth turned it over, night after night, until the day that Eir went back to Asgard. She knew that it was time to leave fair Vanaheim, but she quailed at the direction that her footsteps were to take. Through the winter she lingered, and finally as the spring dawned she forced herself to go back to Jotunheim. From there she passed into Midgard, and her feet eventually found the dusty stretch of the Hel-road.

Many stories have been told about the brave ones who walked living down the Hel-road, including that of Hermod who did it in nine days and nine nights. Hermod, however, had one of the best horses that Odin could supply, and a swiftness spell to carry him along. Mengloth walked the Helvegr on foot, so that she would not lose it, with a stout stick and her pack of herbs and healing-magics over her shoulder. As she passed through Niflheim and saw the sheer black cliffs of Helheim in the distance, the Dead grew thicker on the road, passing her like misty fog packed into shapes with arms and legs. Some were old and wizened, and these did not bother her; they had lived a full life and had gone gladly into Death. The war-dead did not bother her so much either, as they had chosen their deaths. It was the young ones taken by disease, especially the children, that made her weep. Once she saw a ghost of a tiny child, its body swollen from the poisonous bite of some creature, toddling along in the mist. She dropped to her knees in the snow to weep at the sight, for she knew both the poison and its antidote.

She passed over the golden bridge of knives, her head held high, and found her way blocked by its guardian. "What business have you in the Land of Death, you that still breathe?" Mordgud asked her, but the armored woman's voice was gentle.

Mengloth lifted her head and breathed the cold air deeply. "I have come to learn from the healers of my ancestors, who have passed Hel's Gate," she said. "If they will speak to me...and if the Mistress of this realm will allow me...then I would bring their knowledge back to the Nine Worlds."

Mordgud smiled, but it was keen wry smile; without much pleasure in it, but with a good deal of respect. She stood aside to let Mengloth pass, but then commented to her retreating back, "Just remember, healer-woman, that we here are not the enemy you battle." Mengloth turned back, startled, but Mordgud had gone up into her tower to await the next gaggle of ghosts.

The giantess moved toward the great dark wall with slow steps, fearing at the last moment that the gate would not open for her, but it did. As she passed through it, chills ran up and down her spine, and a cold wind passed through her, strangely colder even than the snows of Niflheim which she had just left. Indeed, the air here was warmer; she stood on a carpet of autumn leaves looking at a road that wound through an orchard laden with fruit. It looked mouthwatering, but Mengloth knew enough not to taste of it. She followed the road, not sure where to go. It arched over a small bridge, and as she came down the other side, she saw an etin-woman standing in the road, waiting for her.

The woman was not as tall as Mengloth herself, but her presence loomed as huge and dark as the gate that she had just passed. She was clad in simple black, and one side of her face was that of a lovely woman, with long fair hair trailing down her shoulder. The other side was a skull with scraps of flesh clinging to it, and an odd light in the empty socket. One skeletal hand clutched her dark mantle around her, and she regarded Mengloth silently.

The giantess paused, swallowed her fear, and then came forward to kneel before Hela briefly, touching the ground at the hem of that black robe that seemed to blur into the autumn leaves. She stood again, and called the Queen of the Dead by the title that most Jotnar were taught to speak of her. "Your Ladyship. I have come to beg a boon of you."

Hela regarded her without expression, unmoving. The cold wind picked up and whistled the leaves around the shivering giantess. "And why should I grant any boon to one who has declared herself to be my enemy?" she asked, finally. Her voice was low and husky, not loud at all, yet it chilled Mengloth more thoroughly than the wind.

"It is my job to fight death, when I am given to do a healing," Mengloth faltered. "If I did not do so, I would be doing a disservice to those who have come to me."

The wind settled down a bit. Mengloth noticed that it did not disturb Hela's robes or hair in any way, merely fluttering the dried leaves around her. "No matter how great your skill," the Lady of Death said, "there will be times when you cannot heal those who come to you. If you cannot help them, and their lives have become one great round of suffering with no joy left to them, can you grant them mercy?"

Mengloth shivered again, but not from the chill wind. "No, Your Ladyship," she said in a low voice. "...Only you can do that."

"And the evil spirits of disease that you would cast out of a suffering body?" Hela asked. "When you slay them, into whose hands do they pass?"

"Yours, Lady," Mengloth whispered.

"A true healer, then, would see me as a partner in their work," Hela said. "One who would take over when their skill failed. Who would gather the suffering soul to their breast when there was no more earthly remedy to be had."

For a moment, Mengloth was as still as the figure before her, and then she slowly dropped again to her knees in homage. "You are right, Your Ladyship," she said. "You are not my enemy, and I have been wrong to treat you as one." Her head touched the dust and dry leaves. "I suppose that this is the wisdom that I came here to get, though it is painful. I thank you for that, then."

One skeletal hand reached down and took her by the shoulder, hard like a grip of steel, and drew her to her feet. "Let us be partners, then," Hela said. The bony hand withdrew from Mengloth's shoulder and uncurled like five strings of lightly clacking beads. The giantess took the dead hand in hers, head bowed. "There are those who would speak with you," Hela said, and pointed to the distance. A great lake lay there, mists rising from its waters, and there was an island in the center. "Go to them," the Lady of Death said. "You have until the cock crows at sunset to learn all that you can." She turned, then, and limped slowly away. Mengloth's first instinct was to do something to aid her limping foot, then she saw the skeletal toes beneath the hem of the black robe, and bit her tongue and said nothing.

She went to the water's edge, but there was no boat. Dead faces swirled beneath the surface of the water. Hesitantly, she stepped forth onto the lake and found that the water would bear her up, like shifting sand. Carefully she walked across its haunted waves, until she reached the shore.

A row of old giants and giantesses stood there, bones braided into their hair, faces wizened or smooth or lumpy, holding their bags of root and stone and herb in their hands. Holding out their wisdom to her. They converged on her, babbling, as she set foot on the shore...and then she realized that it was already late in the afternoon here in Helheim, and the sun was slanting lower in the sky. There was no way she would be able to hear them all, not when what they had learned might have taken them years to master. Realizing this, she burst into tears.

The ghosts drew back, and one old woman patted her on the arm, comforting her. Mengloth blinked through wet eyes and watched as the old woman picked up a stone and began to mutter to it. The stone glowed for a moment, and then the glow faded away. The other ghosts began, similarly, to seize stones from the rocky island beach and speak to them. The first old hedge-witch held the stone out to Mengloth. "I put my knowledge in this stone for you," she said in a voice like the faint rushing of winter winds heard through stone walls. "Take it with you, and it will speak to you." The giantess held out her shawl, and the stone was dropped in. It was not a small stone. The others followed, stone after heavy stone, until she was weighted down with the great burden of centuries of knowledge.

The bag of her shawl was so heavy that her feet sank into the water up to the ankles as she crossed back over. She left Helheim by the main gate, bent like an old woman under her burden. It took her many days to pass through Niflheim, sometimes carrying her heavy burden and sometimes dragging it behind her. When her shawl wore through, she wrapped them in her cloak and kept going.

In Midgard, a human with a horse and cart took pity on the poor woman and offered to let her ride in the back, but when she heaved her bundle of stones aboard, it broke both axles on the cart, and she wept and apologized, and continued to drag them down the road. By the time she reached Jotunheim, her cloak had worn through and she continued with the stones wrapped in her skirt. The idea of throwing away a single one in order to lighten her load did not occur to her. She had gone to the Realm of Death and back for them, and every one was precious.

Strangely enough, her body did not give out the whole way back. She had always thought of herself as frail, but somehow the great burden, though difficult, gave her strength. When she reached the western mountains that looked out over the ocean, she was ragged and half-naked and filthy, but the muscles of her arms and legs bulged like mountain cliffs, and she strode up the hillside with the fraying skirt full of stone slung over her shoulder like a baby. Her feet led her to Leirbrimir Mountain, named for an old stone-giant who had become so far one with the rock that his great dead body merged and melded with the cliffside. She built herself a hut with a small bed in it on Leirbrimir's jutting brow, around which she placed the stones in a circle, so that they might teach her in dreams.

So it was that Mengloth returned and set up a house for healing. Her fame grew quickly, as folk from many worlds came to her. After a few years, though, she had no peace. Folk harassed her night and day, and would not let her sleep. She crumpled exhausted at night to their pitiful wails, and woke in the morning to their begging, or worse, stolid patience in the face of pain. The women were the hardest; big bellies that needed help with hard birthing, or bleeding that would not stop, or bodies worn out from too many children.

There was also the kidnapping. The first attempt came a year into her practice. As her fame spread, some young Jotun toughs decided that there would be a good deal of *hamingja* in having the greatest healer in Jotunheim as a bride, and decided to take her by force. Mengloth's uncle Fjolsvith intervened and drove them off, but they were quickly replaced by less violent types who tried to wheedle and court her, pushing into her already overcrowded time with patients. She fended them off, but with more and more anger and frustration. When Fjolsvith suggested that she might as well marry one of them, and thus get rid of the others, she laid into him with an angry torrent of words that took everyone who knew her aback. Her uncle pacified her, saying that of course she need not marry if she did not wish to, and that he would continue to protect her from unwanted suitors, if that was what she wanted.

That night, she gave in and let her sight wander once again to Svipdag. She expected to find him home with his wife and family, by their hearthside, but he was wandering through the wilderness, weeping. Her heart was wrenched to see him, but she could not comfort him with arms of flesh, so she concentrated on stroking his head with her invisible hand. Indeed, it did seem to comfort him after a time, and he fell asleep, exhausted, under a tree. It seemed as if his wife had thrown him out, and he was once again homeless on the road.

The next day a whole family of Duergar came to her for healing. It was unusual to see Duergar who had traveled all the way from Nidavellir to see her, but her fame had spread, and their own surgeons could do nothing for them. They were all suffering from a twisting of their bloodlines, passed down from one to the next. While she could not change their blood, she worked hard on them, teaching their bodies to compensate for what worked wrongly. It took several days, and more than once Fjolsvid had to be called in order to keep away various interruptions. When it was done, the patriarch of the Duergar family bowed to her and thanked her. "I was going to pay you in gold," he said, "but there is not enough gold in Nidavellir to equal the gift you have given us. Instead, I think that a better gift would be to build you a place where you could work in peace."

Mengloth smiled gratefully. "That would be a wonder of a gift, indeed," she said. So the Duergar took their leave, but returned in the spring with a whole crew and began to tunnel and carve out the mountain. They built Mengloth a mountaintop fortress to awe those who saw it from below, all towers and peaks and gargoyle-carved overhangs, unlike the rougher and more natural Jotun fortresses. Leirbrimir's stone bones were quickly shaped into a work of art, an edifice of twisting spiral tunnels that opened onto bright, airy rooms with large windows and open courtyards, hidden from the eyes that might spy. They forged a great gate of wrought iron in the form of twining vines, which Fjolsvid called Clanging Thrymjol. Mengloth's uncle was much impressed with the dwarf-made fortress, and jokingly called it Gastropnir, or Guest-Crusher. "It will certainly make my job as your gate-guard much easier," he laughed. Mengloth laughed as well, and after awhile took to using his name for the place out of habit. Leirbrimir's Mountain, however, soon began to be named Lyfjaberg by the locals—the Mountain of Healing.

A year after she had thanked the Duergar building team profusely and seen them on their way, they returned again, this time with a strange visitor. The slender Jotun man who had hired them was flame-haired and green-eyed, and bowed before Mengloth with a flourish. "May we have the hospitality of great Guest-Crusher, milady? I would speak to you of important matters."

"The sons of Solblindi are always welcome here," Mengloth said, "but who are you, stranger, and what is your errand? For you do not look in need of healing."

"I am called Laufey's son, among other things," he said, "and I come on an errand from my godmother, whom you know well—Sinmora, the Mother of Muspellheim." He smiled his three-cornered smile at her. "I believe that you have visited my daughter as well, healer-woman. That must have taken courage."

Mengloth drew in her breath and quickly ushered Hela's father into her hall, followed by the swarm of Duergar, who she sent to the kitchen with orders to give them whatever fine food and drink was to be had. Loki she led into the great open courtyard where she did many of her healings, and bade him give her news of Sinmora.

"She is well and dancing in the coals still," said Loki, "but she would ask of you a boon. I have made for my godfather and my godmother a great weapon; perhaps you have heard of it?"

"Laevateinn," said Mengloth. "Of course we have heard of it. Surt will wield it only if Ragnarok comes, may the Nornir stave it off! What has that to do with me?"

"Sinmora fears for it, where it lies in Muspellheim," Loki said. "Do not ask me why; that is not mine to tell. She wishes to find a new home in which to keep it, one which will not be stormed. And you have this lovely new impenetrable fortress, thanks to the sons of Solblindi." He waved his hand around, taking in all the curving stonework. "If you will guard her treasure, I will build you a special hall for it that cannot be melted away.

Sinmora says to tell you that it will provide enough heat on even the worst winter days to aid suffering ones whose bones are chilled, or who need to be sweated."

"For Sinmora, of course I will do this," Mengloth said, and so it was done. The Duergar set to work the next morning and built a hall with a floor of burnished gold, which was named Lyr, the Hall of Heat. In the center was an iron box melted to the floor, with no lid or opening, with Laevateinn safely within it. Even enclosed like this, its heat was such that the floor an inch around the box was almost molten. Water could be poured on the floor near the door, and hot steam would spring up. Lyr heated the entire hall in winter, making it comfortable for everyone inside.

In the middle of the night, Mengloth woke with a cold feeling in her belly. She knew, somehow, that Svipdag was in danger. With her heart beating like bird's wings, she tried to calm herself and find him. His eyes were closed when she moved behind them, and there was a terrible stillness and pain in his body. Moving outside of him, she saw him battered and bleeding, near death. His wounds had become unwholesome, and she cursed herself that she was so far away. *If I was there, I would know how to treat him, and he would live,* she mourned, and beat at the air with transparent fists. She screamed at the women who surrounded him, tried to call out what herbs should be used, what should be done, but they did not hear her. She wept in frustration, waving her useless arms at the fallen Svipdag, but they could not touch him.

Then, suddenly, she became aware of an etin-woman in the room who had not been there a moment ago, staring her right in the eye. "Who are you," the woman demanded, "that you are so concerned for my son?"

Mengloth belatedly recognized Groa, Svipdag's mother—but the etin-woman had never been able to see her before! "I am Mengloth," she said, startled, and then almost lost her tongue in shyness, but Svipdag's dire condition spurred her past caring. "I know how to heal him, but I am far away! If I cannot make them hear, he may die!"

"He will certainly die," said Groa sharply, "and I will not have that, not my boy. I shall make those foolish geese listen." She lifted a pot from the wall and flung it at the women, and they scattered shrieking as it smashed onto the floor. Mengloth wondered why Groa did not simply call out to get their attention, and then she knew why with a cold sinking feeling in her belly. Svipdag's mother was dead. Recently dead, from the look of her. Whatever calamity had killed the star-hero had also slain his wife, and nearly slain their son. This was her ghost, come back to save her boy once more.

Groa lifted her arms and with an effort of will, made herself visible to the women in the room. They cried out, but did not run—one of them, her niece, flung herself on her knees and asked her aunt what could be done for her son. Mengloth hurriedly imparted the directions, and Groa translated them, a ghostly apparition in the air. Mengloth wondered why the dead woman could make herself visible when she, still alive, could not—but put it down to the strangeness of being dead but not yet having walked the Hel-road. Sighing and exhausted, she returned to her limp body, satisfied that her beloved would be safe.

She kept an eye on him, even though it had to be only quick glances— the ghost of Groa still hung often about her son's bedchamber. When he became well enough that he could see her, his mother told him that he ought to seek out a bride. "Why, what bride should I have, Mother?" he asked the shade in surprise.

"Mengloth, of Lyfjaberg mountain, ought to be a fair bride for my son," she told him, and then faded away. Mengloth, who was surreptitiously watching, nearly fell back into her own body with surprise.

Svipdag snorted. "I am no hero," he said, and then burst into tears. "I could not even save my mother and father when they were attacked. I should be dead, along with them! I am a worthless son, and I cannot win some famous giantess. With what? I am no good with any weapon, nor have I wealth, or land, or even a glib tongue." He sighed, and Mengloth's heart plummeted. "No, I'll wait until some troll-wench living in a log will have me; it's all I can aspire to." And he rolled over and wept himself to sleep.

At this point, Mengloth retreated in sorrow and did not go to him again. The walls of Gastropnir seemed to close her in, but she threw herself into her work and determined to forget about him, Svipdag, unknowingly her oldest friend. She was unable to forget him, though, no matter how hard she tried—and he, in turn, was unable to forget the name that rang through his mind. *Mengloth*. Again and again, he found himself whispering it. On his own, he began to ask folk what they knew of her, the healer of Lyfjaberg Mountain...and the more he heard, the more he felt driven to find her and woo her.

This is ridiculous, he told himself, but his mind came back again and again to the ghost of his mother, hovering beside his sickbed and telling him that Mengloth should be his wife. *I know nothing of her...but why do I feel as if I know her?* Finally he decided that the only thing for it was to do what he had always done: consult his mother about the matter. He hunted up an old spell for raising the Dead, burned a few bits of her hair left in a comb, and dragged her spirit out of Helheim to answer his questions.

Groa came to him, of course—he was her favorite son—and she begged nine days with him from Hela, who granted it. During those nine days she taught Svipdag nine charms to make something of a hero of him. He had never shown any aptitude for magic before, but he threw himself into learning those nine charms with all the will in his body. Then he set off for Lyfjaberg, to win the hand of the mysterious Mengloth through whatever means he could.

Mengloth, in her turn, was eaten up with impatience. She paced the halls of Gastropnir, shredding the hems of her gowns in her nervousness. Strangely enough, the closer he drew to her, the less easy it was for her to sense him, until she cast her aura around frantically and could no find him at all. It almost made her panic, and she spent a sleepless night... but the next day one of her women noted that there was a strange youth outside chatting with Fjolsvid.

The giantess sat bolt upright. "With Fjolsvid! How long has he been there?" She flew to the window, but the pair had moved under the eaves and she could not see them.

"Quite a long time. They've talked a great deal. It could just be a client," the healer-assistant said helpfully. "Fjolsvid tends to interview them rather severely. And they've been there talking for an hour." All Mengloth's household, by now, knew the gossip that Aurvandil's youngest son was coming to court their rather reserved mistress who had turned down so many others, and that for once she was not disinclined to the idea. Various romantic stories were circulating about it, although Mengloth thought privately that none of them even came close to the reality of the situation.

Mengloth dropped back into her chair, trying not to shake. At that moment she heard Clanging Thrymjol open, and Fjolsvid's heavy tread up the stairs. Her hands clenched on the arm-rests. Fjolsvid's large head peered around the corner. "There's a young man here who claims to be Svipdag, m'dear," he laughed.

She glared at him and said between her teeth, "If you are joking with me, Uncle, the next time you need stitching up, I shall pour hot sauce in your wounds. No, actually, I shall rip your eyes out."

"I'd make a poor gate-guard then, wouldn't I?" he grinned at her, not in the least put off by his niece's sudden fit of venom. "No, dear, it's who he says he is himself. How was I to know? The young fool kept beating around the bush, asking all sorts of foolish questions, giving all sorts of odd names. I almost set the dogs on him," he added cheerfully.

Mengloth was still for a moment, and then she bolted from her chair. Fjolsvid's grin grew wider as he heard her feet take the stairs two at a time.

In the entrance to the main hall, she skidded to a halt, seeing herself in the polished reflection of a silver bauble. Her hair was pulled back severely, but with straggling wisps escaping; there were dark shadows around her eyes from sleepless worry; she was clad in her usual rumpled gown with her favorite jangling mess of mismatched necklaces. Not the sort of fair maiden Svipdag was used to at all, she supposed. Not a fair maiden at all, really. The wind went out of her entirely. She patted at her hair, and then slumped, giving up. This was ridiculous. He would take one look at her and make vague excuses. She knew Svipdag; he would not court a woman just for her wealth or standing. He was too much of a romantic.

So, she told herself, *get it over with. You've waited this long; even with the worst outcome, you'll be able to get some sleep and get on with your life.* She squared her shoulders and rounded the corner. *Why was it easier to walk through Hel's Gate?*

A young man stood in the entryway, looking around at the Duergar-wrought carvings with blinking eyes. He was taller than she thought he would be—*of course, you were either hovering over him or seeing through his eyes, not looking up at him*—and his hair was even more of a bird's nest than her own, and his clothes even more rumpled. He looked up when she arrived, startled, then his eyes turned inward with a look she recognized as panic—the panic that happens when one realizes that all one's carefully rehearsed lines have completely flown out of one's head. It was probably the same look that she had on her own face. "Milady—" he began.

"Don't." She cut him off with a gesture. "I know why you're here. It's because your dead mother told you that you ought to have me as a wife."

He blinked again. She clasped her hands to keep them from reaching out to him. "Are you a seer, Lady?" he asked.

"...No. I am only a healer. But I know who you are."

He collected himself and bowed to her. "I am Svipdag, son of the Star-Bright one Aurvandil—"

She cut him off again. "I know all that. I've been waiting for you for twenty years." She realized how mad that must sound, and suddenly buried her face in her hands. "Oh, this is ridiculous! I suppose I ought to explain, but I expect you wouldn't believe me—"

She felt her hands being pried from her eyes, to be clasped in his. Chills ran up her arms at his touch. "You need not explain, Lady. The Norns have decreed that we two are to be together, or so my mother said, and she ought to know, being on the wrong side of Hel's Gate." He grinned at her, his lopsided grin, and added, "I'm only glad that you didn't set those dogs on me. Not every etin-maid accepts her fate so reasonably."

Mengloth swallowed. "We have always been together," she whispered, "though you knew it not." Five ways of explaining it to him ran through her head, and she dismissed them all in favor of falling into his arms and onto his lips. To her great relief, it didn't seem awkward at all.

On their wedding night, after they had taken joy in one another and Svipdag had fallen asleep, Groa appeared one last time. She rested a hand on her son's brow and smiled. Mengloth opened her eyes and saw her mother-in-law, and spoke up, no longer frightened of the sorceress, alive or dead. "Why did you prepare Svipdag to take me like a city in siege," she asked, "when you knew that I would have done anything to bring him to me?"

Groa smiled in the dark, showing her white teeth. "Because I know my son," she said. "Because I know boys, which you do not, living here in this house of women. If a boy wins a girl too easily, her surrender is of no value—whereas if he thinks that he has conquerered her, he feels more secure and is more likely to stay. All that I did, I did to bring you two together...after a lifetime of you following him around."

Mengloth started, and flushed, and Groa chuckled at her in the dark. "Yes, yes, I knew about my son's little guardian spirit, although for the longest time I knew not who you were. I was glad of you, though, because I knew that he would need a guardian spirit. Take good care of him, now that you have him."

Her arm tightened around her sleeping husband. "The best," she said.

"Then the best is what I wish you," said Groa, and vanished into the night. Neither Svipdag nor Mengloth ever saw her again, but sometimes the hair on the back of Mengloth's neck would stand up, and she would look around, but see nothing. Svipdag himself gave up his attempts at being a hero, and settled for being a husband, at which they both discovered, to their mutual delight, that he excelled. And if the fragile artworks of Gastropnir had to be placed at a greater height, or tied to their shelves, Mengloth never voiced a word of complaint.

Mother of Gods

by Laure Gunnlod Lynch

estla hummed gently as she reached down into the cradle that held her newborn triplets. Her shining cascade of snow-white hair—as white as the soft fur that lined the cradle—spilled down over her shoulders to tickle the pink faces of the tiny boys who gazed up at her, their blue eyes as sharp as the sky on a winter morning. Such clarity would have been shocking if they had been ordinary infants, but they were not. These were her three sons by Borr, her strong, handsome husband who was not like any other Jotun man she had ever known, and who many believed was not truly of their kind at all but the first of some new race. Her scrying had told her that from his seed would come three great ones, the three who she now bent over to snuggle and kiss, one by one.

In return for her caresses, the middle child, with snow-white hair like her own, grabbed at her finger. The eldest, whose hair was a cross between the flame-red of his father's and her own mother's white-gold, tried to grope for her breast, thinking it was time for a meal. The youngest, whose hair was all flame, grabbed a handful of her hair and yanked hard. But Bestla only laughed lightly and, turning away from the cradle for a moment, picked up the wooden bowl of water she had set on a nearby table, along with a fresh-cut birch twig.

Then she turned back to her boys, regarding her youngest first. "You have the fiery hair of your father, my child, and from the sparks in your eyes, no doubt his fiery temper as well. And yet I can see that you will also have a mischievous sense of humor. You will bring joy and laughter wherever you go; yours is the power of the fires of the hearth, yet those very flames can become the fires of destruction if allowed to rage out of control." Lightly, she used the birch twig to sprinkle him with a few drops of water. The baby laughed. "You are Lodurr, for you will bring your warmth to all that you touch. And you are also Ve, for even by your mischief you will prove to be the salvation of your kin and their means of survival—when you are not also their undoing."

She turned her attention to her middle child. "You are snow-white like me, my child, and I suspect you have also inherited my will, which is as strong and hard as ice. The powers of water are yours, to shape and to give form to all that you touch, and yet you must take care not to let those powers flow away from you—or worse, dissipate and turn to steam. You will always live in the shadow of your two brothers and your other kin, and yet your gifts are indispensable. You are like the ice of Niflheim that met and interacted with the hot steam of Muspellheim in Ginnungagap at the beginning of all the worlds. You are the medium that allows creation itself to occur." Gently, she sprinkled him with water. "You are Hoenir, for your role in shaping what will come, but you are also Vili, for your spirit is strong and will become the unseen backbone on which your brothers depend."

Finally, she turned to her oldest child, who met her gaze with something alarmingly close to a challenge in his startling blue eyes. "You have eyes of flame, my child," she spoke softly. "Blue flame that cuts like a sword. They mirror the brightness and wildness of your soul. The skies will be yours, and the winds, and all the powers of air and mind and consciousness. You will be the brightest of the bright and the highest of the high, but you will also never hesitate to descend to the darkest depths to accomplish your aims. I see a great wyrd for you, but also a terrible one. You will sacrifice yourself for wisdom again and again, and will be despised by many who have gained the most from your gifts. You will be lord of your brothers, and yet ever on the outskirts of your clan. The wild blood is strong in you, my son, the warg blood that will sing in your veins and make you long for the wild, cold places from which you sprang, here in Niflheim. You will dwell in all worlds while belonging to none and bestowing gifts on all. You will fight tirelessly for the preservation of those who have no love for you and who trust you little better than a common outlaw. And yet you will rise above them all." With a wave of the twig, she sprinkled him. "You are Odin, the frenzied one, the ecstatic one. Your gifts are inspiration and madness alike, and many more will hate and distrust you than adore you for them. Yet you are also Will and Holiness, for you combine in yourself the gifts of your two brothers as well as your own. I love all of my sons, but of the three you are the greatest. And my heart tells me that you are also the one for whom I shall most often weep."

But by now, all three boys were yawning and blinking, ready for sleep. With a smile, Bestla tucked their coverlet of white fur around them, as somewhere in the snow-capped mountains, a lone wolf began to howl.

Gunnlod's Tale

(as told by Bragi to Elizabeth Vongvisith)

unnlod was the daughter of Suttung, famed far and wide even as a young maiden for the loveliness of her voice. She could sing with such power and passion that her listeners felt moved to tears by sad ballads, or laughed heartily at jesting tunes, or longed to commit brave deeds when she sang heroic songs of days past. Those passing near the windows of Suttung's great house often paused, smiling, to listen as her songs came to them from inside the walls of her home. However, Suttung's daughter herself was seldom seen.

Gunnlod was not particularly fair—she was actually rather plain-looking—but Suttung kept her carefully hidden from all but their kinsfolk and closest retainers. He loved Gunnlod dearly, but that love was tinged with possessiveness, for she was his dead wife's only offspring and he was very jealous of the company his daughter kept. He chased away those who came calling in the hopes of wooing Gunnlod, and tried to persuade his daughter not to enter into a match with another. "For love is sweet while it lasts, but see how suddenly it can be taken away from you," he would say sadly, gesturing to the empty chair next to his own in their great hall, the chair that Gunnlod's mother had once occupied as mistress of Suttung's household, before illness and fever had taken her life. Suttung had not so much looked at another woman since his wife's death.

"My father," Gunnlod would say, "I am unwise in the ways of the world, and I have no desire to leave you, but I know this: love, no matter how brief, is too precious to deny. You are my beloved father and I respect your wishes, and so I have stayed away from men, but I will yet love when love comes to me." And Suttung would sigh and mutter that his daughter knew not of what she spoke. She did not quarrel with him, but smiled her calm smile and kept her peace.

One day, word came to Suttung's house that his sire Gilling had been slain by a certain pair of dwarves. There was much sorrow and wailing at this news. Enraged, Suttung left his household to seek revenge for the deaths of his father and mother. Before he departed, he said to Gunnlod, "If I do not return, remain here, my daughter, and see to the welfare of our household and our people's affairs. But mark my words, Gunnlod: love is fleeting and leaves naught but sorrow in its wake, and you would do better never to let its snares entrap your heart."

"I will love when love comes to me," Gunnlod said again, "but otherwise, I shall do as you ask, father." Suttung, shaking his head, went away and slew the dwarves who had killed Gilling and his wife, and brought back with him the magical mead of poetry the dwarf brothers had brewed of Kvasir's blood. But while he was away, word got around that Gunnlod held the stead alone, and soon a bevy of would-be suitors formed outside the door, each asking to come in and plead his case to the mysterious woman with the lovely voice, for each was convinced that she who sung so sweetly would make a fine mate. Suttung had not reckoned with this. Gunnlod did not allow them to see her, and her men drove off by force those who were too tenacious to heed her polite requests to leave.

Suttung considered the mead his greatest treasure—after Gunnlod his daughter. He knew that the Aesir would probably attempt to regain the mead from him, and he was sore vexed to hear that the moment he left Jotunheim, suitors had come to try and take her away from him. So he contrived to keep both his prizes far from the reach of everyone. He had a mazelike tunnel built, running into the very earth beneath his house, with a large chamber at the heart of the mountain. He had it lavishly furnished for Gunnlod's comfort, though it could have no windows and no fire, so deep under Hnitbjorg did it lay. He ordered her women to remain with her, and had brought to them food and drink and whatever else they desired, as often as they wished. Here he bade Gunnlod stay and guard the mead herself.

Gunnlod's women wept, for they missed the light of day, and it was cold within the mountain's heart, though the chamber soon warmed a little from the presence of their bodies. But Gunnlod herself did not mourn, and soon her sweet voice echoed round the cavernous chamber and through the long, labyrinthine passages, back up into Suttung's hall. He and his folk smiled when they heard it, and Suttung's heart was a little relieved, for he had indeed felt some measure of guilt for entombing his beloved daughter in that way. But he knew Gunnlod would not sing if she was truly miserable, so his heart was lightened.

So she remained there for many months. At last Gunnlod said that it was unfair to her women to share her exile, and she sent them all back. They were secretly relieved, but continued to wait on her, tending to her needs and bringing her word of the world outside. When they asked her if she was well, Gunnlod would only say, "I am well, and I am waiting," which mystified them. And they whispered among each other how strange it was that Gunnlod sang nearly constantly, filling her prison and the house above it with music. When she was not singing, she refused all visitors, and shut herself up for long hours, and her doings were known to no one.

Suttung himself came to see his daughter one day, when Gunnlod was silent. As he entered her chamber, he saw her sitting on a low stool with a basin of water on the floor before her. She did not notice his entrance, and she sat gazing into the bowl dreamily. He narrowed his eyes, and was about to speak when he heard his name being called from the house far above, and so without saying anything to Gunnlod, he quietly went out of the chamber and back through the long, twisting passages to find out why he was being sought.

"Someone comes here with your brother," he was told by one of his men. Suttung frowned and went out of the hall, his gaze following the man's pointing finger. Two figures were coming down the road that led to his brother's farm—the familiar shape of Baugi, and a stranger. Suttung's scowl deepened. "At least Gunnlod has ceased to sing," he thought, "so that this stranger cannot hear her voice and ask unwelcome questions." But he felt uneasy nonetheless. It was common knowledge that Gunnlod was never seen outside of her father's walls, but Suttung did not know how well known was the existence of the mead in the secret chamber, too. "Make ready for our guests," he told his man, who nodded and rushed off, shouting for fresh ale to be brought.

Suttung went back inside and waited in his chair next to his wife's empty one for the guests to come in. They did so, and Suttung saw that Baugi's companion was an ill-favored Jotun who said his name was Bolverk.

"He has done the work of my nine thralls who were killed, and then some," Baugi said, shrugging. "And so I came here, on my word, to ask you for what he wants in return—a drink of the mead you took from the dwarves."

Suttung started a bit, and his expression darkened. "No," he said, wondering how this stranger knew of the mead of Kvasir. "That I will not give."

Baugi, after a long look at his brother, shrugged again. "I have done as you asked, Bolverk," he said to the other. "I have asked Suttung. I cannot alter his answer." He turned and left the hall. Bolverk the stranger gave Suttung a long look too, which made Suttung even more uncomfortable. Then he turned away. As they left, Suttung saw Bolverk move close to Baugi, whispering urgently in his brother's ear. "That one will cause trouble," he said to himself. And then he paused, for Gunnlod had begun to sing again.

Outside, Baugi walked away from his brother's great hall. He was a man of somewhat more modest means than Suttung, and he had much to attend to on his own farm. "Stay a moment," said the stranger called Bolverk. "I would ask another favor of you."

"I have done what you requested. It's not my fault Suttung said no," Baugi said. But Bolverk was persistent.

"I have heard that you have the means to drill through the very mountainside, to make a way into the tunnel that lies beneath and leads to the chamber where is hidden the mead of Kvasir's blood, and Gunnlod, Suttung's daughter. Will you do this for me, my friend? I should have some satisfaction, after all, for all my hard and earnest work."

Baugi grumbled and wondered how Bolverk knew of that place, but after much discussion, eventually he agreed. They climbed back up the slopes of the Hnitbjorg to a spot where they could not be seen by onlookers below, or from within Suttung's house. Here Baugi, who had helped his brother create the secret tunnel, drilled a tiny hole that led right into one of the passageways. At once, a faint sound could be heard coming from within—a woman singing. They listened to it for a few seconds and then Baugi turned to go.

"So our bargain is concluded," he said, smiling because he thought there was no way Bolverk could make use of such a small opening, and thus he did not feel he had done Suttung any disservice.

"Indeed," Bolverk said, with an answering sly smile that Baugi did not entirely like, but he merely nodded, bade the other farewell, and began to climb down the mountainside. Bolverk waited until he was out of sight, then he shifted his shape—for this was really Odin in disguise. Abandoning his Jotun form, he took instead the likeness of a serpent and wriggled into the hole, dropping to the floor of the passage beneath. There he changed back into his Aesir form, one-eyed and fair of face, and stood on his feet again. It was absolutely dark all around him; Suttung's people carried their own torches in and out whenever they went to visit or tend to Gunnlod. Odin stood still in the blackness and listened.

Suddenly, the music altered; before, it had been a merry May dance tune, but now the mysterious woman lowered her tone and began to sing of love. Her voice was like warm honey, sweet and rich and beguiling. Odin paused. Gunnlod's reputation as a superb singer was well-deserved; even the rumors had failed to do justice to her gifts. Her song tugged at Odin, so that it was with only half his own will that he began to walk in search of the owner of the voice, even though his mind was still focused on getting the magical mead away from Suttung. He wandered for a long time in the darkness, coming closer and closer to the sound of Gunnlod's voice. Finally, he saw a faint light up ahead, and quickening his pace, he came to an archway in the rock. He paused, just outside of the glow of light he saw coming from within.

"Come in, stranger," Gunnlod said quietly. There was a trace of laughter in her voice. Odin stepped forward into the light, and then paused, blinking at the sudden brilliance.

The chamber was spacious, nearly as large as Suttung's own hall far above. Torches lit it so that the interior was as bright as day. It was furnished with much fabulously carved and inlaid wooden furniture—chairs, tables, and a large curtained bed. Gold and silver cups, basins, pitchers and other wares sparkled all around. Elaborate hand-woven tapestries—imported from far outside Jotunheim—hung on each of the four walls, as did an array of fine weapons, obviously well-used and carefully tended. There was a large chest for Gunnlod's clothes, and she herself sat in the center of the room upon a stool so richly inlaid it looked to be carved of solid gold. She was garbed in a fine gown, and her hair was loose, falling down her back in lustrous brown waves. She was rather ordinary-looking otherwise, but dignified, holding herself proudly as she gazed upon the stranger. Behind her, in the shadows against a far wall, Odin saw a cauldron and two plain clay jars, looking out of place among all the fancy trappings, but he knew that therein lay the treasure he sought.

"I have waited for you a long time," Gunnlod said. "Welcome, you who are called Bolverk."

"How do you know me, when your father has kept you hidden from the eyes of men?" Odin asked, moving closer. He drew off the hood that shaded his handsome features. He saw Gunnlod take a swift breath, but her expression did not change.

"I have the seer's gift, to some small degree. I have been here for many a long month, guarding my father's treasure and looking into the future." Gunnlod gestured toward a water-filled basin of silver that sat on the floor nearby. Odin glanced at it, then his gaze went back to the woman. He smiled at her.

"And why have you waited to greet me with welcome instead of with fury?" he asked, nodding toward a sword that hung near Gunnlod's bed. "I imagine you can use that as well as you have used your scrying-bowl—"

"I can," Gunnlod replied coolly.

"—or indeed, your magnificent voice. I heard you sing as I approached, and I was... touched by its beauty."

Gunnlod smiled. "You think to woo me, and so obtain my father's greatest treasure."

"I think to win both his great treasures," Odin said, moving still closer. He was startled by Gunnlod's sudden laugh, a bitter one that brought him up short. She had risen to her feet, and stood as tall as he did. He gazed at her speculatively.

"I know what you desire," Gunnlod said. "Let us be frank. I am unworldly, but I am wise in my own way. You hope to seduce me and win the mead of poetry. I have seen this. I have also seen that you are the only man I will ever love, and that you will leave me, and that my father was right about one thing. Love's absence... is pain." She bowed her head. Odin waited. Gunnlod spoke again without looking at him. "I have foreseen that this meeting will leave me filled with longing for you for the rest of my days. Yet from it, I will obtain my greatest joy. So... ask anything of me, king of Asgard, and I shall grant it. I am willing to pay the price." She lifted her head, and her eyes were proud, and she was not ashamed.

Odin considered. Then he said, "Lady, you have indeed been frank and I would not force from you what you are willing to offer freely, without giving something in return. Therefore, give me three drinks of the mead brewed of Kvasir's blood, and I shall remain here three nights with you as your lover, and whatever else may come of this," he shrugged, "I will not begrudge, nor expect you to begrudge me."

Gunnlod said, "I agree." Then she bade Odin conceal himself behind her curtained bed, and she called for her women and told them not to disturb her for three days and three nights, merely to leave food and drink enough for that time, and that she would call them if she needed their help. They protested, but she said that she would be well, and finally they did as she asked. And Odin remained with her for those three days and nights, and their talk was only of love, and her singing during that time was the sweetest and most beautiful that any had yet heard.

Finally, at dawn after the third night, Odin rose and said to Gunnlod, "I must take my leave of you now. Give me what I have asked for." Gunnlod nodded. Her heart was heavy, but she was too proud to ask Odin to reconsider or to come see her again, and she knew he never would. She led him over to where the mead lay. Odin drank once from the cauldron and each of the two jars, and taking Gunnlod's hand, he squeezed it in farewell, but did not speak. Then he left her without a backward glance, and disappeared into the darkness, hurrying away into the passage to make his escape.

Gunnlod swallowed hard and fought down her tears, and she was about to call her women when her gaze fell upon the now-empty containers, and she knew what Odin had done. She stood quietly for a moment, thinking. Then she opened her mouth and called out to her father that all the mead of poetry had been stolen, but she did not say that her heart had been stolen along with it.

Suttung heard Gunnlod's call, and looking outside, saw an eagle making its way rapidly away from Hnitbjorg. He changed himself at once into another eagle and flew off in hot pursuit, his people shouting encouragement to their lord as he vanished into the sky after the thief. He chased Odin all the way back to Asgard, but could not get in and was driven away by the Aesir. Suttung returned to his home, and upon resuming man's form, he immediately strode down the passage to where Gunnlod sat waiting for her father's return. He was furious, for he knew that she must have allowed Odin to take the mead in exchange for dalliance with her.

"We have lost the mead of poetry thanks to your lover's wiles! What have you to say, my daughter?" Gunnlod was silent. Suttung shouted, "See what love has wrought for you, for our folk! We have gained nothing from this!"

"Not nothing, Father," Gunnlod said softly. She looked calmly at Suttung's angry face. "I am carrying his son, and he will be of our blood as well as the Ill-Worker's. He will be your heir and mine, and he will be called 'best of poets' one day. Is this not compensation for the loss of the mead?" But Suttung would not listen. He was so angry that he forbade Gunnlod to leave her chamber ever again. He set guards to watch night and day at the entrance to the passage, and had the hole drilled by Baugi closed up, and none but her women were allowed to come and go. Suttung himself did not go to visit her again.

Gunnlod was grieved by all this, but she bore her father's decree without complaint, and remained there in her underground room where she had known the embrace of her one love. In time, she gave birth to a son. He was neither physically remarkable nor handsome, but strong and healthy, and though Suttung did not comment on the birth of his grandson, in his heart he was pleased, and his anger toward Gunnlod began to soften. But he still did not relent, and so Gunnlod and her son, whom she named Bragi, remained in the chamber under the mountain.

One day, when Bragi was nearly a year old, Gunnlod waited until her women went away, and she went to the corner of the room where the empty cauldron Odrorir and the jars Son and Bodn lay, dusty and forgotten. From deep within Bodn, she withdrew a small, corked bottle. She had concealed this in various places within her chamber over the long months, and now she took it over to where her small boy sat gazing at her with bright brown eyes.

"Drink this, my son," she said. Gunnlod uncorked the bottle, and from it she fed Bragi the last precious drops of the mead of poetry, which she had been saving from the moment she saw her as-yet-unborn son in her seer's mirror. Bragi drank obediently, and from that day forth, he was changed. He spoke more readily and beyond his years, and the women who waited on Gunnlod marveled at his progress. When he was a little older, he began to learn to sing. Gunnlod, who adored her son above all other things, taught him all the songs she knew, save for the one she had used to lure Odin to her side. That she kept for herself.

One year passed, then another, and seven winters after Bolverk had come to Baugi's farm, the two of them, Gunnlod and Bragi, were still living inside their secret chamber in the mountain. The entire household and many of those outside it now knew that Gunnlod's son was a prodigy and that none of his like had ever been heard in Jotunheim before, for despite his youth, Bragi was already a better singer than even his mother. He was also unusually intelligent for his age, and he delighted in hearing the stories his mother and her women told, and could repeat them, word for word, with very little trouble. Suttung had never been down to see his grandson; his pride would not allow it, but the more he heard of Bragi's skill, the more curious he became. Finally, he told Gunnlod's women to bring the boy up.

Suttung waited in his hall until the young boy was brought before him. Bragi was very pale, for he had never seen the sun, and he blinked, squinting in the brightly lit hall, but he appeared healthy, and his face was so like Gunnlod's that Suttung's sternness slipped a bit as he gazed on his grandson.

"Sing for me, child," he said, and Bragi obediently opened his mouth and began to sing a simple shepherd's tune. His voice swelled the air around him, a high, clear child's soprano, and there was something beyond beauty in it. The folk of the household stopped in their tracks; the birds outside quit singing and gazed through the windows in silence, and even the sun outside came out from behind the clouds in the overcast sky above. The fire quieted its merry crackle, and the wind slowed its creaking of the house. Far below, Gunnlod was likewise silent, listening to her boy sing. Suttung felt his heart swell with affection for the child of his own blood.

"Stay with me," he said, "and gladden my household, for I am growing old and I would like to see your young face here every day."

"But what about my mother?" Bragi asked, and was dismayed to see his grandfather's expression grow stern again.

"She disobeyed me, and she must be punished," was all he said. "But you do not deserve to be punished as well, for it was none of your doing."

"I cannot leave Mother," Bragi said, shaking his head. "I am sorry, my grand-sire." And he turned away and went back down to Gunnlod's hidden chamber.

Suttung was displeased, but he gave orders that Bragi should be allowed to come and go as he wished, and Gunnlod herself bade Bragi to leave her and go into the household now and then, for she worried for her son, growing up in a sunless room underground. And so Bragi spent some of the time with his mother, and some of the time with his grandfather. He was allowed to go outdoors, and was often taken with Suttung or other members of the family on short journeys, and he soon added to his song-hoard and tale-hoard, so that by the time he was twelve, he was the most skilled of storytellers and a singer beyond compare. Older skalds bowed when they saw him, and everyone whispered about Bragi and his mysterious parentage, for few knew who had fathered him on Gunnlod, and the tale of the mead's theft was a closely guarded secret.

Bragi never stopped asking his grandfather to relent and allow Gunnlod to come out of her chamber, but Suttung always refused, more out of stubbornness now than real anger. Then one day, when Bragi was nearly full grown, a stranger appeared at the top of the road leading to Hnitbjorg. Suttung stood gazing out the window with his grandson as the stranger came closer. It was not one of the etin-folk, but a tall man clad in a long, muffling cloak and a wide-brimmed hat.

"There approaches the one who sired you, my grandson." Suttung said stiffly, for the sight of the stranger filled him with anger and resentment. Bragi gave him a startled look. Gunnlod had never told him who his father was, only that he had come and gone and that she did not expect to ever see him again.

The stranger came to Suttung's hall, where he was welcomed, and he identified himself as the father of Bragi. He approached the boy and stood looking at him. Bragi was not very tall, and resembled his mother more than his father in that he was rather plain and unimpressive-looking, but perhaps the stranger saw more in the boy than was apparent on the surface, for he smiled as if well pleased, and his eye glittered under the shadows of his hat.

"Come with me to my land and my own people. I regret that I did not come for you sooner, but I had no wish to rob your mother of her greatest joy," the stranger said.

Bragi considered. "I would not leave my mother a prisoner here, and it is by my grand-sire's leave that I come and go in his household, as I am not yet of age." He turned to Suttung, who sat watching all this with a very sour look on his face. Suttung longed to kill the stranger, whose identity he knew very well, but since the latter was the father of his own grandson, the lord of Hnitbjorg felt that he must refrain, since he loved Bragi well and did not wish to upset him.

"What is your will, Grand-sire?" Bragi said.

"I say that you shall remain here now, but when you are a grown man, you may go where you choose," Suttung said. The stranger bowed curtly to him, and then grasped young Bragi's shoulder.

"Come to me when you are of age," he said. "You will be welcome in my land and have no fear of anyone there." He departed the hall. Bragi went down to his mother's chamber and told her all that had passed. A sad smile crossed her face, but it vanished quickly when Gunnlod saw that her son had noticed it.

"I will miss you, my son, but I think your father is right. You should go to him, at least for a little while, and learn the stories of his folk as well as those of Jotunheim which you already know. I think you would do well to go wherever you can to learn as much as you can, for you are a skald better than any other, and it is only fitting that you know all the tales you can hear." Gunnlod said wisely. And then she told Bragi the story of his own siring, and how Odin had contrived to win both the mead and her love, and left her after three nights.

When Bragi reached manhood, he went to Suttung and said, "Grandfather, I wish to leave your household and go to the land of my father."

Suttung agreed, though he resented Odin's claim over his beloved grandson. "As you wish. You are a man now, and master of your own life."

"There's one thing I would ask of you first," Bragi said. "Let Mother come out of the mountain. Surely your wrath has been appeased by now.

Surely she has paid for giving the mead away to my father. She has spent the whole of my youth below the ground. Let her return and live among our kinsfolk again. I would feel happier knowing that she is not so alone when I go far away from this land and my family."

Suttung frowned. "That I cannot do. Gunnlod my daughter broke her word by acting as she did. I will not allow it." Bragi pleaded, but Suttung would not relent, and eventually he was forced to give up. He went to his mother and said, "I will return, and I will find a way to make my grandfather's heart soften towards you, Mother. Farewell."

Gunnlod smiled at her son. "I am well, Bragi. Go into the world, and see what you shall see, and learn what you would learn, and don't mourn for me." So he left her and went to Asgard, where Odin and Frigga welcomed him into their household. He learned all the stories and songs the Aesir were willing to share with him, and made many more that they delighted in hearing. He became even more renowned for his skill. But Bragi did not forget his imprisoned mother, nor his words of farewell to her. After many months, he returned to Jotunheim and made his way into the land of his mother's kin, and came again to Suttung's house, where he was welcomed as eagerly and warmly as if he had been a visiting king.

"Will you not let my mother go?" Bragi entreated his grand-sire. "She should have long ago been the occupant of that seat," he said, indicating the empty chair next to Suttung's own in the great hall. "She is the lady of this household and the mother of one they are calling 'best of poets.' Surely she deserves better honor than what you have shown her."

But old Suttung was still stubborn, and they argued long, then quarreled bitterly. Finally Bragi said in exasperation, "Then I will take her place, if only for a little while. I am the result of her deed even if I had no part of it, and I should bear at least some of her punishment. Let my mother emerge from her prison for nine days each year, and let me remain instead in that chamber where I was born, if you feel someone must still pay the price for the loss of Kvasir's blood-mead after all this time." Suttung would not hear of this at first, but Bragi was so persuasive that he finally gave in, secretly glad for the excuse, though it pained him to send his grandson down into the hidden room under Hnitbjorg.

Bragi went to his mother and told her to leave her chamber, and that he would take her place for nine days. She likewise protested, but Bragi finally made her go out and she went through the passageway up into Suttung's house, where she was received with joy by all but her father, who would not speak to her.

Nine days Bragi sat beneath the mountain, singing and playing his lute when he was not sleeping, and hardly anything got done within Suttung's household because people were always stopping to listen to that magnificent music. Bragi's voice was deep, rich and mellow as old brandy, so smooth that hearing it was a pleasure even when the words were sung in some unfamiliar tongue. Meanwhile, Gunnlod was allowed free run of Suttung's considerably large dwelling and even ventured outside, where the sunlight warmed her face for the first time in many years.

At the end of the nine days, Bragi came back from inside the mountain. He hoped that his grandfather had been persuaded to relent by being in the company of his beloved daughter once more, but Suttung was as hard as ever, and Gunnlod was made to return to her chamber underground. Bragi was glad that his mother had been temporarily freed from exile, but he was unhappy at his grand-sire's stubbornness, and it was with sadness that he returned to Asgard again.

Each year for many years after that, Bragi would go back to Jotunheim and remain for nine days in Gunnlod's chamber while she went free. He did this without complaint, but eventually word of this curious arrangement reached Odin's ears, and he sent for the skald and questioned him about this state of affairs. Bragi said that it had been his idea, and Odin frowned. "I don't like this. You are honored among my people and your mother's folk and by many others besides, and it is unfit that someone of your reputation and worth should submit to something so lowly."

"Yet my mother has endured it since before my birth," Bragi pointed out, "and you have said nothing of her reputation or her worth."

"True," Odin said matter-of-factly. "Your mother is a good woman, but your grand-sire is a hard man. Is there nothing you can say to persuade him to let Gunnlod go free permanently?"

"I have tried every argument I can think of, but nothing has reached him. He has been unforgiving ever since the mead of poetry was taken from under his very household."

Odin smiled knowingly at that, but rearranged his expression upon seeing Bragi's face. He thought for a minute, while Bragi waited in silence. "Perhaps your grand-sire is not truly angry at your mother at all, but for her," he said at last. "I hear he never took another to wife after her mother died many years ago."

"That is true," Bragi said.

"And has Gunnlod herself never loved another?" Odin asked delicately.

"You know that she hasn't, Father. Besides, how could she, imprisoned and seeing no one but myself and her women for so long? And while she walks free for that short time each year, my father keeps a close eye on her, as he did when she was young." Bragi said helplessly. "I don't understand what you mean."

"I mean that it may not be for pride that your grand-sire has kept Gunnlod locked away for so long, but for sorrow's sake," Odin said. "But I think I know how to persuade him to let Gunnlod out for good. Listen to me..." And Odin began to sing a song Bragi had never heard before. He was surprised, for it was in the Jotun tongue and was not one of the Aesir's. When Bragi had memorized it, Odin said, "You know what to do with this. You may tell your mother that it is a gift, and that despite what she might believe, I have not forgotten her." So Bragi left Odin and spent many long hours crafting new words to go along with the old ones.

When Bragi came to Suttung's house later that year, he again replaced his mother in her imprisonment, and after Gunnlod walked free, he settled himself within her richly furnished chamber and took up his lute. He began to sing a song no one had ever heard coming from within that mountain. It was the story of a woman who had seen her lover in a vision and knew that like the image she saw, her man's love would be fleeting and impermanent. Yet she risked everything for that brief love, nonetheless. And within this song was another, the one which Gunnlod had sung to entice Odin to her side, knowing all the while that he would never stay with her, that she would long for him all her life, and that she was willing to give him both of her father's treasures for the sake of knowing his love for that short time.

Bragi sang as he had never sung before, and his voice swept up through the passages of the mountain like a living thing, carrying the full power of his words to the ears of all who listened. The folk in the household above remained stock-still; some of them were weeping openly. Gunnlod stood staring into the fire, thinking of three days and nights that had brought her true joy, and the even greater joy that her son had given her in the long years after. Suttung listened, and for the first time he understood that his daughter had known all along what he had never realized—that love is precious in itself, and that it is no less precious for being impermanent, and that its loss, while painful, is no cause to deny it. He glanced at the empty seat by his side, and then at his daughter's face as she looked into the flames without seeing them and his old heart softened at last.

When the song ended, a great shout went up from those listening, and Suttung himself went down to the chamber to fetch Bragi up. They returned through the secret passageway to the sound of their kinsfolk applauding and cheering, and Suttung, for the first time in many years, reached out for Gunnlod and brought her close to where he stood with Bragi. He said to her, in front of everyone, "My daughter, I have been cruel. I have punished you wrongly for something I had no right to judge. Will you forgive me? What may I do to restore your love and good faith?"

"There is nothing you can do, Father," Gunnlod said flatly, and for a moment, there was silence. But then she smiled. "I foresaw this, that from my love for Bolverk would come my greatest joy. And that has come to pass, for my son Bragi stands here now—beloved, famed and honored by our own folk and others throughout the worlds. It is he who has managed to free me from my prison and to free you from yours, and so my joy is complete."

Then she turned to face her father squarely, and there was steel in her gentle voice. "I am done with seeing, and now I wish to live my life quietly and freely, in my own way. I will not remain in your household, Father. I will leave this place and go up into the mountains, and there make my home with those of our folk who will come with me." Several people immediately stepped forth to volunteer. "I hope that one day, you will find another to sit where my mother once sat," she added, nodding at Suttung's wife's empty seat. "For that place was never mine, not so long as you were unwilling to let go of her loss." And with that, Gunnlod made ready to depart her father's household, and Suttung did not stop her from doing as she pleased, and he never tried to do so again.

Gunnlod went into the mountains, and her women and some of the men in Suttung's household went with her. And there she still dwells, in a house far above the hidden chamber in the rock where she had known love, and isolation, and happiness. The next time Bragi saw his mother, he told her how he had learned her love-song, and what Odin had asked him to say to her. She did not reply, but smiled her calm smile, and her house was ever full of music after that. To this day, if you travel in the mountains around Hnitbjorg, you can hear her voice, sounding as beautiful as ever. Sometimes if you are lucky, you can hear Gunnlod and her son singing together, and the very wind itself will slow and the birds grow silent as those two voices dance with each other, around and around in the free air of the mountains.

Thor and Jarnsaxa

by Alice Karlsdottir

nce upon a time, when the world was young, Thor the Thunderer, son of Odin, decided to go and see the world, though he was then but a lad. His father could not refuse him, as he well knew the joys of wandering himself; yet he sought to counsel his son in the ways of the world. "Thor, my son," said the All-Wise, "in you rests the strength of the earth and the might of the wind; none in the Nine Worlds is mightier than you; but, you are young, and, I fear, not much given to reflection; it may go harder with you than you think."

"Bah, Father! I care not for thinking, but for deeds. I know you have sought much for wisdom," the lad hastily amended, "but as for me, I would seek my own way in the world."

"That is as it should be; nevertheless, I will give you three tokens to take with you; perchance you may find some use of them when you are in trouble." With these words, Odin All father gave to his eldest son a raven's feather, a wolf's hair, and a flintstone. "Here, carry these with you. If you come into difficulty, take the feather and break it in half; it will bring you aid. If again you find trouble, take the hair and snap it in two; thus will you find help. When in the direst danger, take the flintstone and strike a spark on it. But only use these gifts when you cannot find the way to success by yourself."

Thor took his father's gifts and thanked him; but he secretly felt he would have no need of such magician's tricks. And so, provided with a stout oak staff and a good lunch, Thor set out from Asgard.

To and fro over the Nine Worlds he wandered, doing many mighty deeds and seeing many wondrous sights. And in all this time, he prevailed by his own might and courage, and left his father's gifts in the bottom of his wallet. At last he came to the borders of Jotunheim, home of the Giants, the sworn enemies of the Aesir. "Ha! I am not afraid to venture further!" cried Asa-Thor. "I am not afraid of anything!" (He was, as I have said, yet young.) With that, he picked up his staff and strode down the rocky path that lead through the realm of the Jotuns. Here he did many brave deeds and saw many wondrous sights, and in all this time, he prevailed by his own might and courage, and left his father's gifts in the bottom of his wallet.

At last, he came to a castle on a rocky cliff. It was late in the day, and his provisions were by now running low. "I will venture forth and seek shelter for the night. Jotuns though they are, even they must surely follow the laws of hospitality!" (He was very young.) When Thor came to the door, he found a huge iron knocker, so heavy it would have taken thirty mortal men to lift it; but Red-Beard (although he had but a youth's beard then) lifted it with ease. Once, twice, thrice he knocked on the heavy stone door.

Finally he heard a woman's voice bellow, "Who is it that knocks so loudly on my uncle's door?"

"It is I, Asa-Thor, Odinsson," Thor bellowed back. "I come to seek the guest's right. Open the door, if you dare." The heavy door swung open in a snap, and there stood a fair maiden, tall as an oak and ruddy as red mountain clay, with eyes bright as coals.

"If I dare? I dare anything! I am Jarnsaxa, the Giantess, and I have often longed to see one of the Aesir. Hmm... you are not so handsome as I would have thought," the Giantess went on, heedless of the sparks in Thor's eyes. "Still, you look all right, though your manners are not of the best. I would not be so bold to proclaim my parentage in this house, for this is the home of my uncle, the fierce mountain Giant. He has little love for the Aesir.

However," said the maiden, her voice lowered to a mere shout, "I am not ignorant of how to behave in the world; and, you do look all right. I will let you in and hide you, and perhaps all will be well."

Asa-Thor was loath to hide from the Giant, but he let himself be persuaded by the maiden. She bade him sit to dinner before her uncle came home. She placed before him a roast ox, and before you could blink twice, Thor had eaten half of it; but the maiden ate the other half as fast as he. Then she set before him an oven of beer, and before you could cough, Thor had downed it with one draught; but the maiden meanwhile emptied another oven just as big without so much as a blink. Then she gathered up all of the dishes on one arm and tossed them into the trough so hard that the timbers groaned. By this time, Thor was thinking that never had he seen so fine a girl, and would have said as much when they heard the rumbling footsteps of Jarnsaxa's uncle. The girl was quick to hide Thor under the bed, despite his protestations. She then went to the fire and began to turn the spit.

When her uncle came into the room, he roared, "I smell the blood of the cursed Aesir, the murderers of my kinsmen!"

"Shut your mouth and be quiet, or you will make me spoil my work," said the maid; "What you smell is an old bone that a raven dropped down the chimney this morning."

Then the old Giant called for his dinner, but when he saw how little there was, he roared at his niece. "Be still," she roared back, "for the dogs carried one of the oxen away while I was busy; I have told you not to keep them in the house."

The giant was but ill satisfied, but he once more sat down to the table and called for drink. When the girl brought it, he was vexed even more to see how little there was. "I suppose you will tell me the wind blew the beer out the window! Now I am certain some stranger has been here at my table. You wicked girl, I'll cuff you for lying!" At this moment Thor jumped out from under the bed, for he would not let Jarnsaxa be hit for all the gold in Svartalfheim.

"You need not stir yourself," said Jarnsaxa; "I am used to this ill-tempered old man. He know better than to strike me!"

"Nonetheless, I will let neither man nor woman fight my battles for me," said the young God. "Here am I, Thor Odinsson!" he cried, turning to the Giant; "I am not afraid of you or anyone else in the Nine Worlds. It was I who ate your meat and drank your ale; and such was my right, by all that's proper and good. But this maid is too fair to remain here alone with a cross old man like you; I think it will be better for her to come with me."

"You might ask me first before making plans like that," interrupted Jarnsaxa.

"Would you rather stay here then?" muttered Thor crossly.

"No, I think you are quite right; I am tired of sitting at home and seeing no one but my uncle. It is time I got out into the world a bit."

"I think you both are too much in a hurry; you might both remember that, as head of the family, I must be consulted in such a matter," snorted the old Giant. He was a very fierce giant, but yet he secretly trembled at the sight of Asa-Thor. But he was also crafty, and wise in the ways of magic and deceit, and it was his plan to trick the Red-Haired God and find some devious means of destroying him. "I see no reason for Jarnsaxa not to leave home, but I must know first if you are a worthy companion for her. I will set three tasks for you; if you can fulfill them, Jarnsaxa may go with you; but if you cannot, your head is forfeit."

"Don't bargain with him," whispered Jarnsaxa, 'He's nothing but an old cheat."

But Thor said, "Bring on your tasks! There is nothing I cannot do!" (Ah, he was young, and eager to show his prowess to Jarnsaxa, I fear.)

"It's a bargain then!" crowed the old Giant; and he and the Asa shook hands on it.

The Giant thereupon took Thor to the cellar, where he threw a barrel of wheat and a barrel of barley upon the ground. "There, young stripling; these must be separated, each with its own kind, within the space of three hours, or your head is forfeit!"

Now Thor could perform any feat of bravery or courage, but this task, requiring deftness of hand and cunning, was quite beyond him. As he was brooding over his fate, he happened to think on his father's gifts, and, taking the raven's feather out of the bottom of his wallet, broke it in half as Odin had instructed him. In an instant, there appeared before him the largest raven he had ever seen, with feathers as black as darkest Niflheim and eyes that blazed like the eternal fires. "Who are you, that seem neither God nor mortal?" Thor exclaimed.

"I am neither God nor mortal," said the raven. "I am your father's friend and am sent here to help you out of trouble. What is your will?"

Thor told him then of the impossible task that had been given him. The raven thereupon gave three loud cries, and all birds that fly through the heavens instantly came to his bidding, and one by one they sorted the grains, each with its own kind. Within the space of one hour they were done and gone. "This is surely a wonder!" cried Thor. "How can I repay you?"

"Only this small thing; that I may share your meat whenever you sit to table."

"This seems a small thing indeed," said Thor; "it shall be done!"

When three hours had passed, the fierce old Giant sharpened his axe and went downstairs, prepared to slay his young guest, according to their agreement. But there he found all the grain in barrels, each according to its own kind, and Thor sitting and eating all his store of smoked meat. The giant was sorely vexed, but concealed his rage and pretended to be pleased by the God's success. But then he took him to the pasture, where there were a thousand goats and a thousand sheep wandering over hill and dale. "Separate these flocks, each according to its own kind, in the space of three hours, or your head is forfeit!"

When left alone, Thor made some attempt to gather the animals; but the sheep were too silly to be guided, and the goats were so headstrong that they ran away from him until he huffed and puffed and turned red, and felt most foolish. Suddenly he remembered his father's gifts, and took the wolf's hair from the bottom of his wallet and snapped it in two, as Odin had instructed. In an instant there appeared before him the largest wolf he had ever seen, as grey as slate and with eyes like lightning. "Who are you, that seem neither God nor mortal?"

"I am neither God nor mortal," said the wolf. "I am your father's friend and am sent here to help you out of trouble. What is your will?"

Thor told him of the impossible task that had been given him. The wolf thereupon gave three loud cries, and all beasts that walk the earth instantly came to his bidding, and one by one they frightened and bullied the sheep and the goats into their own flocks, each according to its own kind. Within the space of one hour, they were done and gone. "This is surely a wonder."' cried Thor. "How can I repay you?"

"Only this small thing; that I may share your mead whenever you sit to table."

"This is a small thing indeed," said Thor; "it shall be done."

When three hours had passed, the fierce old Giant sharpened his axe and went to the pasture, prepared to slay his young guest. But there he saw all the beasts in their herds, each according to its own kind, and Thor sitting in the middle drinking all the goat's milk. The Giant was even more vexed than before, but concealed his rage and again pretended to be pleased. "I see you are determined to have my niece, and, so fond am I of you, I shall give you an easy task for the last. All I require is that you pass one night in my bed; but if at any time you feel afraid and flee the room, you forfeit your head!" But the Giant really was planning treachery; for as soon as the young God was asleep, the Giant planned to take his axe and slay Thor in his bed.

But Jarnsaxa, who knew her uncle well, suspected some such trick and alerted Thor to his danger before he retired to bed alone (and sorely he wished he could have slept in Jarnsaxa's bed instead of her uncle's). So before he retired, he took the flint out of his wallet and struck a spark on it. In an instant, there appeared before him a slender and handsome youth, dressed in gay clothing and with wicked green eyes. "Who are you, who seem neither God nor mortal?"

"Well, as to that," smiled the youth; "I am your father's friend and am sent to help you out of trouble. You seem to be having quite a bit of it lately. Well, now, what is your will?"

Thor then told him of his last task, and that he suspected the Giant of treachery. "Right you were to call on me," said the youth; "I know of treachery well, and I can tell you plainly that this Giant means for you never to leave his house alive. Now you must listen closely and do exactly what I say, and it may be all will still turn out well."

"I know well myself what to do with a traitor," cried Thor, waving his oak staff in the air.

"Hold your tongue, you green youth!" cried the youth, stifling a laugh. "This is no time for boldness, although well I know that none can match you in strength and courage. But this Giant is well versed in cunning and magic, and it is not in combat that you can overcome him."

So Thor listened to the youth's direction. He took a large Oak log from the fireplace, and placed it in the bed in his stead, arranging the coverlets so cunningly that it looked as if the Thunderer himself was indeed sleeping on the Giant's pillow. Next, he took from the Giant's dresser a stone, a thorn, and a gold ring, as the youth bade him, and put them into his pocket. Then he took his stout oak staff and hid himself behind the door.

Just as the clock struck twelve, sure enough, there came the Giant through the door, creeping softly in the dark with his axe upraised. When he came to the bed, he dealt such a blow where Thor's head should have been that it would have killed a stone. "Asa-Thor, how fare you?" called out the giant.

But the youth, who had concealed himself under the bed, answered in Thor's voice, "Oh, passing well, passing well; only, it seemed as a gnat landed on my head in my sleep!"

The Giant was well startled at these words, for he deemed Thor to have been dead. "Maybe I did not deal him a hard enough blow; for it is said that he is strongest of all the Aesir," said the Giant to himself. So he raised his axe behind him and dealt a blow three times harder than the first, so that the whole room shook; a mountain would be killed by such a blow. "Asa-Thor, how fare you?" called the Giant, being certain the God was surely dead this time.

But the youth under the bed called out in Thor's voice, "Oh, passing well, passing well; only, it seemed as if a fly landed on my head in my sleep!"

At this, the Giant was quite frightened, for he could not imagine what kind of being could have withstood such a blow; still, he thought to himself, "Well, much have I heard of Thor's strength, not to mention his hard head; but this time, I will kill him surely." And with that, he swung his axe around his head three times, and dealt the bed such a blow, nine times harder than the others, that it would have shattered the World-Tree itself and brought time to an end. "Asa-Thor, how fare you now?" called the Giant.

But the youth under the bed said, "I would be well indeed, if I could but get some sleep in this bed; for if I but close my eyes, these winged insects will be lighting on my face, and the sound of them whirring round my head is enough to drive me mad!"

"Why," said the Giant, turning pale as a corpse, "what did these insects feel like?" For he could not believe Thor was still alive.

"They felt something like this!" cried the real Thor, rushing out from behind the door and fetching the Giant such a blow on his pate with his stout oak staff that the evil old creature was cleft in two. Then Thor and the youth and Jarnsaxa took provisions, and all the silver and gold that was her dowry. Outside, Jarnsaxa had hitched her two goats to a cart, and, jumping inside, they all sped away toward the border of Jotunheim.

They had but gone an hour's journey, when the youth said to Thor, "Look behind us over your left shoulder and tell me what you see."

Thor looked and said, "I see a cloud of dust and many horses coming after."

"That is the kin of the old Giant you slew; they are craving vengeance of us, but we'll fix them." And he bade Thor to throw the stone he had taken from the old Giant's dresser over his right shoulder; when Thor did this, the stone became a tall mountain, which the Giants had to knock down with their clubs before they could continue; meanwhile, Thor, Jarnsaxa, and the youth rode on. But after another hour had passed, the youth said again, "Look behind us over your left shoulder and tell me what you see."

Thor looked and said, "I see a cloud of dust and many horses coming after."

"That is the kin of the old Giant you slew; they have gotten over the mountain and are craving vengeance of us, but we'll fix them." And he bade Thor throw the thorn he had taken from the old Giant's dresser over his right shoulder; when Thor did this, the thorn became a wide bramble-forest, which the giants had to tear up with their fists before they could continue; meanwhile, Thor, Jarnsaxa, and the youth rode on, and they made good use of their time, for they were nearly at the borders of Jotunheim within the space of another hour. But then the youth a third time said to Thor, "Look behind us over your left shoulder and tell me what you see."

Thor looked and said, "I see many horses and riders, fierce Giants armed with sword and club, and they are almost upon us!"

"That is the kin of the old Giant you slew; they have gotten over the mountain and through the forest, and are craving vengeance of us; but we'll fix them for good." And he bade Thor to throw the gold coin he had taken from the old Giant's dresser over his right shoulder; when Thor did this, the coin multiplied into piles and piles of gold. When the Giants saw this, they all halted their journey and began to fight over the riches, so fiercely that they had soon slain each other and not a one remained alive. But one old troll-woman, the mother of the old Giant Thor had slain, was not to be pacified with gold, but kept riding, and almost jumped right into the chariot, had not Jarnsaxa dealt her a blow on the head with one of her massive girdle hooks, which struck the old woman dead on the spot.

"By Asgard, this is the wench for me," roared Thor as they passed out of Jotunheim into the world of men. "I will marry you."

"You are too hasty. I said nothing of marriage," exclaimed Jarnsaxa. "I have long wanted to see something of the world myself, and I am not sure I am ready to settle down. Besides, you and I are from two different worlds, and, while we now have many things in common, someday when you are grown, you will want a queen fit to sit with you in Asgard, and then you would only be ashamed of your Giant wife." Thor protested that such a thing would never be, but Jarnsaxa was firm, and he could see she was determined to go her own way (she was pretty but very stubborn). "Still," she went on, "you grow better to look at hourly, and you are a brave and lusty boy and have besides a fine appetite. I would not mind staying with you for a while, so what I propose is this: we will not wed, but be lovers; and you will go your way, and I will go mine; but whenever I long for you, I will call you from the heart of the mountain; and whenever you long for me, you will call me from the peak of the heavens; and thus, from time to time, we will be together."

This seemed a fair plan to Thor (who was really much too young to be thinking of settling down himself), so they pledged their troth to each other, and spent three days and nights together in the hidden groves of the forest; and at the end of that time, Jarnsaxa took three red hairs from the beard of Asa-Thor and wove herself a ring which turned to the finest red-gold as soon as Thor placed it on her finger. But Jarnsaxa gave to Thor a ring of iron, which he placed on the middle finger of his right hand; and whenever he thought of his fair and lusty Jarnsaxa, the ring gave forth sparks, and Thor would rumble through the heavens to meet his lady.

Then Thor bade farewell to Jarnsaxa, and she to him; and the Red God climbed into his chariot drawn by goats. But he said to the youth who had helped him, "This surely was wondrously done. How can I repay you?"

"Only this small thing," said the youth, "that I may travel with you on your journeys and see the wonders you see; and you shall lend me your strength, and I shall lend you my cunning, and together we will see the world. For," he muttered under his breath, "I think in games of wits, you could use an ally."

"This seems a small thing," said Thor, "and now I begin to see there may be some use for cunning after all, although I do not think it as fine as battle. Therefore, friend of my father, go with me and be my companion; what is your name?"

"My name is Loki, and I think you will never lack merriment nor rest easy as long as I ride in your wagon; I travelled with your father ages before this, and will travel with you, for I can never keep still long." And that is how Loki came to travel with Thor the Thunderer, and also how Thor won the love of the Giantess Jarnsaxa.

But as for Jarnsaxa, she went to live in the heart of the mountain, where she watches over the work of the dwarves, that they do not become lazy again as they were when Odin found them in the beginning of time. She later bore Thor two fine sons Magni and Modi, whom he took to live in Asgard and be his heirs; and ever did the Aesir treat Jarnsaxa with honor and courtesy, as befitted Thor's first love; and ever did Asa-Thor hasten to seek Jarnsaxa when the storm of love was upon him.

Vengeance's Son

*(as told by Rind to Raven. Odin didn't argue with it—
he sighed and said, "Let her have her say; she's owed it.")*

he eight silvery hooves of Sleipnir beat a rhythmic pattern against the clouds as Odin hurtled through them. The air over the northeastern mountain chain of Jotunheim was frigid; he had gone from an Asgard summer to a Jotunheim winter in moments as he crossed the Thund Thvitr, and the tears froze to his cheeks and beard. He wiped them away with a hand that only trembled a little. *Not now,* he told himself. *I am the Lord of Asgard, and there is work to be done, desperate work. I cannot afford the luxury of mourning until it is all over. Let my poor Frigga do that work for me, until I can close myself in my high tower at Valaskjalf and weep and rage for my son. My best, my most beautiful son. No, not now. Think of what lies before you.*

The thinking side of his mind closed out the fresh memory of blood and his wife's screams, the fallen golden figure—*No.* Like a flutter of black wings, thought took over. *There are only a few women of any sort in the Nine Worlds who have the gift of traveling through time. Hyndla, but she is too old, and well guarded besides. That seer in Muspellheim, but she has two husbands who would get in the way. I will not even think about the Hag of the Iron Wood, no, that way lies disaster. Unn, sixth of the nine daughters of Ran...* He spared a warm thought for the pretty mermaid, but then it ran away like water on a stone. Aegir let him get close to his daughters once; that would never happen again. *No, it has to be Rind, Billing's child. She is young enough, unmarried since her last husband died, and she has the Gift.*

Sleipnir's hooves slowed as they came in sight of the great stone hall that was Billing's winter home. Billing would not be there to interfere; he spent the winter in Vanaheim, trading and building up his obscene wealth. Odin had checked in his tower's mirror, just before leaping onto his horse. Still weeping, but scheming already. Scheming desperately. Asgard was in an uproar. For the moment all was mourning, but by tomorrow there would be talk of revenge. No, by tonight, he amended that thought, remembering the red rage in Thor's eyes, even as he wept in a bewilderingly childlike manner. *And he will be expecting it, expecting Thor and Heimdall and all my other sons. For all that he has played the shivering fool in the past, none of them really understand how powerful he is. And he knows them, knows their weaknesses. If he is fighting for his life on his own terrain, he might kill them. Yet only a son of mine can avenge another son... I need a son that no one knows about, and I need him now.*

He dashed the last of the tears from his beard, hoping that his eyes were not too red, hoping that there would be no foolish maids to get in his way, hoping—the thought crept in behind his schemes in spite of everything—that Eir had managed to get one of her potions into Frigga and that the poor woman had been brought to bed. All the work she had done to keep Baldur safe, by Urd's Well... He had not the heart to tell her that it would all be for nothing. He had not the heart to tell her anything about the whole situation. It would have rent apart their marriage. The heaviness of his great secret weighed on his heart like an iron anvil.

The eight-legged horse spiraled down into the courtyard, and Odin leapt from his back, gathering all his power into one great charm. There was no time for wooing, no time for sweetness. And anyway, he had tried that before with Rind, and got nowhere. *Why must it be her, the one whose love I could not win, no matter how hard I tried? Are the Norns laughing at me?* Well, what he could not win, he would take. There were too many things at stake. He could not afford to think of niceties at this moment. The situation was too dire.

As he strode forward, the door to Billing's winter hall opened, and an etin-woman stood in the doorway. Yes, she had seen the shadow of his horse, she knew who her visitor was. There was no time for disguises, anyway. Every minute counted. His hands twitched with the galdr that he was ready to throw, as soon as he could assess the situation.

Rind was tall, taller than he remembered, clearing him by a head. But slender, statuesque. Not one of the usual giantesses who have shoulders that could bring down pine trees and great ham-fists that could crush a man's skull. Her skin was white, with that faint blue cast that those of nearly pure frost-etin blood kept, even when they had been born outside of Niflheim; her features, though not beautiful, were narrow and not bad-looking. Her black hair swept down to her knees, and she was clad in layers of white and grey that fluttered in the winter breeze and emphasized her height and slender body. A movement of her hand, and the breeze was still, at least in the courtyard. "Well met, Master of the Aesir," she said, and there was an ironic tilt to her voice. Odin remembered how damned intelligent Rind was; a brilliant woman indeed. "What brings you here on this day of all days? For surely this cannot be a mere pleasure visit."

"Indeed not," said Odin forthrightly. "I need your aid, Mistress Rind, and the hour is urgent. I must speak with you. Will you not let me in, so that we can discuss it?" The galdr required that he be in her home, with nowhere for her to retreat to. Since she had already proved herself immune to his charm, he tried instead to look honest and straightforward.

She stared at him for a moment, and then nodded. "You may come in, and drink my father's ale, and speak to me," she said, "but remember that I owe you nothing."

"I am well aware of that," he said. He did not smile; there was enough dishonesty in this without that. As he stepped across the threshold, he lifted his hand and traced a rune, and sent it straight at her. It flashed pink for a moment before it found its unwitting mark, and Odin let out his breath as the aim proved true. This, at least, had gone properly.

Her dark eyes grew wide, and she sucked the air into her lungs in a great breath. For one moment, a terrible cramp overcame her, which was the first part of the spell—making sure that her women's parts were suddenly, fully fertile—and then it subsided. She let her breath out hoarsely, and then clutched her hands to her breasts. The second part of the spell was one of desire. It was designed to make her want him between her legs, want that more than anything. Her thin fingers clawed the air for a moment, jerked towards her lap as if to claw at the offending, disobedient parts, and then with an effort of will, she moved them away and balled them into fists. He watched her dark eyes closely; first bewilderment, then realization, then rage. Faster than he expected. She was a brilliant one indeed, with a frightening amount of self-control, he thought with admiration. "You bastard," she gritted out between clenched teeth. "My husband is not a year in his grave, and you would do this to me?"

"The sooner that we get it over with, the sooner you will have your body to yourself again," he said soothingly. "I promise that I will make it a pleasure for you, Mistress. I would not do this if it were not necessary."

"I will fight this," she said between gritted teeth. "I will have my servants cast you out, and then there will be an end to this!"

He shrugged. "You can try," he said. "But did you think that I would throw a geas on one such as you that would end with me merely out of sight? No, it would overpower you and you would come crawling to Asgard, begging. You don't want that humiliation, and frankly, I don't want it for you. You are too good to be lowered in that way. By the end of the day today, it will all be over, and we will be done with each other. That is all I want—this one day. Will you give it to me?"

Her hands clawed at her skirts, and she cast him a venomous look. He marveled at how staunchly she fought a spell that had taken every ounce of his power. Calculations ran through her head; he could almost hear them ticking over. In spite of the screaming in her loins, her head was still cool enough to consider her options. *What a cold woman. Will she stab me in the height of passion, I wonder? She would be one who would be capable of that, I think.* The thrill of the danger ran through him, and did not deter him for a moment.

Finally her breathing slowed, and she lifted her head. "If I go willingly with you," she said gratingly, "I will ask this as my price: Honesty. You will tell me everything, Bolverk. Everything."

Her voice was caustic as she deliberately called him by the name that he had used to seduce poor Gunnlod. Bolverk. Evil-worker. In spite of himself, he flinched. The first stab, he thought, and her aim is also true. "She chose her own way," he said, momentarily thrown off guard. "Her love was real. There was no magic involved."

She growled, deep in her throat, and the wind suddenly screamed outside the hall and battered at the windows. "Honesty," she snarled. "I am no fool, *Bolverk*. I know that your son lies dead on Gladsheim's floor. The birds took that news in a thousand directions as soon as it happened. All of the Nine Worlds know that Baldur travels the Helvegr. I cannot imagine that you came here to take me against my will merely to salve your grief!"

For a moment Odin stood entirely still; he had not realized that he would not be catching her unawares. Then his shoulders slumped. Honesty. At this point, he might as well. "I need a son," he said.

"You have dozens," she retorted.

"I need a son who has not yet been born, who can be trained to kill my son's murderer. A son whom that slayer has not yet met, who will be able to take him unawares. Whose mother can travel through time, so that I can send her away, and at the end of this day she will be able to return with him full-grown and ready to be Baldur's avenger."

Her eyes widened and then narrowed as she realized the full scope of his machinations. "All this to slay a helpless blind man?" she asked mockingly.

He held her eyes with his. "You and I both know that Hodur was only the unknowing tool of someone else." *And this, though it is no lie, this you will not get the full truth of. Let it stay at the point where this will lead you.*

She looked away. "You want a son trained to kill Flame-Hair?" she murmured, shaking her head. He saw how, in spite of herself, her body moved towards him like a magnet. He caught her around the waist and stroked her back reassuringly, and she did not move away.

"It is the only way that I can think of," he said. And then she gave in, and he bore her away to her bed, although her body was tight as stone and she would not kiss him. It did not take long, and he could smell that she had conceived his son. She lay there among her white furs, shaking, and asked him, "I must stay away a long time, then, if I am to raise a son to be his brother's avenger. I may become lost in time. How will I get back?"

"I shall hold your thread," he assured her. "I will not allow you to become lost. This is too important."

Rind beat a fist upon the bed. "My father will be furious," she said. "Perhaps it is best that I am gone until my son is old enough to go to Asgard, and let me be done with this, and with you. But it will be many years, away... Where in the past shall I go?"

"Not in the past," he told her. "In the future."

She gasped and sat up, clutching her robes about her. "The future? But that is unknowable. I cannot travel to the future."

"I can send you," he said. "I have consulted more seers than you can imagine. I know the shapes of many different futures. I will give you the picture of the place; all you need do is to go there. And at the end of the day, I will fetch you back."

Rind stood up, turning her back to him. Her dark eyes, he saw now, were sweeping about her room, planning what to take and what to leave. Her body no longer welcomed him; from its closed-in stance he saw that it was quite the opposite. *Cold woman,* he thought again. *Only such a one could raise a son that could get a jump on Loki. My blood brother, I am sorry,* he mourned to himself, *but these are desperate times. I play many games, and I must sacrifice for the greater good. I must sacrifice my son... and my brother.* The tears threatened to overwhelm him again, but he stilled them in an act of supreme will. *I will not weep in front of this ice-woman whose life I have just ripped apart. That, at least, I will not do. It would be an insult to both of us.*

It was the end of the day for Odin; the sun was setting like a bowl of blood running down onto the fields. Sunna mourned too, he realized; she had loved Baldur. The morning's carnage had given way to the afternoon's work, as many hands toiled to build the greatest funeral boat ever built in his land, out by the shore. The place had seemed deserted when he had returned; all had gone to the coast for the boat-building, and only his wife and her women remained to cleanse and watch over Baldur's corpse. He had given Frigga what moments he could of comfort, hoping that she would not notice, in her grief, that he bore a giantess's scent freshly upon him. Then he had called for Hermod, the only son he could spare, and sent him off to ride the Hel-road, to beg for his brother's life. It was a long shot, and Odin privately doubted that it would work—Hela was too implacable, there was no bargaining with that cold bitch, colder even than Rind—but it had to be tried, if only to show Frigga that he had done everything possible.

He sat on his throne in Gladsheim, staring out over the empty hall; one hand idly stroked Freki's head while the other held tight to an invisible thread—Rind's soul-string. It did not lie quiescent, but jerked and danced like a mad thing; time was running much faster on the other end. He did not wonder what she was learning, there in the future. If he had thought too much about that, he would have considered it unwise to send her, and then the whole situation would be moot. There would be time enough to ask about that, later; to get what he could from her.

The last rays of the sun sank behind the hills, and Odin could see the lights of the procession coming back from the shore. Even with their grief, the people must eat. He slipped off of his throne and went out into the courtyard of Gladsheim, gazed at the twilight sky for a moment, and then pulled on the thread in his hand as hard as he could, praying desperately that it would not snap off.

It did not. One moment he was alone, and the next Rind was there in a blast of cold wind, wrapped in white furs that sparkled with rain. Her dark eyes met his levelly; there were lines around her eyes and she seemed older, more worn. "It took you long enough," she said.

"Is he here?" Odin asked, almost holding his breath. *Had this mad, impossible ploy worked?* "Is he grown and with you?"

In answer, she gestured behind her with a sardonic smile. A youth stepped forward, tall and slender like his mother, but still young—the faintest trace of hair lay on his lip. Tangled black hair brushed his shoulders, and he bore a sword. His face was serious, awed, smudged with grime. "Vali," she said, "this is your sire. I will not call him your father, for he did none of the work of fathering you save for the first five minutes. But you are of his blood, and you exist because he wished you to, so greet him now if you will."

"Mother," the youth protested. "I cannot go among these people in their great hall now! I have just come from the hills, I have not washed my face or combed my hair—they will think me a swineherd fresh from the pens!"

Rind smiled ironically, coldly. "Do not be ashamed, my son," she said. "At least you come by your filth honestly."

Odin stepped forward, exultant. The lad was well-favored, and clearly Aesir, and he had no doubt that Rind had taught him to fight. Perhaps there was a chance that this would work. "My son," he breathed. "Do you understand your purpose here?"

The lad drew in his breath. "I am to avenge my brother's slaying," he said, in a low voice.

"You are correct, my son," Odin replied. "And after that work is done, you have a place with me and your brothers in Asgard forever. I will not shirk my responsibility to you. Whatever life-pension you wish, I will give it to you." He took Vali's arm and led him into the hall, which was filling now with the boat-builders, come back for food and drink. The hall was quieter than normal; people spoke in low voices as they seated themselves. Frigga was up from her bed, seeing to the food and drink, but her face was shadowed and her hair disheveled. "My people!" he cried out. "Attend me! This is Vali, my son, who was born to avenge Baldur's death and slay his killer! Make way and give him honor!"

Across the room, Thor's head jerked up, eyes glittering. He would be angry, seeing his chance at vengeance ripped from his fingers; Odin opened his mouth to call out to his eldest son and calm him, but then noticed that Vali had left his side. Turning, he saw Hodur being led out to eat by two of Frigga's handmaidens. Odin's blind son seemed even more stooped and grey with the burden of the murder he had inadvertently committed, and perhaps wondering who among them blamed him. *I will absolve him publicly tonight*, Odin thought, and then saw Vali moving toward Hodur's grey, shaking form.

The youth approached him almost respectfully, and touched him on the shoulder. "My brother," Odin heard him say, "I am sorry." The words were not spoken loudly, but they somehow fell into a lull in the conversation and everyone looked up. Even Thor was distracted.

And then Vali's sword leaped from its sheath and whinged through the air, and through Hodur's neck. The blind man's head toppled from his shoulders, and his body collapsed like a pile of rags. Frigga's scream rent the shocked silence. A second son lay dead, less than a day after the first. Odin's heart banged in his chest, and everything seemed to slow down.

Vali stooped and lifted Hodur's head, and held it high. "I have slain the one whose hand slew my brother," he called out, only a little uncertainly. "I have fulfilled my oath to my sire." His eyes sought Odin's, and blinked; his forehead creased in worry at the expression the All-Father knew must be on his face.

Wrenching himself out of his paralysis, he whirled around to see Rind's cold, cold eyes. "I have kept my word," she said, with only a little spite in her voice. "I have delivered up a son-avenger to you. That is all you will get from me. Vali is yours; do what you will with him." Leaning closer, she whispered, "If you wish to murder your blood-brother, Lord of Asgard, you will have to do it yourself, with your own hands, and you know it. No one else can do it for you." Then she turned and was gone, just before Hodur's spreading blood reached the place where they stood.

Odin looked down, opening and closing his empty hands as if groping for something that he had lost. *Gamble lost. Vengeance for vengeance. In my pain and desperation I underestimated her. And now, since I had not yet absolved Hodur, Baldur is avenged and Loki is... free?* For a moment hope leaped in his heart, but then he quashed it sternly. *I am the King of Asgard, and many futures are in my hands. If I must shave off pieces of my heart, one at a time, to twist the future as I would have it, then it must be done. It is the price of rulership.*

But I cannot kill him, not with my own hands. I cannot. I could more easily slit my own throat. It was a hard admission, but true. No one would understand, but he could not be the one to slay that wild spirit. And, he realized, sending another to do it would still be his hand. There could be no fooling himself on that matter, not any longer. Rind's aim had been true. *I deserved it. I did her great wrong. A man can do many foolish things, in his grief. Now pay the price of your folly, Great King. Be good to her son.*

As he moved forward to say the right things to that poor bewildered young man, a hapless pawn between two cold sparring wills, one thought flickered willy-nilly through his mind. *Did she see something, in the future, that forced her decision?*

That, I suppose, I shall never know.

He thought that he heard a chuckle from someplace that was not in the room, and wondered if the Norns were laughing at him again.

Runemasters of the Tree
(as told by Asvid)

very once in a while, a door is opened into Ginnungagap, and something comes through.

The first opening of the door was Surt, and no one speaks of this, not even Surt. There were others, but they are lost in the mists—of Niflheim, of history. It may be that the Vanir opened the door and entered, and made their own world. It is certain that the Alfar came from outside, from whatever layered fey-worlds birthed also the Sidhe and other elven races. The door opened, and something—someones—came through

But to open that door from the outside is one thing. To open it from the inside, to call something in through the blackness of Ginnungagap, that is something else entirely. Only once has it been done in the Cosmos of the Tree, and that was when Odin offered himself up as a sacrifice, and wrenched the door open from his side, and pulled through the spirit-powers that are the Runes.

It is known that Odin hung nine days on the Tree. What is not known is that when he opened that door with the force of blood and pain and suffering, his life force trailing down the tree to be taken up as thread by the Norns and spun into a great spell, the runes that came to him were not the only ones that came.

They were the first spirits through the door, aye, and they came all as a set together into his bleeding hands, but others followed thick and fast. Some buried themselves like meteors into the earth of many of the Nine Worlds, where they still remain to be found and uncovered. Some shot past into Ginnungagap, perhaps to circle the Tree, perhaps to become stars, perhaps to vanish into the blackness.

At the moment that Odin opened that door, everyone in the Nine Worlds looked up. Some knew what had happened, and gasped, or their faces froze intently as they sensed the influx of power. Some knew nothing, except that the air was strange and still, as if every particle was holding its breath. After a while, perhaps they shook their heads and went back to work, their skin prickling but none the wiser. There were four, though, who knew more than this. Four, in all the Nine Worlds, besides Odin himself. They did not know of his act until it happened, and at that time their minds were elsewhere...but the rune-spirits who had been released into the world scented them out, found them, and filled them.

In Alfheim, Dain was the head of a great Alfar house, a prince among the Fair Folk, but he had hidden himself in the cellar of his great hall, a knife clutched in his hand. His beloved lady was dead and gone, her soul swept away to Hela, and there would be no seeing her again. She would not reincarnate among his people, as most of them did. His heart was a deep, empty well of desolation, and he had no more will to live. "She was my life," he whispered to himself. "Half my soul is gone with her." Though his folk would cry out and stop him if they knew, he was toying with the thought of giving himself also to Hela, to be with his beloved again. *In Death I will find you again,* he thought. The knife traced the edge of his wrist, and its sharp point caught, releasing a few drops of blood to stain the edge of his flowing sleeve. The pain felt good. *Take me to my beloved, then.* He placed the knife at the side of his throat, and began to press.

In Nidavellir, Dvalin, one of the first fathers of the Duergar, was gravely ill. Every remedy had been tried, and all had failed. His wives and children knelt around his bed, weeping over his wasted form. He had fought for long weeks, gained ground and lost it again, but now he was tired and weak and it was overtaking him. In spite of this, he fought still, his hands clutching weakly at the bedclothes as he struggled to stay alive. "I—will—not—give—in!" he gritted through his teeth, and all wept to see such strength and courage brought low. His breath grew harsh in his throat, rough and ragged, but his eyes still stared wide at the single lamp that lit the darkened room like a crack of sunlight.

In Midgard, Duneyr lay dying in a ditch. Cunning man, herbmaster, the patchy bits of lore that had trailed down from greater beings had come to him. A gentle man, he spoke to the spirits of the plants and the wights that lay beneath the ground...but mortal men seldom trusted those who worked with magics, even small magics. And all the Gods help you if their grudging trust was betrayed...say, for example, by a patient whom you could not save. He had tried to heal the lord's sickness, and the man had made an almost miraculous recovery from his deathbed, but the fool had taken this miracle as reason enough to go back to his old ways of drinking too much ale, eating only rich meats, and bestirring from his chair only to grasp at the breast of passing servant-girls. The ill-tasting medicines that Duneyr had given to him were quickly forgotten, and it was only a matter of months before he relapsed, and died. Desperate for someone to blame, his sons sought out the herb-man with murderous intent, and here he lay broken, dying of internal wounds too great for he himself ever to have healed. *This is wrong*, he whispered soundlessly. *Surely I was not meant to die this way, O Norns? I have helped many, I deserve this not!* His last thought, as sight faded from him, was that his daughter would be waiting dinner for him, and it would likely burn. He could almost see the spark from that flame...

In the great forest of Jotunheim, Asvid lay gasping on the ground. Enemies of his clan had come upon him and they had fought, fought gloriously, but they were too many and had outnumbered him. Still, he had killed over twenty before they had hammered his great, solid mountain giant's body down into the soft forest earth. *My father might be proud of me,* he thought, *if he were not beheaded and stuck down a well. Or perhaps he would not be proud to know that I had fallen just yards away from his cave.* If he turned his head, agonizedly, he could see the dark mouth of Mimir's cave, under an arch of stone next to the great bulk of the World Tree's protruding root. *Forgive me, Father,* he said silently. *I came to see you for the first time since my childhood, and it has meant my death, and I will not even be able to meet you.*

His wounds were bleeding out, now, and he was beginning to fade. Even as the spinning tree limbs filmed over in his sight, he felt something strange. The dark claimed him, but in that dark was a window of light, opened in the Universe. With a sense of awe, with senses stretched by being no longer wholly in his body, he realized that this was a hole opened by someone's sheer force of will, an arm reached through the Well of Wyrd and an aperture rent in the very fabric of Ginnungagap. Through it spilled a cascade of sparks, souls, lights, colors, shapes that started to take form only as they passed from that place to this. He saw hands reaching out, heard the screams of the one-eyed form bound to the Tree in his agony, saw him seize a double handful of those light/color/shape/soul/sparks, and fall back away and out of sight.

His own cry echoed that of the one-eyed one, and he reached forward as well with his great hands, grasping after them like a drowning man after a rope. He knew not what they were, nor why he must hold them; only that it was more important than anything else he had ever done with his life. As he touched them, they burned his hands, and he fell back, gripping them to what had been his heart. They took on form in his hands, his blood, his scent; they became symbols that he could understand. As his flesh eyes opened onto the canopy of trees, he vaguely heard other voices cry out like a high, wailing song in the darkness....

...and Dain, his lifeblood pouring from his throat, realized what Odin the Aesir King, gone these nine long years, had done. His unseeing eyes saw the magics like gilded, glowing threads wending their way into the world, and in the darkness, light entered his heart for the first time in many days. As his scream died away, those threads twined themselves around his fingers, and he pulled them in to him, weeping. *Was this the Universe giving me weregild for the loss of my beloved?* he wondered, as the elf-runes took form between his fingers, healing him, taking life from his spilled blood and giving it back to him. He laughed, for the first time, as if reborn, and barely heard the hoarse cry that faded as soon as sounded...

...and Dvalin sat bolt upright in bed, face white and bloodless as that of a corpse, fingers reaching out and seizing something in midair. "Yes!" he shouted, and then his emaciated features bent into a gaunt grin, and before his unseeing eyes lights formed in the air. His family cried out, also, in fear and wonder, and hid their faces before his croaking laughter. His first wife buried her face against his knee in gratitude, understanding only that somehow, her husband would live, and that was enough. The dancing shapes that firmed with his breath, between his hands, that would matter later....

...and Duneyr was the only one who did not scream. Instead, he smiled, softly, wondering in his delirium whether he had been saved by firefly-lights. But no, they were no longer fireflies, just symbols chalked in ash on stone, marked in blood in the dirt, written in wrinkles on his hands, sliding in lines of energy across the ground. He understood them, although he did not know how. But that seemed like something to explore once he was home, safely away from the road and the eyes of those filled with hate. Struggling to his feet, he marveled at how light he felt; if he was not certain that this was his body, he would never have believed that he was still alive. Alive, and with a stomach to eat supper with his daughter, and perhaps not even late after all. As he walked down the familiar road, his stride stronger with each step, he did not even find it unusual that the symbols appeared in the dust of the road ahead of him, one in each muddy footprint, like serpents that squirmed from one pool to another. After all, stranger things had happened to him that day, like being snatched back from the road to Hel.

Odin came down from the Tree and went home to Asgard, where Frigga welcomed him with open arms, and returned to his throne. That part of the story, everyone knows. The other parts were quieter, for no one trumpeted the returns of the others, save perhaps the family of Dvalin, and the great old Duergar himself preferred to shrug it off as merely a recovery from illness. Where he had once been a boastful sort, brash and loud, he was now found to be quiet and full of wisdom; he ceased to lead war parties, but stayed home and counseled those who came to him, and more often than not he counseled against a direction that would take lives. The Duergar-runes he taught to a scant handful of his folk, the craftspeople whom he judged not only the finest in art but the most upright in morals as well. They in turn limited their teaching of them, at his request, to a small and secret number. Each of them swears in turn never to let them pass into the hands of outsiders, and if it has ever happened, it would have been done by one who broke that terrible oath, and would be slain by his brothers were it known.

Dain walked out of the depths of his castle like a cloud parting with the great light of the sun, his face suffused with a new hope, and he opened his hands and taught the Alfar-runes to any Alf who would come to him. Where before he had been a great lord, he now gave up his castle and lived with no home, traveling from place to place and teaching. All doors in Ljossalfheim were opened to him, and he was much loved. For years this was his mission, and he became famed for it among his own people, although they too kept this knowledge apart from other races. It is even said that alone of all the light-elves, he willingly went to Svartalfheim and taught these runes even to their darker kindred, so intent was he that they were the inheritance of all Alfar... and it is also said that he alone among the Ljossalfar is as welcome there as in the world of his birth.

Duneyr taught no one of the runes. He wrote them down, carved them onto trees and stitched them onto his clothing, but he used them not where other mortals could see, and he never spoke to anyone of his experience. His heart had been made too distrustful of the goodness of any other man, and he feared that the runes might be used for ill by those with malice in their hearts. At first he feared even to use them himself, but one day he came home to his hut where he lived alone (for he had left his daughter's hearthside out of fear for her safety) and found a giant sitting by his fire. "Greetings, Man," said the giant, standing to greet Duneyr, but not fully for the ceiling prevented it. "How are you named, my friend?"

For a moment Duneyr could not speak, so surprised was he, but then he stammered, "I am called Duneyr." Since something else seemed to be needed, he said, "It means 'restful' in the old tongue. My mother named me so for being the easiest of all her babes."

The giant laughed. "Restful you are, I am sure, but I am equally sure that your life has not been so to you! Well, you may call me Durathor, as that means Sleeping, and we shall be a pair, you and I!"

"If I may ask, sir," the slender, frail, grey-haired man said haltingly, sidling about the room without taking his eyes off of his tall, burly, black-bearded guest, "what have we in common that we should be any kind of pair?"

Durathor's eyes held his with a keenness that seemed to cut through his soul. "You know that as well as I, friend. You and I were both dying on the day that One-Eye tore a hole in the Darkness, and we both received into our hands that which cannot be easily Named. One-Eye, myself, you, a fair-haired Alf, and an old Duergar. We are all the same, in that way... or at least, the four of us who simply took the leavings from One-Eye's table. Ah, but what leavings they were, aye?" His eyes unfocused for a moment, seeing a memory inside his head. Duneyr knew exactly what he was seeing.

"What would you have of me?" he whispered. "I—I have done nothing, worked no ill with that which came unlooked-for—"

"That's just it, my friend. You have done nothing, all these years. I, I was a great warrior, did you know that? But then the runes came to me, and I carved them into the bark of the tree, of the root that springs forth near my father's spring. After that I gave up fighting, and became a magician, and healer. I passed the runes on to those I deemed worthy among my folk. Dvalin and Dain, they have done the same...Garm's pawprints, Dain has spread them across the length and breadth of his land!

Even One-Eye is teaching his runes where he will. Yet you have not passed on this gift to anyone."

Duneyr sat by the hearth and stared into the fire. "There are none that I deem worthy," he said. "I do not know your people, or the Alfar or the Duergar, or least of all the great Aesir, but I know mortals. We are vicious and untrustworthy, all of us, save for a few...and they are weak."

"Weak, like yourself, my friend?" A great hand came down upon Duneyr's shoulder. "Then I will give you another gift. I will teach you to be strong, and perhaps in time you will feel safe enough to give from generosity, and not from fear."

So it was that Duneyr and the giant who called himself Dunathor became fast friends. Although Duneyr protested that he could not possibly learn the skills of a warrior, being of middle age and grey-haired and stiff in the joints and nearsighted in the eyes, Dunathor insisted that it was not impossible. Slowly, slowly, he learned to use his body as a weapon, and to use the runes as weapons as well. His friendship with the giant was strong enough that one day he offered to teach Dunathor the rune-magics that he had learned, and so the two traded knowledge. So it was that some human-magic made its way into Jotun runelore, and vice versa. It was then that they realized that both sets had one in common: the rune that Duneyr called Odin's spear, and Dunathor called Odin's horse, but which meant the world tree on which he had made his sacrifice. Because he had been the one to open the door, each set of runes would bear this rune in his name, save his alone.

Eventually, Duneyr came across the sons of the ill-fated lord on the road, and instead of ducking his head and enduring their jeers, he knocked them off their horses with his quarterstaff, and placed a *galdr*-curse on them that turned their lives to muck until they begged his forgiveness, which he gave, being still a gentle man at heart.

But news came into Midgard of folk who knew the casting of magical runes, and Duneyr knew that those runes were not the same ones that he knew. "'Tis One-Eye, teaching to those who pray to him," said Dunathor. "You have waited too long, my friend; some folk have them now, after all. And you can guarantee that there will be battles of galdr-magic."

"Then perhaps the time is right," said Duneyr, "to pass these on." And he laid a geas upon his runes, that all who use them might be peaceful and kind of heart. But the geas would not stay on the Jotun-runes, the etin-staves that he had learned from Dunathor. "We are not a peaceful people," Dunathor laughed at him. Still, he went out and taught the runes to three whom he deemed to be gentle and good of heart, but he would teach no more than this, no matter what his giant-friend said.

Years passed, and Duneyr became an old man. One morning he awoke to find Dunathor at his hearth, as was not unusual, but with him stood an elderly Duergar and a tall golden Alf of great beauty. "You time will come soon, my friend," said the giant. "Of all of us, you have the shortest life, so I would have you meet the rest of this group of unlikely brothers."

"We have spoken among ourselves for many years," said the old Duergar, puffing on his pipe. "Alone among all others, we four have experienced the opening of Ginnungagap...well, we four and Odin, and he keeps his own counsels."

"But it is time," said the Alf, "to speak of the winds." At Duneyr's confusion, he went on, "I do not mean the air that blows through the sky, but rather the currents that swirl through the Tree, between worlds. You know whereof I speak, do you not?"

Duneyr nodded. He did know, and he had wondered if indeed those currents could be used to do again what Odin had done. He saw that the others had read his thought, and were nodding. "Indeed they might, and by far worse wights than One-Eye," said the giant that he knew as Dunathor. "That is why we have all agreed to give up our worldly lives and become guardians of those winds, that no others may interfere with the fabric between the Tree and Outside."

"We come today to ask you as well," said Dain. "Will you join us, and give up your mortal life and existence, and guard this with us?"

"We had not planned it quite yet," said Dvalin, "but we have all been using our runes for an oracle, and we knew that your time would be soon."

The grey-haired man nodded. "I know it too," he said. "Let it be so, then! I would have a cause that goes beyond death, to protect these worlds. I have learned," and he smiled at the giant, "that fighters can be useful."

"So be it, then," said Dunathor. "And since there can now be no secrets between us, know that my real name is Asvid, son of Mimir of the Well. Come, my friend!" And he held out his hand, and Duneyr his friend took it, and the four of them joined hands in a circle and made a great magic, so great that it blew his small cottage to pieces. From its wreckage came four deer—one graceful dappled fallow deer, one short, stocky chestnut-coated roe deer, one great shaggy black elk... and one red deer that followed the other three with a bit of hesitancy, having never flown through the air before, nor yet left his world. The four stags circled in the sky over Midgard, the red deer looking back over his shoulder only once more, and then they were gone.

Of Odin and his runes, much is known...at least in comparison to the others. Asvid, Dain, and Dvalin are all known and honored among their people for being the first true runemasters, but little is spoken of them outside of those worlds. As for Duneyr, no mortal man ever heard his story, though his friend Dunathor had passed it into the stories of the Jotnar, where it survives to this day. His runes are used by Jotun runemasters, and they know to bless and thank the mortal healer who passed them on, though it is said that to use them for long will make the most ardent warrior turn to peaceful pursuits. On the other hand, most of Duneyr's runes have been lost among humans, or are hidden in the minds of only a few, secretly passed down...except for a scant handful of the Jotun runes passed to him by his friend Dunathor, which survive sometimes tacked onto the great original runes of Odin, for mortals are wont to force traditions together into one pot, hoping to make a stew that will turn out to be the ultimate truth.

What was known by even fewer was the fate of the four Guardians. They are known in later lore only as the Deer of the Four Winds, yet few understand what that means, just as few understood that the experience of being dragged back from Death's door by Odin's brave and brash act had bound them all together in a way that superceded their loyalty to their own peoples. Never before or since had a Jotun, an Alf, a Duerg, and a mortal man all pledged friendship together, and it took the rending of the cosmos to do it. Still, they guard the currents of time and space, unseen and unrewarded, and so it is meant to be.

All hail the Deer of the Four Winds! May they never tire in their task.

Index

Printed and bound by CPI Group (UK) Ltd, Croydon, CR0 4YY

05/03/2024

03726716-0003